Battle of Camperdown. P. 389.

UNIVERSAL NAVAL HISTORY.

COMPRISING

THE NAVAL OPERATIONS
OF THE PRINCIPAL MARITIME NATIONS

OF THE

WORLD,

FROM THE EARLIEST PERIOD TO THE PRESENT TIME.

ENLIVENED BY SKETCHES OF
SEA BATTLES, REMARKABLE ADVENTURES, SHIP-WRECKS, AND PERILOUS VOYAGES,

WHICH RENDER SO INTENSELY INTERESTING THE

HISTORY OF THE OCEAN.

BY JOHN FROST, LL.D.
AUTHOR OF "PICTORIAL HISTORY OF THE WORLD," "PICTORIAL HISTORY OF THE UNITED STATES," "BOOK OF THE NAVY," "LIVES OF THE COMMODORES," ETC., ETC.

WITH THREE HUNDRED ILLUSTRATIONS.
REPRESENTING THE MODE OF BUILDING OF ANCIENT AND MODERN VESSELS, PORTRAITS OF DISTINGUISHED NAVAL COMMANDERS, SEA FIGHTS, ETC.
FROM ORIGINAL DESIGNS
BY W. CROOME, AND OTHER EMINENT ARTISTS.

NEW YORK AND HARTFORD:
H. E. ROBINS AND COMPANY.
1851.

PHILADELPHIA:
STEREOTYPED BY GEORGE CHARLES.
No. 9 Sansom Street.

CONTENTS.

THE naval history of the world possesses many points of interest to the general reader. It marks the gradual progress of civilization in the great maritime nations. It displays the power of human ingenuity, skill, perseverance, and courage. It exhibits the rise and the decline of many great states. It affords many lessons of the vicissitudes of national prosperity and adversity; and it presents numerous examples of individual heroism and ability.

In the compendium of naval history which I have attempted in the following work, I have confined myself necessarily to the grand features of the subject, avoiding minor details, and passing over entirely the affairs of obscure and unimportant communities, who have exercised no influence on the destinies of the civilized world.

From the large number of historical works which I have deemed it important to consult, I have gleaned all that I considered important to the elucidation of the subject; but I have considered it unnecessary to encumber the page with numerous references to authorities. Standard authorities, such as Thirlwall, Gibbons, Sir Harris Nicholas, and others, of equal authenticity, have been my main reliance.

It has been my aim to give a clear, succinct, and, at the same time, entertaining account of the progress of naval affairs, from the earliest times to the present day, and I have made the history as complete as the space alloted me would permit.

The reader will notice the slow progress of navigation in the early ages, and the laborious and persevering efforts required for the advancement of the art of naval construction, the frequent loss of whole fleets and armies from the imperfect means of resisting the disastrous effects of storms and tempests; and the unsatisfactory knowledge, or rather the total ignorance of the ancients respecting the true form of the earth; and it will also be seen that all these defects were remedied by the discovery of the mariner's compass, and the consequent progress of the art of navigation, and the rapid extension of geographical research.

The modern history of the navies of the world presents a totally different aspect from that of the navies of ancient time. Vast enterprises are now undertaken and executed in a few weeks, which in ancient times would either have been wholly impracticable, or would have required years for their completion.

Civilization, which in ancient times advanced by slow and painful efforts, is now rapidly advanced by the increased intercourse between distant nations, and the wide diffusion of science and the arts, consequent upon improvements in the art of navigation, and the existence of large and powerful fleets for commerce, and navies for aggression and defence. To trace the progress of naval affairs, and the consequent diffusion of civilization and science, from the earliest times to the present day, will, it is believed, afford the reader sufficient entertainment and instruction to compensate him for the time occupied in the perusal of the following pages.

My acknowledgements are due to my friend, Mr. Croome, for the tasteful and beautiful style in which the volume has been embellished by his faithful pencil. His delineations, it is believed, will serve to impress indelibly on the reader's memory the leading events in the naval history of the world.

With a few words of explanation on a certain point, I will now take leave of the reader.

In the first chapter I have given the scripture account of the ark, with the commentaries of approved writers. I give their opinions, to be received by the reader for what they are worth. My own view of the passages of scripture relating to the ark are different; but I do not deem the present a fitting occasion for offering them to the public.

TO give, within a moderate compass, a history of the naval operations of all the great maritime powers of the world, from the earliest period known to historical writers to the present time, may be considered a bold undertaking. It, nevertheless, may be accomplished in a manner calculated to afford a view of the subject, such as will satisfy the curiosity of the general reader. In attempting it, the writer will have recourse to ancient and modern writers who have treated the subject incidentally in connection with the civil and military history of the various ancient and modern nations. He will thus bring together on one volume the naval events recorded in many hundred volumes, and present a complete Universal Naval History—a work which, as far as he is aware, has not hitherto been attempted.

In the progress of the work, while he will avoid unnecessary and tedious details, he will endeavor to condense into one comprehensive sketch the naval history of each ancient nation, and each conspicuous naval power of the middle ages. The modern history will more naturally divide itself into epochs, during which several naval powers are engaged in the same wars.

Incidental notices of the progress of commercial enterprise and discovery, and anecdotes of individual prowess and skill will occur notwithstanding the limited size of the work; and a history of naval construction will form a separate article at the close of the work.

It will be perceived in following this course of history that seafaring pursuits, discovery, colonization, trade and maritime commerce by exciting a spirit of rivalry among different nations, invariably give rise to naval war, and occasion the construction of powerful fleets and the occurrence of great naval actions. But the same strong passions which carry nations to a high point of power and dominion on the ocean, ultimately lead to their downfall; and the traveller who muses over the prostrate ruins of Tyre, Sidon, Carthage, Athens, and other renowned cities of first rate naval powers, learns from their rise and fall that there is a Supreme Power which rules the destinies of mankind and sets limits to the attainments of human ambition. We trust that a perusal of these pages will imprint upon the reader's mind considerations of the same salutary tendency. It is in vain that we read the records of past ages if we do not learn from them lessons of moral virtue, religion, and justice.

NOAH'S ARK.

RETURN OF THE DOVE TO NOAH'S ARK.

CHAPTER I.

THE ARK OF NOAH.

THE first vessel constructed for sailing or floating upon the water, of which we have any record, is the ark built by Noah for safety during the universal deluge. The description of this structure, concerning which there has been much discussion, is contained in the following verses of the book of Genesis, chapter vi.

"Make thee an ark of *gopher wood;* rooms shalt thou make in the ark, and shalt pitch it within and without with *pitch.*

"And this is the *fashion* which thou shalt make it of: The length of the ark shall be *three hundred cubits,* the breadth of it *fifty cubits,* and the height of it *thirty cubits.*

"A window shalt thou make to the ark; and in a cubit shalt thou finish it above; and the door of the ark shalt thou set in the side thereof; with lower, second, and third stories shalt thou make it."

There is much difference of opinion about the form of the ark. The common figures are given under the impression that it was intended to be adapted to progressive motion; whereas no other object was sought than to construct a vessel which should *float* for a given time upon the water. For this purpose it was not necessary to place the ark in a sort of boat, as in the common figures; and we may be content with the simple idea which the text gives, which is, that of an enormous oblong box, or wooden house, divided into three stories, and apparently with a sloping roof. The most moderate statement of its dimensions makes the ark by far the largest of vessels ever made to float upon the water. As the measurements are given, the only doubt is as to which of the cubit measures used by the Hebrews is here intended. It seems that the standard of the original cubit was the length of a man's arm, from the elbow to the end of the middle finger, or about eighteen inches. This was the *common* cubit; but there was also a *sacred* cubit, which some call a hand's breadth (three inches) larger than the common ones; while others make the sacred cubit twice the length of the common. The probability is that there were two cubic measures beside the common; one being of twenty-one inches, and the other of three feet. Some writers add the geometrical cubit of nine feet. Shuckford says we must take the common or shortest cubit as that for the ark; Dr. Hales, taking this advice, obtained the following result: "It must have been of the burden of 42,413 tons. A first rate man-of-war is between 2200 and 2300 tons; and consequently, the capacity or stowage of eighteen such ships, the largest in present use, and might carry 20,000 men, with provisions for six months, besides the weight of 1800 cannon and all military stores. It was then by much the largest ship ever built."

The wood whereof the ark was built is called in the Hebrew *gopher wood*, and in the Septuagint *square timbers*. Some transfer the original *cedar*, others *pine*, others *box*, *&c.* Pelletier prefers cedar on account of its incorruptibility, and the great plenty of it in Asia; whence Herodotus and Theophrastus relate, that the kings of Egypt and Syria built whole streets thereof instead of deal. The learned Mr. Fuller, in his Miscellanies, has observed, that the wood whereof the ark was built was nothing but that which the Greeks call κυωαριςςος, or the *cypress tree;* for, taking away the termination, *kupar* and *gopher* differ very little in sound. This observation the great Bochart has confirmed, and shown very plainly that no country abounds so much with this wood, as that part of Assyria which lies about Babylon.

The dimensions of the ark, as given by Moses, are 300 cubits in length, 50 in breadth, and 30 in height; which some have thought too scanty, considering the number of things it was to contain; and hence an argument has been drawn against the authority of the relation. To solve this difficulty many of the ancient fathers, and the modern critics, have been put to very miserable shifts: But Buteo and Kircher have proved geometrically, that, taking the common cubit of a foot and a half, the ark was abundantly sufficient for all the animals supposed to be lodged in it. Snellius computes the ark to have been above half an acre in area. Father Lamy shows, that it was 110 feet longer than the church of St. Mary at Paris, and 64 narrower: and if so, it must have been longer than St. Paul's church in London, from west to east, and broader than that church is high in the inside, and 54 feet of our measure in height. Dr. Arbuthnot computes it to have been 81,062 tons. It contained, besides eight persons of Noah's family, one pair of every species of unclean animals, and seven pair of every species of clean animals, with provisions for them all during the whole year. The former appears, at first view, almost infinite; but if we come to a calculation, the number of species of animals will be found much less than is generally imagined; out of which, in this case, are excepted such animals as can live in the water; and Bishop Wilkins shows that only 70 of the quadruped kind needed a place in the ark.

By the description Moses gives of the ark, it appears to have been divided into three stories, each ten cubits or 15 feet high; and it is agreed on, as most probable, that the lowest storey was for the beasts, and the middle for the food, and the upper for the birds, with Noah and his family; each storey being divided into different apartments, stalls, &c., though Josephus, Philo, and other commentators, add a kind of fourth storey, under all the rest; being, as it were, the hold of the vessel, to contain the ballast and receive the filth and feces of so many animals: But F. Calmet thinks, that what is here reckoned a storey, was no more than what is called the keel of the ships, and served only for a conservatory of fresh water.

Many doubts have been entertained concerning the capacity of the ark, and learned commentators have entered into discussion relative to the number of its apartments and the quantity of living things it contained. But these discussions only exercise ingenuity. It may have been divided into apartments for each species of animals, and it may not. It is evident, that precise notions as to the form, divisions or capacity of the ark cannot be obtained.

In what place Noah built and finished his ark is no less a matter of disputation. But the most probable opinion is, that it was built in Chaldea, in the territories of Babylon, where there was so great a quantity of cypress in the groves and gardens in Alexander's time, that that prince built a whole fleet out of it for want of timber. And this conjecture is confirmed by the Chaldean tradition, which makes Xisuthrus (another name for Noah) set sail from that country. The time taken to build the Ark is also much disputed, some making it 52 years, others 78, 100 and 120. The Mahometans say it was made in two years.

We will now turn to the history of the ark and its occupants as given in the Bible. We are informed that the Lord resolved to destroy "man and beast, and the creeping thing, and the fowls of the air," which he had created, because they were corrupt, and he repented that he had made them. But Noah, "a just man and perfect in his generations," "found grace in the sight of the Lord," and he was commanded to build an ark, that when the destroying deluge was sent upon the earth, he and his family—eight persons in all—together with a male and female of every species of living things, might find safety. Noah did as he was commanded. He was six hundred years old when the deluge began. He entered the ark, with his wife, his sons, and his sons' wives, and was followed by a male and female of every species of beast, fowl, and "things that creep upon the earth."

Seven days after Noah's entrance into the ark, the deluge began. "The fountains of the great deep were broken up and the windows of heaven were opened." The flood continued forty days and forty nights. Every thing was destroyed, save the ark which floated in safety upon the waters. After the flood had answered its purpose, the waters began to abate, and at the end of one hundred and fifty days, the ark rested upon the "mountains of Ararat." This mountain, it is generally thought by commentators, lies in Armenia. It is one of the vast chain of Taurus, situated nearly in the centre between the Black and Caspian seas. Its summit is 17,260 feet above the level of the sea, and is always covered with snow. The mountain has a magnificent appearance; the neighboring ones being insignificant in comparison. It is separated into two heads, which form distinct cones. This, perhaps, account for the plural expression "mountains," in the Bible.

The waters continued to decrease, and soon the tops of the mountains were seen. At the end of forty days after the ark rested on Mount Ararat, Noah opened the window of the ark, and sent forth a raven, which went to and fro until the waters were dried up from the earth. He then sent forth a dove to see if the waters were abated from the face of the ground. But the dove found no rest for her foot and she returned. At the end of seven days, the dove was again sent forth from the ark, and in the evening she returned with an olive leaf in her mouth. From this, Noah knew that the waters were abated. At the end of seven more days, he again sent the dove forth, but it never returned. The covering was then removed from the ark, and the face of the ground was found to be dry. At the command of God, Noah and his family, followed by all the varieties of beasts, fowl, and creeping thing left the ark, and once more walked the dry land. Such is the history of the ark as given by Moses in the book of Genesis.

EGYPTIAN AND ROMAN SHIPS.

CHAPTER II.

EGYPT.

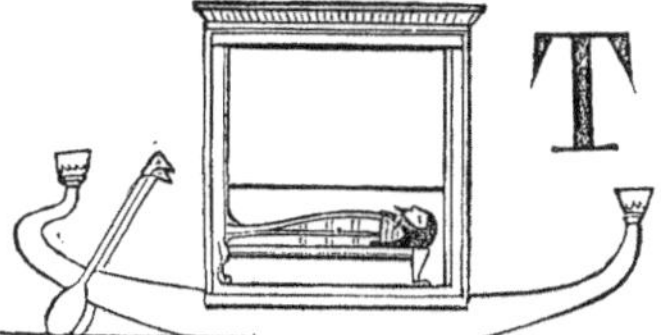

THE next subject of our attention will be the naval history of Egypt, although it is a matter of doubt to which the priority is due—the Egyptians or the Phœnicians. It is certain, that Egypt never became as powerful a maritime country as Phœnicia. Indeed the commerce of its hundred-gated Thebes depended principally upon the traders of the latter country, for a great number of years. But nature appears to have destined Egypt for a commercial country. Its situation, a fertile district, abounding in the necessaries of life, between the arid deserts of Asia and Africa, has in all ages given it a value which in any other position it could not have. The country, however, is destitute of material for building large vessels, and that would seem to have been an obstacle in the way of their becoming extensive navigators. But instances of their colonization of places on the European coast of the Mediterranean are recorded by historians; and, wherever the material may have been obtained, or the vessels built, the earliest records of the Egyptians furnish accounts of several naval expeditions of considerable importance.

The first Egyptian naval expedition of which we have any knowledge, took place in the reign of Ramses III. or Sesostris, the greatest monarch of his time. Filled with the spirit of conquest, Sesostris equipped mighty fleets upon the Red Sea, to attempt the extension of his dominion in the eastern and northern countries. According to Diodorus Siculus, one of the fleets numbered 400 sail. One was also built upon the Mediterranean, which conquered Cyprus, the coast of Phœnicia, and several of the Cyclades. The fleet built upon the Red Sea, conquered all the coast of the eastern shore, but its progress was arrested by shoals and difficulties, which the navigators were not skilled enough to surmount. Some centuries after this, in the reign of Apries, the Pharaoh Hophra of scripture, an Egyptian fleet conquered the Cypriot and Phœnician fleet united; and the rich city of Sidon, in Phœnicia, was taken by a land and naval force.

In the reign of Ptolemy, surnamed Euergetes, or the Beneficent, a mighty expedition was sent against the Asiatic kingdoms of Mesopotamia, Babylonia, Sufia, Persia, and all others as far as the kingdom of Bactria. An essential portion of this great expedition was a large fleet, which conveyed the army of horse and foot to Asia. The expedition was successful, and the greater portion of the powerful kingdoms of the western part of Asia were subdued. Judging from the numbers of the army which this fleet transported, it must have been a mighty one indeed; but one description of it is preserved. Some hundred years after this invasion of Euergetes, Ptolemy Lathyrus ascended the throne of Egypt, but his right was disputed by Ptolemy Alexander, at the instigation of his mother Cleopatra; Alexander was driven out of the kingdom, and took refuge in the island of Cos. Having gathered together a number of ships, he attempted to return to Egypt; but Tyrrhus, the admiral of Lathyrus sailed to meet him, and, after a short engagement, Alexander was defeated and obliged to fly to Myra, in Lycia. From Myra, the prince steered towards Cyprus, hoping the people of that island would aid him. But Chareas, another of Lathyrus's admirals, coming up with him while he

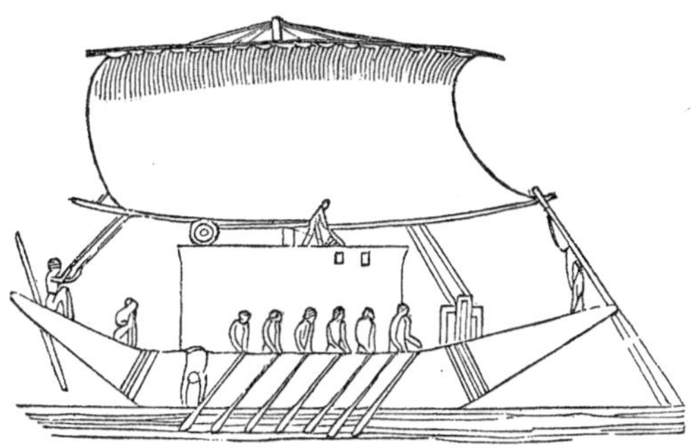

EGYPTIAN SHIP.—FROM THE MONUMENTS.

was ready to land, an engagement ensued, in which Alexander's fleet was dispersed and himself killed.

If the pictures of the Egyptian ships which are found upon their ancient monuments, are at all correct, the vessels composing their fleets were of nearly the same construction and equipment as those afterwards built by the Romans. They were not fitted for voyages of any length, nor did the Egyptians attempt any such. The navigation of the Red Sea, the coasts of the Indian Ocean as far as the Ganges, and the Mediterranean Sea, was the full extent of their undertaking. The vessels were high at the bow and at the stern, and made to represent fabled sea animals. They were low enough to enable rowers to work to advantage, and, consequently, too light to withstand heavy seas. The boat which was used in the navigation of the Nile was, however, of very ingenious construction, and was probably the best for that purpose. The Nile is full of shoals, which would afford constant obstruction to boats of the ordinary construction. But the Nile-boat, or Baris, described by Herodotus, met with little difficulty in its navigation. The keel was not straight, but a portion of a parabola, the curve of which is almost imperceptible. Hence, when the middle of the boat would be upon the sand bank the two extremities would be afloat, and the boat was easily cleared. The sails of these boats were large and heavy. These vessels continued in use until a late period, when steamers were introduced upon the Nile.

After the defeat and dispersion of the fleet of Ptolemy Alexander,

EGYPTIAN FERRY BOAT, SUCH AS WERE USED ON THE NILE.—FROM THE ANCIENT MONUMENTS.

805.—EGYPTIAN SWAMP BOAT.—FROM A SCULPTURE REPRESENTING THE CUTTING OF THE PAPYRUS.

we have no account of any naval transactions until the time of the famous Cleopatra. Civil war having broken out in Rome, headed by the rival generals Cæsar and Pompey, all the maritime countries of the eastern Mediterranean contributed their quotas of ships to swell the size and strength of Pompey's fleet. Among the rest, Egypt sent a considerable number. Of this fleet, which was commanded by M. Bibulus, we shall give an account in the naval history of Rome. We may mention, however, that upon receipt of the news of Cæsar's victory at Pharsalia, the Egyptian portion of Pompey's fleet withdrew from his service. After the conquest of all the places held by Pompey's adherents, Cæsar returned to Rome; and among the shows with which he amused the Romans, was a battle between an Egyptian fleet and a Tyrian fleet. The size of these fleets may be conjectured, when it is stated, that there were on board of each, two thousand rowers and one thousand fighting men, who engaged with each other, and fought with all the horrors of real warfare. Some of the vessels forming the fleet were quadriremes, or vessels having four rows of oars —the largest then built.

After the formation of the Triumvirate at Rome, Mark Antony left Italy, and proceeded to Asia. Some accusations having been brought against Cleopatra, the Egyptian queen, charging her with assisting the cause of Brutus and Cassius, she was summoned to meet Antony at Tarsus. In compliance with the summons, the queen set out in a magnificent ship. Every thing seemed contrived to produce the effect upon the susceptible triumvir which Cleopatra desired. If the descriptions of the ancient authors are to be credited, it was truly a gorgeous pageant. The hull was splendidly decorated with the costliest carvings and gold and silver. The sails were made of costly silks, and spangled with stars to represent the sky. From the stem of the vessel, a large representation of a sea shell was raised, which formed the back of Cleopatra's throne. There, under a silken canopy, arrayed as Venus, and surrounded by beautiful boys and girls, representing Cupids and Graces, reclined the fascinating queen, for whom Antony lost the empire of the world. The sailors and rowers were beautiful maidens, and as they rowed with their silver oars, they kept time to music. Perfumes were given off and loaded the winds that moved the silken sails. Persons, representing the fabled deities of the sea, swam round the vessel in her course, and filled the air with music. The vessel reached its destination, and the queen was magnificently received by the enchanted Antony; and from that time, he became Cleopatra's slave.

The Egyptian fleet bore a prominent part in the sea-fight at Actium, by which the ruin of the cause of Mark Antony was completed. That general having resolved to make one bold effort before the sovereignty should be yielded to Octavianus, united his Roman galleys with the Egyptian fleet, and sent the whole to meet the fleet of Octavianus. But the treacherous Queen Cleopatra had given secret orders to the commanders of the fleet, and as Antony stood on a height overlooking the scene, he had the mortification of seeing the Egyptian ships desert his cause, and with some of the Roman galleys pass over to the fleet of Octavianus. The remainder of Antony's ships made a short fight, but numbers were too overwhelming for them, and they either surrendered or were demolished.

With the dynasty of the Ptolemies, of which Cleopatra was the last, the importance of the naval power of Egypt fell. The country then became a province of Rome, and its history must form a part of the history of that great empire.

The Arabian caliphs, who conquered Egypt in 642, and ruled it until 1169, do not seem to have given much attention to naval affairs. One or two of its cities were taken by the fleets of the crusaders, but the Egyptians had not the power to make any considerable resistance. Under the government of the powerful Saladin, who destroyed the rule of the caliphs, a navy formed a principal part of the defence of the empire. While Saladin was in Palestine battling with the crusaders, a powerful fleet of European ships appeared on the Red Sea, which threatened the cities of Mecca and Medina with the utmost danger. The news of the appearance of this armament no sooner reached Cairo, than Abu Becr, Saladin's brother, who had been left as viceroy, caused another to be fitted out with all speed, under the command of Lulu, a brave and experienced officer. Lulu soon came up with the Christian fleet, and a dreadful engagement ensued. The battle was obstinate and bloody. But the superior strength and skill of the Egyptian commander prevailed. The Europeans were defeated, and a great number of them, being taken prisoners, were butchered in cold blood. This proved such a terrible blow to the Europeans, that they never after ventured on a like attempt.

CLEOPATRA'S VOYAGE TO MEET ANTONY.

The fleets of Saladin contributed much to the extension of his conquests, and they were generally successful. But occasionally they met with a severe check. After the capitulation of Jerusalem, in 1187, Saladin marched with his victorius army to lay siege to Tyre. As that port was blocked up by five of his men-of-war, he anticipated an easy conquest. But he was mistaken, for, one morning, at break-of-day, a Christian fleet fell upon his squadron and entirely defeated it. Not a single vessel escaped the pursuit. During the engagement, a considerable number of Mahometans threw themselves into the sea, and most of them were drowned. This defeat, together with a repulse by land, forced the sultan to raise the siege.

Soon after the arrival of Richard Cœur de Lion, in the Holy Land, with a great reinforcement to the crusaders, the English sunk a Mahometan ship of vast size, having on board 650 soldiers, and a great quantity of arms and provisions, going from Berytus to Ptolemais. Of the soldiers and sailors who were on board this vessel, only one person escaped, who, being taken prisoner by the English, was despatched to the sultan with the news of the disaster. The ship alluded to in this statement must have been of a size superior to any then built by the European nations, and proves the skill which the Egyptians had attained in the art of ship-building.

Upon the death of Saladin, and the subsequent accession to power of the Mamelukes, the empire of Egypt declined rapidly. In 1517, the Turks invaded and conquered the country. Under their rule, which continued until 1768, the commerce of the country was greatly reduced, and the naval power also. In 1768, Ali Bey declared his independence of the Sublime Porte, and took vigorous measures to increase the extent and power of Egypt. He wanted to render the country of the greatest commercial importance, and resolved to get possession of Gedda, the port of Mecca. To this end, he fitted out some vessels at Suez, and manning them with Mamelukes, commanded the Bey Hassan to sail with them to Gedda, while a body of cavalry advanced by land. The expedition was completely successful, and served to stimulate Ali Bey to greater achievements. All his plans, however, were defeated by the defection and revolt of his general, Mahommed Bey, who defeated the army of Ali and took the monarch prisoner.

After the death of Ali Bey, in 1775, Mahommed Bey assumed the supreme rule. Under his government, however, the army was more the subject of attention than the navy. In July, 1798, the French, under Napoleon Bonaparte, invaded Egypt. While the land forces were obtaining the most signal triumphs over the Arabs, Perree, with three armed sloops, a chebeque and galley, attacked their flotilla and set fire to the admiral's ship. But soon after this, the French fleet met with the most complete overthrow, at the mouth of the Nile. We shall defer the account of Nelson's victory until we come to the history of the British navy.

In 1806, Mehemet Ali succeeded in acquiring the supreme authority in Egypt. He was desirous of governing the country upon the European plan. Armies and fleets were organized under the direction of Europeans, in the service of Mehemet Ali, and the power of the pacha became formidable. In 1824, he sent his son, Ibrahim, at the head of an army of 16,000 men, together with a fleet under the command of Ismael Gibraltar, to conquer the Morea and establish a negro colony there. The latter, with the cupudan pacha, was defeated in several naval actions, in September, 1824, by the Greek admiral Miaulis, and Canaris, the commander of the fire-ships. But a second Egyptian expedition succeeded in March, 1825, in effecting a landing at Modon, and captured Navarino, Tripolizza, and other places. Ibrahim then laid waste the Morea, and sent its inhabitants as slaves to Egypt. In October, 1827, a third expedition of the pacha was blockaded in the harbor of Navarino, by the combined French and English fleets, under Admirals Codrington and De Rigny. Shortly after the combined Turkish and Egyptian fleets were destroyed by the allied fleets of France, England, and Russia. Many of the ships in the Egyptian fleet were purchased by the pacha in France, with which country he maintained the strictest friendship. Since the Greek revolution, the navy of Egypt has not been engaged in any affair of importance. By the liberal and enlightened policy of Mehemet and his son Ibrahim, it has been organized and constructed upon the models furnished by the navies of France and England.

THE RUINS OF TYRE.

PHŒNICIAN VESSEL.

CHAPTER III.

PHŒNICIA AND CARTHAGE.

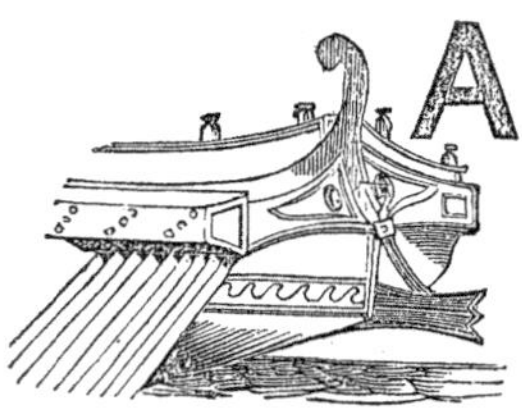

AFTER following up the naval history of Egypt, we next turn our attention to that of the greatest commercial country of antiquity. The title Phœnicia was given to a number of independent cities situated upon the eastern coast of the Mediterranean Sea. Each of these cities was an independent state, but they were generally united in a federative league, first under the presidency of Sidon, and afterwards of Tyre. Phœnicia contained Sidon, the oldest commercial city in the world; Tyre, afterwards so rich and powerful; Aradus, an insular city; Tripolis, so called because it was colonized by the three former cities jointly; Byblus and Berytus, which last is still a good harbor. The narrow and short line of coast, indented with excellent bays and harbors, was covered with lofty and wooded mountains, that jut out into the sea and form bold promontories. Several islands stud the coast, on which cities and commercial establishments were founded as well as on the main land.

Great obscurity shrouds the early accounts of the Phœnician cities, and Tyre is the only one whose history can be satisfactorily traced. During the reign of Hiram, the contemporary of Solomon, Tyre acquired the supremacy of Phœnicia, and became the most flourishing commercial emporium in the world.

The Bible informs us that King Hiram furnished Solomon with a number of ships, manned by Phœnician mariners, which were to sail to the south and east in the Indian Ocean, and traffic with the nations to be found on its coast, principally for the benefit of the king of Israel. The Edomites, living on the Elanitic Gulf, were accustomed to the navigation of the Red Sea, and were subject to Solomon. But they had not the nautical skill and daring of the Phœnicans, and were therefore unacquainted with the navigation of the broad and dangerous Indian Ocean. The interest which Solomon took in the expedition, may be judged of from the fact that he went in person to the port of Erungeber, at the head of the gulf, to superintend and witness the departure of the fleet. It returned in the third year, laden with the rich treasures of the south and the remote east. There were vast quantities of gold and silver, while the bulk of the cargo was composed of elephants' teeth and various sorts of valuable wood and precious stones.

Under Hiram's successors, some important colonies were founded in Africa. Pygmalion's murder of Sichæus, the husband of Dido, led to the foundation of Carthage. Dido, aided by numerous Tyrians, escaped by sea, with her husband's treasures, and took refuge on the northern shores of Africa. There she built the city of Carthage, which soon rivalled Tyre itself in commercial prosperity. The Tyrians exercised their authority over the surrounding cities with so much cruelty, that they applied to Assyria for aid. The Assyrians were unable to cope with the Tyrians at sea; but Nebuchadnezzar king of Babylon, so exhausted Tyre by a constant blockade, that it was almost wholly abandoned by its inhabitants, who erected the city of New Tyre upon a neighboring island. After Cyrus had conquered Babylon, the Phœnician cities submitted of their own accord. But though they became dependencies of the Persian empire they retained their native governments. Tyre supplied the strength of the Persian naval power.

The commerce of the Phœnicians was carried farther into Africa and along the coast of the Mediterranean Sea than that of any other nation; and their naval strength was in proportion to the extent of their commerce. The prophet Ezekiel, whose account of Tyre is the most perfect record extant of its ancient condition, mentions many countries that supplied the Tyrian army and navy with warriors. Their colonies extended along the coasts of the Mediterranean and occupied the principal islands. Sicily and Sardinia appear to have been only naval stations for the vessels of the Phœnicians. It is probable that they had naval stations along the western coast of Spain. The cities founded by them in northern Africa—Carthage, Leptis, and Utica, attained to great wealth and power, rivalling even Tyre itself. In the eastern seas they had establishments on the Persian and Arabian gulfs; and their trade by sea to the mouth of the Nile in Egypt, was of great importance.

IT is supposed that the Phœnician commerce upon the Mediterranean began in piracy; for, in the infancy of Greece, there is frequent allusion to the kidnapping practised by the corsairs from Tyre and Sidon. But when Corinth and Athens became powerful enough to have fleets of their own, they became the rivals and political enemies of the Phœnicians. The first naval engagement of which we have record or description took place between the Tyrrhenian and Carthaginian combined fleets and the fleet of the Greek colony of Phocea. The Persians attacked the city of Phocea, in Ionia, but the people managed to remove their effects and escape with them on board of their galleys. They proceeded to the island of Corsica, part of which had been already occupied by the Carthaginians, and prepared to establish themselves on the coast. The Carthaginians and Tyrrhenians, dreading the rivalry of the enterprising Phoceans, entered into an alliance for their destruction, and sent one hundred and twenty sail to drive them from Corsica. The Phoceans had but half that number of vessels, yet, such was their skill, that they gained a brilliant victory. The Carthaginians, however, gained their object, for the Phoceans, thinking themselves too weak to sustain a repetition of the attack, left Corsica and sailed to the coast of Gaul.

As the power of Carthage increased, that of Tyre, and the rest of the Phœnician cities declined, and the colony soon became far superior to the mother country. The attention they paid to naval affairs soon gave the Carthaginians the command of the western Mediterranean. They became eminent for their skill in ship-building. The vessel most common in their service was the *trireme,* or galley with three banks of oars; but we read of their using ships with five banks, and, in one instance, seven. The rowers were slaves bought by the state for this particular purpose; and, as they required constant practice, they formed a permanent body which was not disbanded in time of peace. The office of admiral was rarely united to that of general, and the naval commanders, even when acting in concert with the military, received their orders direct from the senate.

After the sea fight off Corsica, the Carthaginians had a jealous dread of Grecian valor and skill. When, therefore, Xerxes was preparing to invade Hellas, they readily allied themselves with the Persian monarch, and agreed to attack the colonies while he warred against the parent state. Accordingly, an armament was prepared, whose magnitude showed the power and wealth of Carthage. It consisted of two thousand ships of war, three thousand transports and vessels of burden, and a land army amounting to three hundred thousand men. The command of the expedition was given to Hamilcar. A landing was effected at Panormus (the modern Palermo), and, as soon as the troops were refreshed, Hamilcar led them to besiege Himera. We have not space for the details of the land operations; but it will suffice to say, that the undisciplined Carthaginians were defeated, and Hamilcar killed, by Gelon, king of Syracuse. The vessels in the harbor were then set on fire, and the greater part of the vast fleet was destroyed. The remnant made good their retreat. (B. C. 586.)

After this terrible defeat the Carthaginians made no more warlike naval demonstrations until B. C. 416. In that year they received an embassy from the Segestans, seeking their protection from the Syracusans. The Carthaginians eagerly seized upon this pretext, and a new expedition was sent against Sicily, under the command of Hannibal, the grandson of Hamilcar. The expedition was crowned with success. Two of the Sicilian cities were taken by storm, and the inhabitants put to the sword. This so elated the Carthaginians, that they contemplated the conquest of the whole island. Inules, the son of Hanno and Hannibal, at the head of a powerful armament, proceeded

DESTRUCTION OF THE CARTHAGINIAN FLEET.

to besiege Agrigentum. The siege lasted eight months; during which, the assailants and the citizens endured great privations, and suffered severely from famine. But the Agrigentines forced their way through the Carthaginian lines, and nearly all escaped. After this, the Syracusans totally defeated the Carthaginians in a night attack; and few escaped the horrible slaughter.

Upon the death of the elder Dionysius, his son, a profligate prince, ascended the throne of Syracuse. The Carthaginians thought this was a favorable time to effect their favorite scheme of getting possession of Sicily. Accordingly, a great armament was fitted out, of which Mago was appointed chief commander. At the first attack, Mago made himself master of Syracuse harbor; but distrusting the faithfulness of his Greek levies, who had been solicited to desert by the Greek general, Timoleon, he at once abandoned Syracuse and returned home.

Indignant at this desertion of the object of the expedition, the Carthaginians demanded the death of Mago; and he committed suicide to escape their wrath. New forces were raised to retrieve their losses in Sicily, and Hannibal and Hamilcar were appointed to the command. The army consisted of seventy thousand men, and the fleet of two hundred war galleys, and a thousand ships of burden. But the Grecian general, Timoleon, was too formidable an opponent. With a small force, he surprised the Carthaginian army, and totally routed it. The fleet returned to Carthage.

New dissensions in Syracuse afforded the Carthaginians a fresh pretext for meddling with the affairs of Sicily. Agathocles, a demagogue of mean birth, had acquired great influence among his countrymen, and by the secret aid of the Carthaginians, he became master of the state. But he soon declared his purpose to expel his benefactors from the island. The Carthaginians immediately sent Hamilcar with a powerful army against this new enemy, and he succeeded in shutting Agathocles within the walls of Syracuse. A large fleet blockaded the harbor of that city, and every thing promised success to the Carthaginians. But Agathocles baffled all their plans by adopting extraordinary measures. An army of liberated slaves was raised by him, and money placed at his disposal by the Syracusans. A fleet was prepared in secret, and when all was ready, Agathocles announced his design of transporting troops to Africa, and thus compel the Carthaginians to abandon Sicily, on account of the peril at home. He eluded the blockading squadron, and arrived in Africa, before the Carthaginians knew of his purpose. To fill his soldiers with resolution to conquer or die, he cut off all chance of retreat by burning the transports. Victory soon declared in his favor, and the Carthaginians were once more forced to quit Sicily. After the failure of this expedition, no more attempts were made to get that island into their possession. But intrigue accomplished afterwards what force had failed to do, and Sicily acknowledged the supremacy of Carthage. The naval history of Carthage is so closely connected with that of Rome during the Punic wars, that we will defer it until we come to the history of the latter country. It will be sufficient here to mention, that the navy, the source of the greatness and power of Carthage, was neglected during the wars with the Romans and the strife of internal faction, and to this cause, as much as to her defeats by land, must we ascribe the ultimate success of Rome and the total destruction of Carthage.

CARTHAGINIAN BOAT.

PRESENT APPEARANCE OF THE PIRÆUS, OR HARBOR OF ATHENS.

ANCIENT GRECIAN GALLEY.

CHAPTER IV.

THE NAVAL HISTORY OF GREECE FROM THE EARLIEST TIMES TILL THE BATTLE OF SALAMIS.

THE position of the Grecian states was advantageous for purposes of navigation. It was washed by the Ægean Sea upon the east, by the Mediterranean on the south, and on the west by the Ionian seas. The Ægean, studded with islands, brought it into close intercourse with Asia Minor and the Phœnician frontiers. The voyage to Egypt was neither long nor difficult, though it had not so many resting places to the mariners. From the western side, there was a short and easy passage to Italy. The entire line of the extensive coast was indented with bays and harbors, offering every facility for navigation; while the two great gulfs that divided Hellas, or northern Greece, from the Peloponnesus, or southern Greece, must, in the very earliest ages, have forced naval affairs on the attention of the inhabitants.

The Pelasgi, who are supposed to have been the first inhabitants of Greece, were a nation of hunters and shepherds, and gave no attention to naval matters. Their conquerors and successors, the Hellenes, were of a more enterprising character, if we may give any credit to the traditions of the Heroic Age. The history of the period extending from the entrance of the Hellenes into Greece to the taking of Troy, is filled with accounts of wars, expeditions, and adventures. The details of these expeditions may be fabulous, but there must have been some foundation in fact for the principal events which are recorded. The exploits of Bellerophon and Perseus are the first in tradition. Both of these heroes are said to have sailed from Greece, and to have crossed over to Egypt, and sailed along the coasts of that country and Syria. Hercules succeeded them; but his exploits were all upon land. Theseus is said to have sailed to Crete to deliver Athens from the yoke of Minos, who, every ninth year, exacted a tribute of Athenian youths and virgins, and doomed them to perish in the jaws of the Minotaur. With the aid of Ariadne, the daughter of Minos, he vanquished the monster of the labyrinth; but on his homeward voyage, he abandoned his fair guide on the shore at Naxus. The arrival of Theseus at Athens, proved fatal to Ægeas, who was deceived by the black sail of the victim ships, which Theseus had forgotten to exchange for the concerted token of victory; and, in despair, he threw himself from the Europian rock.

Minos, the ruler of Crete, is a conspicuous character, in the traditions of the Heroic Age. He is said to have exercised a supremacy over the sea and the neighboring islands, and to have given to Greece the first model of a well-ordered state. He raised a great navy, scoured the Ægean, subdued the piratical Carians and Leleges, made himself master of the Cyclades, planted various colonies, and conducted a successful expedition against Attica, where he imposed tribute. He is even said to have carried his arms against Sicily, where he was cut off and his fleet destroyed. The leading events of his career are confirmed by Herodotus and other ancient historians. The dominion of the Cyclades was an almost indispensable condition of the naval power attributed to Minos, and the tradition that they were subject to his rule is confirmed by numerous traces. The maritime power of Crete is said to have declined after the death of Minos.

But the most astonishing features of the early mythical history of Greece were the Argonautic expedition and the siege of Troy. The first deserves close consideration. Though the story is wrapped in the mists of fable, yet that such an expedition may have been undertaken is as probable as the credited events in the career of Minos. The story is briefly thus:

In the generation before the Trojan war, Jason, a young Thessalian prince, had incurrred the jealousy of his kinsman Pelias, who reigned at Iolcos. The crafty king encouraged the adventurous youth to embark in a maritime expedition full of difficulty and danger. It was to be directed to a point far beyond the most remote which Greek navigation had hitherto reached in the same quarter; to the eastern corner of the sea, so celebrated in ancient times for the ferocity of the barbarians inhabiting its coasts, that it was commonly supposed to have derived from them the name of *Axenus*, the inhospitable, before it acquired the opposite name of the *Euxine*, from the civilization which was at length introduced by Greek settlers. Here, in the land of the Colchians, lay the goal, because this contained the prize, from which the voyage has been frequently called the adventure of the golden fleece. Jason having built a vessel of uncommon size—in more precise terms, the first fifty-oared galley his country had ever launched—and having manned it with a band of heroes, who assembled from various parts of Greece to share the glory of the enterprise, sailed to Colchis, where he not only succeeded in the principal object of his expedition, whatever this may have been, but carried off Medea, the daughter of the Colchian king, Æetes.

If this legend were to be believed, we should have the Greeks, in the infancy of their navigation, reaching the extreme limit which was long after attained by the adventurers who explored the same formidable sea and gained a footing on its coasts. This, however, is more probable than some of the other features of the story. The golden fleece was a sacred relic, nailed to an oak in the grove of Mars, at Colchis—at least, such is the tradition.

The Grecian expedition against Troy was the last event of the mythical period. According to the Iliad of Homer, Agamemnon, king of Greece, allied with Achilles, set out on the expedition with twelve hundred ships and 100,000 men, headed by the flower of the Grecian chivalry. The vessels were of rude construction, having only half-decks, and stays instead of anchors. But with this vast armament the besieged Troy could not be taken until the lapse of ten years. If the main incidents of the Iliad are to be taken as historically true, as many historians think they should be, the naval power of the Greeks, in the Heroic Age, was extensive, beyond what it was when Athens and Sparta were at their height of wealth and power. But the numbers of the armament are, doubtless, exaggerated, as observed by Thucydides.

During the long period of warfare between the Grecian states which followed the return of the expedition against Troy, we find nothing pertaining to naval affairs recorded. After the Dorians had succeeded in asserting their supremacy over the neighboring states, two expeditions are said to have proceeded from Peloponnesus to Crete. One of these issued from Laconia, the other from Argolis. Both expeditions succeeded in establishing colonies on the island, without resistance from the Cretans. The Dorians, or Spartans, as they were afterwards called, were essentially a warlike nation, and this disposition was confirmed and promoted by the laws enacted by Lycurgus. But the sea was never an element congenial to the Spartan spirit, and the sea-service was generally left to the Helots.

After the termination of the second war between the Spartans and Messenians, a portion of the inhabitants of the conquered cities of Messenia, betook themselves to their ships; but they were uncertain in which direction to steer their course. One of their leaders proposed that they should seize zacynthus, and from its ports infest the coasts of the Spartans. But the advice was rejected. Finally, it was resolved to seek the city of Rhegium, on the straits that separate Italy from Sicily; and, accordingly, the Messenians sailed to Rhegium, and making themselves masters of that city and the one upon the opposite side of the straits called zancle—they established a permanent colony.

THE Athenians engaged in commercial pursuits at a very early period of their history, and being of a more enterprising character than the Spartans, they soon attained considerable wealth and power as a people. One of their first naval expeditions was that led by Solon against the Megarians, in the island of Salamis, which was completely successful. Pisistratus, who usurped the government of Athens, just before Solon's death, appears to have maintained a con-

VIEW OF CORINTH.

siderable naval force; for, besides the conquest of the island of Naxus, he engaged in another expedition to a more distant quarter, the object of which may have been to provide a place of safety for himself and family upon a sudden change of fortune, but it was principally designed to increase his reputation at home. After the expulsion of the Pisistratidæ, a war broke out between Athens and Ægina. The latter had grown to be a wealthy and prosperous maritime state. The Æginetans were assisted by the Thebans: and while the Thebans ravaged the northern frontier of Athens, a squadron of war galleys left Ægina and stopping at various ports of the Attic coast, plundered many of the maritime towns, and did great damage.

Thucydides fixes the beginning of the seventh century, B. C., as the time of a considerable improvement in ship-building, which was first adopted in Corinth, and was imparted by a Corinthian, named Amenocles, to the Samians. Of the precise nature of this improvement we are not informed; but it is said to have given a new impulse to navigation, and to have enabled the Greeks to pursue their voyages farther and with more safety.

The prominent events which preceded the first war between the Grecian states and Persia are principally of a naval character. Naxus, the largest of the group of islands. called Cyclades, had become populous and powerful towards the close of the sixth century before our era. It maintained a considerable navy and could bring eight thousand men into the field. Aristagoras, the ruler of Miletus, was desirous of bringing the island under his control, but the undertaking surpassed his means. With the aid of Artaphernes, satrap of the Asiatic coast of the Ægean, he obtained the assistance of the king of Persia, the enterprise promising to bring the Cyclades under the government of that powerful monarchy. Two hundred ships and a Persian force were equipped and placed under the command of Megabates, a Persian of high quality. The expedition was ordered to sail to Miletus and take on board the Ionian force which had been raised by Aristagoras. In order to lull the enemy into security, Megabates made towards the Hellespont; but off the coast of Chios, he brought the fleet to anchor, meaning to take advantage of the first fair wind and run to Naxus, and surprise the principal town. While he was in this station, he one day made the round of the fleet to inspect the discipline observed by the inferior officers. On one ship, a Mydian, he found no watch and the commander absent. He immediately sent for him, and ordered him to be fastened to the side of his own galley, and his head passing through one of the port-holes, which were opened in the ancient vessels for the oars as in ours for the ordnance. Information of this degrading treatment of an officer was conveyed to Aristagoras, who immediately demanded his release. Megabates refusing to comply, Aristagoras went and set the officer at liberty. Indignant at this act of defiance, Megabates resolved to defeat the expedition. He secretly sent to warn the Naxians of their danger, and they forthwith made great preparations for defence. When the Persian fleet arrived before the town, they were in a condition to bear a long siege. The siege was continued four months, and then no progress being made, and the funds of the expedition all expended, it was raised, and the fleet returned.

ARISTAGORAS having resolved to revolt against the power of the Persian monarch, soon after his return to Miletus, applied for aid to Sparta and Athens. The Spartan king refused to join him, but Athens consented. A decree was passed to send a squadron of twenty ships to the Ionians, under the command of Melanthius, a man of the highest reputation. Aristagoras sailed back to Asia before the Athenian squadron, which was joined by five ships from Etruria. The expedition sailed to Ephesus, where the troops were landed. After various successes, the invaders were overwhelmed by numbers, and forced to retreat. The Athenians then sailed back to their own country.

Darius, the Persian king, was incensed at the daring of the Athenians, and resolved upon an invasion of Greece. But the first step was to subdue the revolting Ionians. The fleet of the Ionians, though abandoned by its allies, was not inactive. It first sailed to the north, where its presence induced Byzantium and the other cities of the coasts between the Euxine and the Ægean, to rise against the Persian government. The Persian general, Daurises, however, soon reduced the maritime cities to submission. A great fleet was equipped in the harbors of Phœnicia, Egypt, Cilicia, and Cyprus, and an attack

EXPEDITION OF MELANTHIUS.

upon Miletus, by sea and land, planned by Artaphernes. The Ionians resolved to abandon Miletus, and exert all their strength to drive the enemy from the Ægean, and the fleet was appointed to assemble at Ladé. Ladé was then a small island; by the depositions of the Mæander it has now become part of the plain which separates the site of Miletus from the sea. Here the naval force of the confederates met: Chios sent the largest squadron, a hundred galleys: the Lesbians, though their privateers were still at Byzantium with Histiæus, seventy: the Samians could still raise as many as sixty; but Phocæa, though she had not lost her old spirit, could equip no more than three. The united navy amounted to 353 triremes. The hostile fleet which was on its way from the East numbered 600. Notwithstanding this vast superiority in numbers, the Persian generals, when they considered that of the Ionians in nautical skill, felt that they were by no means sure of victory, and would fain have avoided the approaching conflict.

During the interval in which the hostile fleets were watching each other, neither willing to begin the decisive conflict, Dionysius, the commander of the Phocæans, observed that the naval camp at Ladé was far from displaying the order and good discipline which so critical a juncture demanded. In a general assembly he pointed out to his countrymen the danger of insubordination and supineness, and prevailed on them to commit themselves to his guidance. When he was invested with the chief command, he did not suffer a day to pass without devoting several hours to martial exercises. He drew out the fleet in order of battle, practised the rowers in the evolutions of a sea-fight, and kept the marines at the same time under arms in the places where their services would be required. After seven days of this laborious training, the troops began to murmur at what they easily persuaded themselves was a profitless hardship, and to rail at Dionysius as an ambitious meddler. It seemed intolerable that a man who had only brought three ships to join the fleet should domineer over all the rest: the Persians themselves could not lord it more tyrannical over their slaves; and they resolved to shake off the authority of Dionysius, and to assert the rights of freemen. Instead of going abroad to execute his commands, they henceforth dispersed themselves in parties over the island, and reposed during the heat of the day under tents which they pitched on the most agreeable spots. The Samian commanders were disgusted with this folly, for some of them, who were before inclined to accept the terms offered by the Persians, made use of it as an argument to draw the others over to their views. The end was, that they sent to their banished tyrant, Æaces, the son of Syloson, and declared their readiness to close with his late proposals. It was agreed that they should desert in the battle.

The Persian fleet now sailed confidently to the attack: the Ionians met them without suspicion of treachery. But in the beginning of the action the Samians quitted their post, and bore away to Samos. Only eleven captains refused to obey their superior officers, and kept their places; they were afterwards rewarded by a monument in the market place of Samos. The example of the rest, however, was followed by the Lesbians, and as the alarm spread, by the greater part of the fleet. The Chians almost alone remained firm amid the general consternation; but their skill and valor were at length overpowered by superior numbers, and they were compelled to fly. Those whose galleys were disabled from escaping the pursuit of the enemy, ran them aground at Cape Mycalé, and left them. They bent their way northward; but, passing through the Ephesian territory in the night, while the women were celebrating a festival, they were taken for robbers who had come with sacrilegious intentions, and were all cut to pieces by the Ephesians. Dionysius of Phocæa had fought till the struggle became desperate, and had taken three of the enemy's ships; when forced to fly, he sailed to Phœnicia, and sank several merchantmen, and, laden with spoil, steered for Sicily.

The Persian fleet continued its victorious career towards the Hellespont. The cities north of the Ægean were successively overpowered, and sank in the flames. The men of Byzantium and Chalcedon did not wait for the enemy's attack, but left their towns to found a new one called Mesembria, on the western coast of the Euxine.

Soon after this Persian victory, Mardonius, son-in-law of Darius, succeeded Artaphernes in the government of Ionia, and he adopted measures to keep it in subjection. The ambassadors whom he sent to Athens to demand submission were received with lofty scorn, and both sides prepared for hostilities of an active kind.

Mardonius had come with a mighty armament, which was designed to wreak the vengeance of Darius upon Athens and Eretria, and at

RECEPTION OF THE AMBASSADORS OF MARDONIUS.

the same time to spread the terror of his name, and to strengthen his power in Europe. A large fleet was to sweep the Ægean, and to exact obedience from the islands, while Mardonius himself led the land force into Greece, and on his way subdued the Thracian and Macedonian tribes which had not yet submitted. The fleet first directed its course to the Island of Thasus, which still drew a large revenue from the gold mines first opened there by the Phœnicians, as well as from others on the opposite continent. The wealth of the Thasians had tempted Histiæus, and his attack had induced them to increase their navy and to strengthen their fortifications. They now yielded to the Persians without a struggle; and the next year, when Darius, suspecting that their preparations were aimed against himself, commanded them to throw down their walls, and to surrender their ships, they acquiesced with equal readiness. But the Persian armament was soon after checked in its progress by a violent storm which overtook it off Mount Athos, and was thought to have destroyed not less than three hundred vessels and twenty thousand lives. Mardonius soon afterwards thought it prudent to end the expediton, and he returned to Asia.

In the third year after the last disastrous campaign (B. C. 490,) a force was collected in Cilicia, and placed under the command of two new generals, Datis, a Mede, and Artaphernes, son of the satrap of Lydia, and hence, as the king's nephew, superior in rank, but probably inferior both in age and military experience to his colleague, who seems to have been the real leader of the expedition. On the Cilician coast they found a fleet of six hundred triremes, together with horse transports: the whole army was taken on board, and sailed first to Samos, and thence, instead of making the round of the Ægean, which Herodotus thinks would have been preferred as the safer course but for the dread of Mount Athos, crossed directly to the Cyclades. Naxos, which had baffled the attempts of Aristagoras when seconded by the power of Persia, was the first and principal object of attack. The Naxians lost their courage at the appearance of the huge armament, abandoned their walls, and took refuge in the mountains. The Persians carried off all who had not time to escape, and committed the city and its temples to the flames.

The fleet held on its course through the islands, receiving their submission and taking from each a re-enforcement and hostages, and then sailed to Eubœa to accomplish one of the two great objects of the expedition. The first town before which it appeared was Carystus: it rejected the demands of the Persians, and would not serve them against its neighbors and brethren.

After the fall of Carystus the Persians laid siege to Eretria: the men who wished to sell themselves to the enemy prevailed on their fellow-citizens to abandon the design of flight, and, as they could not venture to meet the invading army in the field, to sustain a siege. For six days they made a brave defence, but on the seventh the gates were treacherously thrown open. The infamy of this deed fell on two men whom Herodotus describes as among the most eminent citizens; and perhaps its baseness was mitigated by political motives, which may have led them to regard Athens as an enemy more formidable and hateful than the Persians. The conquerors exactly fulfilled the commands of the king, the more rigorously that the fate of Eretria might strike terror into the Athenians. The city, with its temples, was plundered, burned, and razed to the ground: according to one tradition, which, however, rests on the half-poetical testimony of Plato, the Persian host swept the whole territory of Eretria, as it had done in Samos, and other islands. The captives, however, collected, were lodged in a safe place till they could be carried to the king; then the whole armament steered its course to the coast of Attica.

It was the aged tyrant Hippias who, as he had most earnestly urged the expedition, now guided the barbarian against his country. By his advice the fleet came to anchor in the Bay of Marathon, where it was sheltered from the northern gales by a promontory which runs out from the foot of Parnes. The army was landed, and there was fought the battle of Marathon, in which thirty thousand Greeks overthrew five hundred thousand Persians. After the rout was complete, the only hope of the Persians was to get aboard of their ships. The victors took seven of the galleys; but the rest put off with the remainder of the army. Instead of shaping their course eastward, the invaders steered towards Sunium, with the evident intention of proceeding to the southern coast of Attica. But the victorious army perceiving their object, marched for Athens, and arrived there before the Persian fleet appeared off the coast. The invaders then returned to Asia.

After the overthrow of the Persian hosts, the spirit of the Athe-

THE BRIDGE OF BOATS OVER THE HELLESPONT, USED BY XERXES.

nians was raised to the highest degree of heroic daring. Miltiades obtained a fleet of seventy ships, with which he attacked the island of Paros; but after a long siege, he was forced to abandon it and return to Athens. In the meantime, Darius had been succeeded upon the throne of Persia by his son Xerxes, and mighty preparations for another expedition into Greece were made throughout the dominions of Persia. For eight years, all the western part of Asia was employed in raising and equipping the greatest armament upon record. The Hellespont was bridged by Greek engineers to allow of the passage of the host.

Early in the spring of 480 B. C., the expedition set out under the command of Xerxes. The vast numbers of the land forces were reviewed, and then the king went on board a Sidonian vessel, where a golden tent had been prepared for him, to inspect the fleet; and he caused its divisions and numbers to be registered. The fleet consisted of one thousand two hundred and seven ships of war, and besides the native crews, each was manned with thirty marines, Persians, Medes, or Sacians. But as they moved southward, both army and fleet received additions from the seaports of Thrace and Macedonia, which Herodotus computes at three hundred thousand infantry and one hundred and twenty triremes—thus making the whole number of Xerxes' host on land about two millions of men, and one thousand three hundred and twenty-seven ships in the fleet.

From Doriscus, the army pursued its march along the coast, accompanied by the fleet. At Acanthus, Xerxes stopped to survey a wonderful canal constructed by his order, by which the fleet was saved from the danger of doubling Mount Athos, where the fleet of Mardonius had been wrecked. At that place, the army and the fleet parted for the first time. The army struck across the Chalcidian peninsula to Therme, where, after the naval armament had coasted the intervening bays and had strenghened itself with ships and men drawn from the Chalcidian ports, the two forces again met. During the stay of the fleet at Therme, Xerxes, indulged his curiosity by sailing to the mouth of the Peneus, and viewing the remakable defile through which it issues from the Thessalian plains.

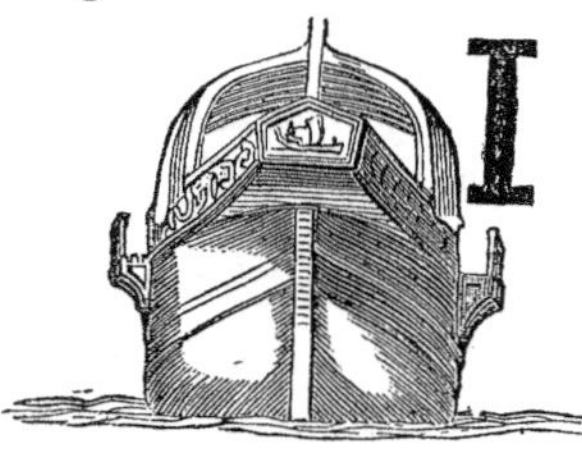

IN the meantime, the Grecian states were not idle. Jealousy and hatred prompted the Argives and Thessalians to remain quiet during the struggle, but most of the other states, under the lead of Athens and Sparta, made preparations for defence. Themistocles, the leading man at Athens, always had the increase of her maritime power as his first object, and at this particular juncture, he made efforts to raise a fleet of sufficient strength to meet the Persians. The Corcyreans whose naval force was among the most powerful in Greece, promised to send a fleet to take part in the conflict; and they accordingly manned sixty ships. But their squadron was detained, they afterwards alleged, by contrary winds, which prevented it from doubling Malea, and arriving before the hour of need was over. The Spartan deputies from the Grecian Congress which had been called, proceeded to Syracuse, and applied to King Gelo for assistance. He offered to aid them with two hundred triremes and thirty thousand men, on condition that he should command the allied forces. The conditions prevented the alliance, and the Spartans returned.

When the news came that the Persians were at Pieria, on the borders of Thessaly, more than two-thirds of the whole naval force of the allies set sail for the north coast of Eubœa.

The northern side of Eubœa afforded a commodious and advantageous station: it was a long beach, called, from a temple at its eastern extremity, Artemisium, capable of receiving the galleys if it should be necessary to draw them upon the shore, and commanding a view of the open sea and the coast of Magnesia, and consequently an opportunity of watching the enemy's movements as he advanced towards the south; while, on the other hand, its short distance from Thermopylæ enabled the fleet to keep up a quick and easy communication with the land force. Here, therefore, 271 triremes were stationed under the Spartan admiral Eurybiades. A Spartan had been appointed to the command, though the Lacedæmonians sent only ten ships, by the desire of the allies, who refused to obey an Athenian. Yet Athens manned 127 ships, and also supplied the Chalcidians with twenty others. It may have been principally the jealousy of Ægina that led to the determination not to submit to Athenian command. The force she sent on this occasion, eighteen triremes, bore no proportion to her power, and to the end of the war she husbanded her navy under the plea of protecting her own shores. Corinth contributed forty sail, Megara twenty, and the rest were chiefly drawn from the Dorian cities of Peloponnesus, which, though not hostile to Athens, could not acknowledge an Ionian leader without a considerable sacrifice of national prejudices.

While the Persian army was waiting at Pieria till a road had been opened for it through the thick forest that clothed the sides of the Cambunian Hills, or soon after it had crossed over into Thessaly, a squadron of ten fast sailing ships was despatched from the fleet of Therme to obtain intelligence about the movements of the Greeks. Off the island of Sciathus they fell in with three Greek ships, which were there stationed on the look-out, one an Athenian, the others of Trœzen and Ægina. They took to flight at the sight of the Persians, who pursued and captured the Trœzenian, and, after a brave struggle, the Æginetan. The victors selected the comeliest man they found among their Trœzenian prisoners, and sacrificed him at the prow of his ship for an omen of victory: this fearful superstition, however, did not prevent them from paying a generous respect to the valor of Pytheas the Æginetan, who, after his ship was taken, fought till he was almost cut to pieces. The Athenians ran their vessel aground in the mouth of the Peneus, and made their way home through Thessaly.

This first appearance of the enemy was speedily announced by fire-signals from Sciathus to the Greeks at Artemisium. The alarm it excited was so great, that the admiral resolved on quitting this station, and retiring to Chalcis, where a few ships might defend the Euripus: before he sailed away, he set watches on the heights of Eubœa, to secure the earliest intelligence of the hostile armament. The Persian squadron, after setting up a stone pillar to mark a dangerous rock in the channel between Sciathus and Magnesia, returned to Therme with the report that the coast was clear. On this information, the whole fleet got under way eleven days after Xerxes began his march from Therme, and the same evening came to anchor on the southern coast of Magnesia. From the mouth of the Peneus to the Gulf of Pagasæ the whole coast is rugged, and destitute of harbors, and even of good roadsteads, but more especially at the foot of Ossa and of Pelion. Night overtook the Persians before they could reach the Pagasæan Gulf; but under the brow of Pelion they found a beach, stretching from the town of Canastæa to the Cape of Sepias, and here they resolved to wait for the morning. As the low shore was of small extent in proportion to their numbers, only a small part of the ships could be drawn up on the beach; the rest rode at anchor, their sterns turned towards the sea, line within line. The night (it was the middle of summer) was fair and calm; but when the dawn was beginning to break, a ripple and a swell of the sea gave notice of an approaching change. As the wind rose from the northeast, those who paid heed to the signs of the weather, and could find a place of shelter, secured themselves from the coming storm; but on the rest it burst with irresistible fury. The ships were torn from their anchorage, driven against each other, and dashed upon the cliffs. The tempest raged with unabated violence for three days and nights. The commanders began to fear lest the Thessalians should be encouraged by the general confusion to fall upon them, and complete their ruin; and they hastily formed a high fence out of the wrecks round the fleet that was drawn up on the beach. At length the storm subsided; but for many miles the shores were strewed with wrecks and with corpses. The ships of war destroyed were reckoned, on the lowest calculation, at 400: the lives, the transports, the stores, the treasure lost, were past counting. When the sea grew calm, the remains of the fleet doubled the southern headland of Magnesia, and put into the Gulf of Pagasæ.

WRECK OF THE PERSIAN FLEET.

The day after the gale got up, while it was at its height, the Greek scouts, who had been left to look out for the enemy, came to Chalcis with such a description of its effects, that every one believed the whole armada to be almost utterly ruined, and after a thanksgiving and a libation to Poseidon, the fleet returned to its former station at Artemisium, to complete the victory which the gods had begun. It arrived in time to capture fifteen Persian ships, which had been detained at Sepias after the departure of the main body, and as they followed in search of it, seeing the Greeks off Artemisium, took them for friends, and only discovered their error when they had gone too far to retreat.

The loss the Persians had suffered, though it amounted to a number exceeding that of the whole Grecian fleet, was scarcely felt in their huge armament. When, from their station at Aphetæ, they perceived the slender force of their adversary, their only concern was to prevent him from escaping: they could not imagine that he would venture on a contest. They, therefore, without delay, detached a squadron of 200 sail, with orders to make for the north, that their object might not be suspected, but when they had got out to sea beyond Sciathus, to bear away to the south, round the southern extremity of Eubœa, and then sail up the channel, and cut off the retreat of the Greeks. The Greeks, on their part, who had persuaded themselves that they should scarcely find an enemy to combat, were at first thrown into consternation by the sight of the power opposed to them, and it is said that Themistocles had great difficulty in restraining them from again turning their backs, and seeking shelter in the Euripus. But whatever foundation it may have had, the Greeks not only stayed, but soon recovered from their first astonishment, and did not shrink from looking the enemy in the face. They had received early information of his plans from a man named Scyllias, who deserted to them from Aphetæ, and was so famous as a diver that he was commonly believed to have traversed the whole intervening space, about ten miles, under water. The news reached them in the morning, and it was determined to wait till midnight, and then sail to meet the squadron which had been sent round Eubœa. In the mean while the Persians did not move from their station at Aphetæ, for they feared lest they should scare their puny enemy to flight: they deemed their own ships superior, not only in numbers, but as sailers. The Greeks were surprised at their inaction, and having waited till noon expecting an attack, they then resolved to venture out and try their strength. The Persians were astonished at their foolhardiness, and hastened to meet and enclose them. They formed a circle round them; the Greeks first drew their line into a smaller circle, with their prows facing the surrounding enemy, and then, at the signal, darted forward, like rays, to pierce and break the wall of ships that encompassed them. The Persians were thrown into disorder by the attack, and lost thirty ships, but the combat was still undecided, when the approach of night put an end to it. Each party returned to his station with altered feelings, the Persians perplexed and disheartened, the Greeks with new hopes. They had gained, not, indeed, a clear victory, but a pledge of one; confidence in their own strength, and insight into the enemy's weakness.

In the following night another violent summer storm, accompanied with torrents of rain, thunder and lightning, terrified more than it hurt the Persians at Aphetæ, where the road was choked with the wrecks and the bodies that were driven in from the scene of the action. But the same storm overtook the squadron that was sailing round Eubœa with perhaps greater fury, and off a part of the coast infamous in ancient times under the name of Cœla (the Hollows.)

Their resolution was confirmed the next day by the arrival of an Athenian who had been stationed at Thermopylæ with a light galley, and now came with the news that the Spartan king, Leonidas, was slain, and all his men killed or taken, and that the Persians were masters of the pass, which was the key to Phocis, Bœotia, and Attica.

While the storm of destruction was pending over Greece, Athens had sent to Delphi for advice. The oracle advised the Athenians to trust to their "wooden walls," for the city would be destroyed. The wooden walls were explained to mean the fleet, which, since it had been increased by Themistocles, was deemed the surest bulwark of Athens. The Athenians resolved to follow the advice, and on the approach of the Persians, removed their families and movable property to their ships and then sailed to Salamis, Ægina, and Træzen, where they were kindly received.

The fleet assembled at Salamis was re-enforced by a squadron, composed partly of additional ships furnished by the same states which had contributed their succor at Artemisium, and partly of a small

THE ATHENIANS ABANDONING THEIR CITY AND TAKING TO THE FLEET.

number sent from other quarters; among these were four from Naxos, which had been intended by the Naxians for the service of the barbarians; but Democritus, who commanded one of them, and was a man of great influence in this island, persuaded his countrymen to neglect the orders they had received at home, and to join the Greeks. The most remote cities of the Greek continent that took a part in the national cause were the Corinthian colonies of Leucas and Ambracia. To the west of the Adriatic, Croton alone showed itself touched by the danger of Greece: it sent one ship; though, perhaps, this merit belonged to the commander, Phäyllus, who had obtained three victories at the Pythian games, and probably equipped his ship at his own expense. The whole armament thus strengthened, with the addition of two deserters, amounted to 380 ships.

Eurybiades still held the chief command. He had called a council of war to deliberate on the position to which it would be most advisable to await the enemy's approach. Almost all voices concurred in the opinion that they ought to leave Salamis, and take up a station nearer the Isthmus. But the Athenians strenuously opposed the measure, and after much debate, the wisdom of Themistocles triumphed, and the fleet remained at Salamis.

Six days after the Greeks had left Artemisium the Persian fleet arrived in the Attic bay of Phalerum. In passing through the channel of Eubœa, it is said that the Persian admiral, seeing himself locked in by the land, which seemed to close the Euripus, suspected that his pilot, a Bœotian named Salganeus, had purposely drawn him into a snare, and hastily put him to death.

Xerxes went on board one of the ships with Mardonius, and summoned the chief commanders of the fleet into his presence, to deliberate on the expediency of seeking an immediate engagement. Among a number of vassal princes who conducted their squadrons in person, was a woman, Artemisia, a queen of Caria. She alone, according to Herodotus, perceived the rashness of hastening a contest by which every thing might be lost, and nothing would be gained but what might reasonably be looked for without one, if time were allowed for the disunion and dispersion of the Greeks, which would inevitably take place when the want of provisions should have driven them from Salamis to the Isthmus. Artemisia, if these were her views, thought like Mnesiphilus; but there was no Themistocles in the Persian council. The king resolved on attacking the enemy without delay. He attributed the checks his fleet had met with at Artemisium to the remissness of servants acting at a distance from the eye of their master. In the approaching conflict his presence would stimulate the brave and overawe the timid. That same day he ordered the fleet to sail up towards Salamis, and to form in line of battle; but the hour was so late that there was only time to perform the evolution without advancing into the straits. It was resolved, however, that the battle should take place on the morrow.

The sight of the Persian Armada drawn up in the order of battle created an alarm among the Greeks equal to the former one, which Themistocles had labored to counteract. The Athenian commander, finding persuasion fruitless, resolved to save the Athenians in spite of their allies, and their allies in spite of themselves. While the other commanders were debating passionately, he sent a message to the Persian commander, informing him of the panic among the Greeks and that they were bent on flight; and he suggested that the Persians could cut off the retreat of the Greeks, by surrounding them. The object of this stratagem was to make the Greeks fight, if for nothing else, for their own safety. The bait took, as Themistocles wished, and the movements of the Persians were so prompt that the island of Salamis was completely surrounded, while the Greeks were engaged in discussion. Nothing then remained but to brace every nerve for the battle.

When morning came, the Persian fleet was seen covering the sea between Psyttaleia and the mouth of the channel, and the army lining the shores of the Gulf of Eleusis. On one of the heights of Mount Ægaleos, the last limb of the long range of hills that, branching out from Cithæron, stretches to the coast fronting the eastern side of Salamis, a lofty throne was raised for Xerxes, from which he could view the fight, quicken the tardy, and goad on the backward by the terror of his presence, and dispense instant punishments or rewards, as justice might demand. By his side were his scribes, to register the names of those who caught the king's attention, by any signal exploit. The Greeks had different motives to animate them, and a different presence to cheer them. Before they embarked, Themistocles addressed them in a speech, the substance of which, as Herodotus reports it, was simply to set before them, on the one side, all

BATTLE OF SALAMIS.

that was best, on the other, all that was worst, in the nature and condition of man, and to exhort them to choose and hold fast the good.

As they were about to take their station, a vessel arrived from Ægina, which had been sent the day before, when the resolution of defending Salamis was adopted, to implore the assistance of Æacus and his line, the tutelary heroes of Ægina.

The Greeks awaited the advance of the Persians in the Straits, which in the narrowest part are no more than a quarter of a mile wide. As the Persians approached, the Greeks backed their galleys, probably till they saw the enemy closely pent in the brief space, which permitted only a small part of his force, more than triple their own numbers, to be brought into action together. Then the ship of the Æacids, or, as was more generally believed, an Athenian, commanded by Ameinias, darted forward and struck one of the Persians. This was the signal for a general engagement. The Persians exerted their utmost efforts, and did not yield to the Greeks in courage and perseverance; every man fought as if the eyes of the king were upon him. But the valor of the Greeks, if not directed by superior skill, was cooler and more deliberate, for it had not to struggle with any of the impediments which threw their antagonists into confusion and took away their presence of mind. Several causes contributed to this effect. The Persian vessels, those especially in the foremost line, were taller and larger than those of the Greeks, and were so much the more exposed to the action of a strong breeze which regularly blew up the channel at a certain time of the day. Themistocles is said to have foreseen the advantage that might be derived from it, and to have delayed the battle to the hour when it was expected to get up. The Persians ships were turned by the wind and the waves, their evolutions were thwarted, and their sides exposed to the attacks of the enemy's prows. While those in front were thus embraced, the commanders of the hindmost, impatient to signalize themselves in the presence of the king, pressed forward to the scene of action, and often fell foul of their friends whom they met retreating. Some of the Phœnicians, whose galleys had been disabled by the shock of some Ionian triremes, which had been accidentally driven against them, went on shore, and complained to the king of what they called the treachery of the Ionians. The loyalty of the Ionians was not unsuspicious, and Xerxes listened to the charge, till an extraordinary exploit of one of their galleys convinced him of their fidelity, and excited him against their accusers. The Ionian had struck and sunk an Attic ship, when she was herself attacked and borne down by an Æginetan: her deck, however remained above water, so as to allow her crew still to stay on board. From this situation her men cleared the deck of the Æginetans with their javelins, and boarded and captured the ship which had sunk their own. When the king saw this, he commanded that the Phœnicians, who had calumniated the bravest and stanchest of his servants, should lose their heads.

Though the complaint of the Phœnicians was probably groundless, it cannot be doubted that the confusion which soon began to prevail in the Persian fleet was greatly aggravated, and rendered more mischievous by the variety of forces that composed it. The Ægyptians, the Phœnicians, the Cilicians, the Cyprians, the Ionians, and the other nations that fought in it, were united by no bond but their compulsory service of the same master; and, as they could feel no interest in the cause they were forced to support, so they could be little concerned about any damage they might inflict on their brother slaves which did not endanger their own safety, and must have been always ready to sacrifice every other object to this. An adventure, which Herodotus describes, was probably not the only instance of this spirit which the battle afforded. The Carian heroine, Artemisia, was chased by Ameinias, who did not suspect the value of the prize he had in view; for the Athenians, indignant, it is said, at being invaded by a woman, had set a price of 10,000 drachmas on her head. She was flying with many others—for it was when disorder had become general among the Persians—and, hard pressed by her pursuers, saw before her the galley of the Calyndian Damasithymus. Without scruple she struck and sunk it: not a man of the whole crew was saved. Ameinias, believing that he had been chasing a friend, turned away from her; while Xerxes, who saw the occurrence, but only learned the name of Artemisia, loudly expressed his admiration of her courage and skill.

The event of the battle was really decided at the first onset, which threw the unwieldy armament into a confusion from which it could never recover, and which so many causes co-operated to increase. Yet it appears to have been long before the resistance of the mass, whether active or inert, was finally overcome; and night had begun to draw

XERXES RETREATING TO HIS SHIPS.

in ere the remains of the Persian fleet took refuge in Phalerum, to which the Greeks attempted not to pursue it. When the vanquished enemy began to seek safety in flight, a squadron of Æginetan ships, which had stationed itself near the mouth of the channel, met the fugitives, completed their defeat, and cut off many who had escaped from the conflict unhurt.

ANCIENT PERSIAN BOAT.—FROM A BAS RELIEF AT TAKT I BOSTAN.

HEAVY ARMED CAVALRY.

CHAPTER V.

CONCLUSION OF THE PERSIAN WARS.

THE day after the great sea-fight at Salamis—the most glorious in Grecian history, Xerxes resolved to return to Asia. The Persian fleet received orders to sail for the Hellespont with all speed, to guard the bridges till the king's arrival. As they sailed in the dark by Cape Zoster, they were deceived by the appearance of some rocky islets, which are scattered near the coast, and taking them for Greek ships, fled, panic-struck, in different directions. The error was detected in time to prevent a dispersion, and they pursued their course to the Hellespont without further interruption. About the middle of the next day, the Greeks received information of the departure of the Persian fleet. They instantly gave chase; but proceeding as far as the Cyclades without catching sight of them, the Greeks returned. The Persian fleet wintered at Cuma and Samos, while Mardonius, with three hundred thousand of the best Persian troops wintered in Thessaly.

When the spring had opened the sea, the Persians united their fleet at Samos, under the command of three new admirals. Their whole force amounted to three hundred ships, of which the Ionian squadron formed a part. They watched the Ionians with suspicion. A revolt in Ionia, seconded by the victorious Greeks, would give them full employment. Their suspicions and fears were not ill grounded. When the Grecian fleet, consisting of one hundred and ten ships, met at Ægina in the spring, under the command of Leotychides, king of Sparta, the successor of Demaratus, and Xanthippus, son of Ariphron, the prosecutor of Miltiades, some Ionian refugees, who had failed in an attempt against Strattis, the tyrant of Chios, came over to solicit aid for the purpose of restoring Ionia to independence. They had already applied to Sparta, and seem to have been referred to the judgment of the allies. But the only point they could carry with the commanders of the fleet was to prevail on them to advance eastward as far as Delos, and even this movement was made with great reluctance, and perhaps to many seemed too bold. The intercourse between Ionia and Greece had not been active enough to render the eastern coast of the Ægean familiar to the Greeks, particularly to those of Peloponnesus. Beyond Delos, their imagination covered the sea with hostile forces, and Samos lay as far out of their self-traced field of action as the Pillars of Hercules. Thus mutual fears kept the interval between the two islands open, and the two fleets at rest, though in an attitude of defence.

But the contest was decided upon the land, by the total rout of the vast army of Mardonius at Platæa. The allies then decided to maintain a fleet of one hundred galleys to prosecute the war against Persia. On the same day that the battle was fought at Platæa, the commander of the allied fleet, one of the Spartan kings, received messages from Samos, inviting him to proceed to the coast of Ionia and thus assist in a revolt of the Ionians. Lotychides rejected the first proposal, but subsequently agreed to comply; accordingly he set sail for Samos.

On arriving there, he found one part of the prediction of the envoys fulfilled. The Persian admirals did not venture to meet him on the sea, and, at his approach, sent away the Phœnician squadron, and with the remainder of the fleet sailed across to the mainland to seek the protection of the land force which was stationed, under the command of Tigranes, on the coast, at the foot of the mountains that end in the promontory of Mycalé, opposite the southern extremity of Samos. The ships were drawn up on the beach at the foot of the mountain, and enclosed within a wall hastily constructed of stones and timber. The army was posted on the shore in front of it. The Greeks were at first confounded by the retreat of the enemy, and by the new position he had taken, and debated for a time, whether they should return to Delos, or make for the Hellespont. At length, however, they resolved not to give way to the unexpected obstacle, but to cross over to Mycalé and offer battle. When they came near the shore, Leotychides repeated the stratagem which Themistocles had used on the retreat from Artemisium for a similar purpose. When his galley was within hearing of the Persian troops, he addressed a proclamation by the voice of a herald to the Ionians, in which he exhorted them, in the approaching battle, to remember first the liberty of their country, and next the watchword which he gave them. All who heard him he desired to convey the same summons to the absent. This contrivance succeeded in the principal object; the Persians believed that a plan of desertion and revolt had been already formed among the Ionians, to be carried into execution at the first favorable opportunity, and that they had just received the signal. When, therefore, Leotychides, finding that the enemy had no intention of coming to an engagement at sea, landed his men to attack them on the shore, they disarmed the Samians, who were most strongly suspected of disaffection, and removed the Milesians from the camp, under the pretext of posting them on the top of Mycalé to guard the passes. The Persians were drawn up at the foot of the mountain behind the breastwork, which, according to their usual practice, they formed with their serried shields.

The Greeks attacked and defeated them and then returned to their fleet, and steered to the Hellespont, where it was supposed the bridges were still standing. They had been removed, and then Leotychides and the Peloponnesians proposed to sail home. The Athenians refused, and while their allies left them, they made an attempt to recover their ancient dominion in the peninsula of Chersonesus. They blockaded Elæus all winter, and at last succeeded in completing the conquest. The fleet then returned to Attica.

After the Persian defeat, the power of Athens rose rapidly and surely. Her maritime rivals, Ægina and Corinth, soon became jealous of her greatness, and Sparta was not long behind them. To establish the dominion of Athens upon the sea was the final aim of the policy of Themistocles. The navy was considerably enlarged, and the harbors improved and fortified.

In the year following the fall of Sestus (B. C. 477,) the allied fleet again put to sea; its entire force is not recorded, but the Peloponnesian states equipped twenty ships, Athens thirty, which were commanded by Aristides and Cimon the son of Miltiades, who was now fast rising towards the place which his father had once held in the public esteem. Pausanias was at the head of the whole armament. It first sailed to Cyprus, and wrested the greater part of the island from the Persians, and then steered for the north of the Ægean, and laid siege to Byzantium, which soon surrendered.

The Spartan portion of the fleet withdrew soon after this, in consequence of the conduct of Pausanias, and the acknowledgement of the supremacy of Athens, by the smaller states.

In the year 466, B. C., Cimon obtained a most brilliant naval victory over the Persians. A great sea and land force had been collected at the mouth of the Eurymedon, in Pamphylia; the fleet, according to Ephorus, who is most moderate in his numbers, amounted to three hundred and fifty, and the Persian commanders expected to be joined by eighty Phœnician galleys from Cyprus. Cimon having strengthened his fleet by successive reinforcements, as he slowly moved along the south coast of Asia Minor, till it amounted to two hundred and fifty galleys, provoked the enemy to an engagement before the arrival of the Phœnicians, and having defeated them, and sunk or taken two hundred ships, sailed up the river to their camp, and landing his men, flushed with victory, completely routed the Persian army, and carried away the rich booty which they left in their tents. According to the author whom Plutarch follows, he still found time for another victory the same day, and having sailed to meet the Phœnician squadron, which had not heard of the defeat of their allies, fell in with it, and destroyed the whole.

A war broke out in the year 457, B. C., between Athens on one side, and Ægina and Corinth on the other. Both Ægina and Corinth were powerful maritime states and were jealous of the increase of the

GALLEY FROM POMPEII.

Athenian naval strength. The Athenians defeated the allied fleet of their enemies off the Island of Ecrypbalea, in the Saronic Gulf; and, shortly afterwards, Leverates, the Athenian commander, defeated them again in a great sea fight, near Ægina, and took seventy of their galleys. In 455, B. C., the Æginetans were obliged to capitulate to the Athenians and surrender all their ships, and thus was a rival naval power humbled. In the same year—an Athenian armament of fifty galleys, with four thousand heavy armed troops on board, sailed round Peloponnesus under Tolmides, burned the Spartan arsenal of Gythinsu, took a town named Chalcis, belonging to the Corinthians, and defeated the Sicyonians, who attempted to oppose the landing of the troops. But these successes were counterbalanced by defeats in Egypt. Megabyzus, the Persian general, forced the Greeks to take refuge in an island in the Nile, where he besieged them for eighteen months. At length, he contrived to turn the stream, which separates the island from his own side of the river, into new channels, and conducted the work so rapidly, that the Greek galleys were all left aground, and were fired by the Athenians themselves, that they might not fall into the hands of the Persians. The greater part of the Greeks were dispersed or killed. But the misfortunes of the Athenians did not end with the destruction of their fleet and army on the Nile. They had sent a squadron of fifty galleys to the relief of their countrymen, which, arriving before the news of the recent disaster had reached them, were surprised by a combined attack of the Persian land force and a Phœnician fleet, and but few escaped to bear the tidings to Athens.

About five years after the events above related, Cimon was appointed to the command of a fleet of two hundred galleys, with which he sailed to Cyprus, and sent a squadron of sixty galleys to the assistance of Amyrtæus, the Pretender, while he himself, with the rest, laid siege to Citium. Here he was carried off by sickness, and, on account of the want of supplies, the armament was compelled to raise the siege. But Cimon's spirit still animated his countrymen, who, when they had sailed away with his remains, fell in with a great fleet of Cilician and Phœnician galleys, near the Cyprian Salamis, and, having completely defeated them, followed up their naval victory with another which they gained on shore over the troops landed from the ships, of the enemy. After this, they were joined by the squadron which had been sent to Egypt, and all sailed home.

Numerous naval expeditions, on a small scale, were undertaken by the Athenians, during the sway of Pericles, and they were generally successful. The Samians having quarrelled with Miletus, the Miletians sought the aid of Athens, and Pericles sailed with fifty galleys, and with the assistance of a party of Samos overthrew the government and established a democracy. He then returned. But the Samians applied to the Peloponnesian states for assistance. While they were deliberating on the propriety of interfering, Pericles, accompanied by nine colleagues, crossed the sea with a fleet of sixty sail, to suppress the revolting Samians.

They had learned that a fleet was expected to come to the assistance of the Samians from Phœnicia, and some galleys were sent to look out for it, while another small squadron was despatched to bring up the re-inforcements to be furnished by Chios and Lesbos. Though his numbers were reduced by these detachments to forty-four galleys,

Pericles did not shrink from engaging with a Samian fleet of seventy, including twenty transports, as it was returning from Miletus, and gained a victory. Shortly after he received an addition to his forces of forty ships from Athens, and five-and-twenty from Chios and Lesbos, which enabled him to land a body of troops sufficient to drive the enemy into the town, and to invest it with a triple line of intrenchments. Yet it appears that, even after the siege was formed, another sea fight took place, in which the Samians, who were commanded by the philosopher Melissus, were victorious. The advantage, however, must have been very slight, or soon followed by a reverse; for we find that, while the hopes of the Samians rested on the Phœnician fleet, and they despatched five galleys to hasten its movements, Pericles thought himself strong enough to take sixty ships and sail along the coast of Caria to meet the expected enemy. The Phœnicians did not come up; but during his absence the besieged drew out their remaining galleys, and surprised the naval encampment of the Athenians, sunk their guardships, and defeated the rest, which were brought out in disorder to repel the sudden attack. This success made them masters of the sea, and enabled them to introduce supplies into the town. They retained the ascendant fourteen days; it was, perhaps, nearly so long before the Athenians were able to convey the news to Pericles. On the return, the state of things was reversed, and the Samians once more closely besieged. But the effort they had made seems to have excited some alarm at Athens, and to have induced the Athenians to put forth more of their strength. A squadron of forty galleys, under three eminent commanders, Hagnon, Phormio, and Thucydides, was followed by one of twenty sail under Tlepolemus and Anticles, and this by thirty others from Chios and Lesbos. Yet even this overpowering force did not deter the Samians, though the succors expected from Phœnicia did not arrive, from venturing on another sea fight, which was soon decided, so as to leave them no means of doing more than remain on the defensive. They held out nine months, and were then so reduced by famine, that they capitulated, and delivered all their ships into the hands of the Athenians.

After his return, Pericles conducted a large and gallant armament into the Euxine Sea, for the purpose of displaying the power of Athens, and strengthening her influence among the cities and nations

GRECIAN WARRIOR IN ARMOUR.

on those coasts. The city of Synope was distracted by a civil war between the partisans and opponents of Timesilaus, and the friends of liberty applied to Pericles for aid. He left them thirteen galleys, under the command of Lamachus, a brave and active officer, and through their means, the democrats triumphed. Pericles introduced a regulation for the purpose of keeping the crews of the Athenian ships in training, which provided that a squadron of sixty galleys should be sent out every year, and kept at sea eight months. This contributed a great deal to the efficiency of the navy.

Before the expiration of the Thirty Years' Truce between Athens and Sparta, a war occurred between the maritime states of Corinth and Corcyra. The Corinthians set out to relieve their colony of Epidamnus with a fleet of seventy-five ships, and two thousand heavy armed men.

When they had reached the mouth of the Ambracian Gulf, they were met by a herald sent in a boat, by the Corcyræans, to forbid them to advance farther; a message which was of course disregarded. In the mean while the Corcyræans manned all their galleys which were fit for service, amounting to eighty sail, and put out to meet the enemy. The Corinthians were totally defeated, with the loss of fifteen ships, and returned home, leaving the Corcyræans masters of the sea. The victorious fleet sailed first to the Corinthian colony, Leucas, where the troops ravaged the land, and then to Cyllene, the arsenal of the Eleans, which was burned, in revenge for the aid which Elis had furnished to the Corinthians. The allies of Corinth on the western coast were so infested by the Corcyræans, that the Corinthians were obliged, in the course of the summer, to send out another fleet to protect them, which continued to watch the enemy's movements, sometimes from Actium, and sometimes from Chimerium in Thresprotia. But though the Corcyræans took a station at the opposite headland of Lucimne, no offer of battle was made on either side, and on the approach of winter both returned home.

Great preparations were made by both parties for renewing the contest, and ambassadors sent to the Athenians to secure assistance. But the Athenians desired to see these two naval powers waste their strength in a war, and they only entered into a defensive alliance with the Corcyræans.

The preparations which the Corinthians had been making from the time of their defeat now enabled them, with the help of their allies, Elis, Megara, Leucas, Ambracia, and Anactorium, to send out a fleet of one hundred and fifty galleys, which proceeded to the Thesprotian port Chimerium, where they encamped, and were joined by a considerable number of the Epirots, who were generally friendly to them. The Corcyræans, whose force amounted to one hundred and ten galleys, took their station, with the ten from Athens, at a little island —one of a group called Sybota, or the Swine pastures—while their troops, reinforced by one thousand heavy armed Zacynthians, were encamped on their own coast at Leucimne. A few days after, the two fleets met in order of battle, the Corinthians, in the left of their own line, being opposed to the ten Attic ships, which were placed at the extremity of the Corcyræan right.

The engagement which ensued—the greatest, Thucydides observes, that had taken place between Greeks to that day—was, however, more like a battle on shore than a sea fight. For on both sides, according to the ancient practice, the decks were crowded with heavy armed troops, and archers, and dartmen, and, after the first onset, the ships, for the most part, remained wedged together in a compact mass, on which the men fought as on firm ground, no room being left for the *diecplus*, the evolution which was the chief display of skill in the naval warfare of the Greeks, by which the enemy's line was suddenly pierced and the oars of the adverse galley swept away. The Corcyræans on the left, however, soon put to flight and dispersed the enemy's right wing, which was formed by the Megarian and other allies of the Corinthians, and pursuing them to the shore with twenty galleys, landed near the camp, where they plundered and fired the deserted tents. But the remainder of their fleet was overpowered by the superior numbers of the Corinthians. The Athenian commanders, fearful of transgressing their instructions, at first abstained from mixing in the fight, and contented themselves with threatening the enemy by their presence at the points where their allies were hard pressed. Gradually, however, as victory declared itself on the side of the Corinthians, and the danger of the Corcyræans grew more imminent, the Athenians were drawn into the combat, and at length took as active a part against the Corinthians as the Corcyræans themselves. The first object of the Corinthians, when the main body of the Corcyræans had been put to flight, was to wreak their vengeance on the survivors who

GREAT BATTLE BETWEEN THE CORCYRÆANS AND CORINTHIANS.

were clinging to the wrecks; and they were so eager in the slaughter, that they destroyed several of their of their own men belonging to the vessels which had been sunk in the defeat of their right wing. Then, having chased the enemy to land, they returned to the coast of Epirus, with all they could take up of their slain, and with their disabled galleys; and having deposited them there, in a desert harbor called, like the islands, Sybota, again put to sea, and made for Corcyra. The Corcyræans, though they had lost seventy vessels and had only destroyed thirty, were yet resolved, in defence of their territory, to meet the attack with their remaining force. It was late in the evening; but the pæan had already been raised for battle, when the Corinthians suddenly retreated at the sight of another squadron which was advancing, unperceived by the Corcyræans, towards the scene of action. These proved to be twenty Attic ships, which had been sent by the Athenians through fear that the first force might be insufficient for the protection of their allies; and the Corinthians imagined that a greater armament might be behind.

The next day the Corcyræans, with the thirty Attic ships, sailed towards the port where the Corinthians lay, to offer battle. The Corinthians came out and drew up their fleet in fighting order; but, though still greatly superior in numbers, they did not wish to risk an engagement on a desert coast, where they had no means of repairing their vessels, and found it difficult to guard their prisoners. They were bent on returning home; and, being fearful that the Athenian ships would bar their progress, they sent a messenger to them to inquire if they designed to violate their faith of treaties by preventing the Corinthians from returning to their own country. The Athenians replied, that they would not prevent them from sailing in any other direction but towards Corcyra. The Corinthians then erected a trophy and returned home.

GREEK AND ROMAN SOLDIERS.

CHAPTER VI.

THE PELOPONNESIAN WAR.

IN the year 431 B. C., war broke out between the rival states of Athens and Sparta. All the Grecian states were ranged on the different sides. Athens was complete mistress of the sea, and upon that element she placed her principal reliance for success. At the commencement of the war, she had three hundred galleys in sailing condition. The strength of Sparta was to be found in her land forces—having never given much attention to naval affairs. While their king led a large army into Attica, an Athenian fleet of a hundred galleys, with a thousand men of arms and four hundred bowmen on board, set sail to ravage the coasts of the Peloponnesus. They were joined by fifty Corcyræan ships, and by others from the same quarter. They visited the coasts of Laconia with fire and sword, and then proceeded to Elis, which they ravaged for two days, defeated a body of troops sent against them, and when the fleet was compelled to take shelter from a gale in the port of Pheia, they made themselves masters of Pheia itself;

STERN OF A GALLEY—FROM A PAINTING ON THE WALLS OF POMPEII.

but as the Eleans were coming up with their whole force, they hastily re-embarked and the fleet sailed northward.

While this great fleet was still at sea, a squadron of thirty galleys was sent into the Eubœan channel to protect the coasts of the island, which were infested by privateers from Locris. The Athenians made a descent on the Locrian coast, and routed a body of Locrians who attempted to oppose their landing. To divert the public mind as much as possible from the plague which had broken out at Athens, Pericles set out at the head of another expedition against Peloponnesus, which consisted of a fleet of one hundred galleys, with four thousand heavy-armed Athenians on board. He was joined by fifty galleys from Chios and Lesbos, and three hundred horse were embarked in transports, now for the first time formed out of old ships. With this force, while the enemy was ravaging Attica, he sailed to the coast of Epidaurus, wasted the greater part of its territory, and made an unsuccessful attack upon the town. He then slowly coasted the Acté and ravaged the fields of Trœzen, Halice and Hermione. But a pestilence broke out in the fleet and Pericles was compelled to return to Attica.

In the year 430 B. C., a Peloponnesian fleet of one hundred galleys, with one thousand heavy-armed Lacedemonians on board, under command of Cnemus the Spartan navarch, or high admiral, sailed to the island of Acarnania, the inhabitants of which were allied with the Athenians. The greater part of that fertile island was ravaged, but the people could not be terrified into submission. This led the Athenians to send a squadron of twenty galleys, under Phormio, to guard the entrance to the Corinthian Gulf. The Peloponnesian allies, resolved to form an expedition against Acarnania and Naupactus, and for this purpose, there assembled at Leucas, in the Corinthian Gulf, a fleet of forty-seven galleys, while a large land force marched to attack Acarnania. This fleet advanced along the coast of Achaia. It was watched by Phormio, who, however, did not attempt to impede its progress until it had passed through the mouth of the gulf, and was sailing towards Acarnania. The commander of the allied fleet did not think Phormio would attack them with only twenty galleys, and therefore they were surprised on the morning after leaving the gulf of Corinth, to see the Athenian ships coming towards them.

As they had not looked for a sea fight, their ships were not in fit condition for one, being encumbered with soldiers for the invasion of Acarnania. But seeing that an engagement was inevitable, they prepared to receive the enemy's attack. They ranged their ships in a circle, the largest which they could form without leaving any opening, the sterns turned inward. Within they placed all the smaller craft which accompanied them, and five of their best sailers, to move as occasion might require. The Athenians advanced in a single line, and as they made the round of the circle with threatening demonstrations, gradually reduced it to a narrow compass. But Phormio had ordered that none of his ships should begin the attack until he gave the signal. He foresaw that the enemy would not be able long to preserve his order, and that the ships and boats would run foul of one another; and he expected that a wind, which commonly blew out of the gulf about sunrise, would complete their confusion. All turned out as he calculated. As the breeze got up, the Peloponnesian gal-

PHORMIO DEFEATING THE PELOPONNESIANS.

leys, straitened in their room, were driven against one another; from the various accidents that ensued an uproar arose, which drowned every word of command; the rowers, from want of practice, were unable to use their oars in the swell of the sea, and the galleys no longer obeyed the rudder. In the midst of this disorder, Phormio gave the signal for attack. The enemy could offer no resistance; all who were not sunk in the first onset took to flight; the Athenians gave chase and captured twelve galleys, with the greater part of the crews. Those which escaped proceeded to the Elean arsenal of Cyllene, where they were joined by Cnemus, who brought with him the squadron which had been assembled at Leucas. Phormio carried his prizes into the harbor of Molycrium, and after raising a trophy on the nearest Rhion (as each of the two points at the mouth of the gulf was called,) and dedicating one of the captured vessels to Poseidon, he returned to Naupactus.

The news of this great victory was received by the Spartans with indignation, and they attributed their defeat to their commander's misconduct. Timocrates, Brasidas and Lycophron were sent to cooperate with Cnemus in getting another and larger fleet together. They soon equipped and manned a fleet of seventy-seven galleys, not, like the former, with a view to operations on shore, but for naval action. Phormio, on the other hand, had sent the news of his victory to Athens, with a request that he should be reinforced, as he expected a battle every day. But his request was unheeded, and he was left to meet the whole force of the allies with twenty ships. The Peloponnesians, schooled by their recent defeat, were resolved not to venture out in the open sea. Phormio saw no chance of victory, or of safety except in ample sea-room. The two parties manœuvred and practised their men for six or seven days. But the Spartans grew apprehensive that a reinforcement might arrive from Athens, and resolved to bring the Athenians to an engagement without delay. Accordingly, upon the night before the contemplated attack, the commanders addressed their respective forces, and used every means to raise the spirits dampened by previous defeat. But they only succeeded in part.

At daybreak the Peloponnesian fleet was seen moving eastward along the shore, the right wing taking the lead, in a column of four ships abreast. The object of this manœuvre was to threaten Naupactus, and thus to draw Phormio round the Molycrian point, and then, suddenly facing about, to coop him in, and capture the whole squadron. But, to provide against the contingency by which some of his ships might get the start of their assailants, and make their escape to Naupactus, twenty of the best sailers in the Peloponnesian fleet were placed in advance of the column to intercept the fugitives. The object was attained only in part. Phormio, as was expected, was alarmed for the safety of Naupactus, and in spite of himself was fain to follow the enemy by a parallel movement along the opposite coast, where a body of Messenians from Naupactus was on its march to support him. The Peloponnesian commanders no sooner saw his whole squadron within the gulf in a single file, close to the shore, than they ordered their column to turn and advance, in a long line, at the utmost stretch of speed, to the attack. Nine of the Athenian ships were driven ashore, one was taken with its whole company; the other crews, for the most part, escaped by swimming; but the empty vessels would all have been captured or destroyed, if the Messenians had not come up, dashed into the sea in their armor, and forced the victors to abandon several of their prizes. But the remaining eleven, which had outstripped this attack and made for Naupactus, were briskly chased by the squadron in advance. All, however, but one, got the start of their pursuers, and found time to face about and form in a line in front of a temple of Apollo, close to the port. The single galley in the rear was chased by a Leucadian, which was far in advance of the squadron, and had the Spartan Timocrates on board. It happened that just before them a merchant ship was riding at anchor. The Athenian captain, by a dexterous and happy manœuvre, suddenly wheeling round it, struck her antagonist on her broadside, full in the centre, and sank her. The Peloponnesians, in the other galleys, who were coming up in disorderly haste, as to a certain victory, and had already begun to raise the pæan, were disconcerted at this spectacle. Some, who were near the Athenian line, stopped short to wait for those behind; some, incautiously pushing forward, and not acquainted with the coast, ran upon shoals. The Athenians, seeing the enemy thus exposed, thought no longer of defence; by a simultaneous impulse the shout of battle rose, and the word was given for attack in every ship. The Peloponnesians, after a short and feeble resistance, fled towards Panormus. The Athenians took six of the nearest, and recovered those of their own which had been abandoned by their crews on the first attack of the Peloponnesians, and taken in tow. The only prize which the Peloponnesians retained was the galley which they had captured with its crew. With this they decorated the trophy which they raised on the Achæan Rhion. The Athenians raised theirs near the spot from which they had advanced to the attack, which gave them the more glorious and useful victory.

After this discomfiture, the Peloponnesian fleet sailed for Corinth, as the season was too far advanced for naval operations, and the commanders feared the arrival of an Athenian squadron. Phormio was joined, after their departure, by the reinforcement he so much needed. But he did not attempt any thing of importance. He remained at Naupactus until spring, when he sailed to Athens, with his prizes and prisoners.

The inhabitants of Mitylene having revolted from their alliance with Athens, and made great preparations to maintain themselves against her power, Cleippides was despatched, with forty galleys, to reduce the city to subjection. Ten Mitylenian ships were seized by the Athenians, and their crews thrown into prison. The fleet of Cleippides blockaded Mitylene, but granted an armistice asked by the inhabitants. The Mitylenians were desirous of gaining time; and, during the armistice, they sent envoys to Sparta, soliciting assistance. The Spartans promised their aid and the envoys returned.

While this fleet blockaded Mitylene, another consisting of thirty galleys, was sent round Peloponnesus to assist the Acarnanians; this expedition wasted the coast of Laconia on their way to Acarnania, and made the Spartans feel the war near home. And now the Athenians resolved to show, that without recalling either this squadron or the armament at Mitylene, they were ready to meet any naval force Peloponnesus could send against them. They forthwith equipped one hundred galleys, manned partly with their own citizens, and coasting the isthmus, exhibited them to the astonished Spartans, and then proceeded to make a descent on the Peloponnesian coast. The state of the Athenian finances prevented them from keeping such an armament at sea for a great length of time. The whole number of vessels in their service was nearly equal to the number they had at the commencement of the war, and the cost of such a navy was a constant drain on the treasury. The large fleet, and part of the one sent to Acarnania returned to Athens.

The Spartans, in keeping their promise to the Mitylenians, sent their admiral Alcidas, with forty-two galleys to their assistance. But Alcidas was totally unfit for commanding a naval armament. Possessing all the wariness, without the energy of the Spartan character, he manœuvred along the coast of Peloponnesus, and when he reached the Cyclades, he learned that the Mitylenians had capitulated seven days before. The Spartan commander then thought it best to return to Peloponnesus. He was pursued by the Athenians, but succeeded in making his escape. Mitylene was then deprived of all remains of independence. Her navy was seized and served to swell the Athenian naval strength.

The fleet commanded by Alcidas was dispersed by a storm off the island of Crete, but it again assembled in the port of Cyllene, where it was joined by thirteen galleys, under Brasidas. This fleet then sailed towards Corcyra, where an Athenian fleet of twelve galleys was anchored. The Corcyræans were divided into two violent parties, and a portion of them were upon the side of Athens, while the others took part with the Peloponnesians. Nicostratus sailed out, with the Athenian galleys, and was followed by a number of the galleys of the Corcyræans. Two of the Corcyræan galleys went over to the Peloponnesians, and the crews of the others began fighting among themselves. Seeing this disorder, the Peloponnesians divided their own fleet, and with twenty galleys, attacked the Corcyræans as they came up in small numbers, while the remaining three-and-thirty encountered the Athenian squadron. But as Nicostratus, by superior skill, avoided their centre, where he would have been overpowered, and, having taken them in flank, sunk one galley, they formed into a circle and stood on the defensive. Just as Nicostratus was about to execute the manœuvre by which Phormio had won a former sea fight, the twenty galleys which had conquered the Corcyræans, came to the relief of Alcidas, and the Athenians were compelled to retreat, which they did in good order. The Peloponnesian fleet remained master of thirteen galleys and of the sea; but instead of following up his victory, Alcidas drew off to another coast, which he ravaged until he heard of the approach of another Athenian fleet. Then he set out for Peloponnesus.

In the summer of 426, B. C., Nicias, one of the wealthiest Athenians and a prudent general, led an armament of sixty galleys, with two thousand heavy armed men on board, against the island of Melos, in the Ægean, which refused to acknowledge the supremacy of Athens. Nicias ravaged the island, and the coast of Locris, and then returned to Athens. At the same time, a squadron of thirty galleys, under Demosthenes and Procles, was sent round Peloponnesus; and being joined by fifteen Corcyræan ships, and by troops from Zacynthus, proceeded to attack Leucas. After laying waste the surrounding territory, Demosthenes did not think it wise to besiege the town, and sailed away to Sollium to secure the aid of that people in an expedition into Ætolia.

In the middle of the next campaign, 425, B. C., a fleet of forty galleys, under Sophocles and Eurymedon. They were accompanied by Demosthenes as general of the land forces. A point at the northern entrance of the bay, now called Navarino, was fortified by Demosthenes, and five galleys left him to guard the fortress. When the rest of the fleet had left for Corcyra, information was received of the approach of a Peloponnesian fleet, and a large Spartan army, under King Agis. Demosthenes sent two galleys to apprise the Athenian commanders of his danger, and hauled his remaining three galleys up under the fort, and protected them with a stockade. His whole force consisted of the crews of the three ships and about forty Messenians. The Peloponnesian fleet numbered forty-three galleys; but a few only could approach the shore at one time. The fight began at the water's edge, and continued with intervals for two days, at the end of which time, the Athenian fleet arrived from Zacynthus. It had been augmented to the number of fifty galleys. The Peloponnesians neither sailed out to meet them, nor made any attempt to close the mouth of the harbor, but allowed themselves to be surprised by the Athenians while a part of their ships were still on shore, and not even manned. Two were taken, one with its whole company, many shattered, and the Athenians chasing them to the shore, tried to carry off those which they found there empty. But the Spartans, desperately fighting on their own shores, drove the enemy back and recovered all their ships but the five first captured. With these the Athenians erected their trophy. Soon after, the Spartans proposed a truce; by the terms of which, they placed their whole navy of sixty ships in the hands of the Athenians until the return of the ambassadors sent to Athens. But when the ambassadors returned, the victors would not give up the ships. Their own fleet had been further increased to seventy sail, and they knew their power. Cleon arrived with a re-inforcement of land troops from Athens, and then, after a hard fight, the Spartans surrendered.

The Athenians now made their enemy feel the force of their naval superiority. An armament of eighty galleys, with two thousand heavy-armed Athenians, and horse transports, with two hundred cavalry, was sent, under command of Nicias and two colleagues, to invade the territory of Corinth and the eastern side of Peloponnesus. But all the operations of this expedition were upon land. In the next year, another squadron of sixty galleys, under the command of Nicias, was sent to wrest the island of Cytherea from the Spartan rule. The result was, that the island was captured, and the fleet remained seven days on the coast of Laconia, inflicting the most terrible ravages, without meeting with any resistance.

In the meantime, a sea fight took place near Messana, between a Locrian fleet of thirty ships and an Athenian and Rhegian fleet of twenty-four ships, under command of Sophocles and Eurymedon, in which the latter were victorious. But they were repulsed in their turn, in making an attempt to seize the Syracusan fleet at Cape Pelorus. Numerous expeditions on a small scale, for the purpose of reducing their former allies to submission, were undertaken by the Athenians during the remainder of the Peloponnesian war, but none of them are worthy of particular mention.

ANCIENT GALLEY FROM POMPEII.

CHAPTER VII.

THE EXPEDITION OF THE ATHENIANS AGAINST SICILY.

WHEN the war was renewed between the two confederacies, a great armament was raised, through the influence of Alcibiades, who, with Nicias and Lamachus, was appointed to command it. The armament collected at Corcyra. It consisted of one hundred and thirty-seven galleys, besides two Rhodians of lower rate. Athens alone furnished one hundred and sixty fighting galleys, and forty for transport of soldiers. Chios and other allies contributed the rest. The army included five thousand heavy infantry, among whom fifteen hundred were Athenians—seven hundred to serve on board in sea fights. The fleet was accompanied by thirty vessels laden with provision. A hundred boats had been pressed into the service; but a number of merchantmen and of small craft followed on private commercial adventures. The armament was divided into three squadrons, one of which each one of the generals took as a separate command. They sent forward three ships to learn which of the Italian and Sicilian towns were willing to receive them. These ships were to meet them on their way.

In this order, the army crossed over to the Japygian Foreland, and proceeded along the Italian coast to Rhegium. Here the generals deliberated on the best plan of procedure. Nicias, who was opposed to the whole expedition, wished to return to Athens, after coasting Sicily. Lamachus went to the opposite extreme—invasion of Sicily at once, before the people had time for preparation. Alcibiades' opinion, being in favor of a middle course of action, was adopted. Alcibiades manned sixty galleys, and leaving Nicias in command of the remainder, sailed towards Syracuse. The galleys were sent forward to enter the harbor, and reconnoitre. No hostile navy appeared in the harbor; but a Syracusan galley fell into the hands of the Athenians. A proclamation was made, inviting those in Syracuse, who were allies and kinsmen of the Leontines to quit the city and join their liberators. The fleet then returned to Catana, where the whole armament was soon collected. Believing that Camarina could be induced to embrace their cause, the whole armament sailed to that place, stopping at Syracuse upon the way. The Camarinæans disappointed the Athenians, and the whole fleet was forced to return to Catana. There they were met by the state galley, the Salaminia, which brought orders to convey Alcibiades and several others to Athens. His departure deranged the plan which he had formed, and which had been adopted by the other generals. He did not return to Athens, however, but resolved to show how deeply he could injure a country which did not appreciate his services. The armament was then divided into two divisions, one under each general, which proceeded together along the north coast. After various manœuvres, Nicias skilfully took advantage of the excessive confidence of the Syracusans, and effected a landing near that city without opposition. A strong position was selected, the ships enclosed within a palisade, and a hasty work thrown up at a point called Dascon. A battle was fought with a much superior force of the Syracusans, and they were defeated; but Nicias decided that the Athenian reputation had been sufficiently vindicated, which was a part of the object of the expedition, and, therefore, the armament sailed away immediately after the battle. After depositing some spoils at Catana, they proceeded to Messana, where the treachery of Alcibiades prevented their entrance; and they were forced to go into Naxos for winter quarters.

In the next spring, operations commenced in good earnest. A portion of the Athenians were landed near Syracuse, and soon after the whole armament arrived in the great harbor. After various successes of the Athenians on land, the Syracusans were induced to try their fortune upon the sea. A large fleet was manned and exercised, and information received that the Corinthians would assist them by sending them a number of galleys. Nicias began to fear for the safety of the armament, although, so far, successful. The Athenian ships were growing leaky and unsound, through the length of time they had been at sea; and it was necessary to keep them always afloat, as the enemy had an equal number always ready to take advantage of any appearance of weakness. The crews had been thinned by a variety of losses. Nicias sent information of his condition to Athens, and obtained the promise of a great reinforcement. Demosthenes superintended the preparation of the main armament, and Eurymedon was sent forward with ten galleys and one hundred and twenty talents. At the same time, they despatched Cimon, with a squadron of twenty galleys, to Naupactus, to intercept the reinforcements of the enemy.

While Athens was besieged by the Spartans, another great armament was sent by her to reduce Syracuse, which was now defended by the united strength of Sicily and some of the Peloponnesian states. Demosthenes left the Piræus with a fleet of sixty Attic and five Chian galleys, having on board, as the core of the army, twelve hundred Athenian infantry. He waited awhile at Ægina, to collect stragglers, and then proceeded to the coast of Argolis, to join a squadron of thirty galleys, under Charicles, which had been sent forward to call upon Argos for her contingent. After taking them on board, they sailed together as far as Laconia, on the coast of which, opposite Cytherea, a fort was erected to serve as a refuge for runaway Helots. Demosthenes then pursued his voyage toward Corcyra, and Charicles, leaving a garrison in the fort, returned with the squadron and the Argives to the coast of Argos.

While Demosthenes was preparing to sail from Athens, the Spartan, Gylippus, persuaded the Syracusans to try their strength in a sea fight. Eighty ships were manned, and it was concerted that thirty-five of them should advance from the great harbor, while the rest sailed round from the lesser harbor, on the other side of the island, to join them. This, it was expected, would surprise the Athenians, and further the design of Gilyppus to attack their forts on shore. The Athenians manned sixty galleys, and with twenty-five, encountered those of the Syracusans in the Great Harbor, while the rest sailed out to meet the other squadron. The battle began at both points, at the same time. The fight inclined against the Athenians for a while. They were giving way in the Great Harbor, and forty-five Syracusan galleys forced a passage into it. But this threw them into disorder, and exposed them, while entangled, to a renewed attack from the Athenians, who put all to flight and sank eleven galleys. Yet such a victory was little better than a defeat, since it was evident that great difficulty would be met in the introduction of supplies, now that an opposing fleet was constantly stationed at Plemyrium to dispute the passage. Several sharp contests occurred in the Great Harbor, when the Athenians strove to destroy a stockade which the Syracusans erected for the shelter of their ships. A great vessel of burden, well guarded from missiles, and mounted with wooden towers to give more effect to their own, was moored alongside the stockade, to cover the operations of a number of parties in boats, which either forced up the piles or sent down divers to saw them off.

A sea fight took place between those who were advancing to the aid of both parties. The Athenian commander, Conon, had contrived to collect a fleet of thirty-three ships, with which he designed to meet the Corinthian fleet, which was near upon equality in numbers. The Corinthians had armed the bows of their galleys with solid timbers contrived for the occasion, when the vessels of the two fleets met, prow to prow, those of the Athenians, not being thus armed, were stove in by the shock. Seven were thus disabled, yet none went down, and they sank three of the Corinthians, and kept possession of the wrecks. Both parties erected trophies—though a victory belonged to neither.

In the meantime, Demosthenes and Eurymedon, after having strengthened their armament with all the reinforcements they could collect, crossed over to the Italian coast, and visited several towns which received him in a friendly manner; but they seemed more anxious to display Athenian power, than to assist Nicias. That commander had contrived to avert the dangers threatened by the superior strength of the Syracusans and their allies; but when they heard of the approach of Demosthenes and Eurymedon, they resolved to strike a blow which should be decisive. They adopted the contrivance for strengthening the bows of their galleys which had been used with success by the Corinthians, and they calculated that the Athenians would not be able to make use of their skilful manœuvres because of the want of room in the harbor. The mode of fighting, which the Syracusans were skilled in, was by running their vessels stern to stern with the enemy; but the Athenians, through their nautical skill, were enabled to strike their enemy obliquely or on the broadside—usually sinking the opposing vessel. The Syracusans had also the advantage of falling back into the harbor, while the Athenians were compelled to fight in a corner, where they could not back water without falling into disorder.

While Gylippus led the army out of the city against the Athenian fortifications, the Athenians were thrown into alarm by the appearance of the whole Syracusan fleet of eighty sail.

Such was the state of things at Syracuse when Demosthenes and Eurymedon sailed into the Great Harbor to the sound of martial music, with an armament no less gallantly equipped than that which left Athens two years before, of seventy-three galleys, with five thousand heavy infantry, and, according to Plutarch, three thousand light troops. The arrival of this formidable force astonished and dismayed the Syracusans, who, when they reflected that it had left Attica occupied by an invading army, concluded that the resources of Athens were inexhaustible, and were ready to give up all hopes of deliverance.

But the terror inspired by the appearance of the armament was not of long duration. The Athenians suffered a terrible defeat in the night, on land, and this revived the most sanguine hopes in the Syracusans. A number of reinforcements were received, and they determined to bring the Athenians to an engagement, where the very magnitude of their armament would turn to the advantage of the Syracusans. After some days' exercise of their fleet, they began an attack on the Athenian lines, and in the skirmish which ensued, they remained masters of the field. Animated by success, they sailed out next day with seventy-six galleys. The Athenians manned eighty-six galleys and gave battle. In the direct shock, the Syracusans maintained their superiority, which they had gained by their mechanical contrivance, by the multitude of troops which covered their decks and by a numerous flotilla of boats. The Syracusans were victorious in the centre, and, as Eurymedon advanced to turn their left, they suddenly overwhelmed him by their whole force, and destroyed or captured his whole division. After this blow the Athenians were easily put to flight, and they took refuge on shore. The Syracusans who attacked them from the shore were routed, and the remaining galleys rescued. An attempt was then made to send a fire ship into the midst of the Athenian station; this, however, was baffled, but the Syracusans destroyed eighteen galleys with all their crews.

The only care of the Syracusans was to prevent the escape of that great armament which was formerly so formidable. The Athenians could still muster one hundred and ten galleys, and with these it was determined to try another and more desperate engagement. As their manœuvres were useless in the harbor, they prepared for a struggle, as near like a land battle as possible. Grappling irons were contrived to detain the enemy's galleys on the first encounter, till they should be boarded and taken. The command of the fleet was given to Demosthenes, while Nicias remained on land. The latter, however, addressed the Athenians, and exhorted them to make the greatest exertion. On the other hand, the Syracusans devised an expedient to elude the grappling irons. They stretched a number of hides over the sterns of their galleys. They manned a fleet equal to that with which they had gained their last victory, and were confident of success.

The Athenians began the battle with an impetuous attack on the bar at the mouth of the harbor which was guarded by a part of the Syracusan fleet; the rest were disposed all round the harbor, and the shore, except so far as it was covered by the enemy, was lined with their troops. The assailants at the first onset overpowered the resistance of the squadron stationed near the bar, and were proceeding to break its fastenings, when they were interrupted by a simultaneous movement of the whole Syracusan fleet, which fell upon them from all quarters, and the engagement soon became general. The earnestness with which it was maintained was such as had not before been displayed on either side; the preceding battles might have seemed sham fights in comparison. Every man, whether it was skill, or courage, or labor that his post chiefly demanded, vied both with the enemy and his comrades in discharging its duties, as if all depended on his own exertions. But the skill of the officers and the zeal of the men had to contend not only with the resistance of the enemy, but with the obstacles arising from the scene of the combat—the narrowest, Thucydides observes, in which two such armaments had ever met. Innumerable accidents were perpetually occurring to cross the best-planned manœuvres; and the most judicious orders, however promptly obeyed, might produce an effect directly opposite to the intention with which they were given. It was seldom that two galleys found room and time for a regular conflict. The stroke aimed at one was frequently intercepted by another, which was itself engaged in flight or pursuit. Attack and defence were completely diverted by unforeseen objects; and friends and foes were entangled and confounded together in inextricable disorder; during which the decks became a field of battle for the heavy-armed troops. The din of so many shocks distracted the attention of the combatants and drowned the words of command, and the noise was increased by a dissonant clamor of exhortation, entreaty, and remonstrance: on the side of the Athenians, as they urged one another to force the outlet, through which alone they could find a passage home, or not to fall back from the sea, which they had made their own by so many hard struggles, on a hostile shore; on the side of the Syracusans, as they animated each other to prevent the enemy's escape, or expostulated with those that fled before the Athenians, whose only aim was flight. The tumult of sounds was heightened by the voices of the numberless spectators who lined the shore, all intent upon the combat, all deeply affected by its vicissitudes, but with different feelings and according to various views. But at length doubt and anxiety were set at rest; The Athenians were seen chased by the enemy, and making for the nearest land; and the confused clamor of their comrades who witnessed the calamity was changed for one universal wail.

This retreat was disastrous for the Athenians. After the greatest endurance of every kind of hardships, they were forced to surrender to the Syracusans, and thus terminated the ill-advised expedition to Sicily. Nicias was put to death by the victors, but Demosthenes was spared.

CHAPTER VIII.

FROM THE SICILIAN EXPEDITION TILL THE CLOSE OF THE PELOPONNESIAN WAR.

ATHENS, though greatly reduced, still possessed wealth and power sufficient to retrieve her losses. The Spartans, anxious to take advantage of her weakness, sent out a squadron of twenty galleys, for the purpose of getting possession of Chios. The Athenians manned an equal number of galleys, and offered the Spartans battle in the

WESTERN SIDE OF THE ACROPOLIS, ATHENS.

open sea. This, however, was declined, and the Athenians had time to strengthen their fleet with sixteen additional galleys. They then attacked the squadron of the enemy, as it was anchored near the land, and captured one galley. The Spartan commander was killed, and the whole fleet only saved by being hauled on shore, and guarded by the Corinthians. Great exertions were made at Athens to equip a new navy. Twenty galleys were stationed at Piræus, and preparations made for manning thirty more. Several victories were obtained over some of their revolted allies, which served to inspirit the Athenians.

In the autumn following the Sicilian disaster, the Athenians were enabled to collect a fleet of one hundred and four galleys at Samos. They divided it into two squadrons—one of thirty galleys was despatched to Chios, and the other seventy-four remained to command the sea, and carry on the war against Miletus. Both of these squadrons met with success in capturing numerous small squadrons of the Peloponnesians, who had now become powerful upon the sea. Astyochus was appointed high admiral by the Spartans, and while the Athenian fleet lay at Samos, he collected a fleet of a hundred galleys, with which he offered battle. The Athenians declined to accept the challenge, and the Peloponnesian fleet returned to Miletus. The arrival of the other portion of the Athenian fleet increased its number to one hundred and eight galleys with which they offered battle, in their turn, but Astyochus thought it prudent to decline it, though his own force had been raised to one hundred and twelve galleys.

After the recall of Alcibiades, the affairs of the Athenians looked more prosperous. The navy was considerably increased, and several small sea fights took place, in which the Athenians maintained their old superiority. At length, after much manœuvring, a fleet of seventy-six sail, commanded by Thrasyllus, contrived to get the Peloponnesian fleet, of eighty-six sail, in a favorable position near the mouth of the Hellespont. Five days were spent in preparations on both sides, and the Athenians then moved in a single column along the shore toward Sestus, and were met by the Peloponnesians, who perceived their approach from Abydos.

Their right was commanded by Thrasybulus; their left, which was parted from the centre by the headland of Cynossema, by Thrasyllus. The Peloponnesians had two main objects in view: to break the Athenian centre, and to outflank their right wing, so as to prevent them from issuing out of the straits. And, accordingly, Mindarus himself, with his fastest galleys, commanded the left of his line against Thrasybulus, while Thrasyllus was opposed to the Syracusans. The attack on the Athenian centre succeeded; it was overpowered by superior numbers, several galleys were driven aground, and the Peloponnesians landed to follow up their victory on shore. In the mean while Thrasyllus was engaged in a warm combat with the Syracusans, and was prevented by the intervening headland from seeing the distress of his centre; and Thrasybulus was employed in endeavoring to baffle the manœuvres of Mindarus. But, according to Thucydides, the partial success of the Peloponnesians threw them into confusion, which spread through their whole line, when Thrasybulus suddenly turned upon the enemy, who were striving to outflank him, and having put them to flight, attacked their victorious but disordered centre. The Syracusans, who had hitherto maintained their station, though with difficulty, against Thrasyllus, were involved in the general defeat. The narrowness of the channel, as the vanquished found shelter near at hand, prevented the Athenians from making many captures. They took only one and twenty galleys, and lost fifteen of their own. But the value of their victory was not to be measured by these visible fruits. This was the first great battle they had fought since their disasters in Sicily; their success restored the confidence of their seamen, and the news, which was immediately carried to Athens, lightened the dark cloud which had hitherto hung over the prospects of the state.

The victors left their prizes at Elæus, and having staid three days at Sestus to refit, sailed northward to reduce Cyzicus, which had lately revolted. On their way, they captured eight galleys—being part of the squadron with which Helixus had captured Byzantium. The Peloponnesians sailed to Elæus, and recovered those of their galleys left there, which were in a serviceable condition; the rest had been burned by the people of Elæus. They also sent to Eubœa, to order a squadron stationed there, under Hegesandrias, to join them. About the same time, Alcibiades returned to Samos, with thirteen galleys, and claimed the merit of having prevented Tissaphernes, the Persian satrap, from sending the Phœnician fleet to assist the enemy.

The Peloponnesians were particularly unfortunate just at this period. Hegesandrias, the Spartan commander, sent Epicles, with

ALCIBIADES DEFEATING THE PELOPONNESIAN FLEET.

fifteen galleys, to aid Mindarus. This squadron was overtaken by a terrible storm off Mount Athos, and every galley, with all of the crews except twelve men, were destroyed.

The hostile fleets in the Hellespont were still watching each other's movements, waiting, perhaps, for supplies and reinforcements, toward the end of September, when Dorieus, having executed his commission at Rhodes, sailed in with fourteen galleys. Information was immediately given of his approach to the Athenian commanders, who were encamped at Madytus, on the coast of the Chersonesus, and they put out with twenty galleys to attack him; but he ran his squadron aground near the headland of Rhœteum, and defended himself so vigorously that his assailants were forced to retire, baffled, to their camp. This action was observed by Mindarus, who was sacrificing to Athené in the citadel of Ilium, which commanded a view of the coast, and he hastened to embark and join Dorieus with his whole fleet. The Athenians now came out from Madytus to meet them, and an engagement ensued near Abydos, which lasted, with fluctuating success, nearly the whole day. Towards evening, Alcibiades was seen entering the straits with eighteen galleys; and, on the appearance of this squadron, the Peloponnesians took to flight, and were pursued and driven ashore, where, however, they maintained the combat in defence of their ships, and were supported by Pharnabazus, who came to their aid with a body of troops. He displayed the utmost zeal in their behalf, animated his men, not only by his exhortations, but by his example, pushing forward with his horse into the sea, and persevering as long as there was an enemy to oppose. The Athenians, however, succeeded in carrying off thirty of the Peloponnesian galleys, and in recovering those which they had themselves lost, with which they retired to Sestus. Notwithstanding this victory, the want of money was so pressing, that while Thrasyllus sailed to Athens to bear the good tidings and to procure reinforcements, other officers were despatched in various directions to collect pecuniary supplies; no more than forty galleys were left at Sestus.

The object of Alcibiades was now to keep the Peloponnesians from hearing of his increase of force. Making all possible speed, he arrived at the island of Proconnesus, on the next day after being reinforced. There he learned that Mindarus was at Cyzicus, with Pharnabazus and his troops. He prepared his men to fight both on sea and land,

and then set sail, in a thick mist, for Cyzicus. As he approached the harbor, the sun dispelled the mist, and the Peloponnesian fleet was seen exercising, a great way off at sea. When the Peloponnesians discovered that the Athenians were between them and the harbor, they made for the nearest land, and, laying their ships together in a compact mass, defended themselves from the decks; but, at length, Alcibiades, having sailed round to another point of the coast, with twenty galleys, landed his men, and attacked the enemy in the rear. Mindarus himself now landed to repel the assailants; but he fell in the battle, and his men were put to flight. The whole fleet, except the galleys of the Syracusans, which they fired, fell into the hands of the Athenians, who carried them away to Proconnesus. The next day they sailed for Cyzicus, which was forced to submit to a heavy contribution. The town of Chrysopolis, on the eastern coast of the Bosphorus, opposite Byzantium, was fortified, and a custom house established, where all vessels passing from the Euxine were forced to pay a duty on their cargoes. Thirty galleys were left at that place, and then Alcibiades returned to the Hellespont.

In the meantime, by the aid of the Persian, Pharnabazus, the Peloponnesians began to build a new fleet at Antandrus. The timber was obtained from the woods of Ida, and the money was advanced by Pharnabazus. But such was the effect of the overwhelming defeat upon the Spartans at home, that an embassy was sent to Athens, asking for peace. This offer, unfortunately for the Athenians, was rejected. While the Peloponnesians were forming a new navy, Thrasyllus was raising a powerful armament at Athens. It consisted of fifty galleys, one thousand heavy infantry, one hundred horse, and five thousand seamen, serving as targeteers. With this force, Thrasyllus sailed to Pygela, which he attacked without success, but ravaged the country all around it, and destroyed a body of troops which came to its aid from Miletus. He then attacked Ephesus, but was defeated upon land, and was forced to sail away to Lesbos. To make amends for his defeat, however, he attacked a Syracusan squadron of twenty-five galleys, captured four, and chased the rest back to Ephesus. Another Alcibiades, a kinsman of the Athenian commander, was captured in one of the prizes, and he afterwards joined the Athenian forces. The fleet, under Alcibiades, wintered at Lampsacus. During the winter, the Spartans relieved themselves of the annoyance they

ATTACK OF THRASYLLUS ON EPHESUS.

experienced from the garrison at Pylus, the fort in Laconia founded by Demosthenes. They blockaded it by sea, and attacked it by land, so that the garrison was obliged to capitulate, with permission to withdraw. The Athenians sent thirty galleys, under command of Anytus, to relieve it, but he was prevented from reaching it in time, on account of contrary winds.

In the spring of 408, B. C., the Athenian fleet moved from Lampsacus towards the Bosphorus, which now became the theatre of war, both parties struggling for the command of this great thoroughfare of Greek commerce. Byzantium was invested and blockaded, and, after a long siege, during which the besieged suffered great privations, the city surrendered to Alcibiades. Various towns were visited and compelled to acknowledge the supremacy of Athens, and pay heavy contributions. The whole fleet then returned to Athens, where Alcibiades was received in triumph. About two hundred vessels were the fruit of the campaign, together with the richest spoils of all kinds. The galley which bore the commander into the harbor of Athens, was adorned with purple sails, and the rowers kept time by the flute of Chrysogonus, and the voice of Calippides, a tragic actor, both in sacred or theatrical attire. An immense crowd received the hero with shouts, and he was immediately appointed commander-in-chief of all the sea and land forces of Athens.

To show their confidence in Alcibiades, the Athenians voted him an armament of one hundred galleys, fifteen hundred heavy infantry, and one hundred and fifty horse, with leave to name his colleagues. Within four months after his return, the preparations were completed and, with Aristocrates and Adimantus as his colleagues, Alcibiades sailed from Athens for the last time. The Spartans selected a man, who they thought was able to cope with Alcibiades, to be their admiral in the place of Cratesippidas. His name was Lysander, and he had early given proofs of his activity and ability, sufficient to justify his appointment to command, although by birth not entitled to the full privileges of the Spartan franchise. The fleet under his command was increased to ninety galleys. Alcibiades also increased the number of his galleys, and stationed the fleet at Notium, to watch the movements of the enemy. The Peloponnesian fleet was inferior in numbers, and it needed repairs, so that Lysander had it hauled on shore to refit, while he waited an opportunity for action.

This came unexpectedly, by the imprudence of Alcibiades. Hearing that Thrasybulus was at Phocea, he sailed thither to meet him, leaving Antiochus in command of the fleet at Notium, with strict orders not to engage the enemy, even if they offered battle. Antiochus was a skilful seaman, but had little talent for a commander. He thought if he could draw the enemy out into the open sea, a victory would be easily obtained. He, therefore, sailed from Notium, taking only one galley in company with his own, into the harbor of Ephesus, and as he passed close by the prows of the Peloponnesian fleet, offered every kind of contumely, by word and gesture, that could provoke an attack. Lysander at length ordered a few galleys to give him chase; but when he saw Antiochus supported by a detachment from the Athenian fleet, he advanced with the remainder of his own, in order of battle. The Athenians now also brought out their whole force; but they came up in separate groups, without order or plan, and were defeated in detail. The galley of Antiochus himself, which was among the foremost, was soon sunk, and his death probably hastened the flight of the rest. They took refuge in Samos, leaving fifteen destroyed or taken; but the greater part of the men were saved by the nearness of the shore. Alcibiades, on hearing of this disaster, came to Samos, and sailed out with his whole force towards Ephesus, to offer battle. But, even after the recent loss, he was still superior in numbers, and Lysander would not risk the honor of his newly-erected trophy. Alcibiades returned to Samos, rather shamed by the enemy's caution than consoled by the display of his own strength.

Soon after this, the enemies of the Athenian commander-in-chief procured his removal, together with that of his friend Thrasybulus. Conon succeeded him in the chief command, and nine colleagues were appointed. Conon found the fleet superior in numbers to the enemy, but despondency prevailed among the men on account of the recent defeat, and the want of a full regular pay. He was obliged to resort to numerous expeditions to various points on the coast, for the sake of the supplies to be obtained by plunder. The number of the galleys was reduced to seventy, in order that each should have a proper complement of men, the crews having been thinned by desertions.

Lysander could not be prevailed upon to stir from Ephesus until the end of his year of office, when Callicratidas was appointed to succeed him, and he returned to Sparta. Callicratidas drew reinforcements from Chios, Rhodes, and other quarters, and having thus collected one hundred and forty sail, prepared to seek the enemy. But want of money, and the machinations of Lysander's partisans prevented the Spartan admiral from executing his intention. He was compelled to sail to Sardis, and then to Miletus, before receiving sufficient supplies, and then his armament was increased to one hundred and seventy galleys. Conon was thus inferior to his opponent by one hundred galleys, and began a retreat. He was overtaken by the Peloponnesians near the mouth of the harbor of Mitylene, for which he was compelled to steer, and lost thirty galleys. The remaining forty galleys were hauled on shore, under shelter of the walls of the town. Callicratidas was master of both harbors formed by the small island on which old Mitylene was built, and he invested the town by sea and land. Conon, however, contrived to send a galley to Athens with the news of his danger, and a request for assistance. The Athenians knew that the loss of their armament would be irreparable, and they put forth their whole remaining strength. At the end of thirty days they manned a fleet of one hundred and ten sail. All Conon's colleagues took command in person, and every man who could be spared from the defence of the city, was sent with the armament. The colleagues first sailed to Samos, where they strengthened themselves with ten Samian galleys, and with thirty more from other quarters, and then they prepared to seek the Peloponnesians. Callicratidas did not shrink from a decisive conflict, but leaving Eteonicus, with fifty galleys, to blockade Mitylene, he stationed the remainder of his fleet at Malea, the southernmost headland of Lesbos. In the evening of the same day, the Athenians arrived at the Arginusiœ islands, over against Malea. Callicratidas wished to surprise them by a sudden attack in the night, but a thunder storm prevented him, and he waited till daylight.

The Athenians were then ready to meet or receive him; and a battle ensued, which for the number of vessels engaged was the greatest that had yet been fought between two Greek navies. We are informed by Xenophon, that Callicratidas was dissuaded by Hermon, a Megarian, the master of his galley, from venturing on an action against such greatly superior numbers as those of the enemy. The Spartan's answer became very celebrated. It was, as Xenophon reports it, "Sparta would suffer no hurt from his death; but he should be dishonored by flight."

The account which Xenophon and Diodorus give of the order of battle differ from each other in most particulars, but they seem to agree as to the general design of both parties: that the aim of the Peloponnesians was attack, that of the Athenians defence. But Diodorus describes the Athenian line as formed so as to take in one of the islands, which separated it into two divisions; to meet which, Callicratidas disposed his fleet in two squadrons parted from each other by a considerable interval. Xenophon represents the Athenians as advancing to a distance from the shore, but formed in a compact mass of two lines in each wing, and only a little weaker in the centre. Aristocrates commanded fifteen galleys in the extreme left; Diomedon was stationed by his side, and Pericles and Erasinides in their rear, each with an equal number. The centre was occupied by ten Samian galleys, under Hippeus, a Samian commander, and by as many under the ten Athenian taxiarchs, and they were supported in the rear by a smaller number of Athenian or allied galleys. On the right, Protomachus took the lead, with Thrasyllus by his side, and Lysias and Aristogenes behind, each having fifteen galleys under his command.

The Peloponnesians, Xenophon describes as drawn up in a single but unbroken line, to take advantage of their superiority in offensive manœuvres over the unpractised Athenian crews. According to Diodorus, Callicratidas himself commanded in the right of his line, and Thrasondas, a Theban, in the left. Neither author, however, gives any intimation as to the effect which these arrangements produced, nor as to the causes which decided the battle, except so far as its issue may have been connected with the fate of the Spartan admiral, who was killed in a conflict with one of the enemy's galleys, according to Diodorus, after he had sunk that of Lysias—who, however, survived—and had struck and grappled with that of Pericles. After this event the Peloponnesians were completely routed, and fled, some towards Chios, some to Phocæa, leaving seventy galleys and upward destroyed or taken. Among them were nine out of the ten which composed the Lacedæmonian contingent, and were, therefore, probably under the immediate orders and eye of Callicratidas.

The Athenians lost five-and-twenty galleys, and almost all at such a distance from the shore that the men who survived had no chance of safely but in clinging to the wrecks. They seem to have spent very little, if any, time in pursuit of the flying enemy, and the generals, having returned to their station at the Arginusæ, held a council on the course to be next adopted.

The squadron of fifty galleys, which blockaded Mitylene, was informed of the defeat of Callicratidas, by a boat kept for that purpose, and by means of making Conon believe that their friends were victorious, the Peloponnesians made their escape. Finding the harbor clear, Conon sailed towards the Arginusæ, and met the Athenian armament. The whole fleet then sailed to Samos, under Conon, and two of his colleagues, while the others returned home. After this terrible blow, Sparta again made overtures for peace, but again were they rejected. For some cause, not accurately known, all of Conon's colleagues were removed from office as soon as they returned to Athens, and two others, Adimantus and Philocles, were appointed in their stead.

The Athenian fleet now rode the sea without a rival. The remnant of the Peloponnesian navy was scattered among the different ports friendly to their interest. But the friends of Lysander succeeded in getting him appointed again to fill the post of admiral, although the Spartan law was against it. Arcacus was nominally the admiral, but Lysander had secret orders to take the supreme command. Early in the summer of 405, B. C., Lysander arrived at Ephesus, with thirty-five galleys. He immediately set about collecting all the Peloponnesian galleys which were scattered in the different ports, and had a number of new ones built at Antandrus. The Persian prince, Cyrus, assisted him with money, which enabled him to pay his seamen in full and accelerated his preparations. Cyrus also promised to assist him with a number of Phœnician ships.

Lysander thought it best, for the time, to avoid a collision with the Athenian fleet, and accordingly sailed to the south coast of Caria, captured various towns and destroyed the inhabitants of those which were allied with Athens. The Athenian fleet pursued him, but he succeeded in escaping to the Asiatic coast. Soon after this, he captured and pillaged Lampsacus, just before the Athenian fleet of one hundred and eighty galleys reached the Hellespont. Finding that Lampsacus was lost, the Athenians retired to Ægospotami, nearly opposite to that place. Lysander had now collected a large fleet, but still was inferior to the enemy, and, although he ordered every thing to be prepared for a sea fight, he declined the offer of battle from the Athenians. At length his opponents, seeing their challenge constantly declined, grew careless of the Peloponnesians, and wandered far from their fleet in search of food, leaving their ships without sufficient guard. Alcibiades, whose fort was near the place, came down to warn the Athenian commanders of their error, but they would not listen to him. Lysander suddenly pushed across the channel, with his utmost speed. Of the six Athenian generals, Conon alone was on the watch, and his own galley, with eight others, were soon manned. But this only enabled them to make their escape. The rest fell into the hands of Lysander, while Thorax and his troops scoured the country, and captured most of the men. Seeing that all was lost, Conon sailed away, with his eight galleys, to Cyprus; the Paralus, the state galley, carried the news of ruin to Athens. The Peloponnesian fleet then returned in triumph, to Lampsacus, carrying all his prisoners and prizes. All the Athenian generals except Conon, were captured, and, exasperated by the cruelties of the enemy, the Peloponnesians determined to put all the prisoners, except Adimantus, one of the generals, to death. Three thousand men, at the lowest computation, were thus massacred.

Lysander now steered the victorious fleet towards the Greek cities which had opposed the Peloponnesians. Sestus, Byzantium, and Chalcedon, submitted without resistance, and then the victor returned to Lampsacus to refit. His whole fleet now numbered two hundred galleys. A few were sent to different towns, to reduce those who acknowledged the supremacy of Athens. He then sailed to Piræus, the harbor of Athens, with one hundred and fifty galleys, while a land force besieged the city and wasted the surrounding territory.

Lysander offered moderate and reasonable terms to the besieged, but the violence of the internal factions prevented the Athenians from accepting them. They prepared for a vigorous defence. But the oligarchical party triumphed and a peace was concluded, by the terms of which Athens was to be annexed to the Peloponnesian confederacy, to give up all her ships but twelve, and the long walls and fortifications of Piræus to be demolished. Thus was that mighty naval power which had ruled the sea so long crushed, it seemed, forever. Lysander dismissed his allies, after the condition of Athens had been framed by his will, and then returned to Sparta.

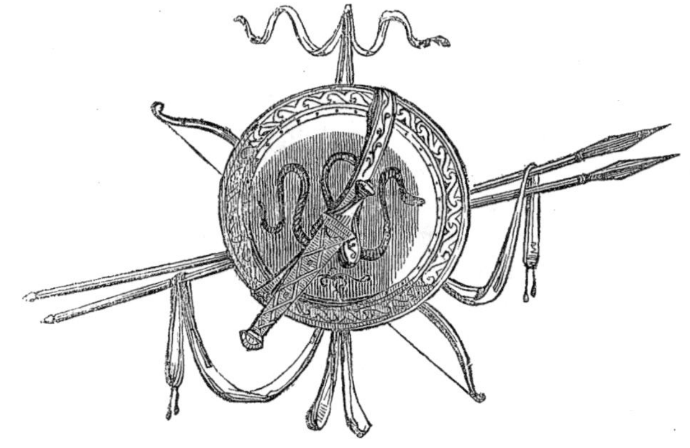

CHAPTER IX.

FROM THE PELOPONNESIAN WAR TILL THE ROMAN CONQUEST.

BY the fall of Athens, Sparta became the mistress of the sea, and maintained her supremacy until it received a severe blow from Conon, the Athenian commander, who had got into favor with the Persians, and been appointed admiral under Pharnabazus. Conon soon collected a powerful fleet of Phœnician and Cilician ships, and forced the Spartan fleet to quit the blockade of Caria. Pharnabazus took command of the Phœnician galleys, and Conon, that of the remainder. As they sailed westward, along the coast of Syria, Conon's squadron, being some distance ahead, they fell in with the Peloponnesian fleet of eighty-five galleys, under Pisander. As the squadron, under Conon, approached, the allies of the Spartans abandoned the left wing, and the remainder of the fleet was driven on shore and captured or destroyed. Pisander remained with his ship to the last, and died like a Spartan, sword in hand.

The victors then cruised in the Ægean Sea, and drove the Spartan harmosts from all the maritime cities on the coast.

In the following spring, 393, B. C., having collected a great fleet and raised a strong body of mercenaries, Pharnabazus embarked with Conon, and, entering the Messenian Gulf, ravaged the richest portions of Laconia, and then sailed to Cytheræ. There an Athenian garrison, under Nicophernus, was placed. Conon then took the chief command of the fleet, and, proceeding to Athens, he patriotically endeavored to rebuild the long walls, and the fortifications of Piræus. The Corinthians were encouraged by these successes to fit out a squadron, which made head against the Spartans for a while, but was, in the end, forced to take refuge in its station at Rhegium. Conon made the most strenuous efforts to restore the maritime power of Athens, and to unite the northern Greeks against the Spartans, and he succeeded, to some extent, in effecting his object. His fleet soon returned to the Asiatic coast, and Conon was thrown into prison, on a slight pretext, immediately on his arrival.

The Athenians were now enabled to fit out a powerful fleet, and their old enterprise seems to have returned to them. They sent Thrasybulus, who had distinguished himself on land, with forty galleys, to overbalance the Spartan supremacy in the neighborhood of Rhodes, and that bold commander sailed to the Ægean and Hellespont, displayed his activity and skill in various conquests, and was killed in the midst of his triumphs. Thus Athens lost the services of both Conon and Thrasybulus, at a time when such men could have revived her former glory. Still Iphicrates upheld the honor of his country on sea and land. The Athenians were master of the Hellespont. The Spartan admirals Teleutias, and his successor, Hierax, cruised in the Ægean Sea, and annoyed the commerce of the Athenians until defeated at Ægina, by Chabrias. Teleutias was a favorite commander among the Peloponnesian seamen. After the defeat of Hierax, he was reappointed to command the fleet in the Ægean. With only twelve galleys, Telutias crossed over from Ægina to Piræus, captured several ships of war and merchant vessels, and escaped without molestation.

In the Hellespont, Nicholœus, with five-and-twenty galleys, was blockaded at Abydos, by an Athenian squadron, of two-and-thirty galleys, under Diodemus and Iphicrates. But the Peloponnesians succeeded in escaping in the night, pursued by the Athenians. Antalcidas, the Spartan admiral, had taken command of the Peloponnesian squadron, and he expected to be joined by twenty galleys from Sicily and Italy. While waiting for these, he heard of the approach of Thrasybulus, with eight Athenian galleys. Selecting twelve of his fastest sailing vessels, he pushed out and overtook the Athenians, and captured the whole squadron. Soon after, by reinforcements from various quarters, the squadron under Antalcidas was raised to eighty sail, and that admiral had thus complete command of the sea. The commerce of the Athenians was diverted to the ports of the allies of Sparta.

During what is called the "Social war," Athens had so far recovered her maritime power as to be able to equip two armaments, each of sixty galleys; but neither of them effected any thing. The three men who had contributed so much to restore the power of Athens, were Iphicrates, Timotheus, and Chabrias. The two first were censured for their conduct of the armament sent against the maritime allies of Sparta, and went into voluntary exile, never to return. The latter was killed in conducting the blockade and siege of Chios. Chares and Phocion then became the principal Athenian admirals. During the war with Macedon, they first attacked a Macedonian fleet lying off Chalcedon, and after a severe fight were defeated, with the loss of several vessels. The news of the defeat roused the Athenians to greater exertions. A squadron of one hundred and twenty sail was raised, and placed under the command of Phocion. This formidable fleet sailed to Byzantium, with the intention of blockading it, but the Byzantines received Phocion with open arms, and he immediately became their general. The commerce of Macedonia was entirely destroyed by the Athenians, and their cruisers even prevented the Macedonians from obtaining the necessaries of life. But when Athens was forced to submit to Philip of Macedon on land, her maritime power became his also. No naval engagement of any importance is recorded until after the death of Alexander the Great. Amidst the struggle for empire, Cassander became master of the port of Athens, and was thus enabled to fit out a considerable fleet, which he sent to the Thracian Bosphorus, under the command of Nicanor. This fleet was at first defeated by the royal navy of Polysperchon; but, being reinforced, Nicanor renewed the engagement, and captured all the enemy's ships, except the admiral's galley.

During the reign of Philip II., of Macedon, (B. C. 222,) a war took place between the maritime cities of Byzantium and Rhodes, in consequence of the heavy tolls exacted by the former for all vessels passing into the Euxine Sea. The Byzantines were beaten in the various sea fights, and forced to abolish the onerous duties. Philip possessed a powerful fleet, and was master of the sea for a short time. But the Rhodians completely annihilated his naval power at Chios, and its revival was prevented by the approach of a Roman fleet and army, which reduced Philip to submission. Greece soon became a Roman province under the name of Achaia, and her naval glory shared the fate of her other powers—it was crushed, and has ever since been inconsiderable.

GRECIAN WAR CHARIOT.

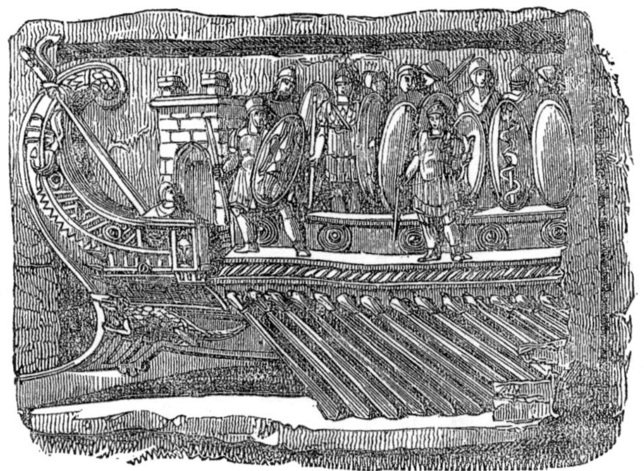

PROW OF A ROMAN GALLEY.

CHAPTER X.

THE NAVAL HISTORY OF ROME, FROM THE EARLIEST PERIOD OF HER POWER, UNTIL THE DESTRUCTION OF CARTHAGE.

THE Greeks had established many colonies on the coast of Italy, before the ambition of the Roman people had extended their power beyond the vicinity of the Tiber, and some of them became flourishing commercial cities. We read in the ancient historians, of the doings of the Etruscans—a piratical people inhabiting the plains of the Po, and that their power was the only source of opposition, on the Italian coast, to the fleets of Dionysius of Sicily. They established numerous colonies on the shores of the Adriatic. But the squadrons of Sicily coasted Italy, and sailed by the mouth of the Tiber, without fear of meeting resistance, or plundered the maritime towns with impunity. Rome possessed no means of preventing their ravages. Her people were not as enterprising as the Greeks, and what ambition they then possessed exerted itself in contests upon land. But when the power of Greece had declined, under the Macedonian yoke, some attempts at raising a navy were rendered necessary by the wants of the Romans. Nothing, however, was effected in that way, until the ambition of the Romans brought them into contact with a mighty maritime state, and then they were made fully conscious of their inferiority in naval matters.

The first war ships used by the Romans were probably obtained from the Greeks. In 282, B. C., we find that two officers were appointed to conduct the naval affairs of the commonwealth. One of these officers—who were to be elected annually—named L. Valerius, was sent, with a fleet of ten ships, to watch the movements of the Tarentines. He arrived unexpectedly before the walls of Tarentum, and seemed to be preparing to force his way into the harbor, when discovered by the enemy, who were engaged at their festival of Dionysia. Esteeming this a violation of a treaty then existing between Rome and Tarentum, the Tarentines immediately manned their ships and sailed out to meet the invaders. They met with no resistance, for the Romans immediately strove to escape. Four ships were sunk, and one taken, with all its crew. L. Valerius, the decemvir, was killed, and, of the prisoners, the officers and soldiers serving on board were put to death, and the rowers were sold for slaves. In the war which followed, the Tarentines were masters of the sea, and, it seems, wasted the coast of Latium; for a Carthaginian fleet of one hundred and twenty sail was sent to Ostia to aid the Romans. The succor was declined, however, and the Carthaginian commander sailed away to the south of Italy, to propose a mediation between Pyrrhus, the Tarentines, and the Romans. The armament afterwards aided the Romans in recovering Rhegium, and destroyed a quantity of timber, which the Campanians had collected for building ships.

The First Punic War broke out about eleven years after the defeat of Pyrrhus, (B. C. 264.) The Romans had neglected their navy after the close of the war with Tarentum, and we hear, at this time, of no decemvirii, or naval commanders, as regular officers of the commonwealth. From the Greek cities in their alliance they obtained a few triremes and penteconters; but they had not a single quinquereme, the class of ships which may be called the line of battle ships of that period. The Carthaginians had a large fleet guarding the strait of

Messana, which the Romans wanted to cross in order to succor the Mammertines. In attempting to accomplish this with their triremes and penteconters, the Romans were easily baffled, and some of their triremes, with the soldiers they were transporting, fell into the hands of the Carthaginians. But Claudius, the Roman commander, succeeded in eluding the vigilance of the squadron, and reached Sicily with a single ship. The defeat of the Carthaginian land forces was followed by the retreat of their squadron; for, in ancient warfare, a fleet was dependent, in a great measure, on land co-operation.

The Carthaginians soon began to exert their naval strength effectively. Many towns on the Sicilian coast which had yielded to the Roman arms were recovered by the Carthaginian fleet, and the coasts of Italy were so often ravaged, that the Romans found it necessary to encounter the enemy on his own element. At the close of the year 261, B. C., they began to fell their timber. But no Italian shipwright knew how to build the line of ships of that period called quinqueremes, and their build was so different from that of the triremes, that the one would not serve as a model for the other. The shipwrights might have been procured from the king of Egypt, but to send thither would have caused too great a delay.

It happened that a Carthaginian qinquereme had run ashore on the Bruttian coast when Appius Claudius was first crossing over to Sicily, and it was noted as a curious circumstance, that the Roman soldiers had taken a ship of war. This quinquereme, which had probably been sent to Rome as a trophy, was now made the shipwright's model, and a hundred ships were built after her pattern, and launched in two months after the first felling of the timber. The seamen, partly proletarians, or citizens of the poorest class, partly Etruscans or Greeks from the maritime states of Italy, were all unaccustomed to row in the quinqueremes, and the Romans, perhaps, had never handled an oar of any sort. While the ships were building, therefore, to lose no time, the future crew of each quinquereme, were ranged upon benches ashore, in the same order, that to us undiscoverable problem, in which they were hereafter to sit on board; the keleustes, whose voice or call regulated the stroke in the ancient galleys, stood in the midst of them, and at his signal they went through their movements, and learned to keep time together, as if they had been actually afloat. With such ships and such crews the Romans put to sea early in the spring, to seek an engagement with the fleet of the first naval power in the world.

The only hope of the Romans for success in a sea fight was an opportunity for boarding. Then the victory of Roman soldiers over African crews would be easy. To facilitate the attainment of their object, they contrived in each ship, what may be called a long draw-bridge, thirty-six feet long by four wide, with a low parapet on each side of it. This bridge was attached, by a hole in one end of it, to a mast twenty-four feet high, erected on the ship's prow, and the hole was large and oblong, so that the bridge not only played freely all round the mast, but could be drawn up so as to lie parallel to it, the end of it being hoisted by a rope just as our cutters' booms are hoisted by what is called the topping lift. The bridge was attached to the mast at the height of about twelve feet from the deck, and being managed with a rope, the bridge was let fall upon an enemy's ship, upon whatever quarter she might approach. When the bridge fell, a small iron spike, fixed in its end, was driven into the deck by the mere weight of the fall, and there held the ship while she was boarded. With these bridges sprung up the masts of their vessels, the Roman fleet made a strange appearance, as all the ancient ships usually lowered their masts previous to going into action.

The fleet, under the command of the consul, Cneius Cornelius Scipio, put to sea in quest of the enemy. But that commander allowed himself to be taken, with seventeen vessels, in an attempt on the Liparæn islands, and was succeeded by C. Duilius. The Carthaginian fleet, under the command of Hannibal, advanced. boldly to meet the Romans, although surprised at the masts and tackle on their ships. But the thirty ships that formed their advance squadron, including that of Hannibal himself, were soon grappled by the Roman bridges, boarded and taken. Hannibal escaped in a boat to the main squadron, which was rapidly coming up. But seeing the efficacy of the contrivance of the Romans, and the fate of their ships, the Carthaginians turned and fled. Their whole loss amounted to about fifty ships sunk or taken, and, in men, to three thousand killed and seven thousand prisoners. The moral consequences of this victory to the Romans were great, indeed. They now became confident of success, both on sea and land, and at once assumed the offensive. Duilius obtained a triumph, on his return, and a pillar was erected to commemorate his victory.

As the Romans extended their naval operations, they unavoidably became acquainted with the violence of the Mediterranean storms; and the terrors of the sea were very dreadful to the people of Italy, who were forced to furnish seamen to man the Roman fleet, a service to which they were unused. Besides their expeditions to Sardinia and Corsica, the Romans gained an advantage over the Carthaginian fleet, in the year, 257, B. C., off the Liparæan islands, for which the consul, C. Atilius, obtained a triumph. These successes stimulated the Romans to such a degree, that they resolved to carry the war into Africa. During the winter great preparations were made for the expedition. A fleet of three hundred and thirty ships was got ready, manned by nearly one hundred thousand seamen, exclusive of soldiers. The two consular armies wintered in Sicily, and the fleet sailed through the strait of Messana, doubled Cape Pachynus, and took the legions on board at Ecnomus, a small place on the southern coast of Sicily. Forty thousand men were here embarked, and the Carthaginians, who had assembled a still larger fleet of three hundred and fifty ships, had already crossed over to Lilybœum, and from thence advancing along the Sicilian coast, were arrived at Heraclea Minor, and were ready to give the Romans battle. Both consuls were on board the Roman fleet. The Carthaginians were commanded by Hanno, and Hamilcar. The contest was obstinate, but at last the Romans were completely victorious. They lost twenty-four ships, in which about two thousand eight hundred and eighty soldiers perished. But they destroyed thirty of the enemy's fleet, and took sixty-four, with all their crews. The remainder of the Carthaginian fleet made all speed to Carthage to prepare to resist the invasion.

The way to Africa was now open, and after victualing their ships with more than usual supplies, as they knew not what port would receive them, the consuls prepared to leave the coast of Sicily for an unknown world. The fleet did not keep together, and thirty ships reached the African shore unsupported. These might have been destroyed before the arrival of the rest, if the Carthaginians, in their confusion, had not neglected the opportunity. The whole fleet assembled under the headland of Hermes, and then sailed southward and disembarked near the place called Aspis, or Clypea, a fortress built by Agathocles. The

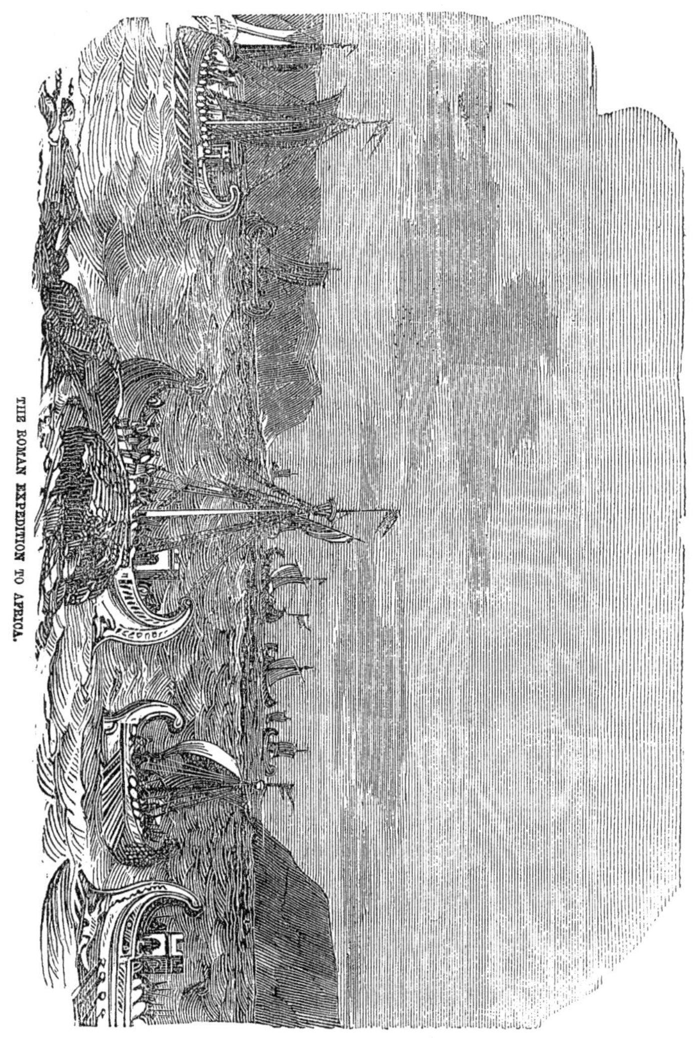

THE ROMAN EXPEDITION TO AFRICA.

ships were immediately drawn up on the beach, after the ancient manner, and secured with a ditch and rampart. The fortress was then captured and the surrounding country ravaged without mercy, until orders were received from the Roman Senate, directing that one of the consuls, with a consular army and forty ships, was to remain in Africa; the other, with the rest of the army, the fleet and the plunder, was to return home. L. Manlius accordingly embarked and returned to Rome, while M. Regulus, with fifteen thousand foot and five hundred horse remained in Africa. After various successes, the army under Regulus was completely routed, and not more than two thousand men escaped to Clypea, which the Carthaginians immediately besieged. A Roman fleet was sent to its assistance, and the Carthaginians, dreading another invasion, equipped a fleet inferior in number to the Romans, and met them near Clypea. The Romans were completely victorious; but they contented themselves with taking the garrison of Clypea on board the fleet, and sailed back to Sicily.

The Romans had now sent fleets to sea for five years, yet they had little experience of its terrors. Their unbounded confidence in themselves made them think that Romans might sail at any season. So, in the month of July, in spite of the warnings of their pilots, they persisted in sailing along the southern coast of Sicily, at the very time when violent gales from the south and southwest make that coast extremely perilous. The fleet was off Camarina when the storm came on. Above two hundred and sixty ships were wrecked, which must have had on board seventy-eight thousand seamen, without counting the soldiers, who were probably twenty-five thousand, and the whole coast, from Camarina to Pachynus was covered with wrecks and bodies. This disaster encouraged the Carthaginians to renew their offensive operations. But the indomitable spirit of the Romans was worthy of the Athenians under similar circumstances. In the space of three months, they fitted out two hundred and twenty ships, and crossing over to Messana, they were joined by the remnant of the other fleet. The whole, under the consuls, A. Atilius and C. Cornelius, sailed along the northern coast of Sicily and took Cephalœdium and Panormus. (B. C. 254.) For this service, Cn. Cornelius obtained a triumph.

Sempronius, the successor of Cornelius, conducted the fleet to the coast of Africa, and plundered the country near the sea; but effected nothing of importance. On his return, the fleet was overtaken by another storm, between Panormus and Laconia, and more than one hundred and fifty ships were wrecked. After this second great disaster, the Romans resolved to tempt the sea no more, and to keep a fleet of no more than sixty ships, to supply the army with provisions, and to protect the coast of Italy. This resolve, hasty and foolish in its inception, was soon broken. In 250, B. C., when Regulus and Manlius were again consuls, the successes of the Carthaginians roused the Romans to exertion. Fifty new ships were built, and a great victory being gained over the Carthaginians, in Sicily, the number was increased to two hundred. This large fleet was employed in blockading the harbor of Lilybœum, during the long siege of that city. The Carthaginians displayed more cool courage and skilful manœuvring on land and sea during this siege, than they had ever shown before. Hannibal sailed from Carthage, with fifty ships, to endeavor to throw succors into the town. He waited his time at the Ægean islands, which lie to the north of Lilybœum. At length the wind blew fresh from the north, setting full into the harbor's mouth; Hannibal placed his soldiers on the decks ready for battle, hoisted every sail, and knowing the channels well, he ran down before the wind to the entrance between the shoals, dashed through the narrow passage, whilst the Romans in astonishment and awkwardness did not put out a single ship to stop him, and amidst the cheers and shouts of the whole garrison and people of Lilybæum, who had crowded to the walls to watch the event, he landed ten thousand men in safety within the harbor. Other officers of single ships passed several times backwards and forwards with equal success, acquainting the Carthaginian government with every particular of the siege, and confounding the Romans by their absolute command, as it seemed, of the winds and waves.

The siege was continued under very unfavorable circumstances, during the winter. The Romans had lost so many seamen in the various attacks upon the town, that their fleet was rendered useless for the want of hands to work it. When the summer came, ten thousand seamen were brought from Rome, and a new consul, P. Claudius, took command. This commander was of a more active temperament than the former ones, but impatient and overbearing. He endeavored to blockade the harbor, but failed; and then, being anxious to distinguish

WRECK OF SEMPRONIUS'S FLEET.

himself, he resolved to attack the Carthaginian fleet, which under Adherbal, as lying in the harbor of Dressanum. His officers foreboded the failure of the attempt, but could not move him from his purpose.

Adherbal did not expect the attack, but so great was his promptitude, that on the first sight of the enemy, he manned all his ships, and keeping close under the land, stood out of the harbor while the Romans were actually entering it. Claudius confounded at this, ordered his ships to put about and stand out to sea again. Some ran foul of each other in doing this, but at last he got clear of the harbor and formed his fleet under the land, with the ships' heads turned to the sea. Adherbal, who had brought his own fleet safely into the open sea, now formed his line of battle and attacked the Romans. We hear no more of Duilius' bridges for boarding; whether the Carthaginians had discovered some means of baffling them, or whether the practised soldiers now on board the Carthaginian ships rendered such a contrivance no longer formidable. Adherbal's victory was complete; Claudius escaped with only thirty ships, and the rest, amounting to ninety-three, were taken; with a loss in men, although some escaped to land, of not fewer than eight thousand killed and twenty thousand prisoners. The conquerors did not lose a single ship, and the number of their killed and wounded was very inconsiderable.

They followed up their victory with vigor. Thirty ships sailed to Panormus and carried off from thence the Roman magazines of corn, which were sent to supply the garrison of Lilybæum. Carthalo arrived with seventy ships from Carthage, and being reinforced by Adherbal, attacked the remains of the Roman fleet which had been drawn up on shore at Lilybœum under the protection of the army, carried off five ships and destroyed others. Meanwhile the other consul, L. Junius Pullus, had sailed from Rome with a large fleet of ships laden with corn and other supplies for the army at Lilybæum, which he convoyed with a hundred and twenty ships of war. Being himself detained at Syracuse to wait for some of the ships of his convoy, and to collect corn from some of the districts in the interior of the island, he entrusted about four hundred of the corn-ships with some of his ships of war to his quæstors, and sent them on to Lilybæum, where the want of corn was severely felt. Carthalo was lying at Heraclea near Agrigentum, looking out for the Roman fleet; and when he heard of their approach he put out to sea to intercept them. The quæstors being in no condition to fight, fled to the small bay of Phintias, not far from Ecnomus, the scene of the great naval battle seven years before, and there mooring their ships at the bottom of the bay, and mounting the artillery of the town on the cliffs on each side of them, they waited for the enemy's attack. Carthalo was disappointed to find them so well prepared, and as their resistance was obstinate he only carried off a few of the corn-ships and returned to Heraclea, watching for the time when they should venture to continue their voyage.

He had not waited long when his lookout ships announced that the reardivision of the Roman fleet under the consul in person had doubled Cape Pachynus, and was advancing along the southern coast of Sicily. Wishing to meet these ships before they could join their other division in the bay of Phintias, he sailed in pursuit of them with all speed. The consul made for the shore near Camarina, dreading an open and rocky coast, and the danger of the southwest gales, less than an engagement with an enemy so superior. Carthalo, not choosing to attack him in this situation, stationed his fleet off a headland between Phintias and Camarinia, and there lay, watching the movements of both the Roman divisions. Meanwhile it began to blow hard from the south, and there were signs of a coming storm which were not lost on the experienced Carthaginian pilots, who urged Carthalo to run in time for shelter. With great exertions he got round Cape Pachynus, and there lay safely in smooth water. But the storm burst with all its fury on the Romans, and overwhelmed both their fleets with such utter destruction, that all the corn-ships, amounting to nearly eight hundred, and one hundred and five ships of war, were dashed to pieces. With two ships of war only did the unfortunate consul arrive at Lilybæum.

These disasters broke the spirit of the Romans. Claudius was recalled, brought to trial for contempt of the sacred omens, and either committed suicide, or met his death at the hands of the executioner. His offence was of this nature. Before sailing to meet the Carthaginians, it was reported to him that the omens were unfavorable, as the sacred chickens refused to eat. "Then they shall drink," was Claudius' answer, and he ordered them to be thrown into the sea. This was the offence for which he was tried; but, doubtless, if he had been successful, he would have received a triumph in spite of it.

The commander who succeeded Claudius was equally unsuccessful, and, being tried for contempt of the auspices, committed suicide. Thus are men punished for being superior to the superstition of the vulgar mass.

After the destruction of the fleet of Claudius, the Carthaginians held the dominion of the sea. But in the twenty-fourth year of the war, (B. C., 242,) the Romans roused themselves for one more effort. So exhausted was the treasury, that the fleet could only be raised by patriotic loans. One, two, or three wealthy persons, according to their means, advanced money to build a quinquereme, which was to be repaid to them in brighter times. By these means, two hundred ships were constructed, upon the model of one of the best sailing of the Carthaginian vessels, captured a few years before. This fleet was placed under the command of C. Lutatius, the consul for that year. The Carthaginian fleet had returned home for the winter, when the Roman fleet sailed, and they entered the harbor of Drepanum without resistance. While the town was vigorously attacked, Lutatius was unceasing in his exertions to perfect his seamen in rowing and manœuvring. Upon receiving intelligence of the siege of Drepanum, the Carthaginians equipped a fleet with all haste, and appointed Hanno to command it. But they had neglected their navy for some time before, and their seamen and soldiers were alike without experience. The ships were also heavily laden with stores for the relief of Drepanum.

Hanno was stationed at the island of Hiera, off the west point of Sicily. He hoped to sail unseen to the coast of Drepanum, and take Hamilcar and the land forces on board the fleet, when he would not fear to meet the Romans. This Lutatius was determined to prevent. That consul being wounded in a skirmish with the besieged, the command devolved on Valerius, the prætor, who was active and skilful.

It was the morning of the 10th of March; the Roman fleet having taken on board picked soldiers from the legions, had sailed on the preceding evening to the island of Ægusa, which lies between Hiera and the Sicilian coast, and had there spent the night. When day broke, the wind was blowing fresh from the west, and rolling a heavy sea in upon the land; the Carthaginians took advantage of it, hoisted their sails, and ran down before the wind towards Drepanum. The Roman fleet, notwithstanding the heavy sea and the adverse wind, worked out to intercept them, and formed in line of battle with their heads to windward, cutting off the enemy's passage. Then the Carthaginians lowered their masts and sails, and prepared of necessity to fight. But their heavy ships and raw seamen and soldiers were too unequal to the contest, and the fortune of the day was soon decided. Fifty ships were sunk, and seventy taken; the rest fled, and the wind, happily for them, shifting just in time, they again hoisted their sails, and escaped to Hiera.

This great victory turned the tide of affairs to the Roman side, and the Carthaginians were compelled to sue for peace. Rome was now mistress of the land and sea.

During the interval between the first and second Punic Wars, the Romans found employment enough to keep their seamen and soldiers in good training. Sardinia, Corsica and Malta were successively seized upon, and, in 219, B. C., the two former were reduced to the state of a province. Illyricum, which borders upon Macedon and Epirus, was at this time governed by Teuta, the widow of King Agron. Her pirates had taken and plundered many ships belonging to the Romans, and her troops were at this time besieging the island of Issa, which was under the protection of Rome. Upon the complaint of the merchants of Italy, two ambassadors were sent to require the queen to restrain her subjects from piracy, and to withdraw her troops from Issa. The ambassadors were murdered. As soon as this became known at Rome a fleet was ordered to be equipped and troops raised. Teuta then seemed anxious to conciliate the Romans; but the Illyrian fleet having gained some advantage over the Achæans, and taken Corcyra, the queen thought herself invincible. An Illyrian fleet was sent to take possession of Issa, then under the Roman protection.

The Roman fleet, consisting of one hundred galleys, under the consul Fulvius, sailed to Corcyra, and took possession of the island and city. Many strongholds along the coast were taken, and the Illyrians lost forty vessels, which were returning home with booty from piracy. The siege of Issa was raised, and the Romans every where victorious, forced the Illyrian queen to sue for peace. This was only granted on the most rigorous terms. The Illyrians were to pay an annual tribute, surrender several important islands, and never to send more than three ships of war at a time beyond Lyssus.

The contest of the Romans and Carthaginians, during the second

BATTLE OF ÆGUSA, OR ÆGUSÆ.

Punic War, was conducted, for the most part, on land. Although possessed of a great fleet of ships of war, Carthage suffered Scipio and his army to pass over to Africa without opposition. The victory of Scipio at Zama, terminated the war in favor of the Romans, despite of the splendid campaigns of the great Hannibal. By the terms of the treaty, Carthage surrendered five hundred vessels of war, being allowed to retain only ten triremes. She was also bound to assist the Romans by sea and land. But the Carthaginians could not long brook such terms as the Romans required them to bear. War was soon declared, and the consuls, Manlius Nepos, and Marcius Censorinus, with an army and fleet were soon despatched by the Romans to begin hostilities.

The fleet consisted of fifty quinqueremes, and a great number of transports. The army numbered eighty thousand foot and four thousand chosen horse. This vast armament was destined for the destruction of Carthage. The city was invested. The inhabitants made the most exraordinary exertions for defence, and repulsed the attack of the Romans. Asdrubal, the commander of the Carthaginians, watching a favorable moment when the Roman fleet drew near the shore, ordered all the old barks in the harbor to be filled with combustibles, and sent among the vessels of the Romans. The device was completely successful; nearly all the fleet was consumed. Asdrubal was victorious in his sallies upon the besieging army and finally compelled it to retire. But these successes were of no avail. Scipio Æmilianus was appointed to conduct the Roman forces, and he soon changed the face of things. Another Roman fleet blockaded the harbor of Carthage, while the city was besieged by land.

The Romans constructed a mole in the old harbor of Carthage, which effectually prevented the entrance or egress of any kind of vessels. But the spirit of the Carthaginians was desperate. With incredible labor, they dug a canal to the sea, by which they could receive the provisions sent to them by their troops in the field. With equal industry, they fitted out a fleet of fifty triremes, with which they sailed out to give the Romans battle. The action lasted all day, without any decisive advantage on either side. The Romans were driven off in a subsequent night attack, in spite of the exertions of Scipio, and then all further attack on the place was suspended. Asdrubal offered to surrender the city upon condition that it should not be destroyed; but this was refused. The destruction of Carthage was determined upon. The siege was renewed early in the spring, and after a most heroic and desperate resistance, the city was taken, and burned and pillaged without mercy. By the orders of the Roman senate, the city was entirely destroyed; and thus that great maritime power, which was so long the rival, and, for some time, the conqueror of the Romans, was blotted from the list of nations.

ROMAN LICTOR AND ROMAN CENTURION.

CHAPTER XI.

FROM THE DESTRUCTION OF CARTHAGE TILL THE SEA-FIGHT ACTIUM.

THE Roman power was next directed against Philip of Macedon, who was compelled to sue for peace at the end of a three years contest. The navy bore but a small share in the operations against that monarch. At the end of the war, the greater part of the Macedonian navy was surrendered to the victors. Soon after the reduction of Macedon, a Roman fleet gained a victory over the fleet of Antiochus the Great, king of Asia Minor, and that prince was forced to give up the greater portion of his navy. From this period until the 680th year of the existence of Rome, we have no record of any naval transactions of any importance. The navy was not neglected during this interval, however, for large fleets were necessary to transport the armies of Marius and Sylla to Africa and Asia Minor.

In the year 74, B. C., the pirates of Cilicia had become so troublesome that it became necessary to adopt measures for their suppression. The Cilicians were bold and skilful seamen, and their country was naturally fortified against invasion. They had an almost inexhaustible supply of ship timber in the cedar forests of Taurus, and convenient harbors for refuge. Their cruises were extended to all parts of the Mediterranean, and they made frequent descents on the coast cities with the object of plunder. A Roman fleet, under Servillius Vatia, scoured the seas and gained several advantages over the light squadrons of the pirates; but they still continued their depredations.

In the year 680, the notorious Verres was appointed to command the province of Sicily as propraetor; and during his administration, a piratical chief named Heracleo, with a light squadron of four vessels, appeared on the coasts of the island, defeated and burned an ill-provided fleet which had attempted to oppose him, and entered in a bravado into the very harbor of Syracuse, which, having surveyed at his leisure, he again put to sea without molestation. The communication between Italy and Greece was intercepted during the whole summer; several officers going abroad, with commissions from the senate, on the public service, were taken, and released for a ransom; and two prætors, with their lictors, while going abroad to take the command of their provinces, fell into the hands of the pirates. Descents were made on both coasts of Italy; the harbor of Gaieta, which was full of Roman vessels, was entered before the eyes of a Roman prætor, and every thing in it was taken or destroyed; the children of M. Antonius, the orator, at the very time, apparently, that their brother was commanding against the pirates, were carried off from the house of their family at Misenum, and were ransomed for a large sum of money. Nay, the mouth of the Tiber itself was not secure from insult; and a fleet, which one of the consuls had been appointed to command, was surprised and taken at Ostia, within twenty miles of Rome. While such were the affronts sustained so near the seat of government itself, it will excite no surprise to hear that Cnidus, Samos, and Colophon, with four hundred other cities, were taken at different times by this daring enemy; and that some of the most famous and richest temples, those of Juno at Samos, at Argos, and at Lacinium in Italy; those of Apollo at Leucas and Actium; those of Neptune at the Isthmus of Corinth, and at Tænarus; and that of Ceres and Proserpine in Samothrace, were violated and ransacked. The commerce and the revenues of Rome were alike intercepted or suspended. The giant power was baffled and despised by these bold rovers of the deep.

"They knew no law—they feared no foe,
And plunder only was their bond."

Expeditions were frequently sent against the pirates, but with only partial success. The war continued until 686, A. U. C. In that year, Pompey was appointed to command the forces employed against the pirates, and he was to hold his office, if necessary, for three years. During the winter, Pompey made immense preparations. He divided the care of the different parts of the Mediterranean among his several lieutenants, resolving himself to superintend their proceedings in every quarter. Before the winter was ended, he put to sea, and deeming it important to open as soon as possible the communication between the capital and those countries which supplied it with corn, he sailed first to Sicily, then crossed over to Africa, and having carefully scoured that coast, he returned to Sardinia, stationing a sufficient fleet off the island, and strong guards at various points. These operations were completed, according to Plutarch, in less than six weeks; and he then returned to Italy, where he remained for a short time, disposing his forces for the protection of both coasts of that peninsula, and sending squadrons and land forces to secure the provinces of Spain, Gaul, and Illyricum. The effect of all these measures was to hunt out the pirates from all their haunts in the western quarters of the Mediterranean, and to drive them gradually back to the seat of their main power in Cilicia. Thither, accordingly, Pompey sailed in pursuit of them; and expecting to meet with a long and obstinate resistance in the strongholds on that coast, he provided himself with every thing necessary for a succession of sieges. But the fame of his personal character went before him; and the vigor of his military operations, combined with the humanity which he had shown to those of the pirates who first fell into his hands, at once deterred the enemy from continuing to oppose him, and encouraged them to trust themselves to his mercy. On his arrival off the coasts of Cilicia, fortresses and ships were successively surrendered to him without a blow. Nor did he deceive the confidence thus reposed in him; but after receiving the submissions of the pirates, after delivering the prisoners whom he found in their hands, and becoming master of all their resources, he took measures for reclaiming the inhabitants of those countries from that rude and wretched state of life which tempted them to robbery. The town of Soli, with some others in the neighborhood, had been lately deprived of their citizens by Tigranes, king of Armenia, who had transplanted them into Upper Asia, to people his new capital Tigranocerta. Into the towns thus deserted, Pompey brought some of the pirates who had surrendered, and settled them in a situation where they might naturally be led to taste and to value the blessings of civilization; while he removed others into some of the districts in the interior, which, perhaps, their own incursions, on former occasions, had reduced to desolation, and placed them where the constant sight of the sea might not tempt them to resume their former occupation of piracy. By this admirable conduct Pompey obtained a glory very different from that usually gained by Roman generals; and in seven weeks from the time of his leaving Italy for the east, he had cleared every corner of the sea from the enemy, and had provided for the stability of his victory by those measures of wisdom and goodness which alone, in public as well as in private conduct, can permanently insure a happy result.

The Roman navy was next employed in the acquisition of Cyprus. The expedition was under the direction of M. Cato, the grandson of Cato, the censor. No resistance was met with. Cyprus had been under the government of an Egyptian prince. But its wealth and fertility, together with the fact that the people were able to build and equip a ship of the largest size without applying to foreign countries for a single article required in her construction, were sufficient attractions for the insatiable Romans. Cato converted the island into a Roman province, and taking possession of the treasures of its former king, he returned to Rome. It is related as an instance of Cato's indifference to triumphs and ceremonies, that when, as his vessel, laden with treasure, sailed up the Tiber, the senate, headed by two consuls and followed by an immense crowd of private citizens came to the shore to welcome him, Cato proceeded without noticing this compliment, until he reached the place where the treasure was to be landed.

When the civil war between Cæsar and Pompey broke out, in 703, A. U. C., Pompey and his forces were besieged in the maritime city of Brundisium. The siege was prosecuted with vigor, and Cæsar, endeavored to construct moles in the harbor to prevent the escape of Pompey by sea. But before this could be done, the ships which had conveyed the consuls into Greece, returned to Brundisium; and Pompey was enabled to embark his troops, and put to sea, in March, with the loss of only two transports which ran aground at the entrance of the harbor, and were in this manner taken. Cæsar was unable to follow Pompey for the want of shipping. But he sent to all corporate towns, to provide a certain number of ships and cause them to be sent to Brundisium, there to be in readiness to transport his army into Greece.

The greater portion of the forces of the commonwealth were now in Greece. The legions of Cæsar were in complete possession of the islands of Sicily, Sardinia, and Cyprus, and the whole of Italy. L. Domitius, on the side of the commonwealth, had collected a squadron of light vessels, manned with his own slaves and dependants and sailed to Massilia, in Transalpine Gaul. The inhabitants of that powerful commercial city placed all their resources at his disposal, as the general appointed by the senate. Cæsar resolved to lay siege to this place; and, accordingly, a month was employed in building twelve ships of war in the neighboring port of Arelate, and in constructing the other works necessary for a siege. The command of the fleet was given to Decimus Brutus, and that of the land force to C. Trebonius, while Cæsar himself, proceeded to Spain. The conquest of the whole of Spain was the work of but forty days. The forces of the commonwealth were all either killed or forced to surrender. The fleet which Varro had collected was given up to the victor, and he embarked his troops on board of it, and returned to Massilia.

In the meantime, Decimus Brutus had totally defeated the naval force of the Massilians, and they were so reduced from scanty sustenance and disease that they surrendered to Cæsar upon his arrival. Domitius had escaped by sea. The seat of war was then turned to Greece, whither Cæsar, with the greater part of his forces immediately proceeded. Pompey was collecting and constructing a vast armament on the coast of Epirus.

To the southward of Illyricum, the mouth of the Adriatic was guarded with a small squadron by P. Cornelius Dolabella, the son-in-law of Cicero; but like others of the young nobility of bad character, engaged in the cause of Cæsar. Inferior as Cæsar was to his adversaries in naval means, he could only expect Dolabella to keep the sea for a time, till the fleets of the enemy should be brought together; after which it became his business to preserve his ships with the utmost care, as Cæsar was ill able to replace them, if they should be taken or destroyed. But whether from want of caution on the part of Dolabella, or from any other cause, he was attacked on the eastern shore of the Adriatic by the ships of the commonwealth, under M. Octavius and L. Scribonius Libo, and was defeated with the loss of his entire fleet. His disaster was only the prelude to another of greater magnitude; for C. Antonius coming up in the hope of relieving him, was surrounded by the victorious forces of the enemy, who putting on shore a portion of their seamen, blockaded him by land and sea, till he was obliged to surrender himself prisoner with all the troops under his command. The soldiers were incorporated with Pompey's army. These successes aided considerably in swelling the number of Pompey's troops and seamen. They gave confidence to the leaders of the commonwealth forces, and diminished that of Cæsar's adherents. Besides the great strength of the land forces of the commonwealth, the navy was one of the largest and best equipped which had yet been collected. There were above five hundred ships of war, besides a greater number of smaller vessels which were continually cruising on the coast. All the maritime countries of the eastern Mediterranean had contributed their quota. This vast naval force was placed under the command of M. Bibulus.

The lateness of the season impressed Bibulus with the belief that no attempt would be made to invade Greece for the present. Surprised, therefore, by the tidings that the enemy were actually arrived on the coast of Greece, Bibulus put to sea in haste from Corcyra, in the hope of intercepting a part, at least, of the transports employed in the passage: but Cæsar had already landed in safety, and Bibulus only succeeded in cutting off about thirty of the empty vessels, which Cæsar had ordered instantly to return to Brundisium. His vexation at his own want of vigilance, combined with his general hatred against Cæsar, led him to commit an atrocious act of cruelty upon the masters and crews of the vessels which thus fell into his hands; for having set the ships on fire, he burnt the men in the same flames. He then lined the coast with detachments of his fleet from Salone to Oricum, a distance of about two hundred miles; and as a mark of his resolution to use every possible exertion, it is said that he lived entirely on board his ship, even at that inclement season. The ancient ships of war, it should be remembered, being calculated chiefly for coasting voyages, and accustomed to send their crews ashore on every occasion to take their meals and to sleep, were very ill provided with accommodations in themselves, and could neither hold a very large supply of provisions, nor afford tolerable quarters on board for the officers and men. To remain, therefore, continually at sea, was attended with great inconvenience, and considerable distress; and thus when Cæsar's occupation of the landing places on the coast, prevented the enemy from coming on shore, or from getting supplies of wood and water, he retaliated upon them to the full the annoyance which he suffered from their blockade. But Bibulus, and the officers and men under his command, bore their privations with the utmost patience and resolution; transports were employed in bringing them regular supplies of wood, water, and provisions, from Corcyra; and when the badness of the weather on one occasion interrupted this communication, they are said to have wrung the dew from the skins with which the holds of their ships were covered, and thus to have allayed the intensity of their thirst. They enjoyed, however, the satisfaction of feeling that they were effectually stopping the passage of the second division of Cæsar's army, which it had been intended to transport without loss of time on board the vessels which had returned to Brundisium, after carrying over the first division. The troops were actually embarked, and had just left the harbor, when a despatch arrived from Cæsar, announcing the strict blockade maintained on the opposite shore by the enemy's cruisers. Immediately the ships returned to Brundisium; and one single private vessel, which had no troops on board, resolving still to attempt the passage, was taken by Bibulus off Oricum, and, according to Cæsar, the whole ship's company, both freemen and slaves, were by his orders put to death. Cæsar thus seemed left to his fate in an enemy's country with only half his army, cut off from all relief, and obliged to depend for subsistence only on the narrow district immediately subject to his control.

Cæsar's system of always acting on the offensive now saved his army. He was so successful that he drove the army of the commonwealth before him to the bank of the Apsus, on which river both armies intended to winter. A little before this, M. Bibulus, who was blockading the towns on the coast, proposed to Cæsar's officers in the town of Oricum, that a truce should be concluded between the fleet and Cæsar's troops stationed along the coast, in order to allow time to negotiate a peace. Information of this proposition was sent to Cæsar, and he hastened to the spot, and had an interview with L. Scribonius Libo, one of Pompey's naval commanders. He immediately perceived that the object of Bibulus was to secure time for supplies to reach the fleet, and therefore, refused to grant the truce.

Soon after this Bibulus fell a victim to his constant exposure and activity. He had thus far prevented the passage of Mark Antony's troops from Brundisium to the assistance of Cæsar; but only by extraordinary exertion and endurance. His death left a vacancy which the dissension's of Pompey's generals prevented him from filling. The bad effects of the omission were soon felt; for each separate commander of a squadron began to act for himself. L. Scribonius Libo, departing from the defensive system of Bibulus, crossed the Ionian gulf with the fifty ships which formed his own division, and proposed to blockade the port of Brundisium itself, by occupying a small island which was opposite to the mouth of the harbor. His sudden appearance enabled him to surprise some vessels laden with corn, which he burnt or captured; he disembarked also a party of troops, with which he dislodged a body of Cæsar's cavalry from one of their posts near the shore; and, elated with these exploits, he wrote to Pompey to assure him that he might safely venture to bring the rest of the fleet into port to refit, for that he himself, with his single squadron, would engage to prevent the passage of Cæsar's reinforcements. A short time, however, proved the emptiness of these promises, for the island which Libo occupied was unable to furnish the ships with a sufficient supply of fresh water; and after the first surprise was over, Antonius stationed his parties of cavalry along the shore in such numbers, that they could not be dislodged, and thus effectually cut off the enemy from all communication with the land. The inability of an ancient fleet to act with success without military co-operation was thus again proved, and Libo was obliged to abandon the blockade of Brandisium, and resume his original station on the coast of Greece.

At length the winter was at an end, and Pompey's naval force had kept the sea through the most unfavorable season of the year with unabated resolution. Their task would now become much easier, and the difficulty of effecting a passage would be proportionably increased to Cæsar's second division. He himself complains that his officers at Brandisium had neglected some opportunities of which they might have availed themselves; and being impatient of their long delay, he wrote to them in very strong terms, enjoining them to put to sea with the first fair wind, and recommending them to steer for the coast of Apollonia, if possible, which, from its want of harbors, was less guarded by the enemy's fleet; adding, that they might there run their ships aground, and that the loss of the vessels was comparatively of no importance. But trusting, above all things, in the effect of his own presence, he made a bold attempt to cross over in person to Brundisium; and having left his army secretly by night, he embarked in disguise on board of a small vessel, and although the weather was very tempestuous, and the wind against him, he endeavored at the utmost hazard to effect the passage of the Ionian gulf; nor was he induced to desist till he found it utterly impossible to accomplish his purpose. His letters, however, had produced a sufficient effect; the soldiers themselves, he tells us, pressed their officers to risk the voyage; and M. Antonius and Q. Fufius Calenus, with four legions and about eight hundred cavalry, at length set sail with a south wind from Brundisium. But, with the wind in such a quarter, they not only failed to reach Apollonia, but could not make even any land southward of Dyrrhachium. They were thus seen from Dyrrhachium by C. Coponius, one of the propraetors who commanded the Rhodian squadrons at that port, and he instantly put to sea in pursuit of them. Flight was their only resource, and they ran before the wind northward, towards the harbor of Nymphæum, which, though open to the south, and threatening the loss of their ships, still held out a chance of their effecting a landing. But, by one of those remarkable instances of good fortune which have occured in naval history on some memorable occasions, the wind suddenly shifted to the southwest, as soon as the transports reached Nymphæum; and thus, owing to the position of the harbor, they were now in perfect safety, whilst sixteen of the enemy's ships, that were most forward in the chase, were all driven on shore and wrecked. Of the crews a considerable number perished, and many were taken by Cæsar's soldiers; but these last, he tells us, he treated with humanity, and dismissed them unhurt to their own homes.

Two of Antonius's transports, being heavier sailers than the rest, were overtaken by the night, and, not knowing what was become of their companions, came to an anchor off Lissus. Otacilius Crassus, who commanded Pompey's garrison in the town, sent off a number of armed boats and vessels to attack them, and summoned them both to surrender. One of them, which had on board two hundred and twenty men of a newly-raised legion, submitted immediately; but the other contained about two hundred veterans, who, although weakened and wretched from the confinement and sickness of a stormy voyage, preserved their courage, and compelled the master of the transport to run the ship on shore. They found a position favorable for their defence; and, after repulsing an attack that was made upon them on the following morning, they reached the main body of the army, which had landed at Nymphæum without loss. Antonius then sent the transports back to Italy, to bring over some reinforcements, and in spite of the exertions of Pompey effected a junction with Cæsar. When Cæsar had cut off the communication between Pompey's army and Dyrrhachium, Pompey collected a large part of his fleet in a small harbor near his position, so as to have complete command of supplies when necessary. This naval superiority prevented Cæsar from receiving supplies from Italy, and his fleet even ventured to attack some of the coast towns, and succeeded in burning some of the transports used in conveying Cæsar's army into Greece.

After the memorable defeat of Pompey, at Pharsalia, he still thought of maintaining his fortunes by means of his fleet; but his application for assistance to those maritime cities and states which had sent quotas to his fleet now proved unsuccessful, and he was forced to sail to Egypt, where he met his death. It seems, that, at the request of the Egyptian king, Ptolemy, his little squadron sailed to Pelusium where it was arranged he should meet the king. On arriving before that city, Pompey found the Egyptian fleet drawn up near the shore and the army on the land. A boat was sent to bring him to the shore, and Pompey, accompanied by a few attendants, entered it and was rowed to the shore. As Pompey arose to get out of the boat, he was stabbed in the back, by a hireling of the Egyptian king, and the blow was followed up by the others in the boat. Pompey died without resisting his murderers and without uttering a cry. Cornelia,

Pompey's wife, and her friends, seeing his fate, immediately put to sea, and succeeded in eluding the pursuit of the Egyptian fleet.

Cæsar had seen the importance of pursuing Pompey to Egypt, and accordingly crossed the Hellespont into Asia, and receiving the assistance of ten ships of war from the Rhodians, and vessels from other ports which had been lately favorable to Pompey's interest, he crossed over to Alexandria. At the same time that Pompey was a fugitive from Pharsalia, his squadrons were very successful in their operations. While one blockaded the harbor of Brundisium, another, under Cassius, burnt the entire fleet of the enemy, amounting to thirty-five ships, in the harbor of Messana. The news of Pompey's defeat deterred his lieutenants from pursuing their advantages, and they retreated to Corcyra, where the remains of the vanquished party were concentrated. Hoping that Pompey would be able to make a stand in some of the eastern provinces, Cato and some of the other leaders determined to carry the fleet thither to join him, and they accordingly set sail immediately. They touched at Petrea, and then proceeded along the coast of Africa, where they heard of Pompey's death. Cassius immediately deserted with the squadron he commanded, and sailed to Syria to submit to Cæsar. Cato now took command of the forces, by common consent, and marched to Mauritania, the king of which country supported the cause of Pompey. The navy of the commonwealth did not possess the exclusive command over the sea as it had before Pompey's death; but it still caused Cæsar's adherents much annoyance, in making descents upon the coast and carrying off vessels and arms.

The victory of Cæsar, at Thapsus, dissipated all the hopes of his enemies, who now made their escape by sea, or submitted to the conqueror. The whole naval force which had been called into the service of the commonwealth was then dispersed, or captured by the squadrons of Cæsar. The cause of the commonwealth was crushed.

After the battle between Antonius and Octavius, at Mutina, the senate wishing to avail themselves of the services of a more trustworthy person than they thought Octavius, appointed Sextus Pompeius, the son of the great Pompey, to the general command of the naval forces of the commonwealth, with an authority on every part of the coast, which like that granted to his father in the war with the Cilician pirates, extended over the country, within a certain distance of the sea. He had retained at Massilia part of the fleet which had belonged to him in Spain, and having speedily increased it after receiving his commission, he sailed to Sicily, deeming that island a favorable situation for his head quarters.

Sicily was at that time held by A. Pompeius Bithynicus, who had received the government of it from Cæsar; but it was occupied, after some resistance, by Sex. Pompeius, and when the proscription began, he was in complete possession of it. He instantly ordered his ships and smaller vessels to cruise along the coasts of Italy, to intimate their presence by every possible signal, and to receive on board every one who applied to them for protection. To tempt the avarice of the soldiers employed in the massacres, he offered to each individual who should preserve any proscribed person, double the sum which the Triumvirs gave for his murder. To those who reached Sicily, he offered every consolation and relief in his power, supplying them with clothing and other articles of which they stood in need, and conferring on those of higher rank amongst them some command in his army or navy. Nor did he ever afterwards, from any selfish consideration, abandon them; but when he concluded his treaty with Antonius and Augustus, he expressly stipulated that all who had fled to him at the time of the proscription, should be allowed to return to their homes in perfect safety. It is delightful to refresh ourselves for a moment with a picture of power actively exerted for objects of benevolence: and to those who revere the memory of Pompey the Great, it is pleasing to think that as his conduct in the war against the pirates was a single instance of wisdom and humanity, amidst the cruelties of other Roman generals, so the virtues of his son afford the principal relief to that dismal scene of wickedness and misery which the party of his enemies were then exhibiting.

The fleet of Sextus Pompeius repulsed the attack of the forces of the Triumvirs, and Sicily was maintained as the refuge of the discontented and the proscribed.

Brutus and Cassius, in opposing the power of Antonius, Octavius and Lepidus, employed their fleets and armies in the eastern Mediterranean, and the eastern provinces of the empire; but upon the advance of the forces of the Triumvirs into Macedonia, they moved forward to meet them. The naval force of Brutus and Cassius was superior to that of their opponents, and they trusted that they could prevent

VICTORY OF MURCUS.

the passage of a portion of the troops of the Triumvirs, by sending L. Statius Murcus, with a considerable squadron to cruise off Brundisium. This squadron was aided by the fleet of Sextus Pompeius. But Antonius succeeded in eluding these fleets, as he had done former ones, and crossed safely into Greece. It appears that L. Murcus was apprehensive of being hemmed in the narrow space between Brundisium and the little island which lies off the mouth of the harbor, and accordingly withdrew his ships so far that the transports, with the legions of the Triumvirs on board, guarded by a number of ships of war, easily passed over to the coast of Epirus. After this successful passage of the enemy, L. Murcus was reinforced by a numerous squadron, under the command of C. Domitius Ahenobarbus. With his fleet thus strengthened, L. Murcus, soon after, fell in with a large force of soldiers, which Cn. Domitius Calinus was carrying over in transports, escorted by only a few ships of war, to reinforce the army of the Triumvirs. The weather proved favorable to Murcus. The wind suddenly dropped, and the transports lay becalmed and helpless, while the enemy's ships of war could use their oars with increased facility in the smooth water. After an obstinate resistance, the whole of the transports were taken, burnt or dispersed; and a force consisting of two legions, two thousand prætorian cohorts, and a numerous body of cavalry were almost entirely destroyed. This success, however, could not effect the issue of the contest between the constitutionalists and the Triumvirs. The battle of Phillippi destroyed the hopes of the former, and Murcus, with his squadron, joined Sextus Pompeius, in Sicily. Cn. Domitius acted for a time as an independent commander, and maintained his seamen by plundering the coast, and committing piracy upon commercial vessels. He then joined the cause of Antonius against Augustus.

The fleets of Sextus Pompeius held undisputed dominion of the sea. They blockaded all the ports and intercepted the supplies on which the assistance of Rome depended, and thus reduced the inhabitants to great distress. The rival generals, Antonius and Augustus, when they concluded a peace, were forced to conciliate Pompeius and give him the possession of Sicily, Sardinia, Corsica and Achaia, with the rank of consul. These concessions were obtained by his naval power alone, which had caused more distress at Rome than the presence of a hostile army in their territory could have done. The peace between

Pompeius and Augustus was soon violated by the jealousy and ambition of the latter. Various attempts were made to invade Sicily, but storms and the fleets of Pompeius baffled every effort.

In the midst of the embarrassment and mortification of Augustus at the failure of his expeditions, Antonius crossed over from Egypt to Italy with a fleet of three hundred ships of war. One hundred and twenty of these ships he was induced to put under the orders of Augustus by the solicitations of Octavia, his wife, although his interest should have urged him to support Sextus Pompeius, and Antonius then returned to Egypt. Augustus ordered Agrippa, his ablest general, to take command of the expedition destined for the conquest of Sicily, and the whole of the year 716, A. U. C., was employed in making naval preparations.

The Italians and the provinces were again oppressed with a fresh load of taxation to furnish the money that was required; while the establishments of all senators, members of the equestrian order, and other wealthy individuals, were called upon to supply a certain number of slaves to man the fleet as rowers. It was on this occasion, also, that M. Agrippa converted the lakes Lucrinus and Avernus, on the coast of Campania, into harbors, in which the ships might be assembled, and where the seamen might be exercised at the oar in perfect safety, alike secured from storms and from the enemy. At length, in the spring of 717, Augustus commenced his operations, being supported not only by the fleet which he had received from Antonius, but by the military and naval force of the province of Africa, which the third member of the Triumvirate, M. Lepidus, was to bring over to his aid. A force thus overwhelming could gain little glory by its victory; but Sex. Pompeius bravely resisted it, and in one engagement totally defeated the enemy's fleet, commanded by Augustus in person, and reduced to the utmost distress the legions which, under the command of Cornificius, had effected a descent on the coast of Sicily.

These successes so raised the pride and the confidence of Pompeius, that he began to style himself the *Son of Neptune*. But this exultation was destined to be of short duration. The distressed legions were relieved by Agrippa, and a great naval action took place soon after, in which the whole naval strength of both parties was brought into the struggle. After a brave resistance against the overwhelming

BATTLE OF ACTIUM.

odds opposed to them, the forces of Pompeius were defeated, and the general himself abandoned the contest and escaped with his family and effects to Peloponnesus.

In the contest for empire between Antonius and Augustus, the whole strength of the east and the west was arrayed in opposition. Antonius collected an army of one hundred thousand foot and twelve thousand horse, and a fleet only half as numerous as that of Augustus. However, his ships were better built and manned with better soldiers. The great decisive engagement was a naval battle. It was fought near Actium, a city of Epirus, at the entrance of the gulf of Ambracia. Antonius ranged his fleet before the mouth of the gulf, and Augustus drew up his fleet in opposition. The two land armies were drawn up on the shore to be spectators of the combat which was to decide who should possess the empire of the world. Actium was to be another Pharsalia to Rome. The battle began on both sides, with great ardor, and was maintained without any advantage being gained on either side, till, suddenly, Cleopatra, attended by sixty of the Egyptian ships, fled from the engagement. Yet the fight was continued with determined bravery till 5, P. M., when Antonius's forces submitted to Augustus, having previously been deserted by their commander.

When Cleopatra fled, Antonius pursued her, in a five-oared galley, and coming alongside her ship, entered it without seeing, or being seen by her. She was in the stern, and he was in the prow. He continued in this situation, either through indignation or shame, for three days, without seeing or speaking to the treacherous queen. When the squadron arrived at the promontory of Tenorus, the two became reconciled, and at once set about endeavoring to retrieve the fortunes of Antonius. After a varied contest upon land, Antonius determined to make a last great effort by sea, and posting himself upon an eminence which commanded a view of the forces, he sent orders to his galleys to engage the enemy. But his seamen were either bribed or anxious to secure themselves, by aiding the most fortunate; for, while Antonious awaited the commencement of the action, he had the mortification to see his galleys salute those of Augustus, and pass over to their side. This completed the prostration of the cause of Antonius, and left his rival in undisturbed possession of the sea and land.

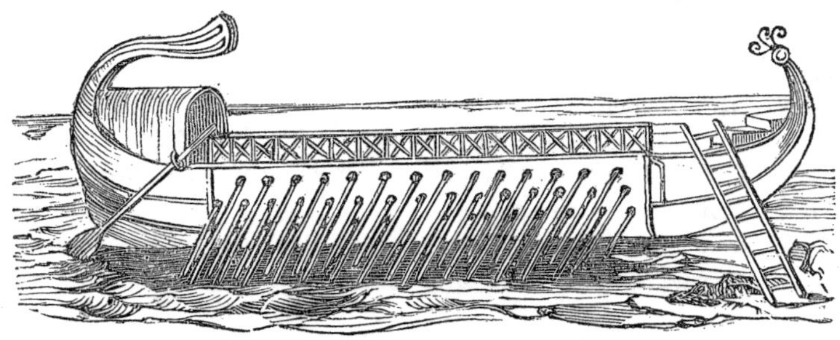

ROMAN TRIREME.

CHAPTER XII.

FROM AUGUSTUS TO CONSTANTINE THE GREAT.

THE navy maintained by Augustus and his successors might seem inadequate to their greatness; but it was sufficient for every purpose. The Romans were never actuated by that enterprising naval spirit which distinguished the Tyrians and the Carthaginians. The ocean was to them an object of terror rather than curiosity. They were possessed of the dominion of the whole extent of the Mediterranean and the policy of the emperors was directed to preserve this dominion peaceably, and to protect their commerce.

Experience seems at length to have convinced the ancients, that as soon as their galleys exceeded two, or at the most three ranks of oars, they were suited rather for vain pomp than for real service. Augustus himself, in the victory of Actium, had seen the superiority of his own light frigates (they were called Liburnians) over the lofty but unwieldy castles of his rival. Of these Liburnians he composed the two fleets of Ravenna and Misenum, destined to command, the one the eastern, the other the western division of the Mediterranean; and to each of the squadrons he attached a body of several thousand marines. Besides these two ports, which may be considered as the principal seats of the Roman navy, a very considerable force was stationed at Frejus, on the coast of Provence, and the Euxine was guarded by forty ships, and three thousand soldiers. To all these we add the fleet which preserved the communication between Gaul and Britain, and a great number of vessels constantly maintained on the Rhine and Danube, to harrass the country, or to intercept the passage of the barbarians.

The first great employment of the naval strength of the Romans, which is recorded, was in the contest between Septimus Severus and Niger for the imperial authority. Byzantium was one of the great passages from Europe into Asia, and besides, being provided with a strong garrison, a fleet of five hundred vessels was anchored in the harbor. This city was favorable to the cause of Niger and maintained it against the whole naval and military force Severus could raise, for three years. This powerful and important commercial city was then entirely destroyed by the conqueror, and thus were the Romans deprived of one of their strongest bulwarks against the barbarians of Pontus and Asia. The effect of this was seen in the reign of Gallienus.

By domestic factions and the fears or private interest of usurpers, the warlike Goths were admitted into the heart of the kingdom of Bosphorus. With the acquisition of a fertile country, the conquerors obtained a naval force sufficient to transport their armies to the coast of Asia. The ships used in the navigation of the Euxine were of a very singular construction. They were slight, flat bottomed barks, framed of timber only, without the least mixture of iron, and occasionally covered with a shelving roof, on the appearance of a tempest. In these floating houses, the Goths carelessly entrusted themselves to the mercy of an unknown sea, under the conduct of sailors pressed into the service, and whose skill and fidelity were equally suspicious. But the hopes of plunder had banished every idea of danger, and a natural fearlessness of temper supplied in their minds the more rational confidence, which is the just result of knowledge and experience. Warriors of such a daring spirit must have often murmured against the cowardice of their guides, who required the strongest assurances of a settled calm before they would venture to embark; and would scarcely ever be tempted to lose sight of the land. Such, at least, is the practice of the modern Turks; and they are probably not inferior in the art of navigation to the ancient inhabitants of Bosphorus.

Nicomedia, Nice, Prusæ, Apamæa and Cuis, cities distinguished for their wealth and splendor met the fate of Chalcedon. The victorious Goths overcame all opposition. The city of Cyzicus had withstood the power of Mithridates. But then it was possessed of wise laws, a naval power of two hundred galleys, and a strong military force. It still retained much of its former wealth and splendor, and offered a tempting prize to the insatiable Goths. They were forced to abandon the project of taking the city, however, by the river Rhyndacus becoming swollen, and the approach of the autumnal equinox, which warned them to cross the Euxine in time.

The success of these expeditions induced the Goths to fit out a third in the ports of the Bosphorus. We are informed that this fleet consisted of five hundred ships, which would seem to be a formidable armament; but as we are assured by the judicious Strabo, that the piratical vessels used by the barbarians of Pontus and the Lesser Scythia, were not capable of containing more than twenty-five or thirty men, we may safely affirm, that fifteen thousand warriors, at the most, embarked in this great expedition. Impatient of the limits of the Euxine, they steered their destructive course from the Cimmerian to the Thracian Bosphorus. When they had almost gained the middle of the Straits, they were suddenly driven back to the entrance of them; till a favorable wind, springing up the next day, carried them in a few hours into the placid sea, or rather lake, of the Propontis. Their landing on the little island of Cyzicus was attended with the ruin of that ancient and noble city. From thence issuing again through the narrow passage of the Hellespont, they pursued their winding navigation amidst the numerous islands scattered over the Archipelago, or the Ægean Sea. The assistance of captives and deserters must have been very necessary to pilot their vessels, and to direct their various incursions, as well on the coast of Greece as on that of Asia. At length the Gothic fleet anchored in the port of Piræus, five miles distant from Athens, which had attempted to make some preparations for a vigorous defence. Cleodamus, one of the engineers employed by the emperor's orders to fortify the maritime cities against the Goths, had already begun to repair the ancient walls, fallen to decay since the time of Scylla. The efforts of his skill were ineffectual, and the barbarians became masters of the native seat of the muses and the arts. But while the conquerors abandoned themselves to the license of plunder and intemperance, their fleet, that lay with a slender guard in the harbor of Piræus, was unexpectedly attacked by the brave Dexippus, who, flying with the engineer Cleodamus from the sack of Athens, collected a hasty band of volunteers, peasants as well as soldiers, and in some measure avenged the calamities of his country.

The hostile operations of the Goths aroused the emperor Gallienus to a sense of his danger, and he appeared in arms against them. But they were in no condition to meet a large Roman army, and a body of them finally capitulated to the emperor on honorable terms. The rest returned on board their vessels and pursued their way back to the Bosphorus.

In the reign of Diocletian, the Franks, in their squadrons of light brigatines, incessantly ravaged the provinces adjacent to the Atlantic. To repel their incursions, it was found necessary to create a naval power; and the judicious measure was prosecuted with vigor by Maximian, the colleague of Diocletian. Gessoriacum, or Boulogne, in the strait of the British channel, was chosen for the station of the Roman fleet, and the command of it was given to Carausius, a Menapian, who had long signalized his skill as a pilot and his valor as a soldier. But the honesty of the new admiral did not equal his talents. He entered into an alliance with the German pirates, attached the fleet to his interest, and sailing over to Britain, boldly assumed the imperial purple and defied the arms of his sovereign. He enlisted the bravest of the youth of the Franks in his land or sea forces, and in return for their alliance, he communicated to the barbarians his knowledge of military and naval arts. Under his command, Britain assumed its natural station as an important naval power.

By seizing the fleet of Boulogne, Carausius had deprived his master of the means of pursuit and revenge. And when, after a vast expense of time and labor, a new armament was launched into the water, the Imperial troops, unaccustomed to that element, were easily baffled and defeated by the veteran sailors of the usurper. This disappointed effort was soon productive of a treaty of peace. Diocletian and his colleague, who justly dreaded the enterprising spirit of Carausius, resigned to him the sovereignty of Britain, and reluctantly admitted their perfidious servant to a participation of the Imperial honors. But the adoption of the two Cæsars restored new vigor to the Roman arms; and while the Rhine was guarded by the presence of Maximian, his brave associate Constantius assumed the conduct of the British war. His first enterprise was against the important place of Boulogne. A stupendous mole, raised across the entrance of the harbor, intercepted all hopes of relief. The town surrendered after an obstinate defence; and a considerable part of the naval strength of Carausius fell into the hands of the besiegers. During the three years which Constantius employed in preparing a fleet adequate to the conquest of Britain, he secured the coast of Gaul, invaded the country of the Franks, and deprived the usurper of the assistance of those powerful allies.

Before the preparations were finished, Constantius received the intelligence of the tyrant's death, and it was considered as a sure presage of the approaching victory. The servants of Carausius imitated the example of treason which he had given. He was murdered by his first minister, Allectus, and the assassin succeeded to his power and to his danger. But he possessed not equal abilities either to exercise the one or to repel the other. He beheld, with anxious terror, the opposite shores of the continent already filled with arms, with troops, and with vessels; for Constantius had very prudently divided his forces, that he might likewise divide the attention and resistance of the enemy. The attack was at length made by the principal squadron, which, under the command of the præfect Asclepiodatus, an officer of distinguished merit, had been assembled in the mouth of the Seine. So imperfect in those times was the art of navigation, that orators have celebrated the daring courage of the Romans, who ventured to set sail with a side-wind, and on a stormy day. The weather proved favorable to their enterprise. Under the cover of a thick fog, they escaped the fleet of Allectus, which had been stationed off the isle of Wight to receive them, landed in safety on some part of the western coast, and convinced the Britons, that a superiority of naval strength will not always protect their country from a foreign invasion. Asclepiodatus had no sooner disembarked the imperial troops, than he set fire to his ships; and, as the expedition proved fortunate, his heroic conduct was univerally admired. The usurper was overthrown in a single battle, and, after a separation of ten years, Britain was restored to the Roman empire.

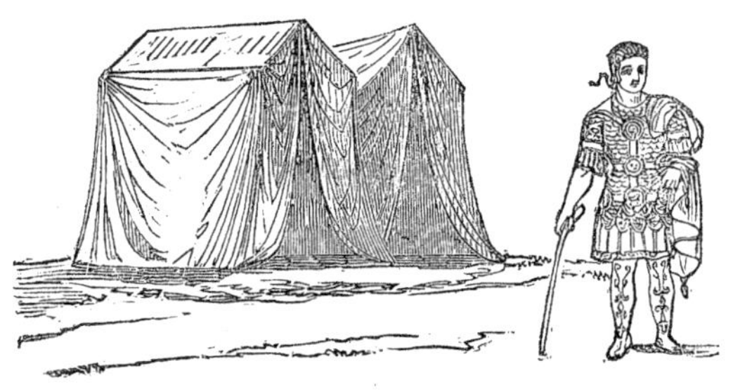

ROMAN TENTS.

CHAPTER XIII.

FROM CONSTANTINE THE GREAT TO THE END OF THE ROMAN EMPIRE.

THE reign of Constantine the Great and Licinius, witnessed a considerable increase of the Roman military and naval power. When the contest between the two emperors began, Licinius was enabled to bring into action, a fleet composed of three hundred and fifty galleys of three banks of oars. One hundred and thirty of these were furnished by Egypt and the adjacent coast of Africa; one hundred and ten sailed from Phœnicia and the isle of Cyprus; and the maritime countries of Bithynia, Ionia, and Caria were obliged to furnish the remainder. The naval preparations of Constantine were inferior. The maritime cities of Greece sent their quotas of ships to the harbor of Piræus, and their united forces consisted of no more than two hundred small vessels; a very feeble armament if compared with those formidable and conquering fleets equipped and maintained by the small republic of Athens during the Peloponnesian War. Since the seat of government had been removed from Italy, the naval establishment of Misenum and Ravenna had been gradually neglected; and as the shipping and mariners of the empire were supported by commerce rather than war, it was natural that they should most abound in the commercial provinces of Egypt and Asia.

The fleet of Licinius held command of the Hellespont, in the narrow strait of which it continued inactive. There its superiority of numbers was of little advantage. The naval commanders of Constantine were ordered to force the passage of the Hellespont, in order that the fall of Byzantium, which was then being besieged, might be hastened.

Crispus, the emperor's eldest son, was intrusted with the execution of this daring enterprise, which he performed with so much courage and success, that he deserved the esteem, and most probably excited the jealousy, of his father. The engagement lasted two days; and in the evening of the first, the contending fleets, after a considerable and mutual loss, retired into their respective harbors of Europe and Asia. The second day, about noon, a strong south wind sprang up, which carried the vessels of Crispus against the enemy; and as the casual advantage was improved by his skilful intrepidity, he soon obtained a complete victory. A hundred and thirty vessels were destroyed, five thousand men were slain, and Amandus, the admiral of the Asiatic fleet, escaped with the utmost difficulty to the shores of Chalcedon. As soon as the Hellespont was open, a plentiful convoy of provisions flowed into the camp of Constantine, who had already advanced the operations of the siege. The city was soon after abandoned by Licinius, and left at the mercy of Constantine.

We are informed that in the expedition against Sapor, the Persian king, the Roman emperor, Julian, besides an army of sixty-five thousand effective and well-disciplined soldiers, was attended by a fleet of eleven hundred ships upon the Euphrates. The military strength of this fleet consisted of fifty armed galleys; and these were accompanied by an equal number of flat bottomed boats, which might occasionally be connected in the form of temporary bridges. The rest of the ships, partly constructed of timber and partly of raw hides, were laden with an immense quantity of arms, engines, utensils, and provisions. A portion of this fleet was used to convey the legions of Julian across the Tigris in a night attack upon the Persian forces. But soon afterwards, by the treacherous advice of a Persian general whom he had taken into his service, Julian was induced to destroy the whole navy which had been transported about five hundred miles, at the expense of so much toil and treasure. Twelve small vessels were saved to accompany, in carriages, the march of the army, and to form occasional bridges for the passage of the rivers. The rest of the large fleet with the greater part of the stores, was committed to the flames. The reasons which induced Julian to make this sacrifice were of a plausible character. The navigation of the Euphrates and the Tigris never extended above Babylon and Opis, and the distance of the last mentioned city from Julian's army, was not great. The labor necessary to force a great fleet against the current of a rapid river, embarrassed with several cataracts, was immense. But plausible as these reasons were, the real motive of advising the destruction of the fleet was treacherous, as was soon proved. The country through which the army was to march was deserted and wasted by its inhabitants, and the supplies of the Romans becoming exhausted, they were forced to make a retreat. Several battles were fought with the immense hosts of Sapor, in one of which the heroic Julian was mortally wounded. The few transports which had been saved when the fleet was burned, now served a good purpose in conveying the dispirited Romans across the Tigris, making many voyages to effect that object. The army under Julian's succesor, Jovian, then easily reached the Roman dominions.

The Goths gave the next occasion for the use of the Roman navy. They had made many incursions into the territories of the empire in the reign of Vallens and Valentinian, but wer egenerally unsuccessful. The provinces of the Danube, especially, suffered from their barbarous devastations. Their final defeat and capitulation took place in the early part of the reign of Theodosius, the successor of Valentinian. After an absence of four years, the Goths returned to the vicinity of the Lower Danube, with acccumulated force. The general who commanded the military and naval powers of the Thracian frontier soon perceived that the barbarians, awed by the presence of the Roman fleet and legions, were anxious to defer the passage of the Danube until the winter; but this he desired to prevent. He sent spies into the Gothic camp to ascertain their strength and to persuade them that by a bold attempt, they might surprise the Roman camp. The barbarians fell into the snare; and the whole multitude hastily embarked in a fleet of three thousand canoes, to make a night attack. The bravest of the Goths led the van; the main body consisted of the remainder of their subjects and soldiers, while the women and children securely followed in the rear. A dark night had been selected for the attack; and they had almost reached the southern bank of the Danube, confident of an easy victory. But, suddenly, they found their progress arrested by an unexpected obstacle; a triple line of vessels strongly connected with each other, formed an impenetrable chain of two miles and a half along the river. While the Goths struggled to force their way against this powerful barrier, their right flank was overwhelmed by the irresistible onset of a fleet of galleys, which were urged down the stream by the impulse of oars and tide. The weight and swiftness of those ships of war broke, sunk, and dispersed the light canoes of the barbarians. Their valor was ineffectual; and the bravest of their troops, with Alatheus, their general, either perished by the swords of the Roman or were drowned in the waters of the Danube. The rest capitulated to the Roman general.

The revolt of Gildo, the governor of the Roman provinces in Africa, during the reign of Arcadius and Honorius was the cause of a war between that general and the parts of the empire which remained faithful to the lawful sovereigns. The vigilant Stilicho collected all the military and naval forces of the western empire. The fleet of galleys and transports sailed in tempestuous weather from the port of Pisa, in Tuscany, and steered their course to the little island of Capraria, where some of the monks who inhabited that island were taken on board the fleet. It is observed in praise of the Roman general, Masuzel, that he passed his days and nights in prayer and fasting. The devout leader, who with such a reinforcement, appeared confident of victory, avoided the dangerous rocks of Corsica, coasted along the eastern side of Sardinia, and escaped the violence of the south wind by casting anchor in the safe and capacious harbor of Cagliari, one hundred and forty-five miles from the African shore. From that point, the passage to Africa was easy. Gildo was vanquished in a great battle, and reaching the sea shore, endeavored to escape in a small vessel; but he was driven back, and, in despair, he committed suicide.

The emperors of Constantinople continued to observe the same system of attack and defence in their navy, as had been practised by the more ancient Romans. But they wisely reduced the height of their galleys, using none but *dromones* of two tiers, having in all one hundred oars. The line of battle was somewhat changed, from a triangle it had become a crescent. The horns pointed rearward, and the admirals were stationed in the centre, and began the attack. The same means of annoyance were still employed. Arrows were thrown from bows, and javelins from engines; huge rocks were projected from machines, often finding their way through the bottom of a vessel, destroying both galley and crew. But the most dreadful weapon then in use was the iron tube, from which the Greek fire was projected in streams upon a vessel and crew of an enemy. This combustible was of such a composition, and of such fearful activity, that nothing could resist it, and water, instead of extinguishing it, only augmented its fury. Though the attack of beaks was still continued, less importance was attached to the point of gaining the wind. In order to escape from the torture of the fire tube, it was usual to grapple at once broadside to broadside, and while the rowers assailed each other with pikes, through their row-ports, the soldiers rushed, with sword and buckler, to the attack, fighting hand to hand. Hence the great numbers of slain in the naval encounters.

After the Goths, under Adolphus, the successor of Alaric, had been induced to quit Italy, by a treaty with Honorius, some degree of tranquillity was restored to the declining empire. This was soon disturbed by the approach of a hostile armament from Africa. Heraclian, count of Africa, who, under distressing circumstances, had supported the cause of Honorius, was tempted to assume the character of a rebel, with the title of emperor. The African ports were filled with the naval forces, at the head of which he prepared to invade Italy; and his fleet did actually surpass that of Xerxes, if, as is stated, the whole number of vessels amounted to three thousand two hundred. Yet with such an armament, the usurper effected nothing. He anchored his fleet at the mouth of the Tiber, and marched for Rome. But was met by one of the imperial captains, and easily defeated. His armament then dispersed, and he, himself, escaped to Carthage with a single ship. He was there beheaded by the Carthaginians, who had returned to their allegiance.

In the fifth century, after the birth of Christ, the Vandals, under Genseric, completely overthrew the Roman dominion in Africa. But the ambition of the barbarians was not satisfied. Genseric resolved to create a naval power, and his resolution was executed with an active perseverance. The woods of Mount Atlas afforded an inexhaustible supply of timber; and the conquered Africans were skilled in the arts of navigation and ship building. After an interval of six centuries, the fleets that issued from the port of Carthage again claimed the dominion of the sea. The daring Vandals were completely successful. They conquered Sicily, sacked Palermo, and made frequent descents on the coast of Lucania. The revolutions of the palace which left the western empire without a defender, and without a lawful prince, stimulated the avarice of Genseric. He equipped a numerous fleet, and cast anchor at the mouth of the Tiber three months after the death of the emperor Valentinian III. The Vandals landed without opposition, and pillaged Rome for fourteen days and nights. All that remained in the city, of public or private treasure, was transported to the vessels of Genseric, and the sack and destruction of Carthage was revenged. The empress and her two daughters were compelled to follow the Vandal king to Carthage; for which port he immediately hoisted sail. Many thousand Romans, chosen for some agreeable qualifications reluctantly embarked on board the fleet of Genseric.

But when the able and virtuous Majorian assumed the imperial purple of the Western empire, the arms of Genseric suffered a reverse. A fleet of Vandals and Moors landed at the mouth of the Liris, or Garigliano; but the imperial troops surprised and attacked the barbarians, who were encumbered with spoil, and drove them, with slaughter, to their ships. To rescue the Italian coast from the depredations of the Vandals, Majorian resolved, like Scipio, "to carry the war into Africa." The ancient spirit of the Romans was aroused. The woods of the Appenines were felled; the arsenals and manufactories of Ravenna and Misenum were restored; Italy and Gaul vied with each other in contributing to the public service; and the imperial navy of three hundred large galleys, with an adequate proportion of transports and smaller vessels was collected in the secure and capacious harbor of Carthagena, in Spain. The king of the Vandals distrusted his ability to resist this armament; but he was saved from ruin by the treachery of some envious subject of Majorian. Guided by secret intelligence, he surprised the imperial fleet in the bay of Carthagena; and burned, sunk or captured the greater portion of it. The work of three years was destroyed in a single day. This exploit enabled Genseric to conclude a treaty with Majorian on advantageous terms.

Under the reign of Ricimer, the successor of Majorian, Italy was exposed to the frequent depredations of the Vandal pirates. In the spring of each year, they equipped a formidable navy in the port of Carthage; and Genseric himself, though at a very advanced age, still commanded in person the most important expeditions. His designs were concealed with impenetrable secrecy, till the moment that he hoisted sail. When he was asked, by his pilot, what course he should steer, "Leave the determination to the winds, (replied the barbarian, with pious arrogance;) *they* will transport us to the guilty coast, whose inhabitants have provoked the divine justice;" but if Genseric himself deigned to issue more precise orders, he judged the most wealthy to be the most criminal. The Vandals repeatedly visited the coasts of Spain, Laguria, Tuscany, Campania, Lucania, Bruttium, Apulia, Calabria, Venetia, Dalmatia, Epirus, Greece, and Sicily: they were tempted to subdue the island of Sardinia, so advantageously placed in the centre of the Mediterranean; and their arms spread desolation, or terror, from the columns of Hercules to the mouth of the Nile. As they were more ambitious of spoil than of glory, they seldom attacked any fortified cities, or engaged any regular troops in the open field. But the celerity of their motions enabled them, almost at the same time, to threaten and to attack the most distant objects, which attracted their desires; and as they always embarked a sufficient number of horses, they had no sooner landed, than they swept the dismayed country with a body of light cavalry. Yet, notwithstanding the example of their king, the native Vandals and Alani insensibly declined this toilsome and perilous warfare; the hardy generation of the first conquerors was almost extinguished, and their sons, who were born in Africa, enjoyed the delicious baths and gardens which had been acquired by the valor of their fathers. Their place was readily supplied by a various multitude of Moors and Romans, of captives and outlaws; and those desperate wretches, who had already violated the laws of their country, were the most eager to promote the atrocious acts which disgrace the victories of Genseric.

The Italians were now destitute of a naval force, and they implored the aid of the nations of the East. But the Western Romans could only obtain the assistance of a cold and ineffectual mediation. Finally,

Ricimir was forced to address the throne of Constantinople in the language of a subject. Anthemius ascended the throne of the Western empire, and a Dalmatian fleet was received into the harbors of Italy. Marcellinus expelled the Vandals from Sardinia. Immense preparations for a naval armament were made by the Eastern Romans. The fleet which sailed from Constantinople to Carthage consisted of one thousand one hundred and thirteen ships, and the number of soldiers and mariners exceeded one hundred thousand men. The command of the armament was given to Basiliscus, the brother of the empress.

The mighty fleet, under Basiliscus, pursued its course from the Thracian Bosphorus to the coast of Africa. The troops were landed at Bona, about forty miles from Carthage. The army of Heraclius, and the fleet of Marcellinus either joined or seconded the imperial commander, and the Vandals were vanquished by sea and land. But Genseric was still equal to his enemies. Basiliscus neglected to follow up his success by marching into the interior of the Vandal dominions, and Genseric artfully obtained a truce of five days. In the interval, he manned his largest ships of war with the most daring of the Moors and Vandals, and they towed after them many large barks filled with combustibles. In the obscurity of the night these destructive vessels were impelled against the unguarded and unsuspecting fleet of the Romans, who were awakened by the sense of their instant danger. Their close and crowded order assisted the progress of the fire, which was communicated with rapid and irresistible violence; and the noise of the wind, the crackling of the flames, the dissonant cries of the soldiers and mariners, who could neither command nor obey, increased the horror of the nocturnal tumult. Whilst they labored to extricate themselves from the fire ships, and to save at least a part of the navy, the galleys of Genseric assaulted them with temperate and disciplined valor; and many of the Romans, who escaped the fury of the flames, were destroyed or taken by the victorious Vandals. Among the events of that disastrous night, the heroic, or rather desperate, courage of John, one of the principal officers of Basiliscus, has rescued his name from oblivion. When the ship, which he had bravely defended, was almost consumed, he threw himself in his armor into the sea, disdainfully rejected the esteem and pity of Gens, the son of Genseric, who pressed him to accept honorable quarter, and sunk under the waves; exclaiming, with his last breath, that he would never fall alive into

HEROIC CONDUCT OF JOHN IN THE ACTION WITH GENSERIC.

the hands of those impious dogs. Actuated by a far different spirit, Basiliscus, whose station was the most remote from danger, disgracefully fled in the beginning of the engagement, returned to Constantinople with the loss of more than half of his fleet and army, and sheltered his guilty head in the sanctuary of St. Sophia, till his sister, by her tears and entreaties, could obtain his pardon from the indignant emperor. Heraclius effected his retreat through the desert; Marcellinus retired to Sicily, where he was assassinated, perhaps at the instigation of Ricimer, by one of his own captains; and the king of the Vandals expressed his surprise and satisfaction, that the Romans themselves should remove from the world his most formidable antagonist. After the failure of this great expedition, Genseric again became the tyrant of the sea; the coast of Italy, Greece, and Asia, were again exposed to his revenge and avarice; Tripoli and Sardinia returned to his obedience; he added Sicily to the number of his provinces; and before he died, in the fulness of years and of glory, he beheld the final extinction of the empire of the West.

After the Western empire had fallen under the dominion of Theodoric, the Goth, a war with the Eastern empire broke out, and was successfully prosecuted by the Gothic king. On the fields of Margus, the Eastern forces were overthrown by an inferior army of Goths and Romans. Exasperated by this disgrace, the Byzantine court despatched two hundred ships and eight thousand men to plunder the sea coast of Calabria and Apulia. They assaulted the city of Tarentum, interrupted the trade and agriculture of the country, and sailed back to the Hellespont, proud of their piratical exploits. Their retreat was possibly hastened by the activity of Theodoric, who covered the Italian coast with a fleet of a thousand light vessels, which he constructed with incredible despatch. But the naval power of the declining empire was best exhibited in the reign of Justinian. That ambitious prince resolved upon the reduction of the African provinces held by the Vandals, and for that purpose extraordinary preparations were made. The illustrious Belisarius was chosen as the commander of the expedition.

Five hundred transports, navigated by twenty thousand mariners of Egypt, Cilicia, and Ionia, were collected in the harbor of Constantinople. The smallest of these vessels may be computed at thirty, the largest at five hundred tons; and the fair average will supply an allowance, liberal, but not profuse, of about one hundred thousand tons, for the reception of thirty-five thousand soldiers and sailors, of five thousand horses, of arms, engines, and military stores, and of a sufficient stock of water and provisions for a voyage, perhaps, of three months. The proud galleys, which in former ages swept the Mediterranean with so many hundred oars, had long since disappeared; and the fleet of Justinian was escorted only by ninety-two light brigantines, covered from the missile weapons of the enemy, and rowed by two thousand of the brave and robust youth of Constantinople. Twenty-two generals are named, most of whom were afterwards distinguished in the wars of Africa and Italy: but the supreme command, both by land and sea, was delegated to Belisarius alone, with a boundless power of acting according to his discretion, as if the emperor himself were present. The separation of the naval and military professions is at once the effect and the cause of the modern improvements in the science of navigation and maritime war.

In the seventh year of the reign of Justinian, and about the time of the summer solstice, the whole fleet of six hundred ships was ranged in martial pomp before the gardens of the palace. The patriarch pronounced his benediction, the emperor signified his last command, the general's trumpet gave the signal of departure, and every heart, according to its fears or wishes, explored, with anxious curiosity, the omens of misfortune and success. The first halt was made at Perinthus or Heraclea, where Belisarius waited five days to receive some Thracian horses, a military gift of his sovereign. From thence the fleet pursued their course through the midst of the Propontis; but as they struggled to pass the Straits of the Hellespont, an unfavorable wind detained them four days at Abydus, where the general exhibited a memorable lesson of firmness and severity. Two of the Huns, who in a druken quarrel had slain one of their fellow-soldiers, were instantly shown to the army suspended on a lofty gibbet. The national dignity was resented by their countrymen, who disclaimed the servile laws of the empire, and asserted the free privilege of Scythia, where a small fine was allowed to expiate the hasty sallies of intemperance and anger. Their complaints were specious, their clamors were loud, and the Romans were not averse to the example of disorder and impunity. But the rising sedition was appeased by the authority and eloquence of the general: and he represented to the assembled troops the obligation of justice, the importance of discipline, the rewards of piety and virtue, and the unpardonable guilt of murder, which, in his apprehension, was aggravated rather than excused by the vice of intoxication. In the navigation from the Hellespont to the Peloponnesus, which the Greeks, after the siege of Troy, had performed in four days, the fleet of Belisarius was guided in their course by his master galley, conspicuous in the day by the redness of the sails, and in the night by the torches blazing from the mast head. It was the duty of the pilots, as they steered between the islands, and turned the Capes of Malea and Tænarium, to preserve the just order and regular intervals of such a multitude of ships: as the wind was fair and moderate, their labors were not unsuccessful, and the troops were safely disembarked at Methone on the Messenian coast, to repose themselves for a while after the fatigues of the sea. In this place they experienced how avarice, invested with authority, may sport with the lives of thousands which are bravely exposed for the public service. According to military practice, the bread or biscuit of the Romans was twice prepared in the oven, and the diminution of one-fourth was cheerfully allowed for the loss of weight. To gain this miserable profit, and to save the expense of wood, the præfect, John, of Cappadocia, had given orders, that the flour should be slightly baked by the same fire which warmed the baths of Constantinople; and when the sacks were open, a soft and mouldy paste was distributed to the army. Such unwholsome food, assisted by the heat of the climate and season, soon produced an epidemical disease, which swept away five hundred soldiers. Their health was restored by the diligence of Belisarius, who provided fresh bread at Methone, and boldly expressed his just and humane indignation: the emperor heard his complaint; the general was praised, but the minister was not punished. From the port of Methone, the pilots steered along the western coast of Peloponnesus, as far as the Isle of Zacynthus, or Zante, before they undertook the voyage (in their eyes a most arduous voyage) of one hundred leagues over the Ionian Sea. As the fleet was surprised by a calm, sixteen days were consumed in the slow navigation; and even the general would have suffered the intolerable hardship of thirst, if the ingenuity of Antonina had not preserved the water in glass bottles, which she buried deep in the sand in a part of the ship impervious to the rays of the sun. At length the harbor of Caucana, on the southern side of Sicily, afforded a secure and hospitable shelter. The Gothic officers who governed the island in the name of the daughter and grandson of Theodoric, obeyed their imprudent orders, to receive the troops of Justinian like friends and allies: provisions were liberally supplied, the cavalry was remounted, and Procopius soon returned from Syracuse with correct information of the state and designs of the Vandals. His intelligence determined Belisarius to hasten his operations, and his wise impatience was seconded by the winds. The fleet lost sight of Sicily, passed before the Isle of Malta, discovered the capes of Africa, ran along the coast with a strong gale from the northeast, and finally cast anchor at the promontory of Caput Vada, about five days' journey to the south of Carthage.

If the Vandal king, Gelimer had known of the approach of an enemy, he might easily have surprised and destroyed a fleet of deeply laden transports, incapable of action, and of light brigantines that seemed only qualified for flight. The Roman soldiers did not blush to confess their dread of meeting the barbarians upon the sea, and Belisarius wisely resolved to seize the first opportunity of landing them on the African coast. Three months after their departure from Constantinople, the men and horses, and the military stores were disembarked, and five soldiers were left as a guard in each ship, the whole fleet being disposed in a semi-circle. When the army took up its line of march, the fleet steered along the coast, seldom losing sight of the army for several days. But as Belisarius moved towards the interior, the naval commanders proceeded cautiously along the coast until they reached the Hermæan promontory, where they received the news of a great victory gained by the army. Faithful to orders, the fleet advanced, with a fair wind, steered through the entrance of Goletta, and occupied, in the capacious lake of Tunis, a secure station, about five miles from Carthage. When Carthage surrendered to Belisarius, the greater portion of the mariners were ordered to join the army, and swell the apparent numbers of the Romans, in the triumph.

But Gelimir kept the field; and sent intelligence of his situation to his brother, who had just conquered Sardinia. Zeno immediately embarked his troops in one hundred and twenty galleys and sailed for the African coast. The Vandals were easily defeated, however, although outnumbering the forces of the Romans. The naval power of Carthage was again crushed, and the Romans were lords of the

BELISARIUS EMBARKING FROM CONSTANTINOPLE FOR THE COAST OF ITALY.

sea. Belisarius then returned to Constantinople and obtained a triumphant reception.

The fleets of Justinian were next employed, under the orders of Belisarius, in the conquest of Italy. Sailing from Constantinople, they captured many of the Italian coast towns and ranged the neighboring country. But there were no opposing fleets to meet them. The Goths gave little attention to naval matters. Totila, the barbarian prince, raised extraordinary obstacles to the invasion of the forces of Belisarius. Upon the Tiber, ninety furlongs below the city, in the narrowest part of the river, he joined the two banks by massy timbers, in the form of a bridge, on which he erected two lofty towers manned by the bravest Goths. The approach of the bridge and towers was covered by a strong and massy chain of iron; and the chain, at either end, on the opposite sides of the Tiber, was defended by a numerous and chosen detachment of archers. But the enterprise of forcing these barriers, and relieving the capital, displays a shining example of the boldness and conduct of Belisarius. His cavalry advanced from the port along the public road, to awe the motions, and distract the attention of the enemy. His infantry and provisions were distributed in two hundred large boats; and each boat was shielded by a rampart of thick planks, pierced with many small holes for the discharge of missile weapons. In the front, two large vessels were linked together to sustain a floating castle, which commanded the towers of the bridge, and contained a magazine of fire, sulphur, and bitumen. The whole fleet, which the general led in person, was laboriously moved against the current of the river. The chain yielded to their weight, and the enemies who guarded the banks were either slain or scattered. As soon as they touched the principal barrier, the fire ship was instantly grappled to the bridge; one of the towers, with two hundred Goths, was consumed by the flames; the assailants shouted victory.

But the skill and courage of Belisarius were prevented from accomplishing their purpose by the misconduct of his officers, and he was forced to fall back to protect his camp. The jealousy of the emperor Justinian prevented Belisarius from obtaining a force sufficient to penetrate into the country, and he wandered, with his small army, along the coast, still displaying all the ability of a great commander. By conquest of some of the maritime cities, Totila obtained a navy of four hundred vessels, which visited the coast of Greece and met with an uninterrupted career of success. The defeat and death of the Gothic prince soon after, put an end to his enterprises, naval and military.

Some estimate of the power of the Greek or eastern emperors, may be formed from the detail of the armament which was prepared for the conquest of the island of Crete. A fleet of one hundred and twelve galleys, and seventy-five vessels of the Pamphylian style, was equipped in the capital, the islands of the Ægean Sea, and the seaports of Asia, Macedonia and Greece. It carried thirty-four thousand mariners, seven thousand three hundred and forty soldiers, seven hundred Russians, and five thousand and eighty-seven Mardaites, whose fathers had been transplanted from the mountains of Libanus. Their pay, most probably, for a month, was computed at thirty-four centenaries of gold, or about one hundred and thirty-six thousand pounds sterling. These forces were inadequate to the conquest of a petty island, yet sufficient to establish a flourishing colony.

The Sclavonian pirates were a source of annoyance to the Greek emperors, and their subjects. The maritime cities which remained faithful to the Roman empire, implored the protection of the Byzantine court; but they were merely advised to pay the barbarians an annual tribute. The kingdom of Croatia had a long sea coast, with capacious harbors, covered with a string of islands, and almost in sight of the Italian shores.

The boats or brigantines of the Croats were constructed after the fashion of the old Liburnians: one hundred and eighty vessels may excite the idea of a respectable navy; but our seamen will smile at the allowance of ten, or twenty, or forty, men for each of these ships of war. They were gradually converted to the more honorable service of commerce; yet the Sclavonian pirates were still frequent and dangerous; and it was not before the close of the tenth century that the freedom and sovereignty of the Gulf were effectually vindicated by the Venetian republic. The ancestors of these Dalmatian kings were equally removed from the use and abuse of navigation: they dwelt in the White Croatia, in the inland regions of Silesia and Little Poland, thirty days' journey, according to the Greek computation, from the sea of darkness.

The Russians were also a source of terror to the remnant of the Romans. In a period of ninety years, the Russians made four attempts to plunder the treasures of Constantinople. The result was various, but the motive, the means and the object were the same in these naval expeditions. Their armaments were singular.

The Greek appellation of *monoxyla*, or single canoes, might be justly applied to the bottom of their vessels. It was scooped out of the long stem of a beach or willow, but the slight and narrow foundation was raised and continued on either side with planks, till it attained the length of sixty, and the height of about twelve feet. These boats were built without a deck, but with two rudders and a mast; to move with sails and oars; and to contain from forty to seventy men, with their arms, and provisions of fresh water and salt fish. The first trial of the Russians was made with two hundred boats; but when the national force was exerted, they might arm against Constantinople a thousand or twelve hundred vessels. Their fleet was not much inferior to the royal navy of Agamemnon, but it was magnified in the eyes of fear to ten or fifteen times the real proportion of its strength and numbers. Had the Greek emperors been endowed with foresight to discern, and vigor to prevent, perhaps they might have sealed with a maritime force the mouth of the Borysthenes. Their indolence abandoned the coast of Anatolia to the calamities of a piratical war, which, after an interval of six hundred years, again infested the Euxine; but as long as the capital was respected, the sufferings of a distant province escaped the notice both of the prince and the historian. The storm which had swept along from the Phasis and Trebizond, at length burst on the Bosphorus of Thrace; a strait of fifteen miles, in which the rude vessels of the Russians might have been stopped and destroyed by a more skilful adversary. In their first enterprise under the princes of Kiow, they passed without opposition, and occupied the port of Constantinople in the absence of the emperor Michael, the son of Theophilus. Through a crowd of perils, he landed at the palace stairs, and immediately repaired to a church of the Virgin Mary. By the advice of the patriarch, her garment, a precious relic, was drawn from the sanctuary and dipped in the sea; and a seasonable tempest, which determined the retreat of the Russians, was devoutly ascribed to the mother of God. The silence of the Greeks may inspire some doubt of the truth, or at least of the importance, of the second attempt by Oleg, the guardian of the sons of Ruric. A strong barrier of arms and fortifications defended the Bosphorus: they were eluded by the usual expedient of drawing the boats over the Isthmus:

and this simple operation is described in the national chronicles, as if the Russian fleet had sailed over dry land with a brisk and favorable gale. The leader of the third armament, Igor, the son of Ruric, had chosen a moment of weakness and decay, when the naval powers of the empire were employed against the Saracens. But if courage be not wanting, the instruments of defence are seldom deficient. Fifteen broken and decayed galleys were boldly launched against the enemy; but instead of the single tube of Greek fire usually planted on the prow, the sides and stern of each vessel were abundantly supplied with that liquid combustible The engineers were dexterous; the weather was propitious; many thousand Russians, who chose rather to be drowned than burnt, leaped into the sea; and those who escaped to the Thracian shore were inhumanly slaughtered by the peasants and soldiers. Yet one-third of the canoes escaped into shallow water, and the next spring Igor was again prepared to retrieve his disgrace and claim his revenge. After a long peace, Jaroslaus, the great grandson of Igor, resumed the same project of a naval invasion. A fleet under the command of his son, was repulsed at the entrance of the Bosphorus by the same artificial flames. But in the rashness of pursuit, the vanguard of the Greeks was encompassed by an irresistible multitude of boats and men; their provision of fire was probably exhausted; and twenty-four galleys were either taken, sunk, or destroyed.

Yet the threats or calamities of a Russian war were more frequently diverted by treaty than by arms. In these naval hostilities, every disadvantage was on the side of the Greeks; their savage enemy afforded no mercy: his poverty promised no spoil: his impenetrable retreat deprived the conqueror of the hope of revenge; and the pride or weakness of empire indulged an opinion, that no honor could be gained or lost in the intercourse with barbarians. At first their demands were high and inadmissible, three pounds of gold for each soldier or mariner of the fleet: the Russian youth adhered to the design of conquest and glory; but the counsels of moderation were recommended by the hoary sages. "Be content," they said, "with the liberal offers of Cæsar; is it not far better to obtain without a combat the possession of gold, silver, silks, and all the objects of our desires? Are we sure of victory? Can we conclude a treaty with the sea? We do not tread on the land; we float on the abyss of water, and a common death hangs over our heads." The memory of these arctic fleets that seemed to descend from the polar circle, left a deep impression of terror on the Imperial city. By the vulgar of every rank, it was asserted and believed, that an equestrian statue in the square of Taurus was secretly inscribed with a prophecy, how the Russians, in the last days, should become masters of Constantinople. In our own time, a Russian armament, instead of sailing from the Borysthenes, has circumnavigated the continent of Europe; and the Turkish capital has been threatened by a squadron of strong and lofty ships of war, each of which, with its naval science and thundering artillery, could have sunk or scattered a hundred canoes, such as those of their ancestors. Perhaps the present generation may yet behold the accomplishment of the prediction, of a rare prediction, of which the style is unambiguous and the date unquestionable.*

At this period, the empire of the world was divided between the Saracens, the Franks and the subjects of the Byzantine emperors. The Saracen squadrons were driven from the coasts of Italy by the Byzantine fleets, but their numbers and their thirst for plunder induced them to return whenever opportunity offered. They were finally expelled from Italy by the Normans, under Robert Guiscard. This ambitious Norman chief then resolved to attempt the conquest of the Roman empire to the east. He procured the services of a person whom he proclaimed as the rightful emperor Michael, and then set about making preparations for the expedition intended to seat him on the throne. After two years' toil, the land and naval forces were assembled at Otranto, the extreme promontory of Italy. Robert was accompanied by his wife, who fought by his side, and his son Bohemond. Thirteen hundred knights of Norman race, or discipline, formed the sinews of the army, which might be swelled to thirty thousand followers of every denomination. The men, the horses, the arms, the engines, the wooden towers, covered with raw hides, were embarked on board one hundred and fifty vessels: the transports had been built in the ports of Italy, and the galleys were supplied by the alliance of the republic of Ragusa.

At the mouth of the Adriatic Gulf, the shores of Italy and Epirus incline towards each other. The space between Brundusium and Durazzo, the Roman passage, is no more than one hundred miles; at the last station of Otranto, it is contracted to fifty; and this narrow dis-

* Gibbon.

tance had suggested to Pyrrhus and Pompey, the sublime or extravagant idea of a bridge. Before the general embarkation, the Norman duke despatched Bohemond with fifteen galleys to seize or threaten the Isle of Corfu, to survey the opposite coast, and to secure a harbor in the neighborhood of Vallona for the landing of the troops. They passed and landed without perceiving an enemy; and this successful experiment displayed the neglect and decay of the naval power of the Greeks. The islands of Epirus and the maritime towns were subdued by the arms or the name of Robert, who led his fleet and army from Corfu (I use the modern appellation) to the siege of Durazzo. That city, the western key of the empire, was guarded by ancient renown, and recent fortifications, by George Palæologus, a patrician, victorious in the oriental wars, and a numerous garrison of Albanians and Macedonians, who, in every age, have maintained the character of soldiers. In the prosecution of his enterprise, the courage of Guiscard was assailed by every form of danger and mischance. In the most propitious season of the year, as his fleet passed along the coast, a storm of wind and snow unexpectedly arose: the Adriatic was swelled by the raging blast of the south, and a new shipwreck confirmed the old infamy of the Acroceraunian rocks. The sails, the masts, and the oars, were shattered or torn away; the sea and shore were covered with the fragments of vessels, with arms and dead bodies; and the greatest part of the provisions were either drowned or damaged. The ducal galley was laboriously rescued from the waves, and Robert halted seven days on the adjacent cape, to collect the relics of his loss, and revive the drooping spirits of his soldiers. The Normans were no longer the bold and experienced mariners who had explored the ocean from Greenland to Mount Atlas, and who smiled at the petty dangers of the Mediterranean. They had wept during the tempest; they were alarmed by the hostile approach of the Venetians, who had been solicited by the prayers and promises of the Byzantine court. The first day's action was not disadvantageous to Bohemond, a beardless youth, who led the naval powers of his father. All night the galleys of the republic lay on their anchors in the form of a crescent; and the victory of the second day was decided by the dexterity of their evolutions, the station of their archers, the weight of their javelins, and the borrowed aid of the Greek fire. The Apulian and Ragusian vessels fled to the shore, several were cut from their cables, and dragged away by the conqueror; and a sally from the town carried slaughter and dismay to the tents of the Norman duke. A seasonable relief was poured into Durazzo, and as soon as the besiegers had lost the command of the sea, the islands and maritime towns withdrew from the camp the supply of tribute and provision. That camp was soon afflicted with a pestilential disease; five hundred knights perished by an inglorious death; and the list of burials (if all could obtain a decent burial) amounted to ten thousand persons. Under these calamities, the mind of Guiscard alone was firm and invincible; and while he collected new forces from Apulia and Sicily, he battered, or scaled, or sapped, the walls of Durazzo. But his industry and valor were encountered by equal valor and more perfect industry. A movable turret, of a size and capacity to contain five hundred soldiers, had been rolled forwards to the foot of the rampart: but the descent of the door or drawbridge was checked by an enormous beam, and the wooden structure was constantly consumed by artificial flames.

The emperor Alexius took vigorous measures to stop the progress of the Normans. He collected an army of seventy thousand men and advanced to meet the invaders. Robert Guiscard resolved to give the emperor battle, despite his vastly superior numbers, and to urge his men to fight desperately, he ordered all their ships to be burnt, and thus cut off their means of retreat. The battle was obstinate and bloody. The shore was lined with the Venetian galleys, which played engines incessantly on the auxiliaries of the Normans who attempted to retreat. But the spirit of the Norman leaders saved them. Gaita, the warrior wife of Robert, displayed the most undaunted heroism and consummate skill, and her husband did every thing to be expected from his great reputation as a commander. The army of Alexius was defeated and the emperor barely escaped with his life. The various losses of the Normans, however, induced Robert to return to Italy, whither with the remnant of the army, Bohemond soon followed him.

The Norman enemy of the Romans soon prepared another expedition. One hundred and twenty vessels were assembled in the harbor of Brundusium, and a new and more powerful army embarked in them. Alexius labored diligently to restore the naval forces of the empire. He obtained from Venice, thirty-six transports, fourteen galleys, and nine galliots, or ships of extraordinary size and strength. By the union of the Greeks and Venitians, the Adriatic was covered with a hostile fleet; but their own neglect, or the vigilance of Robert, the change of a wind, or the shelter of a mist, opened a free passage; and the Norman troops were safely disembarked on the coast of Epirus. With twenty strong and well appointed galleys, their intrepid duke immediately sought the enemy, and though more accustomed to fight on horseback, he trusted his own life, and the lives of his brother and two sons, to the event of a naval combat. The dominion of the sea was disputed in three engagements, in sight of the Isle of Corfu: in the two former, the skill and numbers of the allies were superior; but in the third, the Normans obtained a final and complete victory. The light brigantines of the Greeks were scattered in ignominious flight; the nine castles of the Venetians maintained a most obstinate conflict; seven were sunk, two were taken; two thousand five hundred captives implored in vain the mercy of the victor; and the daughter of Alexius deplores the loss of thirteen thousand of his subjects or allies. The want of experience had been supplied by the genius of Guiscard; and each evening, when he had sounded a retreat he calmly explored the causes of his repulse, and invented new methods how to remedy his own defects, and to baffle the advantages of the enemy. The winter season suspended his progress: with the return of spring he again aspired to the conquest of Constantinople; but, instead of traversing the hills of Epirus, he turned his arms against Greece and the islands, where the spoils would repay the labor, and where the land and sea forces might pursue their joint operations with vigor and effect. But, in the Isle of Cephalonia, his projects were fatally blasted by an epidemical disease: Robert himself, in the seventieth year of his age, expired in his tent; and a suspicion of poison was imputed, by public rumor, to his wife, or to the Greek emperor. This premature death might allow a boundless scope for the imagination of his future exploits; and the event sufficiently declares, that the Norman greatness was founded on his life. Without the appearance of an enemy, a victorious army, dispersed or retreated in disorder and consternation; and Alexius, who had trembled for his empire, rejoiced in his deliverance. The galley which transported the remains of Guiscard was shipwrecked on the Italian shore; but the duke's body was recovered from the sea, and deposited in the sepulchre of Venusia.

The successors of Robert somewhat revived the old maritime power of Sicily. Numerous fleets were fitted out in the ports of that island, and they achieved some important conquests on the coast of Africa; but they were lost in the distractions which produced the decline of the Norman power in the southern part of Italy, and in Sicily. A fleet of seventy vessels, under George, the Sicilian admiral, appeared before Corfu, and both the island and city fell into his power. He then ravaged the coast of Greece and rescued the king of France, who, in returning from an unfortunate crusade, had been intercepted by order of the Byzantine emperor. But, after appearing before Constantinople and defying the emperor, George lost nineteen galleys, which were separated and taken by the fleets of the empire and the Venetian republic.

The emperor Manuel, celebrated as the Alexander and Hercules of his age, determined to make an effort to restore the greatness of the old Roman empire. To this end he equipped a fleet and army, and while he engaged in a war with the Turks and Hungarians, he entrusted the command of the expedition to Italy to Palæologus, his lieutenant. That commander was successful in his campaign; but the sudden enmity of the Venetians being excited, their fleet of one hundred galleys swept the coast of Dalmatia and Greece, and restored the confidence of the Pope Alexander III., who pronounced the final separation of the empire of Rome and Constantinople. The Norman king of Sicily acknowledged himself the military vassal of the Roman empire, and this shadow of dominion procured a truce of thirty years from the Byzantine court. At the end of that time, the king of Sicily invaded Greece with a fleet and army, and gained many victories on the sea of Mamora, or Propontis, and on land. Yet at the end of the war, the Sicilian monarchy was utterly annihilated.

The description of the invasion of the eastern empire by the fleets and armies of the western states belongs to the naval history of those states. It will be sufficient here to state that the invasion convinced the Greeks that the capital of the Roman empire was not impregnable. Her fleets often encountered the skilfully-managed vessels of the Geonese and Venetians; but always without success. The maritime cities on the islands and coasts of the eastern extremity of the Mediterranean Sea, were successively subdued by the Turks, who continued to cast longing eyes towards the rich capital of the eastern empire. A fleet of three hundred vessels, carrying an army of twenty-nine thousand men, under the command of the Turkish emir of Ionia, besieged Thessalonica, threatened Constantinople and pillaged the neighboring country. But it was forced to return to defend the coast of Ionia from the united fleets of Venice, Cyprus, and the Pope. The Turkish communication between Asia and Europe was secured in the reign of Bajazet, who stationed a fleet of galleys at Galipoli, to command the Hellespont. This was one more step towards the destruction of the Roman empire of the east.

At length, Constantine, the last of the emperors, ascended the tottering throne at Constantinople. Mahomet the Second, pursuing, with a greater energy, the designs of his predecessors, determined to effect the destruction or capture of the Imperial city. Constantine was a worthy successor of the great founder of Constantinople, and, impressing some of his own spirit into his degenerate people, he endeavored to make the city as impregnable as it had formerly been. Mahomet made every preparation for the long meditated attack. He constructed a fort on the shores of the Bosphorus, which compelled all vessels passing to pay tribute. One Venetian vessel which refused to comply was sunk; the men escaped in a boat, but they were subsequently captured and taken to the *Porte*, when they were beheaded. The sultan availed himself of the recent discovery of gunpowder and its use. His artillery was superior to any that had yet appeared in the world.

All the Greek cities and fortifications on the Black Sea surrendered on the first summons. Selybria alone withstood a siege or blockade; but on the approach of the dreaded Mahomet himself, all were suppliant. From that place he advanced with his troops in battle array, towards the imperial city, and on the 6th of April, began the siege. The navy of the besiegers was not as formidable as the army. The Propontis was covered with three hundred and twenty sail; but of these, no more than eighteen could be rated as galleys of war; and the far greater part must be degraded to the condition of store-ships and transports. The number of defenders of Constantinople was reduced to four thousand nine hundred and seventy *Romans;* though there was more than one hundred thousand inhabitants. To these were added a body of two thousand Genoese, under the noble John Justiniani. A strong chain was drawn across the mouth of the harbor, and it was supported by some Greek and Italian vessels of war.

The ships of every Christian nation, that successively arrived from Candia and the Black Sea, were detained for service.

The city was inaccessible on two sides of the triangle on which it was built; upon one was the Propontis, and upon the other the harbor. The third side was defended by a double wall and a ditch one hundred feet deep. The cannon of the Turks was opened upon this side, and fourteen batteries thundered against the wall at the same time. The tremendous fire was well returned by the Romans, who were now filled with the ancient spirit. The old battering ram was brought into play by the indefatigable Turks, thus producing a union of the ancient and modern modes of destruction. Through the negotiation of Constantine, the islands in the Archipelago, the Morea and Sicily agreed to furnish the city with supplies. As early as the beginning of April, five great ships, equipped for merchandize and war, would have sailed from the harbor of Chios, had not the wind blown from the north. One of these ships bore the Imperial flag; the remaining four belonged to the Genoese; and they were laden with wheat and barley, with wine, oil, and vegetables, and, above all, with soldiers and mariners, for the service of the capital. After a tedious delay, a gentle breeze, and, on the second day, a strong gale from the south, carried them through the Hellespont and the Propontis: but the city was already invested by sea and land; and the Turkish fleet, at the entrance of the Bosphorus, was stretched from shore to shore, in the form of a crescent, to intercept, or at least to repel, these bold auxiliaries The reader who has present to his mind the geopraphical picture of Constantinople, will conceive and admire the greatness of the spectacle. The five Christian ships continued to advance with joyful shouts, and a full press both of sails and oars, against a hostile fleet of three hundred vessels; and the rampart, the camp, the coasts of Europe and Asia, were lined with innumerable spectators, who anxiously awaited the event of this momentous succor. At the first view that event could not appear doubtful; the superiority of the Moslems was beyond all measure or account; and, in a calm, their numbers and valor must inevitably have prevailed. But their hasty and imperfect navy had been created, not by the genius of the people, but by the will of the sultan: in the height of their prosperity, the Turks have acknowledged that if God had given them the earth, he had left the sea to the infidels; and a series of defeats, a rapid progress of decay, has established the truth of their modest confession. Except eighteen galleys of some force, the rest of their fleet consisted of open boats, rudely constructed and awkwardly managed, crowded with troops, and destitute of cannon; and since courage arises in a great measure from the consciousness of strength, the bravest of the Janizaries might tremble on a new element. In the Christian squadron, five stout and lofty ships were guided by skilful pilots, and manned with the veterans of Italy and Greece, long practised in the arts and perils of the sea. Their weight was directed to sink or scatter the weak obstacles that impeded their passage; their artillery swept the waters; their liquid fire was poured on the heads of the adversaries, who, with the design of boarding, presumed to approach them; and the winds and waves are always on the side of the ablest navigators. In this conflict, the Imperial vessel, which had been almost overpowered, was rescued by the Genoese; but the Turks, in a distant and a closer attack, were twice repulsed with considerable loss. Mahomet himself sat on horseback on the beach, to encourage their valor by his voice and presence, by the promise of reward, and by fear more potent than the fear of the enemy. The passions of his soul, and even the gestures of his body, seemed to imitate the actions of the combatants; and, as if he had been the lord of nature, he spurred his horse with a fearless and impotent effort into the sea. His loud reproaches, and the clamors of the camp, urged the Ottomans to a third attack, more fatal and bloody than the two former. They fled in disorder to the shores of Europe and Asia, while the Christian squadron, triumphant and unhurt, steered along the Bosphorus, and securely anchored within the chain of the harbor. In the confidence of victory, they boasted that the whole Turkish power must have yielded to their arms; but the admiral, or captain bashaw found some consolation for a painful wound in his eye, by representing that accident as the cause of his defeat.

This timely supply raised the hopes of the Greeks. But it was the only succor they received from the West. A moderate armament might have saved the relic of the Roman greatness, and checked the progress of the Turks. It became evident to Mahomet, that the reduction of the city was hopeless unless a double attack could be made from the harbor as well as from the land; but the harbor was inaccessible: an impenetrable chain was now defended by eight large ships, more than twenty of a smaller size, with several galleys and sloops;

and, instead of forcing this barrier, the Turks might apprehend a naval sally, and a second encounter in the open sea. In this perplexity, the genius of Mahomet conceived and executed a plan of a bold and marvellous cast, of transporting by land his lighter vessels and military stores from the Bosphorus into the higher part of the harbor. The distance is about ten miles; the ground is uneven, and was overspread with thickets; and, as the road must be opened behind the suburb of Galata, their free passage or total destruction must depend on the option of the Genoese. But these selfish merchants were ambitious of the favor of being last devoured; and the deficiency of art was supplied by the strength of obedient myriads. A level way was covered with a broad platform of strong and solid planks; and to render them more slippery and smooth, they were anointed with the fat of sheep and oxen. Fourscore light galleys and brigantines, of fifty and thirty oars, were disembarked on the Bosphorus shore; arranged successively on rollers; and drawn forwards by the power of men and pulleys. Two guides or pilots were stationed at the helm, and the prow of each vessel: the sails were unfurled to the winds; and the labor was cheered by song and acclamation. In the course of a single night, this Turkish fleet painfully climbed the hill, steered over the plain, and was launched from the declivity into the shallow waters of the harbor, far above the molestation of the deeper vessels of the Greeks.

As soon as Mahomet had occupied the upper harbor with a fleet and army, he constructed, in the narrowest part, a bridge, or rather mole, of fifty cubits in breadth, and one hundred in length: it was formed of casks and hogsheads; joined with rafters, linked with iron, and covered with a solid floor. On this floating battery he planted one of his largest cannon, while the fourscore galleys, with troops and scaling ladders, approached the most accessible side, which had formerly been stormed by the Latin conquerors. The indolence of the Christians has been accused for not destroying these unfinished works; but their fire, by a superior fire, was controlled and silenced; nor were they wanting in a nocturnal attempt to burn the vessels as well as the bridge of the Sultan. His vigilance prevented their approach; their foremost galiots were sunk or taken; forty youths, the bravest of Italy and Greece, were inhumanly massacred at his command; nor could the emperor's grief be assuaged by the just though cruel retaliation, of exposing from the walls the heads of two hundred and sixty

Mussulman captives. After a siege of forty days, the fate of Constantinople could no longer be averted. The diminutive garrison was exhausted by a double attack: the fortifications, which had stood for ages against hostile violence, were dismantled on all sides by the Ottoman cannon: many breaches were opened; and near the gate of St. Romanus, four towers had been levelled with the ground. For the payment of his feeble and mutinous troops, Constantine was compelled to despoil the churches with the promise of a fourfold restitution; and his sacrilege offered a new reproach to the enemies of the union. A spirit of discord impaired the remnant of the Christian strength; the Genoese and Venetian auxiliaries, asserted the pre-eminence of their respective service; and Justiniani and the great duke, whose ambition was not extinguished by the common danger, accused each other of treachery and cowardice.

Mahomet then stimulated his soldiers to exertion by promises of rich rewards in this world and the paradise of the Mussulman, and prepared for the final effort to reduce the city. The determined leaders of the Romans, although without hope themselves, strove to animate their heroic countrymen and to prepare for a desperate resistance.

In the confusion of darkness, an assailant may sometimes succeed; but in this great and general attack, the military judgment and astrological knowledge of Mahomet advised him to expect the morning, the memorable twenty-ninth of May, in the fourteen hundred and fifty-third year of the Christian æra. The preceding night had been strenuously employed: the troops, the cannons, and the fascines, were advanced to the edge of the ditch, which in many parts presented a smooth and level passage to the breach; and his fourscore galleys almost touched, with the prows and their scaling ladders, the less defensible walls of the harbor. Under pain of death, silence was enjoined: but the physical laws of motion and sound are not obedient to discipline or fear; each individual might suppress his voice and measure his footsteps; but the march and labor of thousands must inevitably produce a strange confusion of dissonant clamors, which reached the ears of the watchmen of the towers. At daybreak, without the customary signal of the morning gun, the Turks assaulted the city by sea and land; and the similitude of a twined or twisted thread has been applied to the closeness and continuity of their line of attack. The foremost ranks consisted of the refuse of the host, a voluntary crowd who fought without order or command; of the feebleness of age or childhood, of peasants and vagrants, and of all who had joined the camp in the blind hope of plunder and martyrdom. The common impulse drove them onwards to the wall; the most audacious to climb were instantly precipitated; and not a dart, not a bullet, of the Christians was idly wasted on the accumulated throng. But their strength and ammunition were exhausted in this laborious defence; the ditch was filled with the bodies of the slain; they supported the footsteps of their companions; and of this devoted vanguard the death was more serviceable than the life. Under their respective bashaws and sanjaks the troops of Anatolia and Romania were successively led to the charge: their progress was various and doubtful; but, after a conflict of two hours, the Greeks still maintained, and improved their advantage; and the voice of the emperor was heard, encouraging his soldiers to achieve, by a last effort, the deliverance of their country. In that fatal moment, the Janizaries arose, fresh, vigorous and invincible. The sultan, himself, on horseback, with an iron mace in his hand, was the spectator and judge of their valor: he was surrounded by ten thousand of his domestic troops, whom he reserved for the decisive occasion; and the tide of battle was directed and impelled by his voice and eye. His numerous ministers of justice were posted behind the line, to urge, to restrain, and to punish; and if danger was in the front, shame and inevitable death were in the rear, of the fugitives. The cries of fear and of pain were drowned in the martial music of drums, trumpets, and attaballs; and experience has proved, that the mechanical operation of sounds, by quickening the circulation of the blood and spirits, will act on the human machine more forcibly than the eloquence of reason and honor. From the lines, the galleys, and the bridge, the Ottoman artillery thundered on all sides; and the camp and city, the Greeks and the Turks, were involved in a cloud of smoke which could only be dispelled by the final deliverance or destruction of the Roman empire. The single combats of the heroes of history or fable amuse our fancy and engage our affections: the skilful evolutions of war may inform the mind, and improve a necessary, though pernicious, science. But in the uniform and odious pictures of a general assault, all is blood, and horror, and confusion.

The immediate loss of Constantinople may be ascribed to the bullet, or arrow, which pierced the gauntlet of John Justiniani. The sight of his blood and the exquisite pain, appalled the courage of the chief, whose arms and counsels were the firmest rampart of the city. As he withdrew from his station in quest of a surgeon, his flight was perceived and stopped by the indefatigable emperor. "Your wound," exclaimed Palæologus, "is slight; the danger is pressing; your presence is necessary; and whither will you retire?"—"I will retire," said the trembling Genoese, "by the same road which God has opened to the Turks;" and at these words he hastily passed through one of the breaches of the inner wall. By this pusillanimous act he stained the honors of a military life; and the few days which he survived in Galata, or the Isle of Chios, were embittered by his own and the public reproach. His example was imitated by the greatest part of the Latin auxiliaries, and the defence began to slacken when the attack was pressed with redoubled vigor. The number of the Ottomans was fifty, perhaps a hundred, times superior to that of the Christians; the double walls were reduced by the cannon to a heap of ruins; in a circuit of several miles, some places must be found more easy of access, or more feebly guarded; and if the besiegers could penetrate in a single point, the whole city was irrecoverably lost. The first who deserved the sultan's reward was Hassan the Janizary, of gigantic stature and strength. With his cimeter in one hand and his buckler in the other, he ascended the outward fortification: of the thirty Janizaries, who were emulous of his valor, eighteen perished in the bold adventure. Hassan and his twelve companions had reached the summit: the giant was precipitated from the rampart: he rose on one knee, and was again oppressed by a shower of darts and stones. But his success had proved that the achievement was possible: the walls and towers were instantly covered with a swarm of Turks; and the Greeks, now driven from the vantage ground, were overwhelmed by increasing multitudes. Amidst these multitudes, the emperor, who accomplished all the duties of a general and a soldier, was long seen and finally lost. The nobles, who fought round his person, sustained, till their last breath, the honorable names of Palæologus and Cantacuzene: his mournful exclamation was heard, "Cannot there be found a Christian to cut off my head?" and his last fear was that of falling alive into the hands of the infidels. The prudent despair of Constantine cast away the purple: amidst the tumult he fell by an unknown hand, and his body was buried under a mountain of the slain. After his death, resistance and order were no more: the Greeks fled towards the city; and many were pressed and stifled in the narrow pass of the gate of St. Romanus. The victorious Turks rushed through the breaches of the inner wall; and as they advanced into the streets, they were soon joined by their brethren, who had, incontinently, forced the gate Phenar on the side of the harbor. In the first heat of the pursuit, about two thousand Christians were put to the sword; but avarice soon prevailed over cruelty; and the victors acknowledged, that they should immediately have given quarter if the valor of the emperor and his chosen bands had not prepared them for a similar opposition in every part of the capital. It was thus, after a siege of fifty-three days, that Constantinople, which had defied the power of Chosroes, the Chagan, and the caliphs, was irretrievably subdued by the arms of Mahomet the Second. Her empire only had been subverted by the Latins: her religion was trampled in the dust by the Moslem conquerors.*

Thus fell the last relic of the great empire of the Cæsars. It had lingered long after its strength had departed, and the Romans, whose military and naval power had conquered the world, met the fate they inflicted upon others.

* Gibbon.

A VENETIAN GALLEY.

CHAPTER XIV.

THE NAVAL HISTORY OF VENICE, PISA AND GENOA.

THE decline of the Roman Empire occasioned the rise of a number of maritime cities, which rose to wealth and power, and established independent governments for themselves. Their greatness depended entirely upon their commercial importance, and it declined as that source of power was diverted elsewhere. Of these cities, the most conspicuous were Venice, Pisa, and Genoa. Their history, by means of their rivalry and mutual hostility, is so interwoven that it will necessarily be comprehended in one chapter.

Pisa was distinguished as a commercial city from the days of the Othos. From her ports, and those of Genoa, the earliest naval armaments of the western nations were sent against the corsairs, who infested the Mediterranean coast. In the eleventh century, she undertook, and, after a long struggle, succeeded in the conquest of the island of Sardinia, then subject to a Moorish chieftain. The cost of the expedition was defrayed by several noble families, who, after the conquest, divided the island into districts, which they held as fiefs of the republic. At a later period, the Balearic isles were subjected to her sway, but she did not long retain them. Her naval power was supported by her commerce. A writer of the twelfth century reproaches her with the Jews, the Arabians and other "monsters of the deep," who thronged her streets.

The crusaders poured fresh wealth into the lap of the maritime Italian cites. In some of these expeditions, the greater portion of the armaments were conveyed by sea to Palestine, and freighted the vessels of Pisa, Genoa and Venice. Pisa maintained a large share of commerce as well as of naval power till the end of the thirteenth century. About that time, we are told, she was in great power; possessing Sardinia, Corsica, and Elba. Her people almost ruled the seas, with their ships and merchandize.

It would have been singular if two neighboring cities, rivals in every mercantile occupation and naval enterprise, should not have been perpetual enemies of each other. It appears, however, that no war broke out between Pisa and Genoa until 1119. From this time they were almost constantly at war. For two centuries, an equality of forces, and of courage and skill, kept the conflict uncertain. Their battles were numerous, and sometimes decisive; but public spirit and resources were called out by defeat, and new armaments took the place of the lost ones. But Pisa was destined to be the Carthage, if Genoa was not the Rome of the war. In a battle off the little island of Meloria, her whole navy was destroyed. This took place in 1284. The resources of the state had been exhausted before, and this was the last effort by private contribution, to equip a fleet. After the defeat, the triumphant Genoese behaved with great cruelty. A large number of prisoners were taken and confined for years in the prisons of Genoa.

From the time of the battle of Meloria, Pisa ceased to be a maritime power. Her commerce dwindled with her greatness and her colonies were easily taken from her by more powerful neighbors; and finally the Florentines purchased a city which had once been equal to their own, for four hundred thousand florins.

The naval history of Genoa is involved in that of Pisa. As allies against the Saracen corsairs, as co-rivals in commerce with those Saracens, as co-operators in the great expeditions of the crusades, or engaged in battle with each other, these two free cities stand in continual parallel. Genoa conquered Corsica at the same time that Pisa reduced Sardinia, and her conquest was longer preserved. She possessed a greater extent of sea coast than Pisa, and her territory was much more extensive. But her commercial prosperity dates from the recovery of Constantinople by the Greeks, in 1261. Jealous of the Venetians, the Genoese assisted Palæologus in overturning that usurpation. They obtained, in consequence, the town of Pisa, over against Constantinople, as an exclusive settlement. This colony frequently defied the Greek capital with its armed galleys and fearless seamen. Extending her commerce into the Black Sea, Genoa aggravated the animosity of Venice. As Pisa's maritime greatness faded, this new power appeared to dispute the dominion of the seas. The first war between Venice and Genoa occurred in 1258. The second was not till after the victory of Meloria had crushed her more ancient rival. It broke out in 1293, and was prosecuted with determined fury and a great display of naval strength on both sides. The usual fleets of the rival powers numbered from seventy to ninety galleys; but the Genoese equipped one armament of one hundred and fifty-five galleys, each containing from two hundred and twenty to three hundred sailors.

The naval exploits of these two powerful republics were brilliant, and exhibited much skill and courage. The forces were nearly equal, and no decisive advantage could be gained on either side. One memorable encounter in the sea of Marmora is worthy of mention. There the Genoese fought and conquered the Venetians, the Catalans and the Greeks.

But the most remarkable war, and that productive of the greatest consequences, was one that commenced in 1378, after several acts of hostility in the Levant, wherein the Venetians appear to have been the principal aggressors. Genoa did not stand alone in this war. A formidable confederacy was exerted against Venice, who had given provocation to many enemies. Of this Francis Carrara, signor of Padua, and the king of Hungary, were the leaders. But the principal struggle was, as usual, upon the waves. During the winter of 1378, a Genoese fleet kept the sea, and ravaged the shores of Dalmatia. The Venetian armament had been weakened by an epidemic disease, and when

Vittor Pisani, their admiral, gave battle to the enemy, he was compelled to fight with a hasty conscription of landsmen against the best sailors in the world. Entirely defeated, and taking refuge at Venice, with only seven galleys, Pisani was cast into prison, as if his ill fortune had been his crime. Meanwhile, the Genoese fleet, augmented by a strong reinforcement, rode before the long natural ramparts that separate the lagunes of Venice from the Adriatic. Six passages intersect the islands, which constitute this barrier, besides the broader outlets of Brondolo and Fossone, through which the waters of the Brenta and the Adige are discharged. The lagune itself, as is well known, consists of extremely shallow water, unnavigable for any vessel, except along the course of artificial and intricate passages. Notwithstanding the apparent difficulties of such an enterprise, Pietro Doria, the Genoese admiral, determined to reduce the city. His first successes gave him reason to hope. He forced the passage, and stormed the little town of Chioggia, built upon the inside of the isle bearing that name, about twenty-five miles south of Venice. Nearly four thousand prisoners fell here into his hands; an augury, as it seemed, of a more splendid triumph. In the consternation this misfortune inspired at Venice, the first impulse was to ask for peace. The ambassadors carried with them seven Genoese prisoners, as a sort of peace-offering to the admiral, and were empowered to make large and humiliating concessions, reserving nothing but the liberty of Venice. Francis Carrara strongly urged his allies to treat for peace. But the Genoese were stimulated by long hatred, and intoxicated by this unexpected opportunity of revenge. Doria, calling the ambassadors into council, thus addressed them, "Ye shall obtain no peace from us, I swear to you, nor from the lord of Padua, till first we have put a curb in the mouths of those wild horses that stand upon the place of St. Mark. When they are bridled, you shall have enough of peace. Take back with you your Genoese captives, for I am coming within a few days to release both them and their companions from your prisons." When this answer was reported to the senate, they prepared to defend themselves with the characteristic firmness of their government. Every eye was turned towards a great man unjustly punished, their admiral Vittor Pisani. He was called out of prison to defend his country amidst general acclamations; but equal in magnanimity and simple republican patriotism to the noblest characters of antiquity, Pisani repressed the favoring voices of the multitude, and bade them reserve their enthusiasm for St. Mark, the symbol and war cry of Venice. Under the vigorous command of Pisani, the canals were fortified or occupied by large vessels, armed with artillery; thirty-four galleys were equipped; every citizen contributed according to his power; in the entire want of commercial resources, (for Venice had not a merchant-ship during this war,) private plate was melted; and the senate held out the promise of ennobling thirty families, who should be most forward in this strife of patriotism.

The new fleet was so ill provided with seamen, that for some months the admiral employed them only in manœuvring along the canals. From some unaccountable supineness, or more probably from the insuperable difficulties of the undertaking, the Genoese made no assault upon the city. They had, indeed, fair grounds to hope its reduction by famine or despair. Every access to the continent was cut off by the troops of Padua; and the king of Hungary had mastered almost all the Venetian towns in Istria and along the Dalmatian coast. The Doge Contarini, taking the chief command, appeared at length with his fleet near Chioggia, before the Genoese were aware. They were less aware of his secret design. He pushed one of the large round vessels then called *cocche* into the narrow passage of Chioggia, which connects the lagune with the sea, and mooring her athwart the channel, interrupted that communication. Attacked with fury by the enemy, this vessel went down on the spot, and the doge improved his advantage, by sinking loads of stones, until the passage become absolutely unnavigable. It was still possible for the Genoese fleet to follow the principal canal of the lagune towards Venice and the northern passages, or to sail out of it by the harbor of Brondolo; but whether from confusion or from miscalculating the dangers of their position, they suffered the Venetians to close the canal upon them by the same means they had used at Chioggia, and even to place their fleet in the entrance of Brondolo, so near to the lagune that the Genoese could not form their ships in line of battle. The circumstances of the two combatants were thus entirely changed. But the Genoese fleet, though, besieged in Chioggia, was impregnable, and their command of the land secured them from famine. Venice, notwithstanding her unexpected success, was still very far from secure; it was difficult for the doge to keep his position through the winter; and if the enemy could appear in open sea, the risks of combat were extremely hazardous. It is said, that the senate deliberated upon transporting the seat of their liberty to Candia, and that the doge had announced his intention to raise the siege of Chioggia, if expected succors did not arrive by the first of January, 1380. On that very day, Carlo Zeno, an admiral, who, ignorant of the dangers of his country, had been supporting the honor of her flag in the Levant, and on the coasts of Laguria, appeared with a reinforcement of eighteen galleys, and a store of provisions. From that moment the confidence of Venice revived. The fleet, now superior in strength to the enemy, began to attack them with vivacity. After several months of obstinate resistance, the Genoese, whom their republic had ineffectually attempted to relieve by a fresh armament, blocked up in the town of Chioggia, and pressed by hunger, were obliged to surrender. Nineteen galleys only out of forty-eight were in good condition; and the crews were equally diminished in the ten months of their occupation of Chioggia. The pride of Genoa was deemed to be justly humbled; and even her own historian confesses, that God would not suffer so noble a city as Venice to become the spoil of a conqueror.

Each of the two republics had sufficient reason to lament their mutual prejudices, and the selfish cupidity of their merchants, which usurps in all maritime countries the name of patriotism. Though the capture of Chioggia did not terminate the war, both parties were exhausted, and willing, next year, to accept the mediation of the duke of Savoy. By the peace of Turin, Venice surrendered most of her territorial possessions to the king of Hungary. That prince, and Francis Carrara, were the only gainers. Genoa obtained the isle of Tenedos, one the original subjects of dispute; a poor indemnity for her losses. Though, upon a hasty view, the result of this war appears more unfavorable to Venice, yet in fact it is the epoch of the decline of Genoa. From this time she never commanded the ocean with such navies as before; her commerce gradually went into decay; and the fifteenth century, the most splendid in the annals of Venice, is, till recent times, the most ignominious in those of Genoa. But this was partly owing to internal dissensions, by which her liberty, as well as glory, was for a while suspended.

The naval history of Venice is more extensive than that of either Pisa or Genoa; and her greatness, founded upon maritime power, was of a longer duration. The situation of the city, "throned on a hundred isles," marked it as a place fitted for attaining the dominion of the sea. It was founded, A. D., 452, by such of the inhabitants of Aquielia, Venice, Mantua, and other Italian cities as escaped the sword of the Huns, under Attila. About thirty years after the building of the city, the Venetians became masters of a fleet, and land forces. They then engaged in a quarrel with the Lombards, and distinguished themselves against the Italian pirates, who had committed depredations on their coasts.

In 764, the Heracleans and Jesulans, subjects to the republic, having formed some designs against the state, put themselves under the protection of Charlemagne. That conqueror not finding it convenient to give them present assistance, settled them in Malamocco, until he could give them more effectual succor. The Venetians, however, disregarding the protection of that powerful monarch, attacked and instantly drove them out of Malamocco. Incensed at this, Charlemagne ordered his son Pepin to declare war against the republic. This was done; but the blow was for some time diverted by Astolphus king of the Lombards, who, committing great devastations in the territories of the pope, obliged Pepin to come to the assistance of his holiness. However, after having afforded the necessary succor to the pope, Pepin prosecuted the war with Venice. Upon which the Venetians declared themselves a free and independent state. But in 804 the war was renewed with the utmost fury. Pepin, having quarrelled with Nicephorus, the Greek emperor, and finding Obeleria, the Venetian doge, inclined to favor his adversary, determined to exterminate the very name of the republic. After having laid waste the surrounding province, he led his army directly to Venice, blocking the city up at the same time by his fleet. The Venetians united and gave the chief command to Valentin, as Obeleria was supposed too nearly allied to Pepin to fight with that good will and cheerfulness the service of his country required. The Venetians, notwithstanding the most obstinate defence, were at length reduced to that part of the city south of the Rialto. While Pepin was preparing to lay a bridge over the canal, they resolved, as a last effort, to attack his fleet. Embarking all the troops they could spare, they succeeded in driving the enemy's fleet aground, and the greater part of their troops perished in attempting to escape; the ships were all, to a few, either taken or destroyed. During this action at sea, Pepin, having thrown a bridge over the Rialto, was attacked on every side by the Venetians from their boats, and others who had posted themselves on the bridge. The battle was long, bloody, and doubtful, until the Venetians succeeded in breaking down the bridge; when all communication being cut off with the troops on shore, the French were to a man either killed or drowned. Pepin was so struck with the intrepidity of the Venetians, that he raised the siege, abandoned the enterprise, and concluded a peace with the republic. He afterwards came to Venice to intercede for Obeleria, but the populace being persuaded that he had acted treacherously, Pepin was no sooner gone than they tore him and his wife to pieces, though she was Pepin's sister. In 839, the Venetians engaged in an alliance offensive and defensive against the Saracens with Michael III., the Greek emperor. A fleet of sixtys galley was immediately equipped, who joined the Grecian fleet and engaged the enemy; but during the heat of the engagement, the Greeks having basely deserted their allies, the Venetians were so completely defeated, that scarcely a single vessel remained to carry the news of their misfortune to Venice. This defeat threw the city into the utmost consternation, as it was not doubted that the Saracens would immediately lay siege to the capital; instead of which they turned their arms against Ancona, which they pillaged and destroyed. The Narentines, however, a piratical people, no sooner heard of the defeat of the Venetians, than they laid waste the coast of Dalmatia, and ravaged the country for a considerable way; at the same time that the city was distracted by internal dissensions and tumults, in one of which the doge was murdered. It was not till the year 881 that the Venetian affairs were thoroughly re-established. By the prudent and vigorous administration of Orso Participato, the power of the Saracens was checked, the Narentines utterly defeated, and peace and domestic tranquillity restored. From this time the republic continued to flourish; and in 903 her reputation for arms became famous all over the world by a great victory gained over the Huns, who had invaded Italy, defeated Berengarius, and threatened the country with total destruction. For a long time after, we meet with no remarkable transactions in the Venetian history; but in general the republic increased in wealth and power by its indefatigable application to maritime affairs and to commerce. About the year 1040 it was ordained that no prince should associate a colleague with him in the supreme power. In 1084 the republic was by the emperor of Constantinople invested with the sovereignty of Dalmatia and Croatia, which, however, had been held long before by right of conquest. As soon as the Crusade was preached up, the Venetians fitted out a fleet of two hundred sail against the infidels; but before this armament was in a condition to put to sea, war broke out with Pisa. The doge Vitalis Michael took upon him the command of the fleet, when, after having defeated the Pisans in a bloody action at sea, he set sail for Smyrna, and from thence to Ascalon, at that time besieged by the Christians. To his valor was owing the conquest of this city, as well as those of Caipha and Tiberias; but before he had time to push his good fortune further, he was recalled on account of an invasion by the Normans of Dalmatia. Here he was equally successful: the Normans were every where defeated; and Michael returned home loaded with booty; but died soon after, to the great grief of all his subjects. He was succeeded by Ordelapho Faliero, under whom the Venetians assisted Baldwin in the siege of Ptolemais, and were the chief instruments of its conquest; and Baldwin, in recompense for the services of the republic, invested her with the sovereignty of that city, which he endowed with many extraordinary privileges, to render his present more valuable. This good fortune, however, was overbalanced by a rebellion in Dalmatia and Croatia. The former was reduced; but, in a battle with the Croatians, the doge was killed, and his army entirely defeated; by which disaster the Venetians were so much dispirited, that they made a peace on the best terms they could, giving up all thoughts of Croatia for the time. Under the government of Dominico Micheli, who succeeded Ordelapho, the pope's nuncio arrived at Venice, and excited such a spirit of enthusiasm among all ranks and degrees of men, that they strove whose names should be first enrolled for the holy war. The doge having fitted out a fleet of sixty galleys, sailed with it to Joppa, which the Saracens were then besieging. The garrison was reduced to the last extremity when the Venetian fleet arrived, surprised, and defeated that of the enemy with great slaughter; soon after which the Saracens raised the siege with precipitation. Tyre was next besieged, and soon was obliged to capitulate; on which occasion, as well as on the taking of Ascalon, the Venetians shared two-thirds of the spoils. But in the meantime the emperor of Constantinople, jealous of the increasing power and wealth of the republic,

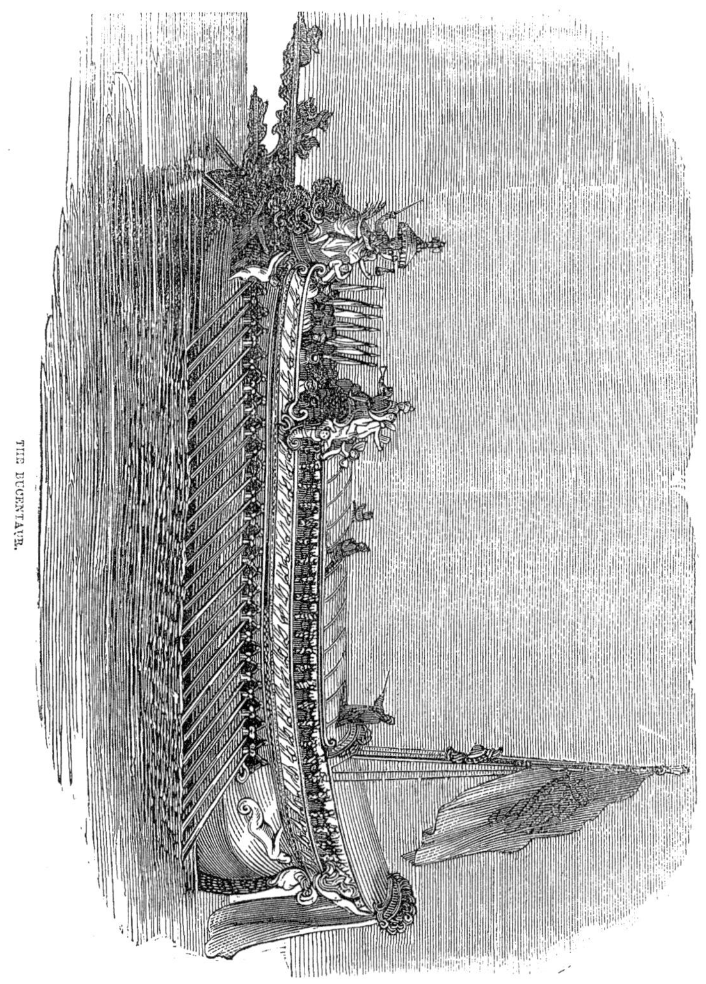

THE BUCENTAUR.

resolved to make an attack upon Venice, now weakened by the absence of the doge and such a powerful fleet. But the senate, having timely notice of the emperor's intentions, recalled the doge, who instantly obeyed the summons. Stopping at Rhodes, in his way home to refresh and water the fleet, the inhabitants refused to furnish him with the necessaries he demanded. Incensed at this denial, he levelled their city with the ground; and from thence sailing to Chios, he laid waste and destroyed the country, carrying off the body of St. Isidore, in those days accounted an inestimable treasure. After this he seized on the islands of Samos, Lesbos, Andros, and all those in the Archipelago belonging to the emperor; and having reduced Zara, Spolatra, and Trahu, places in Dalmatia which had revolted during his absence, he returned in triumph to Venice, where he was received with great joy. The Venetians now became very formidable throughout all Europe. The Sicilians, Paduans, with the states of Verona and Ferrara, felt the weight of their power; and in 1173 they ventured to oppose Frederic Barbarossa, emperor of Germany. The occasion of this quarrel was, that Pope Alexander had taken shelter in Venice to avoid the resentment of Barbarossa, who had conceived an implicable aversion against him, and threatened destruction to their city if they did not give him up. On this terrible menace, it was agreed to equip a fleet, and repel the attacks of such a formidable and haughty enemy. But before the armament could be prepared, Otho, the emperor's son, arrived before the city with a fleet of seventy-five galleys. The doge Sebastiano Ziani sailed out with the few vessels he had got equipped, to give the enemy battle. The fleets met off the coast of Istria, and a terrible engagement ensued, in which the imperial fleet was totally defeated, Otho himself taken prisoner, and forty-eight of his ships destroyed. On the doge's return, the pope went out to meet him, and presented him with a ring, saying, "Take this, Ziani, and give it to the *sea*, as a testimony of your dominion over it. Let your successors annually perform the same ceremony, that posterity may know that your valor has purchased this prerogative, and subjected this element to you, even as a husband subjecteth his *wife*."

Accordingly, this ceremony was annually performed by the doges of Venice, who embarked for that purpose in a magnificent galley, called *Bucentaur*, which is still preserved. The vessel was decorated with all the arts known to the polished Venetians. Carving, gilding, and painting vied with each other for the admiration of beholders, and the pageant annually attracted numbers to witness its grandeur.

In the beginning of the thirteenth century, the Venetians now become very opulent and powerful, by the commerce which they carried on with the rich countries of the East, were invited by young Alexis, son to the emperor of Constantinople, to his father's assistance, who had been deposed by a rebellious faction. In conjunction with the French, they undertook to restore him; and easily succeeded. But the old emperor dying soon after, his son was elected in his room, and a few days after murdered by his subjects; on which the empire was seized by Myrtillus, a man of mean birth, who had been raised by the favor of old Alexis. As the allied army of French and Venetians was encamped without the city, Myrtillis resolved immediately to drive them out of his dominions, and for this purpose attempted to surprise their camp; but being repulsed, he shut himself up in the city, with a resolution to stand a siege. The allies assaulted it with so much vigor, that the usurper was obliged to fly: and though the citizens held out after his departure, they were obliged in less than three months to capitulate. This proved a source of greater acquisition to Venice than all that had yet happened. All the chief offices of the city were filled up with Venetians, in recompense for their services; the allies entered Thrace, and subdued it; Candia, and all the Greek islands, also fell under the dominion of the republic. In the meantime the Genoese, by their successful application to commerce, having raised themselves in such a manner as to be capable of rivalling the Venetians, a long series of wars took place between the republics; in which the Venetians generally had the advantage, though sometimes they met with terrible overthrows. These expensive and bloody quarrels, undoubtedly weakened the republic, notwithstanding its successes. In 1348, however, the Genoese were obliged to implore the protection of Visconti, duke of Milan, to support them against their implacable enemies the Venetians. Soon after this, in 1352, the latter were utterly defeated with such loss that it was thought the city itself must have fallen into the hands of the Genoese, had they known how to improve their victory.

Continual wars with the states of Italy, with the Hungarians, and their own rebellious subjects, kept the Venetians employed so that they had no leisure to oppose the Turks, whose rapid advances ought

THE SIEGE OF CANDIA.

to have alarmed all Europe. After the destruction of the eastern empire, the Turks came more immediately to interfere with the republic. Whatever valor might be shown by the Venetians, or whatever successes they might boast of, it is certain that the Turks ultimately prevailed, so that for some time it seemed scarcely possible to resist them. What contributed also greatly to the decline of the republic, was the discovery of a passage to the East Indies by the Cape of Good Hope, in 1497. To this time the greatest part of the East India goods imported into Europe passed through the hands of the Venetians; but as soon as the above mentioned discovery took place, the carriage, by the way of Alexandria, almost entirely ceased. Still, however, the Venetian power was strong; and in the beginning of the sixteenth century they maintained a war against almost the whole power of France, Germany, and Italy; but soon after we find them entering into an alliance with some Italian states and Henry IV. of France, against the emperor. These wars, however, produced no consequences of any great moment; and in 1573 tranquillity was restored by the conclusion of a peace with the Turks. Nothing of consequence happened in the affairs of the Venetian republic till 1645, when the Turks made a sudden and unexpected descent on the island of Candia. The senate of Venice did not display their usual vigilance on this occasion. They had seen the immense warlike preparations going forward, and yet allowed themselves to be amused by the grand seignior's declaring war against Malta, and pretending that the armament was intended against that island. The troops landed without opposition; and the town of Canea was taken, after an obstinate defence. This news being brought to Venice, excited an universal indignation against the Turks; and the senate resolved to defend to the utmost this valuable part of the empire. Extraordinary ways and means of raising money were fallen upon: among others, it was proposed to sell the rank of nobility. Four citizens offered one hundred thousand ducats each for this honor; and, notwithstanding some opposition, this measure was at last carried. Eighty families were admitted into the grand council, and to the honor and privileges of the nobility. The siege of Candia, the capital of the island of that name, is, in some respects, more memorable than that of any town which history has recorded. It lasted twenty-four years. The amazing efforts made by the republic of Venice astonished all Europe; their courage interested the gallant spirits of every nation;

volunteers from every country came to Candia to exercise their valor, to acquire knowledge in the military art, and assist a brave people whom they admired. During this famous siege, the Venetians gained many important victories over the Turkish fleet. Sometimes they were driven from the walls of Candia, and the Turkish garrison of Canea was even besieged by the Venetian fleets. Great slaughter was made of the Turkish armies; but new armies were soon found to supply their place. Mahomet IV., impatient at the length of this siege, came to Negropont, that he might have more frequent opportunities of hearing from the vizier, who carried on the siege. This war cost the lives of two hundred thousand Turks. Candia capitulated in 1668. The conditions were honorably fulfilled. Morsini, the Venetian general, marched out of the rubbish of this well disputed city with the honors of war. The expense of such a tedious war greatly exhausted the resources of Venice, which could not now repair them so quickly as formerly, when she enjoyed the rich monopoly of the Asiatic trade.

The republic remained in a state of peace, endeavoring to fill her empty exchecquer, till she was drawn into a war, in 1683, by the insolence of the Turks. In this war, General Morsini again had the command of the fleets and armies of the republic, and sustained the great reputation he had acquired in Candia. But the Turks at last succeeded in their object, and when a peace was concluded, the Morea was ceded to them. The struggles and the power attained by this small republic, call the indomitable Athens of antiquity to mind. Both equipped armaments which could maintain the rule of the neighboring seas, and both fell with their naval power. But the Athenians possessed far greater resources than the Venetians. Many wealthy maritime cities were subject to their sway, and were compelled to furnish the material of her vast armaments. The limits of the Venetian territory were gradually reduced after the peace with the Turks, and finally it was swallowed up in the Austrian empire. The commerce of Venice is still considerable, but it is but a shadow of what it formerly was. The most remarkable of the kind of vessels used there, is the gondola, which is employed for business or pleasure, in traversing the "watery streets." Some are splendid in their decorations, and constructed for swiftness and convenience.

While the Italian cities were in the height of their prosperity, an invention came into use which produced as great a change in naval warfare as it did in contests upon land. This was the invention of gunpowder. Though it was not fairly brought into use on board of vessels until the decline of Pisa and Genoa, the Venetians early took advantage of it. The consequence was, the ships were constructed heavier and stronger, in order to bear the weight of the cannon. The former tactics of the admirals of fleets were of course entirely changed, the manœuvres which had formerly exercised this ingenuity and skill being now rendered useless.

MAN-OF-WAR OF THE SIXTEENTH CENTURY.

SHIPS OF THE NORTHMEN.

CHAPTER XV.

THE NAVAL HISTORY OF THE NORTHMEN, OR SCANDINAVIANS.

THE people who inhabited the countries now called Denmark, Sweden, Norway, and Finland, however rude and ignorant they appeared to the luxurious Romans, possessed a greater knowledge of the art of navigation, and greater daring in pursuing maritime expeditions than the polite nations of southern Europe. Their early history is involved in fable; and but occasional glimpses of truth are to be caught from the confirmation of their traditions by the knowledge of the Romans. There is scarce a doubt, that the Huns and the Scandinavians were induced to try the navigation of the sea by the rewards expected from piracy. These intrepid seamen harrassed the shores of Armorica and defied the power of the Roman empire.

The earliest visits to the Orkney islands were made by the Scandinavians. From their barrenness they offered no inducements for permanent occupancy, but their ports offered secure shelter to the ships of the adventurers. The Pictish inhabitants were constantly suffering from their depredations; and, finally, the sea-rovers took up their abode on the islands. Here they fitted out expeditions to ravage every coast from the south of Ireland to the Gulf of Finland. So frequent were these ravages, that, in 888, Harald Harfagre, sailed into these seas with a powerful armament, for the purpose of suppressing them. He subdued the islands of Shetland, of Orkney, of the Hebrides, and the isle of Man, and appointed Sigurd first jarl, or earl, of the Orkneys. This officer severely chastised the pirates who infested the islands; but at his death, they recommenced their depredations.

The celebrated Rollo then proposed to clear the islands from the piratical bands. His proposal was rejected, however, and the command of the expedition next sent out was given to Einer. This chief had but one large vessel, well manned. Yet such his skill and courage, that he triumphed over two pirate chiefs, who, since the death of Sigurd, had held dominion of the islands. This success inspired with envy the sons of King Harald, of Norway; and in 894, one of them, named Halfdan, sailed to the Orkneys with a powerful armament, and forced Einer to secrete himself. In turn, Halfdan was surprised by the jarl, and put to death. This brought on the enmity of King Harald, who sent another powerful armament to reduce the murderer of his son to submission. But the expedition was unsuccessful, and the king was forced to acknowledge the right of Einer to the dominion of the islands. The descendants of Einer continued the predatory excursions to the English and Scottish coasts, which their ancestor had been sent to suppress. The Hebrides islands were also ravaged, and numbers of the inhabitants massacred. The pirates came from Denmark, Norway, and all parts of the north, and they were fierce and daring. In the latter part of the tenth century, through the introduction of Christianity, the excursions of the pirates were much reduced in frequency and effect.

In 861, the Scandinavians made an important discovery. This was the island of Iceland. It was inhabited at the time it was visited by Naddod. That sea-rover left the Faroe Islands with the intention of steering directly to the west of Norway; but a storm arising, drove him far to the northwest, until he reached that largest of the European isles. But he knew not it was an island: he saw that it was covered with snow, and from that circumstance he denominated it *Snoeland*. Though he ascended several high mountains, he could discern no trace of human beings. On his return he acquainted his countrymen with the discovery. The following year it was again accidentally visited by a Swede, Gardar Swafarson, who sailed round it, and ascertaining it to be an island, gave it the name of Gardarsholm. The season was too advanced for him to return; and he passed the whole winter on the coast, living chiefly on the fish which he caught in abundance. The third person that visited it was the Norwegian Floki, surnamed *Rafna*, or the Raven, from the manner in which, according to legend, he found the island. Sailing from the Faroes, he proceeded towards the northwest; but as he was uncertain of the exact direction in which Snoeland lay, he let fly three ravens, which he had previously dedicated to the gods. One of these flew back to the islands which he had left; another returned to the ship; the third proceeded in a right line, and was followed by Floki, until he reached the country which Naddod had discovered. Its name he changed from Snoeland to Iceland.

The first attempt made to colonize the island was in the year 874. Ingulf, the son of a Norwegian jarl, had slain his adversary; and to escape the consequences of the act, he, with his brother-in-law, Jorleif, prepared to visit a region where neither the vengeance of the kindred nor that of Harald Harfagre could pursue him. Deeply imbued with the superstition of the ancient Norwegian worship, he offered due sacrifices to the gods—for in these patriarchal times the privilege of sacrificing descended with that of primogeniture; and when he sailed took with him the ornamented door posts of the apartment in which his household deities were enshrined. These, as he approached the island, he cast into the sea, and vowed, that on the part of the coast to which the elements should drive them, he would establish his colony. In the meantime a promontory on the southeast, still called Ingulfshod, received him; but the door posts, watched by his slaves, proceeded to the southwest, and entered a bay on which the modern

Reykiavik stands. The place in which he had fixed his temporary abode was comparatively fertile; the neighborhood of the bay for many leagues was unusually sterile; yet in spite of all remonstrances Ingulf removed to the latter spot, which he believed to be divinely ordained for him. His companion, Jorleif, chose a more fertile locality to the south; but Jorleif had no reverence for the gods, to whom he never deigned to sacrifice. In the estimation of many, the latter was the wiser man; but in a short time he was murdered by his own slaves, who fled with his substance to some distant islands. They did not escape with impunity: pursued by Ingulf, they paid the penalty of their crime. However great the regret of the chief for the fate of his friend, he piously observed that it was the lot of all who despised the national divinities.

The island soon became the resort of all who would escape the tyranny of kings and jarls, and rapidly increased in population.

Greenland owed its discovery to the Icelandic colony. Towards the close of the tenth entury, Eric the Red, son of Thorwald, a Norwegian jarl, who had been compelled to forsake his country in consequence of a feud, was, for the same reason, obliged to leave Iceland. Whither was he to repair? To Norway he could not; for there were the deadly enemies of his family whom old Thorwald had made. To hide himself in Iceland was hopeless; and in the Orkneys, which were far distant, he could scarcely hope to escape the vengeance of those enemies. He, therefore, resolved to seek a land of which some maritime adventurers had obtained a confused knowledge. Sailing towards the west, he at length discovered a small island in a strait, which he called Eric's Sound, and on which he passed the winter. The following spring, he examined the neighboring continent, which from its smiling verdure—smiling in comparison with the bleak desolation of Iceland—he called Greenland. Filled with the importance of this adventure, he soon returned to that island, and succeeded in collecting a number of colonists, whom he established in the newly discovered land. Yet Greenland was not uninhabited: better for the settlers had it been so; for the wild natives were not friendly to men whom they regarded as intruders on their own domain.

The colony flourished for more than three centuries. But in the beginning of the fifteenth century, the inhabitants were either exterminated by the Indians, or compelled to leave the country.

But the most important achievement of the Norwegian navigators, is said to have been the discovery of North America. The facts are thus recorded by one of the ancient sages of that nation:

Herjulf, a descendant of Ingulf, and his son Biarn, subsisted by trading between Iceland and Norway, in the latter of which countries they generally passed the winter. One season, their vessels being as usual divided for the greater convenience of traffic, Biarn did not find his father in Norway, who, he was informed, had proceeded to Greenland, then just discovered. He had never visited that country; but he steered westward for many days, until a strong north wind bore him considerably to the south. After a long interval, he arrived in sight of a low, woody country, which, compared with the description he had received of the other, and from the route he had taken, could not, he was sure, be Greenland. Proceeding to the southwest, he reached the latter country, and joined his father, who was located at Herjulfsnœs, a promontory opposite to the western coast of Iceland.

The information which Biarn gave of this discovery induced Leif, son of Eric, the Red, the discoverer of Geenland, to equip a vessel for the unknown country. With thirty-five persons he sailed from Herjulfsnœs towards the south, in the direction indicated by Biarn. Arriving at a flat, stony coast, with mountains, however, covered with snow, visible at a great distance, they called it Hellu-land. Proceeding still southwards, they came to a woody but still flat coast, which they called Mark-land. A brisk northeast wind blowing for two days and two nights, brought them to a finer coast, woody and undulating, and abounding with natural productions. Towards the north this region was sheltered by an island; but there was no port until they had proceeded farther to the west. There they landed; and as there was abundance of fish in a river which flowed into the bay, they ventured there to pass the winter. They found the nights and days less unequal than in Iceland or Norway; on the very shortest, (Dec. 21.) the sun rising at half past seven, and setting at half past four. From some wild grapes which they found a few miles from the shore, they denominated the country Vinland, or Winland. The following spring they returned to Greenland.

This description can only apply to the coast of Newfoundland, or Labrador. Vinland was again visited by the adventurous Norwegians under Thorwald, the son of Eric, the Red.

LANDING OF THE NORTHMEN IN AMERICA.

With thirty companions he proceeded to the coast, and wintered in the tent which had sheltered his brother Leif. The two following summers were passed by him in examining the regions both to the west and the east; and, from the description in the Icelandic sagas, we may infer that he coasted the shore from Massachusetts to Labrador. Until the second season no inhabitants appeared; but two who had ventured along the shore in their frail canoes were taken, and most impolitically, as well as most inhumanly, put to death. These were evidently Esquimaux, whose short stature and features resembled those of the western Greenlanders. To revenge the murder of their countrymen, a considerable number of the inhabitants now appeared in their small boats; but their arrows being unable to make any impression on the wooden defences, they precipitately retired. In this short skirmish, however, Thorwald received a mortal wound; and was buried on the next promontory with a cross at his head and another at his feet, a proof that he had embraced Christianity. Having passed another winter, his companions returned to Greenland. The following year Thorstein, another son of Eric, the Red, embarked for the same place with his wife Gudrida and twenty-five companions; but they were driven by the contending elements to the remote western coast of Greenland, where they passed the winter in great hardships. This adventure was fatal to Thorstein, whose corpse was taken back to the colony by his widow.

Several attempts to colonize this Vinland were made by expeditions sent out for that purpose; but all failed. We may observe, that there is nothing improbable in the account of these voyages, and they are narrated by the earliest Scandinavian historians, with all the simplicity and air of truth. Admitting them as true voyages, we cannot but admire the daring of these adventurers. Their vessels could not have been of any great magnitude, judging from the number of seamen they are said to have contained; and the important guide of the compass was wanting. They dared the perils of unknown seas, without any of those things which are now thought to be indispensable in traversing seas which are fully and surely known.

The Scandinavians were masters of the coasts of the Baltic in the neighborhood of the Gulf of Finland. At this time, Russia was split up into a number of small states, the most prominent of which was Novogorod, a flourishing republic which had an extensive commerce, not merely with the nations on the Baltic, but with the Greek empire and Persia. To protect their commerce from the depredations of the warlike tribes around them, the people of Novogorod were forced to call upon the Northmen to send some one who was able and willing to rule over them. Accordingly, Ruric, Sineas, and Truvor, three brothers, were sent for that purpose. They were renowned for their valor and competent to protect Novogorod from the pirates.

One band of these rovers headed by a king—Eric, of Jutland and Trisia, assailed Hamburg, in Denmark. They burned the sacred buildings, and the books which St. Anscar had there collected. In the reign of Magnus, king of Denmark and Norway, the pirates occupied the greater portion of the attention of the governments. He fitted out various armaments, which were all successful in defeating the pirates, but not in entirely crushing them. The Jomsberg pirates were the fiercest and boldest of all, but Magnus burned their capital and reduced them to submission. The same monarch fitted out an armament, proceeded to Denmark, and defeated the usurper Sweyn. All the shores of the Baltic were haunted by the ferocious pirates, and the active Magnus only subdued them after a severe struggle. A more formidable enemy to Magnus appeared in Harald the *Hardrade*, a son of Sigurd, and half brother to St. Olaf. He entered into a league with Sweyn, the object of which was to place Harald on the Norwegian and Sweyn on the Danish Throne. The wealth of Harald hired numerous adventurers, and the two princes ravaged the coasts of Denmark. Magnus prepared an armament to oppose them. But he chose a sure course to secure peace. He offered the valiant Harald half of the Norwegian kingdom, with no doubt of the eventual succession, on the condition of Harald's sharing his wealth with him. The offer was accepted, and Harald deserted Sweyn, who was then compelled to retire. On the death of Magnus, Sweyn attained the object of his ambition, and became king of Denmark. A war between Harald Hardrade, and Sweyn II. followed, as soon as the latter ascended the throne. It lasted many years, and was ruinous to both kingdoms, but especially to Denmark, whose coasts were frequently ravaged. In general the advantage rested with the Norwegian monarch, who, in 1064, obtained a great victory over the Danish fleet at the mouth of the Nissa. With great difficulty Sweyn escaped into Zealand, and began to collect a new armament. Fortunately the mind of Harald was now disposed to peace. Sixteen years of hostilities had brought him little advantage; the fortune of war was dubious; and the Danes, like their king, were averse from a foreign yoke. The two monarchs met, and entered into a treaty, which left affairs just as they had been at the death of Magnus. These were not the only hostilities in which they were engaged. Both undertook predatory expeditions to the English coast; but they could obtain no advantage over the vigilant and intrepid monarch (William I.,) who now swayed the sceptre of that kingdom. Sweyn, too, had the mortification to see his own coasts ravaged (those of Holstein) by the Vandalic pirates, who had renounced Christianity, and who laid both Sleswic and Hamburg in ashes. Before he could reach them they retired.

The successors of Sweyn and Harald found much employment for their armaments in reducing the pirates of Jomsberg and the islands of the Baltic. But no naval expedition on a large scale was undertaken until the people of Jutland, finding their king and nobles unable to protect them, entered into armed fraternities, which were consecrated by religion. They not only defended their own coasts, but equipped a number of vessels to cruise in the Baltic, in search of the pirates. About eighty of the vessels of the rovers were captured. But they were still numerous.

In 1157, Valdemar I., surnamed the Great, ascended the throne of the united kingdoms of Denmark and Norway. He had been tried, and proved to be a valiant, patriotic and active prince. One of his most urgent objects was to secure his coasts against the pagan rovers. In his first expedition, however, he effected little; his armament was inadequate to the undertaking. In the second, he subdued most of the isle of Rugen, and obtained great plunder. In the third, he had for his ally Henry the Lion, duke of Saxony; and both princes overran the maritime coasts of the Baltic, dictating such terms as they pleased. But such expeditions never had any permanent effect. If the pagans submitted, or fled, scarcely was their victor beyond the confines of their territory, than they recommenced their lawless career. It was so with Valdemar; it had been so with the most valiant of his predecessors. Five or six armaments in succession had only the temporary result we have mentioned. He saw that unless he entirely destroyed their strongholds, cut in pieces their gods, and converted them sincerely to Christianity, no peace was to be expected from them. With these intentions, in 1169, he had another armament against the isle of Rugen, and assailed Arcona. It was situated on the northern extremity of the island, and so defended by nature and art as to be thought impregnable. To the inhabitants Christianity had been announced; but no sooner were the visiters departed, than they reverted to their idolatry, and expelled the missionaries. To their gigantic idol, Svantovit, they offered human sacrifices, and believed a Christian to be the most acceptable of all. The high priest had unbounded power over them. He was the interpreter of the idol's will; he was the great augur; he prophesied; no one but himself could approach the deity. The treasures laid at the idol's feet from most parts of the Slavonic world were immense. Then there was a fine white horse, which the high priest only could approach; and in it the spirit of the deity often resided. The animal was believed to undertake immense journeys every night, while sleep oppressed mortals. Three hundred chosen warriors formed a guard of honor to the idol; they too brought all which they took in war to the sanctuary. There was a prestige connected with the temple; it was regarded as the palladium not of the island merely, but of Slavonic freedom; and all approach to it was carefully guarded. Valdemar was not dismayed. He pushed with vigor the siege of Arcona; and was about to carry it by assault, when his two military churchmen, Absalom, bishop of Roskild, and Eskil archbishop of Lund, advised him to spare the idolaters upon the following conditions: that they should deliver him their idol with all the treasure; that they should release, without ransom, all their Christian slaves; that all should embrace, and with constancy, the gospel of Christ; that the lands now belonging to their priests should be transferred to the support of Christian churches; that, whenever required, they should serve in the armies of the king; that they should pay him an annual tribute. Hostages being given for the performance of these stipulations, the invaders entered the temple, and proceeded to destroy Svantovit, under the eyes of a multitude of pagans, who expected every moment to see a dreadful miracle. The idol was so large, that they could not at once hurl it to the ground, lest it should fall on some one, and the pagans be enabled to boast of its having revenged itself. They broke it in pieces; and the wood was cut up into logs for the fires of the camp. Great was the amazement of the spectators to witness this tameness on the part of so potent a god; and they could only account for it by inferring that Christ was still more powerful. The temple was next burnt; and so were three others, all with idols. The numerous garrisons of the island were made to capitulate; the victors returned to Denmark in triumph; and missionaries were sent to instruct the inhabitants in the doctrines and duties of Christianity. At the instance of bishop Absalom, the island was annexed to the diocese of Roskild. This was a glorious and it was an enduring conquest; a fierce people were converted into harmonized subjects, and piracy lost its great support.

But with this vigorous effort, piracy was not extirpated: on the contrary, the Danish coasts were themselves ravaged the following year by the Slavonians. This disaster was owing to the anger of Henry the Lion, duke of Saxony, who had sent a contingent to the corps of Valdemar. He had probably not expected the reduction of Rugen; he certainly was jealous of his ally's success; and, to provoke a breach, he demanded half of the treasures, of the captives, of the hostages, and of the tribute stipulated to be paid. There was probably some justice in the demand; but the king refused to comply with it, and Henry, in great anger, informed the Slavonians that they might consider themselves at liberty to inflict whatever injuries they could on the Danes. How this prince had acquired so great an ascendancy over these people; how they came to call themselves his vassals, is one of those problems which history cannot solve. There must have been treaties, and marriages, and conquests, which chroniclers have omitted. "He was the only prince on earth," says Helmold, "that could put a bridle into the mouth of that ferocious people, and direct them at his pleasure." The vast, restless tribes, from Courland to Mecklenburgh, wanted only this stimulus to rise; and they did rise, in numbers too formidable to be resisted. Valdemar and his ministers suffered the tide to roll on: they had the mortification to witness its ravages on their shores; but when it had spent a portion of its fury, they raised an armament, cleared their shores, passed into the Baltic, and, after some advantages, carried the war into the Vandalic territories. But what salutary impression could be made on a people who, at the approach of an enemy, plunged, with their substance, into the impenetrable recesses of their forests, and returned that moment that enemy retired? Jomsberg, indeed, one of the most flourishing maritime cities in Europe, was taken, and its great treasures became the prize of the victors; but the place has been taken before by Canute, the Great, in 1010, and Magnus, the Good, in 1044. No sooner was it demolished, than it began to rise from its ruins. Valdemar, therefore, perceived that, as he could not exterminate these numerous tribes, who often acted in a general confederation, and were always ready to descend upon his coasts, his only hope was in the friendly interference of the Saxon duke. He, therefore, met that sovereign, conceded all his demands, and had the satisfaction to see Henry issue his mandate, that the Danish coasts should no longer be molested. For some years they were not; but a very precarious surety was that which depended on the will of another person—a person who might, at any moment, change his policy, or whose influence might be destroyed by death.

Valdemar II., surnamed the Victorious, caused a survey to be made of his whole kingdom; and of this important document, the greater portion still remains. There were eight bishoprics, subdivided into parishes, and into Styreshavne or *maritime* districts, each district to furnish a certain number of men, and each sea a certain number of ships, whenever required by the public service. North Jutland had four of these sees—Rypen, Aarhuus, Viborg, Borglum, which together supplied four hundred and fifty vessels. South Jutland, or Sleswic, one see, was divided into one hundred and thirty of these districts, each to furnish a vessel. Fionia, Laland, and Langeland, forming the diocese of Ordinsey, were rated at one hundred. Zealand, Mohen, Falster, and Rugen, which formed the see of Roskild, were rated at one hundred and twenty; Scania, Holland, and Bleking, subject to the archbishop of Lund, contributed one hundred and fifty.

The successor of Valdemar, Eric VI., was continually engaged in civil wars. Swedish fleets ravaged the coasts of Denmark, and destroyed every thing that could be reached. The armaments of the Danes were easily defeated, and Eric was compelled to accept the terms of peace offered by his brother. He sent an expedition against Livonia, but it does not appear that it effected any thing considerable.

In 1360, a war broke out between Magnus, king of Sweden, and Eric, his son. The king of Denmark, Valdemar Atterdag, aided Magnus with all his forces to subdue the rebel son. This was easily effected, and Magnus was triumphant. But he had again recourse to Valdemar to aid him in suppressing a new rebellion against his authority. The inhabitants of Wisby, capital of the isle of Gothland, refused to pay the impost which he had laid upon them; and Valdemar, in obedience to his wish, sailed to chastise them. Wisby was one of the greatest ports in Europe; it was the magazine where the merchandise of the Baltic was kept. Of this much belonged to the Hanse Towns, especially to Lubeck. Immense was the booty which the Danish monarch seized in that town; but why he should plunder the subjects of his ally for his own benefit, is not easy to be explained. Whatever were his own reasons, he soon repented of his violence. The Swedes, indignant with their monarch whom they knew to have been the occasion of the disaster, shut him up in a fortress, called Hako of Norway, to aid them, and declared war against Denmark. To obtain more assistance, they entered into alliance with the enemies of Denmark,—with the counts of Holstein, with the duke of Mecklenburg, and with the Hanse Towns, which were justly exasperated at the plunder of Wisby. The confederated powers put their armaments in motion, and soon reduced Copenhagen. Helsingburg in Scania was besieged, but Valdemar raised the siege and defeated the allied fleets with great loss. Vordingburg was next assailed, but with no better success; and other disasters soon rendered the allies anxious for peace, which was concluded at Lubeck, in 1363. But it was of short continuance. There was a general meeting of deputies from all the towns of the Hanseatic League, above seventy in number; and the result of their deliberations was a new war. It was, indeed, evident, that unless that body secured the free transit of merchandise, there must be an end to all mercantile enterprise, and the worst days of piracy must be restored. Two armaments were soon equipped; and the number of assailants was increased by the adhesion of Denmark's hereditary enemies. Valdemar, terrified, had recourse to negociations. Adolf, count of Holstein, he detached from the league by investing him with the isle of Femeran. The Hanse Towns he propitiated by commercial privileges. A truce was accordingly made, and the king was left to resume his intrigues in the North.

The name of Sigurd I. of Norway, is celebrated in the annals of the North, alike for his pilgrimage to Jerusalem, and his exploits during the voyage. Influenced by the prospect of fame and an immortal reward, Sigurd, with sixty ships, sailed from the North.

During the first winter he remained in England, and was hospitably entertained by Henry I. The second winter, at least the greater part of it, he passed near the shrine of Santiago in Gallicia: he was a pilgrim, no less than a champion of the cross. On his way to Lisbon, he captured some infidel privateers, and destroyed several Moorish settlements on the coast, especially one at Cintra. All who refused baptism he put to the sword. Lisbon, according to the Northern chroniclers, was divided into two parts, one inhabited by the Moors, the other by the Christians. The former he assailed, took it, and with much booty proceeded through the straits of Gibraltar in quest of new adventures. Having passed these straits, he conquered a whole fleet of the infidels, and this was the fifth battle since he left Norway. In vain did the Mahomedan pirates on the African coast resist him; his valor overcame every thing. Landing in Sicily, he was magnificently entertained by Roger, sovereign of the island, who had expelled the Saracens. Roger was of Norman descent: he remembered the land of his sires; and so far did he carry his good will as to insist on serving Sigurd at table. Continuing his voyage, he landed at Acre, and proceeded to Jerusalem, where the offer of his sword was most welcome to Baldwin. From that king he received what he thought a valuable treasure—a fragment of the true cross, which he promised to deposite in the shrine of St. Olaf. He promised, too, at the instance of his new friends, to establish an archiepiscopal see in Norway, to build churches, and to enforce the payment of tithes. His last exploit in these regions was to join in the siege of Sidon; and when that city was taken, half the booty became his. In 1111, the king arrived in Norway after an absence of four years.

That this remarkable expedition redounded greatly to the honor of Sigurd, is certain: he was thenceforth much venerated throughout the North. He married, and attended to the duties of government, especially to the extirpation of idolatry. His expedition (undertaken at the request of the Danish king) against the inhabitants of the isle of Smaland, was one congenial to his feelings. They had received Christianity, but, like many other portions of the Scandinavian population, had returned to idolatry. Even Sweden had its pagans and apostates, some, too, of royal dignity. Great was the punishment inflicted by Sigurd and his ally, Nicholas, on the pagans whom they had vanquished; but mercy to infidels, and still less to apostates, formed no portion of their creed.

LANDING OF SIGURD I. AT ACRE.

CHAPTER XVI.

THE NAVY OF SWEDEN FROM THE FIFTEENTH CENTURY.

IT will now be necessary to consider the kingdoms of Denmark, Sweden, and Norway, which once formed Scandinavia, as separate kingdoms, and to give the naval history of each a distinct place. As the power which, at one time, became the most important, we shall first take up the history of Sweden, from the fifteenth century to the present day.

In 1520, Sweden was restored to liberty, and the foundation of her future greatness laid by the celebrated Gustavus Vasa. The occasion of this revolution was as follows:—In 1518, Christian II. of Denmark, invaded with a design to subdue the whole country; but being defeated, with great loss, by Steno Sture, then regent, he set sail for Denmark. But meeting with contrary winds, he made several descents on the Swedish coast, which he ravaged with all the fury of an incensed barbarian. The inhabitants, however, bravely defended themselves, and Christian was reduced to the utmost distress; one half of his forces having perished with hunger, and the other being in the most imminent danger by the approach of a rigorous winter. He then thought of a stratagem which had almost proved fatal to the regent. Christian offered to go to Stockholm to confer with Sture, on condition that six hostages should be sent in his stead. The hostages were sent, and the wind proving favorable, Christian set sail with them to Denmark. Next year he returned, and drawing Sture into a conferference, had him assassinated. This left the kingdom without a head, and no resistance was made to the progress of Christian, who advanced to the heart of Sweden, destroying every thing with fire and sword. Finally, he procured his election to the throne, and became the most unrelenting of tyrants. At last he departed for Denmark. Soon afterwards Gustavus Vasa, who had been one of the hostages given for Christian's safety by Steno Sture, escaped from his prison, and after a variety of extraordinary adventures, arrived safely in Sweden, and placing himself at the head of a few peasants and warriors, overturned the government of the tyrant, and defeated his armies. Gustavus then laid siege to Stockholm, and petitioned the regency to grant him a squadron of ships to prosecute it with. The armament was granted only on condition that he would oblige himself to pay the expense afterwards. This squadron was dearly bought. It did not go over to the enemy, but in a sea fight, where the Danes were in its power, and might have been destroyed, they suffered them to escape. Soon after, the activity of Gustavus overcame all obstacles, and he was elected king.

When Gustavus Adolphus succeeded to the Swedish throne, in 1611, a war broke out with Denmark, whose designs were perceived by that penetrating prince. The Danes were superior to the Swedes upon the sea, and this gave them great advantages. But such was the spirit of Gustavus, that he forced the Danes to conclude a peace on favorable terms, in 1613. He then resolved to prosecute a war against Poland, which kingdom had given some cause of offence. Accordingly, he set sail for Riga, with a great fleet, containing twenty thousand men. That city was reduced by the armament, after six weeks' desperate fighting. Gustavus then set sail for Dantzic and forced the king of Poland to conclude a truce for a year. After defeating the Danish troops in a number of battles, he sailed for Prussia,

GUSTAVUS ADOLPHUS.

with one hundred and fifty ships. Many battles were there fought, but the usual fortune of Gustavus did not attend his efforts. The obstinacy with which Dantzic held out greatly irritated him. In a sea engagement, the Swedish fleet defeated that of the enemy; after which Gustavus having blocked up the harbor with his fleet, pushed the siege with vigor upon land. The garrison was on the point of surrendering, when a sudden rise of the Vistula ruined the Swedish works, and they raised the siege. When the Poles were forced to consent to a six years' truce, Gustavus kept the port and citadel of Memel, the harbor of Pillau, the town of Elbing, Braneburg, and all that he had conquered in Livonia.

The next object of the enmity of Gustavus was the emperor of Germany, whom he resolved to punish for assisting the enemies of Sweden. The Swedes were well prepared for this great expedition. His troops amounted to sixty thousand men of the most veteran class, and his fleet exceeded seventy sail, carrying from twenty to forty guns and manned by six thousand mariners. The great struggle, however, was upon land, where the genius of Gustavus was triumphant until

CHARLES XII.

the battle of Lutzen, where, although the Swedes gained a great victory they lost their king. During the war maintained upon the continent by Charles X., the two fleets of the Danes and Swedes met and fought for two whole days, without any considerable advantage on either side. Soon after, Charles appeared with a fleet before Copenhagen, and had he commenced the assault immediately, before the inhabitants had recovered from their surprise, the city might have been easily taken. But he gave them time to prepare for a defence. The siege proved tedious, and at last, the city was relieved by the appearance of a Dutch fleet. After this, Charles converted the siege into a blockade, which continued until the end of the war.

In 1676, under the reign of Charles XI., the Swedes received a terrible blow by the defeat of their fleet in an engagement with the combined fleets of Denmark and Holland. In spite of the activity and valor of their king, the conquests achieved by their former generals, were recovered by the overwhelming numbers of their enemies. In 1678, the Swedish fleet was defeated in two engagements. Count Konigsmark, the Swedish general was forced to

DEATH OF GUSTAVUS ADOLPHUS.

PETER THE GREAT.

evacuate Pomerania, and to add to the reverse of fortune, the fleet which transported the army from Pomerania, was wrecked on the coast of Bornholm; by which accident two thousand persons were drowned and the remainder plundered and taken prisoners by the Danes.

The affairs of the Swedes were retrieved on the accession of Charles XII. to the throne. A formidable combination was immediately formed against Sweden by the monarchs who thought to take advantage of his youth. But they found him another Alexander. Having entrusted the affairs of the nation to a council chosen by the senate, Charles set out from Stockholm on the 8th of May, 1700. He embarked at Carlscrona and defeated the fleet of the allies. Having made a descent on Zealand, he proceeded to invest Copenhagen by sea and land, and forced Frederick IV., king of Denmark, to conclude a peace at the end of eleven days. Charles was thus at liberty to turn his arms elsewhere. Hearing that the czar of Russia, Peter the Great, had laid siege to Narva, with one hundred thousand men, he immediately embarked at Carlscrona, though it was then mid winter and the Baltic scarcely navigable, and soon landed at Pernaw, in Livonia, with part of his forces. The Swedes defeated the vast army of the Russians, with the greatest ease, taking all the cannon, twenty thousand prisoners and entirely destroying the remainder.

After many brilliant achievements, Charles, defeated at Pultowa, was forced to fly for refuge to the Turkish dominions, where he remained five years. Nor did his return to Sweden change the aspect of affairs. The czar of Russia, with a fleet of twenty large ships of war, and one hundred and fifty transports, carrying thirty thousand men, threw a part of the Swedish coast into consternation. The fleets of the allied enemies of Sweden blockaded Stralsund, in which town Charles was besieged by numbers greatly superior After performing many valiant exploits, it became evident that Charles must either be persuaded to leave the town, or that he would be buried in its ruins. The danger attending an effort to escape induced the daring monarch to attempt it. Setting out, in a small boat, with sails and oars, he passed all the enemies' ships and batteries, and arrived safe at Ystedt, in Schonen.

Under Gustavus III., the navy of Sweden was put on a more respectable footing; but in the war with Russia, in which that monarch engaged, the contest was maintained principally upon land. The Swedish king showed himself quite equal to his warlike predecessors, Gustavus Adolphus, and Charles XII. No naval engagement has taken place since his death; but the Swedish navy has not been neglected. It now consists of ten ships of the line, fourteen frigates and sloops of war, ten brigs, several steamers, and more than three hundred gun boats. A large number of the trading vessels are so built that they can be fitted out as privateers. The principal naval stations are at Carlscrona and Stockholm.

CHAPTER XVII.

DENMARK AND NORWAY.

IN 1448, Christian I., the founder of the dynasty which has ever since ruled Denmark, ascended the throne. Under his reign, the maritime power of Denmark commanded the Northern seas, and it was principally by means of this naval strength that Christian was enabled to connect Norway with his kingdom. Christian II. was an enterprising though a barbarous prince. To the expedition which he conducted against Sweden we have already alluded. He lost Norway by his barbarous treatment of the inhabitants whose coast he ravaged without remorse. But his reign was short. Under his successors, Norway recovered, and the Danes obtained considerable advantages over the fleets of Sweden. But the accession of Gustavus Adophus turned the tide of success, and the Swedes became as victorious on the sea as on the land. The Danish navy was superior in number of vessels, but the valor of the Swedes compensated for their inferiority in other respects. Christian IV. made peace with Gustavus Adolphus, and remained neutral during the war between Sweden and Germany. But his successors were induced to join the alliance against the power of Sweden, and paid for their presumption. Neither by sea or land could they withstand the nation trained to fighting by the genius of Gustavus. Charles X. forced the Danes to grant a free passage through the Sound to Swedish vessels. But no sooner had the Swedish king withdrawn his forces, than the king of Denmark began to act directly contrary to the spirit of the treaty. Perceiving the hostile designs still entertained, Charles resolved to anticipate them, and appeared before Copenhagen with a fleet, of which we have alredy spoken in the naval history of Sweden.

After the death of the active and able Charles X., the Danes took advantage of the comparative inefficiency of the Swedish forces, and the weakness of a regency, and their fleets were victorious in several engagements with the enemy. They also ravaged the islands of Oeland, Smaland, Unno, and Kuno. But the Danes were no match for the Swedes, even in their distress. They were compelled to sue for peace, which they intended to break at the first opportunity. Again they thought to recover their former possessions and to humble Sweden, when Charles XII. succeeded to the throne. But he defeated their fleet, and reduced them to submission, before they calculated that he would have been ready to leave Sweden. Fear only kept the hostility of the Danes suppressed until the battle of Pultowa had tarnished the glory of the reputation of the Swedish hero. By the peace of 1720, at Fredericksburg, Denmark obtained the toll of the Sound, which seems to have been a very desirable object with the Swedes and Danes. After this period, the Danes enjoyed some degree of tranquillity.

By her accession to the Northern confederacy, in 1800, Denmark was involved in a war with Great Britain, in which the Danish fleet was defeated at Copenhagen, April 2, 1801. The courage of the Danes, however, obtained them a truce, after which a treaty was concluded. In 1807, this state was included in Napoleon's continental policy. England thought it her duty to prevent an alliance between Denmark and France, and, accordingly, a fleet of twenty-three ships of the line was sent up the Sound, August 3d, which demanded of Denmark a defensive alliance, or the surrender of her fleet, as a pledge of her neutrality. Both were refused. Upon this, an army was landed and Copenhagen surrounded. As the king still refused the demands of the British commander, the city was bombarded for three days, and four hundred houses laid in ashes, in the ruins of which thirteen hundred Danes perished. On the 7th of September, Copenhagen capitulated, and the whole Danish fleet, completely equipped, consisting of eighteen ships of the line, fifteen frigates, and a large number of smaller vessels, was surrendered to the British, who carried them off in triumph. The crews which had fought with great bravery were made prisoners of war. Great Britain then offered the crown prince neutrality or an alliance. If he accepted the first, the fleet was to be restored in three years after the general peace, and the island of Heliogoland was to be ceded to the British crown. The crown prince rejected all the proposals, declared war against Great Britain, and entered a treaty with Napoleon at Fountainebleau, October 31. War was also declared against Sweden; but Denmark was forced to conclude a peace with both powers in January, 1814. In 1846, the Danish navy consisted of seven ships of the line, eight frigates, five sloops of war, four brigs, four steamers, and six other vessels, besides eighty-two gun boats. The principal naval station is Copenhagen, the capital. The Danish fleets have lost the command of the Baltic which they once possessed, not by a diminution of their strength, but by the growth of the maritime powers around them.

Norway, for awhile an independent kingdom, then a part of Denmark, and lastly, subject to the crown of Sweden, has but a small, distinct naval history, from the expedition of Sigurd I. to the Holy Land. Its ports were alternately the stations of the Danish and the Swedish fleets, and its numerous and extensive forests and productions afforded the material for the construction of a great number of vessels. In 1821, the Norwegian navy consisted of two frigates, six brigs, and eight schooners.

CHAPTER XVIII.

SPAIN AND PORTUGAL.

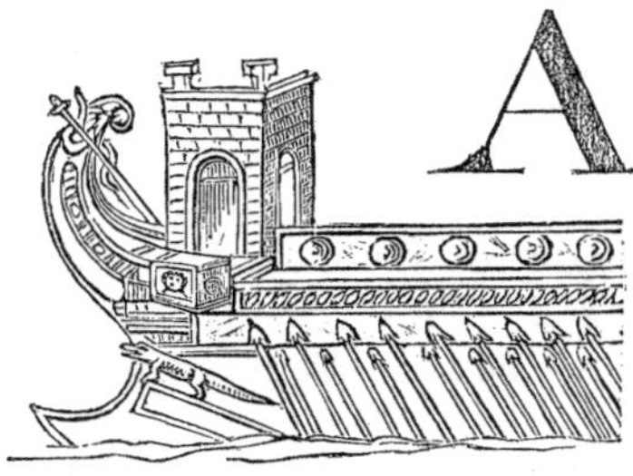

AS in the earliest times, Spain and Portugal were united under the same name and government, and as their naval history afterwards is so closely interwoven, that we should be driven to repetition if they were narrated separately, we shall include them under the same head.

Until the invasion of Spain by the Carthaginians, not long before the commencement of the first Punic War, nothing certain can be affirmed of the Spaniards or their habits. The country was most probably peopled by the Celts, whose barbarism never allowed them to engage in maritime pursuits. They were, doubtless, contented with their navigation of the rivers and the coasts in their light skin-covered canoes. The success of the Carthaginian expeditions, in reducing the country and their final expulsion by the Romans has already been mentioned in the naval history of Rome and Carthage. The attractions of Spain, consisted chiefly in her vast treasures of silver, which were exported in the fleets of the Phœnicians, the Carthaginians, and, lastly, of the Romans.

Nothing remarkable in naval matters occurred in Spain until the civil war between Marius and Sylla. Marius had appointed Sertorius prætor of Spain. As soon as he was overthrown by Sylla, that general sent thither one Caius Annius to drive Sertorius out. As Sertorius had but few troops along with him, he despatched one Julius Salinator with a body of six thousand men to guard the passes of the Pyrenees, and to prevent Annius from entering the country. But Salinator having been treacherously murdered by assassins hired by Annius for that purpose, he no longer met with any obstacle; and Sertorius was obliged to embark for the coast of Africa with three thousand men, being all he had now remaining. With these he landed in Mauritania; but as his men were straggling carelessly about, great numbers of them were cut off by the barbarians. This new misfortune obliged Sertorius to re-embark for Spain; but finding the whole coast lined with the troops of Annius, he put to sea again, not knowing what course to steer. In this new voyage he met with a small fleet of Cilician pirates; and having prevailed with them to join him, he made a descent on the coast of Yvica, overpowered the garrison left there by Annius, and gained a considerable booty. On the news of this victory, Annius set sail for Yvica, with a considerable squadron, having five thousand land forces on board. Sertorius, not intimidated by the superiority of the enemy, prepared to give them battle. But a violent storm arising, most of the ships were driven on shore and dashed to pieces, Sertorius himself, with great difficulty, escaping with the small remains of his fleet. For some time he continued in great danger, being prevented from putting to sea by the fury of the waves, and from landing by the enemy; at last, the storm abating, he passed the straits of Gades, now Gibraltar, and landed near the mouth of the river Bæotis. Here he met with some seamen newly arrived from the Atlantic or Fortunate Islands; and was so taken with the account with which they gave him of those happy regions, that he resolved to retire thither to spend the rest of his life in quiet and happiness. But having communicated this design to the Cilician pirates, they immediately abandoned him, and set sail for Africa, with an intention to assist one of the barbarous kings against his subjects who had rebelled. Upon this Sertorius sailed thither also, but took the opposite side; and having defeated the king named Ascalis, obliged him to shut himself up in the city of Tidgis, now Tangier, which he closely besieged.

For ten years did Sertorius make head against all the forces of Rome, defeating their best generals, including Pompey and Metellus. He appears decidedly the ablest commander of his time, and his personal qualities were worthy of admiration, At last, he was assassinated by his general, Perperna, and his forces were then easily defeated by Pompey.

None of the tribes of barbarians, who successively overrun the territories of Spain during the last years of the empire of the west, possessed the enterprising spirit of the Vandals. The active genius of Genseric, their king, was not contented with the conquest of Spain. His expedition to Africa and his subsequent naval power we have already narrated in the giving the naval history of Rome. The vessels which transported the Vandals over the straits of Gibraltar were furnished by the Spaniards, who were glad, by any means, to get rid of these ferocious invaders. The Visi-Goth sconquered the territory of the Spaniards and founded a ruling dynasty, which continued until the eighth century. They were an enterprising nation, and fitted out expeditions which made considerable conquests in Barbary. But towards the end of the ninth century, the Saracens overran all the Gothic dominions in Barbary, with a rapidity which nothing could resist, and then sailed across to Spain about the year 711. Their force was overpowering, and the Goths were either driven out of the country, or compelled to submit to the rule of the Saracens.

In the long wars which followed between the Moors and the kings of Arragon, Castile, and Leon, the Moors were generally superior to their enemies upon the sea. But they lost the Balearic isles, which were conquered by James I. of Arragon, and gradually declined in power and extent of possessions. The great protection and ready aid of the Moors was found in their kindred beyond the straits. The African Moors always offered their assistance in time of need.

The kings of Castile, Arragon, and Leon did not join in the first crusade, their attention being continually occupied by the Moors, whom they at last reduced to the province of Granada. Neither of these kings gave much attention to naval matters. The Catalonians only seemed to have been enterprising enough to strive for the dominion of the sea. In a war with France and Naples, in 1283, the Catalonian admiral, Roger de Loria, obtained a high reputation by three victories over the combined fleets of the French and Neapolitans. This famous naval commander succeeded Pedro, the son of the king of Arragon, in the post of admiral of all the naval forces of that kingdom. Soon after taking command, he reduced the greater part of Malta, and defeated the French fleet within sight of Naples, taking the prince of Salerno prisoner. He again defeated the fleet of the enemy near Rosas, and wasted the coast of France.

In 1298, the Sicilians revolting from the sovereignty of Jayme II. king of Arragon, proclaimed his brother Frederic, and prepared to sustain his cause vigorously. The king of Arragon passed over to Italy, with a considerable armament, where he conferred with his allies, the pope and the king of Naples. He then sailed to Sicily. In this unnatural war, it is some consolation to perceive that the king was not deaf to the voice of blood. Hearing that Frederic was advancing with a fleet to oppose him, he besought that prince to return to the island, and thereby omit the danger, no less than the disgrace of a battle. But Frederic was not to be intimidated, and the Arragonic fleet sailed to Syracuse, which was besieged. The vigorous resistance of the inhabitants, and the capture of a part of his fleet by the vessels of his brother, compelled Jayme to return to Spain for reinforcements. With a powerful fleet he again appeared off the coast of Sicily; but he was encountered by the Sicilian king, who, after a gallant action, was defeated. Eighteen of the Sicilian vessels and numerous prisoners remained in the power of the victors. There is every evidence, that Jayme could have taken his brother's galley on this occasion, but that nature urged him to connive at his escape. Nor did he improve his advantage. Instead of proceeding at once to the Sicilian coast, he returned to Naples.

During the reign of the same monarch, the Arragonese were involved in a war with the maritime inhabitants of Pisa. The pope had granted the islands of Sardinia and Corsica to the king of Arragon. Two armaments were sent against Cagliari, which important city surrendered after a long siege, and the Pisans were forced to abandon Sardinia. Alfonso IV., who succeeded Jayme II., soon found Sardinia a troublesome conquest. In 1330, the Genoese, incensed that the enterprising Catalonians should have obtained a settlement in seas which they considered as exclusively their right, fomented an insurrection among the islanders, and sent a fleet against the capital. A bloody war ensued. Though the troops of Alfonso were usually successful, his active enemies made some descents on Catalonia and Valentia, which they ravaged with perfect impunity during the absence of his fleet. All attempts at negotiating a peace failed, the Genoese demanding, as a necessary condition, to be indemnified for the expense of their armament.

Scarcely had the war with the Genoese been satisfactorily terminated by Pedro IV., the son and successor of Alfonso, when a war broke out with the king of Castile. It commenced in 1356, on the refusal of the Castilians to restore a prize made at sea, by one of the Biscayan pirates, and the capture of two Pisan vessels in the neutral port of Santa Maria, and was continued with varied success both by sea and land. In 1359, the Arragonese fleet ravaged the coasts of the Castilian dominions, and the Castilian fleet ravaged the coast of Valentia and insulated Barcelona and Ivica. In general, the advantage lay upon the side of the Castilians. A short truce was concluded between the hostile powers, but it was only for breathing time, to recover strength for the contest. A peace was not concluded until 1374. In the meanwhile, Pedro sailed with a formidable armament, and landed in Majorca, whose king he dethroned with ease. But his fleet, combined with the Venetians, was defeated by the intrepid Genoese, in the Thracian Bosphorus. However, this defeat was compensated in 1352, by a naval engagement in which the combined fleets of Catalonia and Venice obtained a signal triumph. When a peace was concluded between the Genoese and Arragonese, each power agreed to abandon to the other, certain ports and dock yards for the construction of ships. The war was ruinous to both parties; as Sardinia would not acknowledge the sway of either, and it was necessary to maintain a large land and naval force to secure even a show of subjection.

While the Arragonese contended with one of the greatest naval powers of that age, the navies of Castile and Portugal were not idle. Upon the death of Pedro, the Cruel, Fernando, king of Portugal, considering himself as the rightful heir to the Castilian throne, assumed the regal title and arms of Castile. But his abilities were inadequate to the contest in which he engaged with the usurper Enrique II. He fitted

GAETA.

out various armaments by sea and land to enforce his pretensions; but the vigor with which Enrique overcame his numerous enemies astonished them. In 1370, Fernando sent a powerful armament to the mouth of the Guadalquiver, where it was defeated by the fleet of the Castilians. The English sent a fleet against the French king, the ally of Enrique; but his activity was still victorious; the English fleet was defeated. Juan, the son and successor of Enrique upon the throne of Castile and Leon, had to contend with the same enemies as his father. Fernando, of Portugal, entered into a league with the duke of Lancaster, in England, the object of which was to dethrone Juan. The young king showed that he was quite equal to the contest. In 1381, off Cape St. Vincent, his fleet triumphed over that of Fernando, and Almeida was forced to submit to him.

As Arragon was continually engaged in hostilities with the neighboring powers, her people became both skilful soldiers and seamen. Her fleets were equal to any which then rode the sea, and numerous victories had established their reputation and caused them to become objects of fear. Under Alphonso V., the Catalonian seamen were constantly employed in the operations against the Genoese and the inhabitants of the islands of the Mediterranean. No single engagement worthy of mention took place upon the sea—the fleets of Arragon being employed in blockading during the siege of the ports of the various islands. In 1432, Alphonso set sail upon an expedition against the Neapolitans. After a successful attack on the isle of Gorbes, where he defeated the king of Tunis, the piracies of whose subjects had long afflicted the people of his coasts, he proceeded to Sicily. There he was forced to wait, on account of the number of his enemies, who now included the Pope, the emperor Sigismund, the duke of Milan, the Venetians, Genoese, and Florentines. On attempting to besiege Gaeta, garrisoned by Genoese and Milanese, he was forced into a naval battle, in which his fleet was not only defeated, but almost annihilated. The king, Alphonso, and his brothers Juan and Enrique were taken prisoners and conducted to the city of Milan, from whence, however, they were soon liberated. The war was renewed, and this time with more vigor by the Arragonese. They defeated the fleet of the duke of Anjou, and invested the capital, Naples. A rapid succession of victories over the combined forces of the Genoese and Neapolitans secured the object at which Alphonso had been aiming—the Two Sicilies, and the Neapolitan throne for his son. Under the reign of this ambitious monarch, the power of Arragon reached its greatest height. Her fleets were invincible, and commanded the western Mediterranean. No important naval transactions are recorded as having occurred during the interval between the death of Alphonso I. and the union of Arragon with Castile and Leon, under Fernando and Isabella. The naval events of their reign, which were of the very highest importance in every point of view, will fall under the reader's notice in the next chapter.

ANCIENT SPANISH GALLEY.

SPANISH AND VENETIAN COSTUMES, SIXTEENTH CENTURY.

CHAPTER XIX.

PORTUGUESE AND CASTILIAN EXPEDITIONS.

DURING the reign of Joam I. king of Portugal, the most brilliant deeds of valor were performed by his martial sons, in the expedition against the Moors of Africa. The fortress of Ceuta, on the African side of the Straits of Gibraltar was the object of this expedition. It was inhabited by pirates whose depredations were a source of great annoyance to the commerce of the Portuguese. The fortifications were strong and defended by the bravest portion of the Mahomedan population. During the progress of the preparations, the greatest secresy was preserved, in order to prevent the increase of the garrison. It

SALA BEN SALA.

was given out, that the armament was to be led against the count of Holland. At length, having collected a considerable number of vessels from most parts, and been joined by adventurers from most nations of Europe, accompanied by his sons and his chief nobles, Joam embarked, proceeded towards the Straits, and about the middle of August, 1415, arrived before Ceuta. Sala ben Sala, the Moorish governor, a man advanced in years, but of undaunted courage, prepared for a vigorous defence. In spite of his opposition, however, the troops were disembarked without loss, and the Moors, who lined the coast were forced to seek the shelter of the fortress. The ardor of the two infantes caused them to pursue the fugitives so closely that both entered the fortress at once. Perceiving that they were accompanied by no more than five hundred Christians, the former

SIEGE OF CEUTA.

sent messengers for assistance, and were soon joined by a few hundred more. By this time, another of the princes, Pedro, had disembarked and hastened to join his brothers, Duarte and Enrique. The Moors had rallied and were fighting desperately for their native hearths. The enthusiasm of the young princes was so great that they got separated from their followers in the pursuit, and Pedro, with four others found himself surrounded by a host. The five heroes maintained their ground until relieved by a party of Christians. The king himself disembarked and then the Mahomedans fled. The Portuguese flag was hoisted upon the ramparts and the success of the expedition seemed complete. A small but select garrison was left in Ceuta, and the king then returned, with the armament, to Lisbon.

No sooner had the fleet of Joam departed, than the Moors commenced their preparations for the recovery of their stronghold. For three years after the reduction of Ceuta, the little garrison, under the conduct of the valiant Don Pedro de Menezes, was constantly called upon to repel the attacks of the enemy. At first they advanced to the harbor, and burnt the few vessels that remained there. But the sallies made by the Portuguese knights drove them off with terrible slaughter. In 1419, the place was invested by sea and land by an army and fleet from Grenada. The valor of the besieged was extraordinary. Fearing, however, that the fortress must ultimately surrender, if not succored, the Portuguese king ordered two of his sons, the infantes Henrique and Joam, to sail, with a considerable armament. As they appoached the place, they perceived that the Mahomedans had landed, and furiously assailed Don Pedro, who, with his brave little band was making terrible havoc among them. The hosts of the enemy were totally routed, whilst the infantes took or dispersed the Moorish vessels, commanded by a prince of the house of Grenada. This splendid success attracted the attention of all Europe. Don Pedro became one of the most celebrated heroes in the history of the days of chivalry.

In the reign of the same prince, Joam I., the Portuguese began their great career of maritime discovery. His son Henrique, who had studied mathematics and navigation, was the first to enter on this course. To facilitate his long meditated enterprise, he fixed his abode in the kingdom of Algarve, on the most elevated point of Cape St. Vincent, a point which he considered favorable to his astronomical observations, and where he founded the Tour of Sages. The first voyage, with two of the frail barks of that period, was undertaken in 1419, and extending only about five degrees of latitude, was unsuccessful. In the following year, however, three vessels being equipped for a much longer adventure, arrived at the Madeiras, which had been previously discovered by Machin, an English navigator. A subsequent expedition penetrated as far south as Sierra Leone, within three degrees of the line. From this time half a century elapsed before any Portuguese vessel ventured beyond these latitudes, though the Canaries were, in the meantime, discovered by some Biscayan mariners. The pope granted to the Portuguese the dominion of the regions which might thenceforward be discovered from Cape Bojador to the Indies.

The reign of Duartes the son of Joam I., was rendered disastrous, by the calamity of the plague and the result of an expedition against Tangier. The restless ambition of Fernando, the king's brother, hurried him into this enterprise. The preparations for it oppressed the people for some time, and the hindrances to the completion of the armament were regarded as ominous of a disastrous termination. The fleet sailed on the 22d of August, and on the 26th arrived before Ceuta. The forces numbered six thousand men, which was considered by some as inadequate to the undertaking, but the princes, Fernando and Henrique burned to distingush themselves, and with their usual impatience they resolved to proceed to Tangier—Henrique by land and Fernando by sea. The fleet arrived first before the town, which was defended by Sala ben Sala, with seven thousand Moors. The Portuguese commenced the siege at once, and continued it thirty-eight days without success. At length, a general assault was ordered. But it failed, despite the valor of the assailants. A large army of the Moors then advanced to force the Portugese to raise the siege. A long and bloody battle was fought, and the valiant invaders were forced to enter into a treaty with the Moors, by which it was agreed to surrender the fortress of Ceuta and their artillery, arms, and baggage. Fernando was to remain as a hostage. They were even then constrained to fight their way to their ships. The once proud armament then returned ingloriously to Lisbon.

After a long and dreary captivity, Fernando fell a victim to the cruel treatment of the Moors. No attempts were made to ransom him or to avenge his death, until 1457, when Alphonso had succeeded

Duarte upon the Throne of Portugal. That king had been very zealous in making naval preparations to assist in a new crusade; but the death of the pope, who so enthusiastically supported the holy war, and the dissentions of the Christian princes, left Alfonso at liberty to direct his forces against the Moors. The ports of Lisbon, Setubal, and Oporto were filled with the vessels of the armament. It was determined to invest Alcacar Seguer. In September, 1457, the armament, consisting of above two hundred vessels, and carrying twenty thousand men, sailed from the three ports, effected a junction at sea, and steered towards the Moorish coasts. On the 17th of the following month, it arrived before Alcacar Seguer, where the disembarkation was effected with but little loss. On the following morning the inhabitants agreed to evacuate the town. The Christians then entered it, and the government was confided to Duarte, de Menezes, son of the heroe of Ceuta. The king of Fez, with a large army of Moors, soon came to attempt the recovery of the place, and Alphonso, thinking his forces too weak to contend with them, ordered Duarte to maintain the town, while he sailed back to Portugal for reinforcements. Nobly did Duarte vindicate his claim, as the son of the valiant Don Pedro. The Moors were repulsed in their assault, with so great a loss, that they retired for reinforcements.

The successful conquest and defence of Alcacar Seguer stimulated Alphonso to make another attack upon Tangier. The armament engaged in this expedition was repulsed owing to the incapacity of Fernando, the king's son, who commanded it. The disastrous result of this undertaking, depressed Alphonso as greatly as his former success had stimulated him. But in 1471, he embarked thirty thousand men on board three hundred and eight transports, and proceeded to invest Arsilla, a fortress on the Atlantic, about seventeen leagues from the Straits of Gibraltar. This ancient and wealthy city was vigorously assailed by the Portuguese and as vigorously defended by the Mahomedans. Most of the inhabitants, scorning submission, perished with arms in their hands. The Portuguese spared none. This success so terrified the inhabitants of Tangier, that they abandoned their city, and it was immediately occupied by the Portuguese. For his successes in these expeditions, the subjects of Alphonso gave him the surname of Africanus. But he appears to have been utterly unworthy of such a distinction.

COLUMBUS.

Animated by the discoveries of the Portuguese, as soon as Ferdinand and Isabella had united the kingdoms of Arragon and Castile, and formed the kingdom of Spain, they were induced to aid and favor all attempts to perform the like services for them. The discovery of the new world by Columbus, attracts the notice of posterity to this reign. To Isabella must be in part ascribed the glory of this enterprise. At first she received with natural coldness the proposals of Columbus; but, overcome at last by the representations of a monk, the friend of Columbus, and still more by the resistless reasoning of the navigator himself, whom she admitted to her presence, she borrowed the sum of money necessary for the armament and bade him depart. This was in April, 1492. In the same month of the following year he returned from his first voyage, bringing the undoubted evidences of his having discovered a new world. He was received with extraordinary honors and appointed admiral of the Indies, with suitable means to support the dignity. With a fleet of eighteen vessels, containing one thousand two hundred seamen, three hundred

LANDING OF COLUMBUS.

CARDINAL XIMENES.

mechanics, twelve priests to convert the heathen, and a large number of horses, sheep, &c., he again left Spain, in September, 1493, and happily reached his destination. On returning from this second voyage, he was driven into the harbor of Lisbon, and was there compelled to acquaint Don Joam with the productions, climate, and riches of the New World. That monarch resolved to fit out some vessels of discovery in the same direction. This led to a dispute with the Spanish sovereigns, which, being referred to the pope, was decided in a singular manner. He seemed to consider that he had a right to divide the globe between the Spaniards and Portuguese. A line three hundred and seventy leagues west of the Cape de Verde islands was allowed as the limit of the Portuguese claim.

After the death of Isabella, Ferdinand was declared regent of Castile, as the Castilians would not recognize a prince of Arragon as their sovereign. He was active and successful. In 1509, at the suggestion of Cardinal Ximenes he proposed an expedition against Oran, on the African coast. The cardinal defrayed the expense and accompanied it. Oran was stormed and forced to receive a Christian garrison. The following year, Bugia, on the same coast, was captured, and Algiers, Tunis, Tremeien, and other places acknowledged the supremacy of the Christians. Another armament reduced Tripoli. The death of Ferdinand in 1516, put an end to his conquests.

While the Spanish sovereigns were thus actively engaged in discovery and conquest, the Portuguese spirit of maritime enterprise was not sleeping. A fort was founded on the coast of Guinea by order of Joam II., and from that time the Portuguese derived an immense revenue from the trade with the natives. To prevent other European vessels from securing any of this valuable commerce, Joam took care that the voyage should be represented as both difficult and dangerous; and impossible to be undertaken in any other vessels than flat-bottomed round smacks, at that time peculiar to Portugal. But the discovery of Guinea was but the beginning of Portuguese enterprise. Joam suspected that by coasting the African continent, a passage to the East Indies might be discovered. He sent two travellers to explore the western coast of Africa, and obtain the necessary information whether the trade with the East Indies would be valuable, and after their return, learned that the natives knew the continent terminated in a great cape far south. Joam then resolved to attempt the passage to India. He fitted out two squadrons—one under the command of Joam Alphonso de Aveiro, the other under Jayme Cam. The first discovered the kingdom of Benin, and there the death of the commodore put an end to the expedition. The other, under Jayme Cam, proceeded to the coast of Congo, and entered into a commercial treaty with the natives. A number of expeditions followed this one as far as Congo; but the discovery of the Cape of Good Hope was not made until 1487. It was discovered by the enterprising and skilful seaman, Bartholomew Diaz. In the following year, Vasco de Gama doubled it on a voyage to India. This latter expedition occupied two years and was filled with "hair-breadth 'scapes." At one time De Gama was forced to cannonade a Mahomedan city in Mozambique, and at another, a mutiny among the crew compelled him to take the helm himself. He arrived safely in Lisbon, however, and his narrations were received with astonishment and delight.

Manuel, who had succeeded Joam II., immediately equipped a fleet of thirteen vessels, which were confided to Don Pedro Alvares Cabral. This fleet was driven westward by a tempest, and the coast of Brazil was discovered. In a second voyage to the same coast, Cabral lost several of his ships. Many encounters took place between the Mahomedan merchant vessels and those of the Portuguese, but the Portuguese were always successful. A number of Indian and Arabian vessels were burned in the harbor of Calicut, and the city bombarded. A small squadron of Portuguese vessels was successful in a contest with a fleet belonging to the Moors and the king of Calicut, as the former was on its way to the Indies.

But the most extraordinary of the voyages undertaken by the Portuguese in their frail vessels, was one, under Vasco de Gama, in 1502. This renowned navigator had been created admiral of the Indies, and he readily undertook a voyage no longer considered dreadful. He set out with ten vessels, and was accompanied by his uncle, Vicente Sodre, with five more. His cousin Estevan de Gama had orders to follow him, with four additional vessels; and, in the following year, six more were despatched into the same seas—three, under Alfonso, and three under Francisco de Albuquerque. Having doubled the

ALBUQUERQUE.

Cape, Vasco resolved to confirm the influence of his country on the African coast, especially in Sofala and Mozambique. He cannonaded Quiloa, in revenge for the treachery displayed by the inhabitants on a former occasion, to his men. Off the coast of Malabar, Vasco was joined by his relative Estevan, which increased his force to nineteen ships; and he then resolved to vindicate the authority of his master. He captured an Egyptian vessel laden with treasure, and took terrible revenge upon the Moors and Hindoos for their treacherous conduct to the Portuguese. Not satisfied with seizing several valuable ships, he cut off the hands, head, and feet of thirty-two Moors, which he sent in a bark, as a present to the governor, and furiously cannonaded the city of Calicut. Leaving his uncle, Sodre, to continue the work of destruction, Vasco then sailed to Cochin, to see after the state of the Portuguese factories there. He soon received an invitation to return to Calicut and make peace with the Moors and Hindoos, which he was credulous enough to believe was sincerely meant. On his arrival,

VASCO DE GAMA.

before he was aware that hostilities were intended, his fleet was surrounded by above a hundred Moorish and Hindoo vessels. Had not Sodre, who had been ordered to cruise off the coast, unexpectedly appeared, the destruction of the Portuguese would have been certain. But, with his kinsman's aid, Vasco soon triumphed over his enemy. Sodre was left with six vessels, to maintain the Portuguese conquests, and Vasco returned home. Four small squadrons, under the Albuquerques, arrived soon after to assist Sodre, but that commander, by neglecting the factories and engaging in piracies had almost caused the ruin of them. The Albuquerques left only one hundred and fifty men in the fortress, when they also returned to Portugal. If the historians of the time speak truly, this little garrison performed wondrous deeds—maintaining the fortress against a large army of Hindoos. Their commander, Pucheco, immortalised himself, and his valorous deeds have been lavishly praised by the Portuguese.

It would be mere repetition to give the history of the various armaments sent out from Portugal to act against the Moors and Hindoos who endeavored to interrupt and destroy their commerce. They all display the skill and daring of the navigators and the naval power of Portugal in a favorable light. The principal admirals who conducted these expeditions were Francisco de Almeida, the Albuquerques, and Lope Soares.

The successes of the Portuguese in the East aroused the jealousy of Ferdinand of Castile; and by the representations of a navigator, named Ferdinand Magellan, (or Fernando de Magalhanes,) he was induced to equip five vessels, and giving Magellan the power of life and death over the crew, ordered the navigator to attempt his favorite project—the discovery of a route to the Indies by sailing southwest from Spain. Magellan embarked at Seville in August, 1519, and doubling Cape de Verde, passed the islands of that name, and plunged into the vast western ocean. Reaching the Brazilian coast, he cautiously proceeded southward. Nothing but the indomitable resolution to succeed, and the ardent zeal he felt in the undertaking could have made the intrepid Magellan persevere, alike in opposition to the elements and his crew. He, at length, passed into the dreaded straits which bear his name, where he lost a number of his crew by severe weather. Having cleared the straits he steered towards the equator, where the air was milder and he hoped to get provisions. As the squadron proceeded through the boundless Pacific, and no land appeared, the crew mutinied; but the energy of Magellan suppressed their conspiracy. He despatched one of his vessels in search of provisions; but instead of obeying this order, the captain returned to Europe. At length, considering the absent vessel as lost, the daring navigator continued his course westward, and, after a passage of fifteen hundred leagues, unparalleled for its boldness, reached the Phillipine islands. Here closed the career of Magellan. Having achieved immortal fame, as one of the conquerors of the deep, he fell a victim to the barbarity of the inhabitants of the isle of Zebu. In many respects, Magellan was the most extraordinary man of his age. All who can appreciate the difficulties he surmounted in traversing so great a distance in unknown seas will render the tribute of admiration.

CHARLES V.

CHAPTER XX

THE NAVAL OPERATIONS OF SPAIN AND PORTUGAL FROM 1516 TO THE PRESENT TIME.

THE reign of Charles V. raised Spain to a degree of importance in Europe which his death considerably diminished, and which could have been sustained only by a successor as ambitious and fortunate as that emperor. The Spanish forces obtained many signal victories upon land during the wars that convulsed Europe, but it does appear that any considerable naval expeditions were undertaken, or even that their fleets met an enemy fit to cope with them.

After the death of Charles, the United Provinces of the Nether-

DEFEAT OF THE SPANISH ARMADA.

lands revolted, and after a struggle succeeded in gaining their liberty. In this quarrel, Elizabeth of England, took part against Philip, which brought on a war between England and Spain, in 1587. The naval and military power of Philip was considered much superior to that of the Queen of England, and he resolved to invade that island. Accordingly, extraordinary preparations were made, and in May, 1588, brought to a conclusion. The Spaniards, confident of success, gave their fleet the name of the Invincible Armada. It affords a good picture of navies as they were in that age. It consisted, at this time, of one hundred and thirty vessels: sixty-five of these were galleons and larger ships; twenty-five were pink-built ships; nineteen tenders; thirteen small frigates, four were galleases; and four galleys. The soldiers on board amounted to nineteen thousand two hundred and ninety-five, the mariners to eight thousand and fifty; of these, three thousand three hundred and thirty soldiers, and one thousand two hundred and ninety-three mariners had been supplied by Portugal: besides which, the rowers in the galleases amounted to twelve hundred, and in the galleys to eight hundred and eighty-eight. There were also on board two thousand four hundred and thirty-one pieces of artillery, and four thousand five hundred and seventy-five quintals of powder: three hundred and forty-seven of the pieces of artillery had likewise been supplied by Portugal. Two thousand volunteers of the most distinguished families in Spain, exclusive of the sailors and soldiers already mentioned, are stated to have accompanied the expedition.

Philip's preparations, in the Netherlands, of a further force, were not less advanced than those of Spain. Besides, a well appointed army of thirty thousand foot and four thousand horse, which the Duke of Parma had assembled in the neighborhood of Nieuport and Dunkirk, that active general had provided a number of flat bottomed vessels, fit for transporting both horse and foot, and had brought sailors to navigate them from the towns in the Baltic. Most of these vessels had been built at Antwerp; and, to prevent the Dutch from intercepting them should they pass by sea, they were sent along the Scheldt to Ghent, thence by the canal to Bruges, and so to Nieuport by a new canal dug for the particular occasion. This laborious undertaking, in which several thousand workmen had been employed, was already finished, and the duke now only waited for the arrival of the Spanish fleet; hoping that, as soon as it should approach, the Dutch and

English ships, which cruised upon the coast, would retire into their harbors.

The details of the regular force which the English assembled to oppose the Armada, both by sea and land, are minutely given in a manuscript now in the British Museum (MS. Reg. 18 C. xxi.,) formerly belonging to the Royal Library. At the time when Queen Elizabeth began her preparations, her fleet did not amount to more than thirty ships, none of them near equal in size to those of the enemy. Ultimately, however, the different descriptions of vessels, large and small, which formed her navy, amounted to one hundred and eighty-one ships, manned by seventeen thousand four hundred and seventy-two sailors. The military force consisted of two armies, one for immediately opposing the enemy, under the Earl of Leicester; the other for the defence of the queen's person, commanded by Lord Hunsdon. The army appointed for the defence of the queen's person amounted to forty-five thousand three hundred and sixty-two, besides the band of pensioners, with thirty-six pieces of ordnance. Lord Leicester's army amounted to eighteen thousand four hundred and forty-nine; the total of both armies to sixty-three thousand five hundred and eleven, besides two thousand foot who were expected from the Low Countries. The forces of the Presidentship of the North remained stationary, in case any thing should be attempted on the side of Scotland; as were also the forces of the Presidentship of Wales.

The Armada was to have left Lisbon in the beginning of May, but the Marquess de Santa Cruz, who had been appointed admiral, at the moment fixed for the departure was seized with a fever, of which he died in a few days; and by a singular fatality, the Duke de Paliano, the vice-admiral, died likewise at the same time. Santa Cruz was reckoned the first naval officer in Spain; and Philip found it extremely difficult to supply his place: he at last filled it with the Duke de Medina Sidonia, a nobleman of high reputation, but entirely unacquainted with maritime affairs. Martinez de Recaldo, however, a seaman of great experience, was made vice-admiral.

In these arrangements so much time was lost, that the fleet could not leave Lisbon till the 29th of May. It had not advanced far in its voyage to Corunna, at which place it was to receive some troops and stores, when it was overtaken by a violent storm and dispersed. All the ships, however, reached Corunna, La Coruna (the Groyne, as it is called by our historians and sailors,) though considerably damaged, except four. They were repaired with the utmost diligence, the king sending messengers every day to hasten their departure; yet several weeks passed before they were in a condition to resume the voyage.

In the meantime a report was brought to England that the Armada had suffered so much by the storm as to be unfit for proceeding in the intended enterprise; and so well attested did the intelligence appear, that, at the queen's desire, Secretary Walsingham wrote to the English admiral, requiring him to lay up four of his largest ships and to discharge the seamen. Lord Howard was happily less credulous on this occasion than either Elizabeth or Walsingham, and desired that he might be allowed to retain these ships in the service, even though it should be at his own expense till more certain information were received. In order to procure it, he set sail with a brisk north wind for Corunna, intending, in case he should find the Armada so much disabled as had been reported, to complete its destruction. On the coast of Spain he received intelligence of the truth: at the same time, the wind having changed from north to south, he began to dread that the Spaniards might have sailed for England, and therefore, returned without delay to his former station at Plymouth.

Soon after his arrival Lord Howard was informed that the Armada was in sight. He immediately weighed anchor, and sailed out of the harbor, still uncertiain of the course which the enemy intended to pursue. On the next day he perceived them steering directly towards him, drawn up in the form of a crescent, which extended seven miles from one extremity to the other. Plymouth was at first supposod to be the place of destination; but it was soon apparent that the Duke de Medina adhered to the execution of the plan which had been laid down for him by the court of Madrid. This was, to steer quite through the channel till he should reach the coast of Flanders, and, after raising the blockade of the harbors of Nieuport and Dunkirk by the English and Dutch ships, to escort the Duke of Parma's army to England, as well as land the forces which were on board his own fleet. Lord Howard, instead of coming to close and unequal fight, contented himself with harrassing the Spaniards on their voyage, and with watching attentively all the advantages which might be derived from storms, cross-winds, and other accidents.

It was not long before he discerned a favorable opportunity of at-

attacking the vice-admiral, Recaldo. This he did in person; and on that occasion displayed so much dexterity in working his ship, and in loading and firing his guns, as greatly alarmed the Spaniards for the fate of their vice-admiral. From that time they kept closer to each other; notwithstanding which, the English on the same day attacked one of the largeat galeases. Other Spanish ships came up in time to her relief, but in their hurry, one of the principal galleons, which had a great part of the treasure on board, ran foul of another ship, and lost one of her masts. In consequence of this misfortune she fell behind, and was taken by Sir Francis Drake; who, on the same day, took another capital ship, which had been accidentally set on fire. Several other rencontres happened, and in all of them the English proved victorious. Their ships were lighter, and their sailors more dexterous, than those of the Spaniards. The Spanish guns were planted too high, while every shot from the English proved effectual. The Spaniards, however, still continued to advance till they came opposite to Calais, where the Duke de Medina, having ordered them to cast anchor, sent information to the duke of Parma of his arrival, and entreated him to hasten the embarkation of his forces. But the duke, though he embarked a few of his troops, informed Medina that the vessels which he had prepared were proper only for transporting the troops, but were utterly unfit for fighting; and for this reason, till the Armada was brought nearer, and the coast cleared of the Dutch ships which had blocked up the harbors of Nieuport and Dunkirk, he could not stir from his then station (at Bruges) without exposing his army to certain ruin. In compliance with this request, the Armada was ordered to advance; and it had arrived within sight of Dunkirk, between the English fleet on one hand and the Dutch on the other, when a sudden calm put a stop to its motions. In this situation the fleets remained for a whole day. About the middle of the night of August the 7th a breeze sprung up, and Lord Howard had recourse to an expedient which had been planned the day before. Having filled eight ships with pitch, sulphur, and other combustible materials, he set fire to them, and sent them before the wind against the different divisions of the Spanish fleet. The Spaniards beheld these ships in flames approaching them with great dismay: the darkness of the night increased their terror, and the panic flew entirely through the fleet. The crews of the different vessels, anxious only for their own preservation, thought of nothing but how to escape from immediate danger. Some weighed their anchors, whilst others cut their cables, and suffered their ships to drive before the wind. In this confusion many of the ships ran foul of one another, and several of them received such damage as to be rendered unfit for future use.

When daylight returned, Lord Howard had the satisfaction to perceive that his stratagem had produced the desired effect. The enemy were still in extreme disorder, and their ships widely separated and dispersed. His fleet having received a great augmentation by the ships fitted out by the nobility and gentry, as well as by those of Lord Seymour, who had left Justin de Nassau as alone sufficient to guard the coast of Flanders, and being bravely seconded by Sir Francis Drake, and all the other officers, he hastened to improve the advantage which was now presented to him, and attacked the enemy in different quarters at the same time with the utmost impetuosity and ardor. The engagement began at four in the morning of August the 8th, and lasted till six at night. The Spaniards in every rencontre displayed the most intrepid bravery; but, from the causes already mentioned, did little execution against the English, while many of their own ships were greatly damaged, and ten of the largest were either run aground, sunk, or compelled to surrender.

The principal galeas, commanded by Moncada, having Manriquez, the inspector general, on board, with three hundred galley slaves and four hundred soldiers, was driven ashore near Calais. Fifty thousand ducats were found on board of her. One of the capital ships, having been long battered by an English captain of the name of Cross, was sunk during the engagement. A few only of the crew were saved, who related that one of the officers on board having proposed to surrender, he was killed by another who was enraged at his proposal; that this other was killed by the brother of the first; and that it was in the midst of this bloody scene that the ship went to the bottom. The fate of two other of the Spanish galleons is particularly mentioned by contemporary historians, the St. Philip and St. Matthew: after an obstinate engagement with the English admiral's ship, they were obliged to run ashore on the coast of Flanders, where they were taken by the Dutch.

The Duke de Medina now not only despaired of success, but saw clearly that by a continuance of the combat he should risk the entire destruction of his fleet. The bulk of his vessels rendered them unfit not only for fighting but for navigation in the narrow seas. He therefore determined to abandon the further prosecution of his enterprise; yet even to get back to Spain was difficult: he resolved, therefore, to sail northwards, and return by making the circuit of the British isles. Lord Seymour was detached to follow in his rear, but from the bad supply of ammunition which he had received from the public offices, was deterred from renewing an attack which, in all probability, would have led to the Duke de Medina's surrender.

A dreadful storm arose, after the Spaniards had rounded the Orkneys, and the whole fleet was dispersed. Horses, mules, and baggage, were thrown overboard to lighten a few of the vessels. Some of the ships were dashed to pieces on the rocks of Norway; some sunk in the middle of the North Sea; others were thrown upon the coasts of Scotland and the Western Isles—the wreck of one being still visible, it is said, at Tobermoray, in the Isle of Mull; and more than thirty were driven by another storm, which overtook them from the west, on different parts of the coast of Ireland. Port na Spagna, on the coast of Antrim, near the Giants' Causeway, obtained its name from this circumstance. (See Trans. of Geol. Soc. vol. iii. plate 10.) Of these, some afterwards reached home in the most shattered condition, under the vice-admiral Recaldo; others were shipwrecked among the rocks and shallows; and of those which reached the shore many of the crews were barbaronsly murdered, from an apprehension, it was pretended, that in a country where there were so many disaffected Catholics it would have been dangerous to show mercy to so great a number of the enemy. Camden says, "They were slain, some of them by the wild Irish, and others put to the sword by command of the lord deputy, for he, fearing lest they would join with the Irish rebels, and seeing that Bingham, governor of Connaught, whom he had once or twice commanded to show rigor towards them as they yielded themselves, had refused to do it, sent Fowl, deputy marshal, who drew them out of their lurking holes and hiding places, and beheaded about two hundred of them."

The Duke de Medina having kept out in the open seas, escaped shipwreck; and, according to the official accounts, arrived at Santander in the Bay of Biscay about the end of September, "with noe more than sixty sayle oute of his whole fleete, and those verye much shattered."

Strype, in his Annals, reckons the Spanish loss upon the coast of England to have amounted to fifteen ships and above ten thousand men, besides seventeen ships and five thousand three hundred and ninety-four men sunk, drowned, and taken upon the coast of Ireland.

The statements, however, published at the time, apparently upon authority, say, "In July and August, ships fifteen, men four thousand seven hundred and ninety-one; sunk, &c., upon the coast of Ireland, seventeen ships, five thousand three hundred and ninety-four men:" making a total of thirty-two ships, and ten thousand one hundred and eighty-five men.

Thus ingloriously failed, from causes impossible to be foreseen, as well as from mismanagement, this expedition of the *Invincible* Armada; proving that—

> "Though man with man may strive with fearful might,
> He hath no armor to contend with Heaven."

Under Philip II., the Spanish power reached its height. He not only ruled Spain and Portugal, but the Netherlands, Naples, Sicily, and Sardinia, the duchy of Milan, the Canary and Philipine Islands, and the immense colonies in America and Africa. Such a kingdom needed powerful naval and military forces to keep it in subjection. But the people of Spain became indolent and enervated, and the wealth brought by their maritime discoveries was the great cause of the ruin of their power. Long wars exhausted their finances, and their forces were inadequate to maintain what they had subdued. Their naval operations were unimportant for many years. The gradual increase of the English, French, and Dutch maritime power destroyed that command of the sea which the Spanish and Portuguese once possessed, and the skill and intrepidity of their seamen seemed to diminish in proportion. France and England triumphed over the Spanish fleets in the wars of the eighteenth century, and compelled her to give up many of her valuable islands, in order to secure peace. These naval affairs will be mentioned in the histories of the victorious nations.

In October, 1804, the English seized the Spanish frigates which were carrying the produce of the American mines to Cadiz, for which war was declared against that power. The victory of Nelson, at Trafalgar completely annihilated the Spanish naval power. Twenty large vessels were captured by the English, and the remainder of the fleet much damaged. In the war which broke out between the Spaniards and the French republicans, the French army which had entered Spain was beaten in two battles by the emperor, and numbers of the enemy and their whole squadron at Cadiz surrendered; but these successes did not save them from being subjected to the power of the conqueror of Europe, for a time.

In 1820, preparations were made by Ferdinand VII. to suppress the American insurgents; but these preparations only served to exhaust the resources of the state; and the insurgent privateers captured Spanish vessels in sight of the coast, while the officers were literally dying of hunger. Cadiz at length obtained permission to fit out frigates, at its own expense, for the protection of its trade, which was seriously threatened with annihilation.

At present, the Spanish navy is scarcely worthy of mention. In 1802, it numbered not less than sixty-eight ships of the line, forty frigates, &c.; but, in 1834, it was reduced to two ships of the line, four frigates, and eighteen smaller men of war; and at present most of these have become disqualified for service. This being the state of facts, the once important and renowned navy departments, as they were styled, of Ferrol, Cadiz, and Carthagena have been abolished, and there is now but one naval station—Cadiz. What a miserable remnant of that power which once ruled the sea! Internal intrigues and the continual strife of factions have diverted attention from this source of greatness. The Portuguese navy is at present reduced to five frigates, four sloops-of-war, and several other vessels of smaller size. In 1783, and still, in 1808, the naval force of Portugal consisted of ten ships of the line, eighteen frigates, &c., all in good order, and, in 1825, it numbered at least five ships of the line, while at present there is none. This is a melancholy neglect, but it is owing to the same causes as the decline of the Spanish naval greatness.

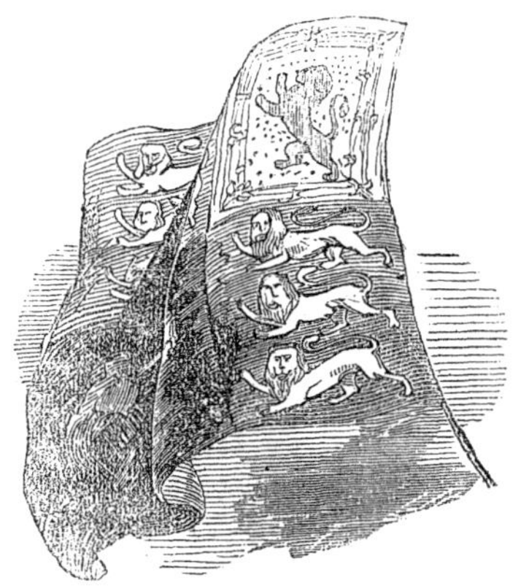

GREAT BRITAIN.

CHAPTER XXI.

THE NAVY OF GREAT BRITAIN FROM THE EARLIEST TIMES TILL THE THIRTEENTH CENTURY.

WE have now to give the history of the rise and progress of the mightiest navy of the present day. Its history involves much of that of France, and wherever it is convenient, the progress of the navy with which the British have mostly contended will be mentioned; this course will avoid repetition and shorten the chapter devoted to the history of the French navy.

The ancient name of Britain—"Clas Merden,"—"the sea-defended green spot," indicated alike her fertility and natural protection. The wants of an insular people soon taught the Britains commerce, and if vessels were not necessary for defence, they were required for fishing and to convey the product of a rude agriculture and still ruder manufacture from one part of the island to the other. If reliance is to be placed upon the voice of tradition, "the roving fleets of Britain," and the invention of a sail and rudder for ships, had been commemorated by her bards.

Though little is recorded of the vessels dignified by the name of "ships," it may be safely inferred that the largest of them was only a sort of coracle, constructed of twigs covered with ox-hides, capable of holding three or four persons, and, in summer, of passing to Ireland and across the British Channel. A small sail on a single mast, a paddle like the ancient clavus over each quarter for a rudder, and a few oars, seem to have completed the furniture of these frail barks, whose farthest voyages did not occupy more than six days.

Some improvements must have been made in the construction of British ships, before the arrival of the Romans; and the description which Cæsar gives of the vessels of the Veneti, a people settled near the entrance of the Loire, may with certainty be applied to those of this country, because it is unlikely that there should have been any material difference between them, and because the Venetan fleet had been reinforced from Britain. "Their ships," says Cæsar, "were built and fitted out in this manner: their bottoms were somewhat flatter than ours, the better to adapt them to the shallows, and to sustain without danger the ebbing of the tide. Their prows were very high and erect, as likewise their sterns, to bear the hugeness of the waves, and the violence of tempests. The hull of the vessel was entirely of oak, to stand the shocks and assaults of that tempestuous ocean. The benches of the rowers were made of strong beams about a foot in breadth, and were fastened with iron bolts an inch thick. Instead of cables, they fastened their anchors with chains of iron; and used skins and a sort of thin pliant leather for sails, either because they wanted canvass, and were ignorant of the art of making sail cloth, or, which is more probable, because they imagined that canvass sails were not so proper to bear the violence of tempests, the rage and fury of the winds, and to propel ships of that bulk and burthen. Between our fleet and vessels of such a construction the encounter was this. In agility, and a ready command of oars, we had the advantage; but in other respects, regarding the situation of the coast, and the assaults of storms, all things ran very much in their favor; for neither could our ships injure them with their prows, so great was their strength and firmness; nor could we easily throw in our darts, because of their height above us, which also was the reason that we found it extremely difficult to grapple with the enemy, and bring them to close fight. Add to all this, that when the sea began to rage, and they were forced to submit to the winds, they could both weather the storm better, and more securely trust themselves among the shallows, because they feared nothing from the rocks and cliffs upon the ebbing of the tide."

Cæsar having resolved to await the arrival of his fleet; it was no sooner seen by the Venetans than about two hundred and twenty of their ships, well fitted for service, and armed with all kinds of weapons, formed a line of battle. The Roman commanders, aware that the enemy's ships were proof against the prows of their galleys, were doubtful how to proceed; and though they erected turrets on their decks, yet, being still overtopped by the lofty sterns of the Venetans, they could not throw their darts on board them, while the missiles of the Gauls, being impelled from an eminence, fell with great violence on their men. In this emergency, the Romans had recourse to a novel artifice. They affixed scythes to long poles, and, having fastened them in the enemy's rigging, rowed off their galleys. The ropes by which the yard of each vessel was suspended were thus cut away; and, the sail falling, their vessels became unserviceable, because the Gauls depended entirely upon their sails and rigging. Thus disabled, the Venetans tried in vain to escape; a dead calm ensued, and the Romans obtained a complete victory.

On his first invasion of Britain, Cæsar, observing that his soldiers were appalled by the manner in which they were encountered, ordered some of his galleys, a kind of vessel less common with the natives, and more easily managed than the transports, to advance a little beyond those ships towards the shore, and attack them in flank. This proved of considerable service; for the surprise occasioned by the form of the galleys, the motion of the oars, and the working of the engines, caused the Britons to halt, and soon after to give way.

Finding that the ships used in the Mediterranean were not suited for northern seas, Cæsar ordered a particular class of vessels to be built for his second invasion of Britain. He directed that they should be lower than his former ones, for the convenience of loading and landing, on account of the shallowness of the British coast; and he increased their width that they might carry a greater number of horses, and at the same time be light and fleet, to which object lowness in the water greatly contributed. On his return from Italy, he found that, notwithstanding the scarcity of materials, no less than six hundred transports had been built according to the above mentioned plan, and that twenty-eight galleys were nearly ready for launching. Strabo says that these ships were of an intermediate size between Cæsar's own swift sailing vessels, and those of burthen which he had obtained in Gaul, that they might be as buoyant as possible, and yet resist the waves, and be left on the strand without injury.

The whole of the Roman fleet assembled at Portus Itius, in Gaul; except forty of the ships, which had been previously wrecked by a storm. The whole fleet reached the coast of Britain about noon; nor did any enemy appear in view. But as Cæsar afterwards understood from the prisoners, though a great army of Britons had repaired to the coast, yet terrified by the vast number of ships, which together with those of the last year's expedition, and such as had been fitted out by particular persons for their own use, amounted to upwards of eight hundred, they retired hastily from the shore, and hid themselves behind the mountains.

Though it is said in one place that eighty transports were sufficient to convey two legions, their size could not have been great; for, like galleys, they were propelled by oars; and, having lost many of those vessels in a gale which arose in the night after his arrival, Cæsar thought it safest, though a work of great labor and difficulty, to draw all his ships on shore, and inclose them within the fortification of his camp, which service occupied his army day and night for ten days.

While the Britons learnt little of marine architecture from the Romans, their conquerors are said to have adopted from the islanders both the form and the name of a peculiar kind of fast sailing boat called "pictæ." These boats, which were very long, like a modern pinnace, were smeared with wax, probably to quicken their passage through the water, and contained about twenty rowers. As their principal use was to gain intelligence, or to dart suddenly upon an enemy, it was desirable that they should remain unseen as long as possible; for which reason their sails and rigging were dyed of a light blue color, to resemble the sea, and their crews wore clothing of the same hue.

No other information exists respecting the Anglo-Saxon navy than what can be gleaned from incidental allusions to the subject in the

Saxon Chronicle and Laws; and, though these notices are neither so explicit nor so copious as could be desired, they are of much interest. Only four kinds of vessels are mentioned by name in Anglo-Saxon records, namely, "ships;" "long ships," "ceols;" "hulks," "æscs;" and "boats;" and as very few pictorial representations of British or Norman vessels before the eleventh century have been discovered, the shape, size, and other particulars of Anglo-Saxon ships can only be inferred from the annexed imperfect representation.

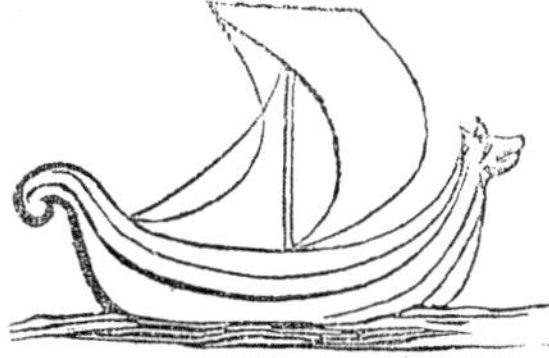

The reign of Alfred the Great was distinguished by several naval expeditions and improvements in the construction of vessels. In the year 897, the south coast was harrassed by the daring, predatory bands of the East-Anglians and Northumbrians, who arrived in a vessel called the "æsco." To oppose these "æsco," Alfred commanded "long ships" to be built. These are said to have been twice as long as the others, with sixty oars and more, and to have been swifter and steadier than any before constructed. The newly invented vessels proved very efficient in protecting the shores from the pirates, and in navigating the tempestuous seas of the north.

The naval power of England is thought to have been twice displayed in a peculiar manner by king Edgar; first, by his having been rowed on the river Dee by eight tributary kings; and secondly, by a charter granted to a Worcester church, in 964, in which he styled himself, "Edgar, king of England, and of all the kings of the islands, and of the ocean lying round Britain, and of all the nations that are included within the circuit thereof, Supreme Lord and Governor." If the monkish historians of the time are to be credited, the navy of Edgar consisted of three thousand six hundred sail, all very "stout ones," divided into three squadrons, one of which cruised on the north, another on the east, and the third on the west side of Britain. Edgar is said to have collected these squadrons every year, and taking command, to have sailed round his dominions with them in the following manner:—Immediately after Easter, he ordered the whole fleet to the west part of the island, and then, sending it back, proceeded with the western fleet to the northern coast, and thence with the northern division he returned to the eastern coast, to prevent the invasions of the pirates and to train his people to war.

It is consistent with the history of a maritime people, that one of their early sovereigns, though himself a usurper, should have owed his crown to the navy. Canute was chosen king by his fleet, and in the Witan, or Great Council at Oxford, which elected his son Harold to the throne, in 1036, it is expressly stated that almost all the thrones north of the Thames, and the "lithomen, or naval men of London," were present. The laws of the Witan, under the reign of Ethelred made many provisions respecting the navy, which shows what consideration the Saxons gave it. Until after the Norman Conquest, the little that is known of naval affairs is contained in the Saxon Chronicle.

The invasion of Julius Cæsar, with at first eighty, and the second time with six hundred ships; the arrival of the Angles in the year 448, under Hengist and Horsa, with "three long ships;" of Ella and his three sons in 447, with three ships; of the two eoldormen, Cerdic and Cyrnic, his son, in 495, with five ships; of Port and his two sons, at Portsmouth, in 501, with two ships; of the West Saxons, in 514 with three ships; of Northmen, out of Harethra-land, with three ships, in 787, the crews of which killed the king's reeve, and which are said to have been the first Danish ships that ever came to England—are the only notices of a maritime nature till the ninth century.

In 883, a Danish and Norwegian fleet arrived on the southern coast of England, and King Edward was defeated in a sanguinary battle with the crews of thirty-five ships at Charmouth. About two years after, the Danes combined with the Welsh and forming a large fleet, they again made war upon Egbert; but they were completely beaten at Hengstown, in Cornwall. The next engagement with the Danes took place in 837, at Southampton, where the eoldorman Walfheard defeated the crew of thirty-five ships; but in the same year, the Danes were successful at Port, in Dorsetshire, and, in 840, the crews of the same number, possibly of the same ships, retained the field, after a battle at Charmouth, with Ling Ethelwolf. Few, if any, of the contests appear to have taken place at sea, and the first known naval battle with the Danes occurred in 851.

The accession of the renowned Alfred, early in 871, forms as memorable an epoch in the Naval and Military, as in the Civil History of Britain. Having both previous to, and after, his accession repeatedly defeated the Danes on land, he proceeded to sea in the summer of the year 875, in command of his fleet; and, in an engagement with seven ships, captured one and put the others to flight. Alfred's next naval exploit was in 882, when he captured four Danish ships after an obstinate resistance; their crews having been "sorely distressed and wounded before they surrendered."

In 885, two sea fights occurred: in the first, sixteen Danish pirates were taken at the mouth of the Stour, and their crews slain; but, as the Saxons were returning with their booty, they met a large fleet of pirates, which defeated them. In the same year, another large fleet attacked the old Saxons; but the Frisians having joined them, the Saxons obtained, it would seem, two victories.

A successful descent of Ethelwald, with all "the ships he was able to get," and to whom the people of Essex submitted in 904; the arrival, in 918, of a large fleet from Brittany, which pillaged part of North Wales, and made the bishop of Landaff prisoner, who was afterwards ransomed by the king for forty pounds,—are the only naval events recorded in the reign of Edward the Elder, who died in 925. He was succeeded by Athelstan, who, after subduing the Anglo-Danes, became the first monarch of all England. In 933 Athelstan invaded Scotland with his fleet, as well as with his army; and his exploits at the great battle of Brumby, in 937, are described in a contemporary Saxon poem. Anlaf, the Northmen's chieftain, is said to have escaped in his vessel; and his followers "departed in their nailed barks, bloody relic of darts on dinges ocean, o'er the deep water, Dublin to seek, again Ireland, shamed in mind."

A rich and appropriate present was made to Athelstan by Harold, king of Norway, about the year 931, of a ship adorned with a golden prow, having a purple sail, and armed with a complete bulwark of golden shields. Athelstan is memorable for being, it is said, the first English sovereign who confederated with a foreign monarch against a common enemy. He entered into a treaty with Louis à Outremer, of France, by which he engaged to assist him in crushing a rebellion, by an English fleet. An English squadron, accordingly, appeared off the coast of Flanders, as soon as the rebellious forces had crossed the Rhine, and not only protected the coast towns, but invaded the territory of the enemy.

The Danish pirates were a constant cause of annoyance to the

Saxons during the reign of Ethelred, the Unready, and their number and courage struck terror into the king's troops, so that they could not be induced to stand before the invaders. In the year 1000, better fortune attended Ethelred in his contests with the Danes, and after some unsuccessful attacks they were glad to accept an offer of peace. No sooner had a truce been agreed to, than Ethelred commanded that every Dane in his dominions should be put to death; and the massacre took place accordingly, on the 13th of November, 1002. This horrible slaughter is said to have been caused by the discovery of a conspiracy to murder the king and the Witan, and take possession of the kingdom.

At last the numerous and devastating incursions of the Danes roused Ethelred to exertion. Great efforts were made to form a navy, and for that purpose a tax was levied upon all. In 1009, these ships were ready, and "there were so many of them as never before had been among the English nation in any king's days."

It has been calculated that the tax must have produced eight hundred ships, and armed thirty thousand men. This numerous fleet was directed to rendezvous at Sandwich, to be in readiness to defend the coast: but Ethelred's usual ill fortune attended him; or, as it is forcibly expressed, "but still we had not the good fortune, nor the worthiness, that the ship force could be of any use to this land, any more than it oft before had been."

Twenty of Ethelred's ships were enticed away by Wulfnoth, a South Saxon, father of the celebrated eorl Godwin; and, when eighty ships under Brihtric were sent in pursuit of him, they were dispersed by a gale of wind, of unprecedented violence, and many of them driven ashore. Wulfnoth, taking advantage of this circumstance, hastened to attack the distressed vessels, and bunt the whole of them. Intelligence of this event having reached the king, who was with the other part of his fleet at Sandwich, the crews were struck with despair; and Ethelred, his nobility, and council having all deserted the ships, the sailors rowed them back to London, "and they let the whole nation's toil thus lightly pass away."

The naval operations during the reign of Canute the Great and Edmund Ironside are unimportant, and the records of them very scanty. Edward the Confessor ascended the throne in 1041, and in 1044, he went to Sandwich with eighty-five ships. In the next year he collected as large a fleet at that port as had ever been seen in England, in consequence of Magnus, king of Norway, having threatened to invade his country. The Norwegian king, however, did not see fit to carry out his intention. The Saxon king put to sea in his ships to operate against the pirates; but it does not appear that any action took place. In the dissentions of the Saxon eorls, in the time of the Confessor, the navy was a favorite resort both for the security it afforded, if in flight, and the facility of moving if becoming the assailant. The celebrated eorl Godwin and his son Harold, afterwards king, were frequently in rebellion against the king, and at one time, by their powerful naval force, threatened to obtain the mastery; but an arrangement was effected with them.

Early in 1066, eorl Tostig, with a large fleet appeared off the Isle of Wight, and levied money and provisions. He then went into the Humber with sixty ships, whence he was driven by the land forces of eorl Edwin; and being forsaken by the butsecarls, he proceeded to Scotland with only twelve vessels. Meeting the king of Norway with three hundred ships, Tostig placed himself under his command, or, as is said, "became his man;" and with their combined force sailed up the Humber to York, where they defeated the English under the eorls Edwin and Morcar. The Northmen were, however, soon after completely routed, their leaders were slain, and driven to their ships by king Harold, after a long and sanguinary battle at Stamford Bridge, in Yorkshire on the 25th of September, in which Harold was wounded. When "the Normen were put to flight, the English from behind hotly smote them, until they came, some to their ships, some were drowned, and some also were burned; and thus in divers ways they perished, so that there were few left: and the English had possession of the place of carnage."

In the spring of that year, the largest fleet and army ever seen in England were assembled at Sandwich to resist the invasion with which England was threatened by the Duke of Normandy. Harold continued at Sandwich for some time; but either from the belief that the ships would not be wanted, or, as the annalist says, because their crews refused to serve after the feast of the Nativity of our Lady, the 8th of September, when their provisions were exhausted, the king allowed them to return to their homes; and the ships were sent to London, many being lost on their passage.

When William, Duke of Normandy, resolved upon asserting his

right to the crown of England, by invading the island, his chief barons and other subjects opposed the scheme; but the arrival of the pope's bull, excommunicating Harold, and sanctioning the claim of William, turned reluctance and indifference into enthusiasm, and the Normans entered warmly into the design. The baron Fitz-Osbert offered sixty ships filled with soldiers, the bishop Odo forty, the bishop of le Mano thirty, with crews and pilots and all the rest of the Norman barons, a number of ships proportioned to their revenues. Money, armor, stores, provisions, and all other necessaries for the enterprise were freely bestowed. England appeared the modern Land of Promise.

William appointed the mouth of the Dive, a small river between the Seine and the Orne, as the place of general rendezvous for his ships and army; and, after being kept there nearly a month by contrary winds, his fleet anchored off Saint Valery, near Dieppe. Heavy rain and bad weather, during which several vessels with their crews had foundered, greatly depressed the spirits of the troops and seamen; and they inferred from these untoward events, and the prevalence of a foul wind, that God was offended with the design, and had thus manifested his displeasure. Fearful that they might abandon the enterprise, William, himself a prey to anxiety, and not altogether free from the superstition of his followers, stimulated their frames by strong liquors, while he fortified their minds by religious associations.

Writers differ much as to the number of the Norman vessels, and of the soldiers they contained. Four hundred ships with large masts and sails, and more than a thousand transport boats, and sixty thousand troops, is the estimate of the learned historian of the event; while other authorities rate the fleet from six hundred and ninety-six to one thousand, but one writer says there were three thousand which carried sails. The great variation in these accounts may probably be attributed to some writers having included, while others omitted, in their enumeration, the smaller transports and boats. An approximation to accuracy might be obtained if the exact number of the soldiers were known; but, as this is also doubtful, there are no means of arriving at the truth on either point. However greatly William's forces may have been overrated, it is certain that he invaded England with a large army both of cavalry and infantry; and, as it made only one passage, the small vessels of which it consisted must have been very numerous.

SHIP OF WILLIAM THE CONQUEROR.

It appears that the Conqueror's ship was distinguished by having at its mast head a sort of square, white banner charged with a gold cross within a blue border, surmounted by another cross of gold, which is supposed to have been the gonfanon given to him by the pope; but it may have been his usual ensign. His ship is larger than any of the others, and contains ten men. The prow is ornamented with a lion's head; and at the stern is the effigy of a boy blowing a horn, and holding in his left hand a gonfanon. It is remarkable that in the list of William's fleet before referred to, this ornament should be expressly mentioned; and the ship itself is there said to have been the gift of his consort, and called "Mora," which is supposed to mean "mansion," or "habitation."

Two other ships of the Conqueror's fleet are thus represented; and they differ only from that of the Duke, by being smaller, by the sails being divided into horizontal compartments, by their being laden with horses, by the absence of any ornament at the stern, and in one of them, also at the prow, and by there being no shields round the gunwales.

As the Bayeux tapestry affords the best, if not the only contemporary representation of ships, it is desirable to describe all the naval subjects that occur in it. The first vessel introduced is that in which Harold sailed for Normandy, in 1065. He appears in a large boat, with seven men and one mast, but without a sail: it is being pushed off from the shore with oars, and has an anchor over the bows. A

THE HORSE BOATS.

smaller boat is near it. He then appears in a ship with one mast, and a very large green sail, going before the wind, containing fourteen men, with shields round the gunwales; and one shield is suspended over the bows. He is next seen landing from another representation of his ship, the sail of which is of four cloths, party colored, and the prow and stern are ornamented with lions' heads. A boy is at the mast head, apparently to look out; two men are pulling, and a man holds an anchor in his hand over the bow. Harold is then seen landing from a boat at anchor, and is arrested by Guy, Count of Poitou. The ship in which Harold returns to England has no peculiarity from the others; but the vessel which brings a messenger to inform William of the death of Edward the Confessor, and Harold's accession, has only four men, one of whom carries out in his hand a small anchor without a stock.

Preparations for the invasion are shown by men hewing timber, and cutting it into planks for ship building. The ships are afterwards launched, and the process is remarkable. Two ropes being affixed to their bows, and drawn through a block on a post; the vessels are pulled by several men to the water. The Conqueror's fleet is represented as consisting of twelve ships of different sizes; and some have from three to eight horses on board. On reaching England, the mast was struck by being lowered forwards, and the horses were landed by leaping over the gunwale; which prove that the vessels were of very small size, and low in the water. All the ships are marked horizontally by four or more lines, perhaps to represent plank; and these divisions are always differently colored,—blue, yellow, red; blue, yellow, red, or blue, yellow; or blue and yellow; the Conqueror's vessel being painted alternately, brown and blue.

William's ship sailed much faster than the rest, and was so far ahead of the fleet, that at daybreak the next morning none of the others could be seen. He, therefore, sent a sailor to the mast head to look for them: "I see nothing but sea and sky," he exclaimed; and the ship was immediately brought to an anchor. A good breakfast and spiced wines having been served, the man was again sent to look out, when he descried four vessels; and, ascending the mast for a third time, "I see," he said, "a forest of masts and sails." As soon as the body of the fleet had come up, William weighed, and his army landed without any resistance, at Pevensey, near Hastings, on the 28th of September, 1066. When the army had disembarked, he ordered his ships to be drawn on shore and destroyed.

Harold was then at York, recovering from a wound. As soon as he heard of the arrival of the Normans, he conducted his forces southward, and though the English army was greatly inferior in numbers to the enemy, he nobly refused to compromise his rights. The battle of Hastings, fought on the 14th of October, gave a new dynasty to England. Harold died like a hero in the midst of the fight. When William had subdued England, he found himself entirely without the means of defending her shores. The greater part of the navy had been carried to Ireland by Godwin and Edmund, the sons of Harold, and William had destroyed the vessels which conveyed his forces across the Channel.

In the five years which elapsed after his accession, William succeeded in supplying the first necessity of a maritime nation, by forming a navy. In 1071 he sent a naval as well as a land force against the rebellious earl Morkar; and in the following year he invaded Scotland both by sea and land, when Malcolm was compelled to make peace, give hostages, and "become his man." In 1073, king William crossed the Channel with an army, and subdued the province of Maine.

The navy received much attention during the reign of Henry the Second, who ascended the throne in 1154. When England was menaced with an invasion, in 1161, by the Count of Boulogne and

Flanders, whose fleet was said to consist of six hundred ships, king Henry was abroad, engaged in a war with France; but Richard de Lucy, the justiciary, collected so large a force on the coast, that the attempt was abandoned. Early in March, 1170, while the king was crossing the Channel from Normandy, so great a storm arose in the middle of the night, that his fleet was dispersed and much damaged. With great difficulty Henry's ship reached Portsmouth, but one of the others, in which his physician, and Henry de Agnellis, a distinguished baron, with his two sons, and some other persons of the royal household, had embarked, foundered. It is said, that the passengers and crew amounted to four hundred; but this statement is either one of the usual exaggerations of the chroniclers wherever they mention numbers, or the ships of the twelfth century were at least four times larger than they are supposed to have been.

Richard the First had taken the cross before his accession; and soon after that event, he agreed with Philip of France that they should proceed together to the Holy Land. Great preparations were made throughout England to provide a fleet and an army for that purpose; and at the beginning of December, 1189, numerous ships were assembled at Dover from all parts of England to convey the king and his followers across the Channel. On the 11th of that month he embarked for Calais, and joined the French monarch at Rheims, when a treaty of friendship and assistance was entered into between the two sovereigns. Richard soon after appointed "justices," or admirals, and issued the first regular code for the government of the fleet. The code consisted of thirty-seven articles, and received the appellation of the Laws of Oleron.

In the mean time a fleet had been collected at Dartmouth from all parts of England, Normandy, Poitou, Brittany, and Aquitaine, in which such of the crusaders as had not accompanied the king by land, and the engines, stores, and other materiel for the army, were embarked. These ships were to join Richard at Marseilles; and the fact is deserving of particular attention, because it is the earliest evidence yet discovered of English vessels having been sent on so distant a voyage. Part, if not all of the ships, sailed from Dartmouth towards the end of April, 1190; but, owing probably to the unfitness of vessels so constructed and rigged to pass the Atlantic ocean, many disasters befel them. For five days the wind continued fair; but on

Ascension day, the 3d of May, before they had crossed the Bay of Biscay, it changed, and blew so violently that the ships were dispersed.

Philip of France had arrived a few days before; and while he greeted his royal ally with every ostensible mark of confidence, he is supposed to have been secretly envious of his magnificent appearance. The late period of the year prevented Richard from proceeding immediately to the Holy Land, and the two kings with their followers, wintered at Messina. Many of the galleys of the English fleet were so much injured by a species of worm called "beom," that it was necessary to careen and repair them.

On the 30th of March, 1191, the French monarch sailed for Palestine; and information being brought to Richard that his mother, the queen dowager of England, and his betrothed bride, Berengaria of Navarre, had arrived at Reggio, on the opposite coast, he crossed the Faro, and returned with the ladies to Messina on the day of Philip's departure. About the same time the fleet was reinforced by thirty busses, bringing soldiers and provisions from England. Either from its being the season of Lent, or from Richard's unwillingness to delay his voyage, he did not solemnize his nuptials at Messina. Every preparation being made, and the troops and stores embarked, he entrusted Berengaria to the care of his sister Queen Joan, and placed them on board a large buss, or dromon, commanded by Sir Stephen de Turnham, the commander of the fleet. On the morning of Wednesday the 10th of April, all the large ships put to sea; and as soon as the king had dined, he followed them down the Faro with the whole of his galleys. The English fleet has been variously described; but most writers agree in stating, that it consisted of thirteen dromons, or very large busses, one hundred and fifty smaller busses, fifty-three well armed galleys, with several galleases, and other light vessels. The busses and ships were of great burthen, wonderful fleetness, and strongly and compactly built. Each of the large ships carried, besides her crew, forty valuable horses, with the necessary armor, and the same number of foot soldiers. The money for the expedition was distributed among the ships and busses in case of accident, and they were stored with provisions of all kinds for one year.

On Thursday, the 11th of April, when off Etna, a calm obliged them to anchor; but a light and favorable breeze springing up the next day, Good Friday, they weighed and made some progress. In the night they were again becalmed; and on Saturday the 13th, the fleet experienced so heavy a gale from the southward, that the passengers and crews alike were sea sick and frightened; and the ships becoming ungovernable, many of them were dispersed. "Despairing," says the historian, "of all human aid, they trusted to God alone." During the whole storm, Richard remained cool and collected, encouraging all around him by his speeches and example. Towards evening the gale abated, and the king's ship, which was indicated during the night by a light at the masthead, brought to, that the scattered vessels might gather around her. "In truth," says Vinesauf, "the king watched and looked after his fleet as a hen doth over her chickens." All, except twenty-five vessels, having appeared in the morning, they proceeded with a fair wind to the island of Crete, where the king anchored on the 17th of April.

Among the missing vessels was the ship in which his sister and bride had taken their passage; but the next day, seeing nothing of those vessels, he continued his voyage. A favorable breeze impelled the fleet "with bellying sails and masts slightly bowed, not unlike a flight of birds; and the following morning they found themselves close to Rhodes." It seems that, either from having missed the port, or from being unacquainted with the coast, the vessels lay to, off that island until the 22d, when Richard landed, and, being taken ill, continued there for some days. Naturally anxious to learn what had become of his sister and Berengaria, he sent galleys in all directions to look for them, and for the other missing vessels. Meanwhile the queen's ship, with several others, had reached Cyprus, which was then in the hands of Isaac Comnenus, styling himself emperor. When the vessel with the two queens on board entered the bay of Lymesol, Isaac invited the ladies to land; but they declined, saying they only wished to know if the king had passed. The emperor then armed four galleys; and the commander of the English ship, suspecting his intentions, immediately weighed and stood out to sea.

On the 6th of May, Richard appeared off the harbor of Lymesol, where he found the ship with his sister and bride on board, and was informed of the manner in which they had been treated by Isaac, and the fate of his three ships and their crews. Indignant at Isaac's conduct, he immediately sent two of his knights to demand satisfaction.

RICHARD CŒUR DE LION CAPTURING THE CITY OF LIMESOL.

The emperor pretended to be highly displeased, and his offensive answer, "Ptruht Sire, I have nothing to do with the king," so excited Richard's displeasure, that he instantly determined to attack the town. Having commanded his people to arm, Richard leapt from his ship into a boat, and was followed by a host of knights and soldiers, in galleys and smaller vessels. Isaac opposed them with a large body of his "griffons," and barricaded the town with doors and windows of houses, old galleys, casks, and other things; but nothing could resist the impetuous valor of the crusaders. Cœur de Lion himself struck the first blow: Lymesol soon fell into their hands; and the emperor, completely defeated, took refuge in the mountains. The next day, the ship with the two queens, and the rest of the fleet, anchored in the port.

The emperor Isaac was compelled to bind himself to serve under Richard, in Palestine, and to surrender all his castles, and pay twenty thousand marks in gold. But he broke the treaty, a few hours after it was made. Richard then sent an army in pursuit of him, and so completely was he defeated that he came and voluntarily submitted himself to the discretion of the conqueror. Richard ordered him to be placed in silver chains, and confined in a castle in Palestine. Cyprus was, therefore, the first conquest in a distant sea made by the English armaments.

The king returned to Lymesol, and soon afterwards his fleet was reinforced. On the 5th of June, he embarked, and with all his galleys, proceeded to the scene of his future glory. Before he reached Palestine, however, he became the hero of a naval battle. On the 7th, when near Baruth, an immense ship was discovered ahead. This ship is described as having three tall, tapering masts, and being elegantly painted. She is said to have had on board, upwards of one thousand five hundred men, selected Turks, for the defence of Acre.

Richard ordered a galley to be sent alongside of the Turkish vessel in order to ascertain her real character; but the Turks almost destroyed her crew with their arrows and Greek fire. Richard instantly led his vessels to the attack. An obstinate conflict ensued, in which the Turks had the advantage, on account of the height of their ship. But one resource remained to the English king. He ordered the vessels of his fleet to strive to pierce the sides of the enemy's vessel with their iron prows. This was executed, and the Turkish vessel sank, and all her crew, except fifty-five were either drowned or slaughtered. Great importance was attached to the capture of this great ship, as, if it had arrived at Acre, the city never would have been taken by the crusaders.

King Richard landed at Acre on the 10th of June, and was received with great enthusiasm by his companions in arms who were besieging the town. Though the English galleys were of great use to the army during the remainder of the crusade, nothing of a strictly naval character took place. Having concluded a truce with Saladin, and being greatly reduced by illness, king Richard determined in September, 1192, to return to Europe. Early in October, the queens Berengaria and Joan sailed from Palestine for Sicily, and on the 8th of that month, Richard took his departure in a larges buss; but owing to contrary winds, he was nearly a month at sea before reaching the island of Corfu. Procuring three galleys on the coast of Romania, he crossed over in a small vessel, and agreed with the masters of the galleys to convey him and his suite to Ragura and Tara. To avoid being recognised, he wore his beard and hair like those of a pilgrim. But his expenditure and retinue being inconsistent with his appearance, his rank was suspected.

Near Vienna, he was arrested by order of the Duke of Austria, and kept in confinement a year and five months. Towards the close of 1193, the king was ransomed and returned to England. No important naval transactions occurred during the remainder of his reign.

KING JOHN'S FLEET UNDER THE EARL OF SALISBURY, SAILING TO THE PORT OF DAMME.

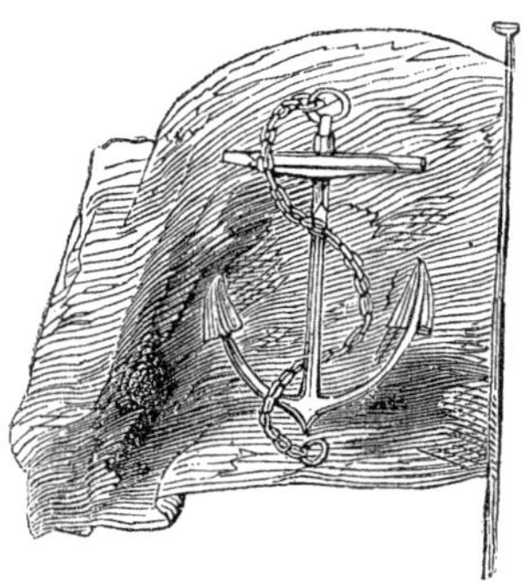

CHAPTER XXII.

FROM 1200 TILL THE DEATH OF EDWARD THE SECOND, IN 1326.

KING John is considered by some as the founder of the British Royal Navy. He made a close approach to a regular naval establishment; and the right of England to the sovereignty of the narrow seas is said to have been solemnly asserted and enforced. Having established himself on the throne, and raised an army, he collected ships enough to convey it to Normandy, and embarked at Shoreham, for Dieppe, about the middle of June. He remained abroad until the 27th of February in the following year, when he arrived at Portsmouth, from Harfleur.

Early in 1213, the pope, after a long controversy with king John, absolved his subjects from their allegiance, and exhorted all Christian princes and barons to unite in dethroning him. The king of France, who was constantly upon the watch for a chance to gratify his ambition, eagerly seized upon this pretence, and made extensive preparations to invade England. John took vigorous measures for the defence of his dominions. By the middle of April he had assembled a numerous fleet and a large army at Dover. In the meantime, a quarrel arose between the king of France and the Count of Flanders, because the latter refused to support Philip in his attempt upon England. The French monarch, to punish the count, entered Flanders with his whole army, and all the ships which were in the Seine, for the purpose of conveying the French troops to England, were sent to the port of Damme. Though the harbor was of "wonderful size," it could not contain all the French ships, which are said to have amounted to seventeen hundred sail; so that many of them anchored on the coast. The Count of Flanders naturally called upon King John for assistance, who immediately ordered his fleet, consisting of five hundred vessels, and having on board seven hundred knights, to proceed to Damme under the command of the Earl of Salisbury, the Duke of Holland, and the Count of Boulogne. Salisbury, greatly surprised to find the port full, and the coast covered with vessels, sent to reconnoitre the strange fleet; and learned that they were French, and that the greater part of their crews had landed and gone inland to plunder. He instantly attacked the ships, and three hundred vessels laden with corn, wine, and arms fell into his hands. The cables of the prizes were cut, and, the wind being off the land, they were soon on their passage to England. About a hundred or more of the others, which were either drawn upon the strand or driven upon the shore, were burnt, and part of their cargoes brought away. Not satisfied with his success, Salisbury and his brave companions landed, and pursued the French for some distance; but King Philip sent so large a force against them that he was compelled to retreat, and hastily embarked. The biographer of that monarch gives a different account of this affair. He says, that, except a few knights and soldiers who were left to protect the ships, all the French forces were besieging Ghent when the English fleet appeared off Damme; that Salisbury and his soldiers rushed into small boats and took possession of the vessels outside the port, and the next day attacked the ships in the harbor as well as the town; that the king quitted Ghent, and drove the English to their ships, slaying and drowning nearly two thousand, and making many prisoners. Important as the capture of the French fleet must have been, since it induced Philip to burn the remainder of his ships and to quit Flanders, this event cannot be considered to have added much to the naval renown of England, and it is chiefly memorable for having been the first engagement between the ships of France and England.

During the summer of 1216, the straits of Dover and other parts of the English channel, appear to have been filled with the vessels of Prince Louis, of France, under the command of the celebrated Eustace, the Monk; for when the pope's legate demanded permission of king Philip to go to England, he willingly promised him protection throughout his own dominions; but he added, "If you should happen to fall into the hands of Eustace, the Monk, or any other of Louis's men, who infest the sea, do not impute it to me should any harm befall you."

Disgusted with the conduct of their faithless sovereign, the English barons offered the crown to Louis, the eldest son of the king of France, who eagerly accepted the proposal. A fleet of six hundred ships and eighty cogs having been collected at Calais, Gravelines, and Whitsand, by Eustace, the Monk, for this service, the prince embarked with a considerable force; but, owing to a strong northeast wind, the ships were dispersed, and Louis was obliged, in his single vessel, to anchor at Stonar, in the isle of Thanet, on the 21st of May. Meeting with no resistance, Louis proceeded with his ships to Sandwich; and after subduing the whole of Kent, except Dover castle, he joined the confederated barons at London.

King John did not long survive this formidable attempt to deprive him of his crown, as he died at Newark on the 19th of October, in the same year.

When Henry the Third ascended the throne, he was but ten years of age; his capital and part of his dominions were in the hands of the invading prince, and many of his most powerful subjects adhered to the cause of his enemies. But never were such difficulties surmounted more rapidly than these. The earl of Pembroke, the guardian of the kingdom, defeated and destroyed the hopes of Prince Louis, and of the English barons who were his confederates. Soon after their discomfiture, the French fleet, which was coming to their assistance, was completely defeated; an event of the greatest interest; for it was the first regular sea fight, worthy of the name, between the ships of England and France, and the precursor of that series of victories which crowned the navy of Britain with glory.

As soon as the news of Louis's defeat at Lincoln reached France, Robert de Courtenay collected an army for his assistance, which embarked at Calais, in a fleet of eighty ships, besides galleys and smaller vessels, under the command of the famous Eustace, the Monk; and on the 24th of August they put to sea, intending to proceed up the Thames to London.

Hubert de Burgh, the king's justiciary and Governor of Dover castle, impressed with the necessity of preventing this formidable force from landing, immediately took measures for the purpose. Addressing the bishop of Winchester, the marshal, and other great personages, he said, "If these people land, England is lost; let us, therefore, boldly meet them, for God is with us, and they are excommunicated." His ardor was not, however, shared by his audience, who replied, "We are not sea soldiers, nor pirates, nor fishermen: go thou and die!" Not discouraged by this answer, De Burgh sent for his chaplain, and having hastily taken the sacrament, he, with an emphatic oath, thus enjoined the garrison to defend their post: "Ye shall suffer me to be hanged before ye surrender the castle, for it is the key of England." Affected to tears by the exhortation, and still more by the fate that seemed to await their chief, they pledged themselves to obey his commands.

Sixteen large and well armed ships, manned with skilful seamen belonging to the Cinque Ports, and about twenty smaller vessels, formed the English squadron. Assembling some of the bravest of his knights, among whom were Sir Philip d'Albini, Sir Henry de Turberville, Sir Richard Suard, and Sir Richard, a natural son of King John, De Burgh led them to the ships, and immediately put to sea.

The enemy were at some distance from Calais when the English sailed, but all the accounts of the engagement are defective in nautical details, while the few that do occur are very obscurely expressed. It appears that the wind was southerly, blowing fresh; and that the French were going large, steering to round the North Foreland, little expecting any opposition. The English squadron, instead of directly appraching the enemy, kept their wind as if going to Calais; which made Eustace, the French commander, exclaim, "I know that those wretches think to invade Calais like thieves, but that is useless, for it is well defended." As soon as the English had gained the wind of the French fleet, they bore down in the most gallant manner upon the enemy's rear; and the moment they came close to the sterns of the French ships, they threw grapnels into them, and, thus fastening the vessels together, prevented the enemy from escaping;—an early instance of that love of close fighting for which English sailors have ever since been distinguished.

The action commenced by the crossbow men and archers, under Sir Philip d'Albini, pouring volleys of arrows into the enemy's ships with deadly effect; and, to increase their dismay, the English threw unslaked lime, reduced to a fine powder, on board their opponents, which being blown by the wind into their eyes, completely blinded them. The English then rushed on board; and cutting away the rigging and haulyards with axes, the sails fell over the French, to use the expression of the chronicler, "like a net upon ensnared small birds." Thus hampered, the enemy could make but a feeble resistance; and, after an immense slaughter, were completely defeated.

Besides, Robert de Courtenay, William de Baris, Ralph de Tornellis, and other distinguished persons, the English captured one hundred and twenty-five knights, and more than a thousand soldiers of inferior rank. The loss sustained by the English is no where mentioned, but it does not appear to have been great The action was in all points of view glorious to the skill and valor of the victors.

Prince Louis succeeded to the throne of France, in July, 1223, and being called upon by the English government to fulfil his promise to restore Normandy, Maine, and Anjou, he peremptorily refused to do so, entered Poitou and then took possession of Rochelle, and other towns. It was therefore determined to send a considerable force to Poitou, under the Earl of Salisbury, and Prince Richard, the king's brother, who was soon after created Earl of Cornwall and Count of Poitou. Warlike preparations were accordingly made, and vessels ordered to be provided for the conveyance of troops to France. The fleet assembled at Portsmouth, in May, 1226, but, in consequence of the conclusion of an armistice for twelve months, between France and England, it did not assume the offensive.

Towards the close of 1241, Henry, instigated by his mother, who had married the Count de la Marche, determined to assist the count in his quarrel with the French monarch; and on the return of the Earl of Cornwall from the Holy Land, in January 1242, it was agreed that the king should conduct an army into Poitou in person. Great preparations were made for the expedition. Henry went to Portsmouth on the 21st of April. Having completed his arrangements and taking with him thirty casks filled with money, the king sailed from Portsmouth on the 10th of May, accompanied by the queen, his brother, the Earl of Cornwall, seven other earls, and three hundred knights; but the wind failing, the fleet was obliged to anchor again. On the next day, however, they put to sea, and before the 16th, arrived at St. Matthew, in Brittany, from whence they sailed to Rions at the mouth of the Gironde, where the king landed and proceeded immediately to the city of Pons. Though the French monarch ordered twenty-four well armed galleys to be at Rochelle to resist the invasion, they offered no opposition to the English fleet.

Henry having requested military and pecuniary assistance, reinforcements and supplies were sent to Gascony, under the direction of the Cinque Ports. The nobility of England and Ireland, ashamed to remain idle at home while their sovereign was waging war abroad, wished to join the king, and so many of them embarked for the purpose, that their ships formed a large naval force. As soon as the French sailors and pirates, who were guarding the opposite coast, heard of the expedition, they armed and fitted out ships and galleys, and put to sea to attack the English; but, before the fleets met, both were completely dispersed by a sudden storm. Driven before the wind in great confusion, the crews scarcely knew friends from foes, and consulted only their own safety. The French ships being, however, nearer to their own shore, and the wind more favorable for them, they succeeded in getting into harbor; while the English and Irish ships, "fearing alike," says the honest historian, "the elements and the French, fled in shame, in fear, and bitterness of heart, they knew not where, and came to remote and unknown coasts." So great were the sufferings of those on board, that the Abbot of Evesham, Sir Richard de Burgh, and many others never recovered their health, and, unused to a foreign climate, languished until they died; whence it may be inferred that part of the fleet was driven on the coast of Spain or Portugal. This event was severely felt by the king; and, to revenge himself, he issued orders to the Cinque Ports to commit every possible injury upon the French at sea, as well to merchant ships as to vessels of war. Not satisfied with obeying these commands, the sailors of the Cinque Ports acted with such ferocity, that they "slew and plundered like pirates," as well their own countrymen, returning from pilgrimages, as foreigners, "sparing neither friends nor neighbors, kith nor kin."

The French adopted vigorous and successful measures to protect their shores. After many shameful defeats, the wardens of the Cinque Ports were obliged to apply to the Archbishop of York for assistance; and their statements present a deplorable picture of the English navy. They said, they had been thrice repulsed by the enemy with ships, men, and goods, especially by the inhabitants of Calais that neither the ships of the Cinque Ports, nor even the whole English fleet, were capable of resisting the fleet which the French had prepared; and they entreated the archbishop to consult with the king's council on the imminent danger that threatened the country. They added, that the Count of Brittany, with all the shipping of Brittany and Poitou, well armed and equipped, was waiting to intercept vessels passing between England and the king; that, to increase their distress, the Normans and sailors of Whitsand and Calais scarcely permitted them to fish; that the pirates who guarded the high sea with their galleys would not suffer even pilgrims to return home; and that such was the position of the king, that Bordeaux might be considered his prison, unless money and ships were immediately dispatched to him. At the time when this representation was made to the Archbishop of York, he could hardly venture to send the king's ships of burthen to him; and he, therefore, earnestly advised Henry to settle his affairs there, and hasten to England. The king adopted this advice. He embarked about the end of August, 1243, and landed at Portsmouth on the 25th of September.

The introduction of the mariner's compass is one of the most remarkable events of the thirteenth century. It at once gave the navigator more confidence in making long voyages, and prevented the accidents so common before, when the polar star was not visible.

The reign of Edward the First, who ascended the throne in 1273, was not remarkable for maritime events. A great and enterprising prince, his abilities found sufficient employment at home. Alfonso, king of Castile and Leon, having undertaken an expedition against the Saracens, he sent to request the assistance of his brother-in-law, the king of England. Edward accordingly ordered the authorities of Bayonne to build and equip twelve ships and twenty-four galleys for that purpose. In the conquest of Wales, which was affected during this reign, the fleets of England performed considerable services, in the conveyance of troops and the dispersion of the Welsh pirates.

The first naval transaction of any moment in this reign arose out of a quarrel between two common sailors, and led to the most important consequences. In 1293, two of the crew of an English ship, in some port of Normandy, landed to get water, and meeting with several Norman sailors, a dispute ensued which produced blows on both sides. One of the Englishmen was slain, and the other fled to his ship, followed by twenty of the Normans. The vessel immediately put to sea and was pursued by many of the Norman ships. Shortly afterwards, the French squadron fell in with six English ships, which they attacked, and having captured two of them, they hung their crews, together with some dogs, to the yards of the vessels. They then cruised in the Channel for some time, committing such outrages, that they "made no distinction between an Englishman and a dog." It was never in the nature of English sailors to submit to such infamous treatment; and without waiting for the approval or assistance of their sovereign, they determined to be revenged.

The four ships that had escaped were joined by many others from the Cinque Ports, and eagerly sought the enemy; but not finding them at sea, they entered the Seine, where they were discovered at anchor, and instantly attacked. A sanguinary conflict took place, which terminated in the defeat of the French and the loss of six of their ships. Several other partial engagements occurred, attended "by great slaughter on both sides, shipwreck, and rapine—both thirsting for blood;" but no particulars are mentioned of any of these affairs. It was at length determined to try their strength in a pitched battle, on the 14th of April, at a spot mid-channel between England and France, indicated by anchoring a large and empty ship. The English enlisted the Irish and Dutch sailors in their cause, while the Normans had obtained the assistance of the French, Flemish, and Genoese.

On the appointed day the two fleets, well armed, met at the rendezvous. The weather was very tempestuous: hail and snow fell heavily, accompanied by a high wind; and the chroniclers observe, that the courage of the respective combatants was as unequal as the elements. The English fleet does not appear to have exceeded sixty ships, while their opponents had more than two hundred. After a desperate conflict, "Almighty God," say Knyghton and Hemingford, "was pleased to give the victory to our side:" and they add, with their usual exaggeration, that "many thousands perished by the sword, beside those who went down in their ships, who were almost countless. Our men brought away about two hundred and forty ships laden with spoil."

Though the French appear to have been the aggressors, Philip demanded redress, and summoned Edward to appear before him as his vassal. Edward refused, and Philip took possession of Gascony. This the English king resolved to recover by force of arms. In 1294, effectual measures were taken to maintain the naval power of England. The king divided his fleet into three large squadrons, and placed the ships of Yarmouth and the adjacent ports, which amounted to fifty-three sail, under the command of Sir John De Botetourt; those at Portsmouth, under Sir William de Leybourne; and those of the western ports and Ireland, under a good knight of that country, called Ormond. After an efficient number of vessels were collected at Portsmouth, the army, which consisted of five hundred men at arms and twenty thousand foot soldiers, sailed about the first of August, but the ships having been dispersed off the coast of Cornwall by contrary winds, they were obliged to put into Plymouth, and did not quit that port until the early part of October. No naval battle took place during this expedition.

The first instance of the grant of what are called "Letters of Marque and Reprisal," is supposed to have occurred in 1295. Bernard d'Ongressill, a merchant of Bayonne, then part of the dominions of the king of England, was the owner of a ship belonging to that place, called the "St. Mary," laden with almonds, raisins, and figs, which vessel, while on her passage from Barbary to England, was driven by stress of weather into Lagos, in Portugal. When at anchor, some armed Portuguese came from Lisbon, boarded the vessel, robbed d'Ongressill and the crew, and took the ship and cargo to that city. The king of Portugal having received one-tenth part of the spoil, the remainder was divided among the robbers. By this proceeding, d'Ongressill said he had lost seven hundred pounds; and he prayed Sir John of Brittany, then lieutenant of Gascony, to grant him letters of marque—literally, "license of marking the men, and subjects of the king of Portugal, especially those of Lisbon, and their goods, by land and sea," until he had obtained compensation. Accordingly, in June, 1295, the king's lieutenant granted d'Ongressill, his heirs, successors, and descendants, authority for five years to "mark, retain, and appropriate," the people of Portugal, and especially those of Lisbon, and their goods, wheresoever they might be found, until he had obtained satisfaction. This license was confirmed by the king on the 3d of October, with the condition, that it should cease as soon as restitution had been made.

In 1297, Edward resolved to assist the Count of Flanders against the king of France. He embarked in a cog, called after himself, the "Edward," at Winchelsea, on the 22d of August. The king took with him a large fleet, and an army consisting, if we may credit the chroniclers, of fifteen hundred cavalry, and fifty thousand foot soldiers, of whom thirty thousand were Welsh. He landed at Slugo on the 27th of August, but no sooner had he taken up his quarters, than a quarrel arose among the sailors of his fleet, arising out of old dissentions between the people of the Cinque Ports and those of Yarmouth. The men of the Cinque Ports seem to have begun the affray, by boarding the Yarmouth vessels, slaying their crews, and burning above twenty ships. The king's commands were entirely disregarded; and only three of the Yarmouth vessels could make their escape. This event shows the daring and lawless habits of English sailors at the close of the thirteenth century. The king returned to England in March, 1298, and no further important naval operations are recorded until his death, which took place in July, 1307.

King Edward the Second had been affianced before his father's death, to Isabel, the only daughter of the king of France, and he lost no time after his accession in claiming his bride. He sailed from Dover on the 22d of January; and on the 28th of that month, his nuptials were celebrated at Boulogne in a most splendid manner. The king returned to Dover on the 7th of February. In the war with the Scots, under Robert Bruce, a fleet of fifty ships, under Sir John de Caunton, was of much service in supplying the English troops engaged in the war, and in clearing the sea of the numerous pirates which infested the coast. Several small squadrons were fitted out during the Scottish war, to harass the coasts of the enemy, but they effected nothing worthy of mention.

In the war with France, which broke out in 1324, the greater portion of the contest was maintained upon the sea. Each power made every exertion to display its naval strength. Edward commanded

EDWARD I. E BARKING FOR FLANDERS.

V

the authorities, in the various ports of his realm, to equip every ship for war, and with all their might to attack and destroy the ships belonging to the king of France, so that the French, being the originators of the war, might feel its effects.

A disgraceful peace was concluded with France in May, 1325, Edward yielding the point which gave rise to the war. But an inexorable hatred existed between the two kings, and hostilities were soon renewed.

No fact in the naval history of the thirteenth and early part of the fourteenth century is more remarkable, than the piratical habits of the sailors of England and other countries. During a truce or peace, ships were boarded, plundered, and captured by vessels of a friendly power, as if there had been an actual war. Even English merchant ships were attacked and robbed, as well in port as at sea, by English vessels, and especially by those of the Cinque Ports, which seem to have been nests of robbers; and, judging from the numerous complaints, it would appear that a general system of piracy existed, which no government was strong enough to restrain. Remonstrances and demands for satisfaction were constantly made by one sovereign of another, for some aggression committed by his subjects at sea; and when justice was not obtained, letters of marque and reprisal were granted, which were, in fact, permission for individuals to take the law into their own hands, and to obtain compensation for their own private injury from any innocent countryman of the aggressor.

The title of "Admiral" is attributed to no less than twenty-one persons in the reign of Edward the Second. Few of these individuals, however, are deserving of much consideration, either from their station, or their services; and some of them were so obscure, that little is known of their history, except that they held the office of admiral. The most prominent, both for rank and service, were Sir Simon de Montacute, Sir John de Cromwell, Sir John Sturmy, Sir John of Argyle, and Sir John de Caunton.

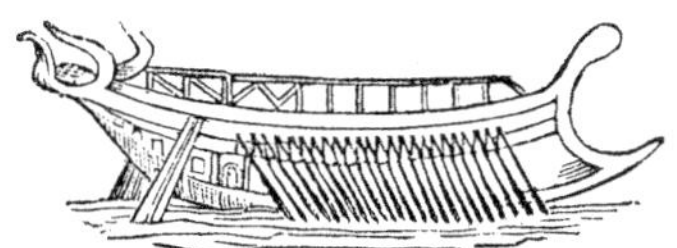

CHAPTER XXIII.

FROM THE DEATH OF EDWARD THE SECOND TILL THE DEATH OF HENRY THE FIFTH.

THE name of Edward the Third is identified with the naval glory of England. Though the sagacious Alfred, and the chivalrous Richard commanded fleets and defeated the enemy at sea, Edward's glory was still greater. He gained, in person, two signal victories—fighting on one occasiou, until his ship actually sunk under him, and was rewarded by his subjects with the proud title of "King of the Sea."

The isle of Cadsand, near the entrance of the Sluys, was garrisoned by many Flemish knights and esquires, who did so much mischief to the English by intercepting them on their passage to and from England, that Edward determined to dislodge them. Accordingly, in

November, 1337, Henry, Earl of Derby, and Sir Walter Mauny were ordered to proceed to Cadsand, with five hundred men-at-arms and two thousand archers. They embarked at London, and with the first tide, reached Gravesend. On the 10th of November, the expedition arrived off Cadsand, and, the wind and tide being in their favor, they prepared to attack the place "in the name of God and St. George." "Then," says Froissart, "they sounded their trumpets, quickly armed themselves, put their vessels in order, and placing their archers forwards, sailed rapidly towards the town." The Flemings, to the number of five thousand, under Sir Guy of Flanders, brother to Louis, Count of Flanders, "a good and sure knight, though a bastard," made every preperation for receiving them, and drew up his troops on the dykes and sands.

As the ships approached the harbor, the English archers shouting their national war cry, shot their arrows with such effect, that the Flemings who defended the entrance were compelled, with many wounds, to retire. The troops then landed, and a hand to hand fight ensued, with hatchets, swords, and glaives. Though the Flemings displayed great bravery, they were at last defeated, with the loss of a thousand men, and Sir Guy of Flanders was made prisoner. The victors then sacked and burnt the town, and carried the plunder and prisoners to England. When the king was informed of their success, he showed great satisfaction."

Having resolved to assert his rights to the crown of France by an invasion, Edward collected a large fleet and army at Orwell, and sailed for Antwerp, where he arrived on the 16th of July, 1338. The French squadrons committed terrible devastations on the English coasts, and captured some large ships. They were assisted by the Genoese and the Spaniards. The inhabitants offered a determined resistance to the invaders, but their numbers were generally overpowering. In July, 1339, a fleet of thirty-two galleys appeared off Sandwich; but finding the inhabitants prepared for them, they did not dare to land, and diverged to Rye, where they did much mischief. An English fleet approaching, the French ships took to flight, and were chased into Boulogne. Not satisfied, however, with forcing the enemy into port, the English entered the harbor, took several of the French vessels, hung twelve of their captains, burnt part of the town, and returned with their prizes to England. Soon after, Sir Robert Morley, an

English admiral, burnt five towns in Normandy and no less than eighty ships. But the general superiority of the French upon the sea, at this time, was clearly evident.

No year was more memorable in the naval history of England than 1340. Early in January, Edward the III. formally assumed the title and arms of the king of France, and at once resolved to enforce his claim by the most active measures. He sailed back to Orwell from Flanders, and preparations were immediately begun for a large expedition. Every ship carrying twenty tons and upwards was ordered to be well manned and equipped, and sent to Sandwich for the king's passage. About the 10th of June, when all the preparations were completed, and the horses shipped, Edward was informed that Philip of Valois had assembled an immense fleet at Sluys to prevent his landing. He disbelieved the report, and said he would at all events attempt to cross the Channel. But he was at last induced to wait till he had collected more ships from the northern and southern ports, as well as from London. Within ten days, a fleet of about two hundred sail assembled, and more soldiers and archers arrived than were wanted.

King Edward sailed about one o'clock on the 22d of June, with two hundred vessels, and on his arrival on the coast of Flanders, was joined by the northern squadron, consisting of fifty sail, under Sir Robert Morley. On the 23d of June, about noon, Edward arrived off Blankenburg, ten miles to the westward of the mouth of the Sluys, and discovered the French fleet lying in that port. The opposing fleet numbered one hundred and ninety vessels, nineteen of which were larger than any the English had yet seen.

The French ships were manned with above thirty-five thousand Normans, Picards, and Genoese; and this formidable armament was commanded by Sir Hugh Kiriet, having under him Sir Nicholas Bahuchet, who received the honor of knighthood on the morning of the battle, and the celebrated Genoese admiral Barbenoire.

As the tide did not suit for attacking the enemy, the remaining part of Friday was occupied by the English in deliberation; and towards the evening, or early the next morning, the French fleet removed from Sluys, and proceeded in three columns to Grongne, nearer the entrance of the river. It is doubtful whether Edward was or was not assisted by the Flemings, the English writers having denied it, while those of France assert that the French stood their ground until their enemies were joined by some Flemish ships; and though the king alludes to the Flemings in his dispatch, the passage is rather obscure.

At sunrise on Saturday, the 24th, the two fleets were at no great distance from each other; but the state of the tide prevented the English from entering the port until about noon. No writer has mentioned the direction of the wind, or the exact localities; and there are few of those other nautical details which are indispensable for the perfect comprehension of a naval engagement.

Having gained the wind, the English bore down upon the enemy; and the battle began soon after noon, by Sir Robert Morley, the admiral, attacking one of the van ships, apparently the "Christopher." He was nobly seconded by the ship of the Earl of Huntingdon, which was supported by that of the Earl of Northampton. Sir Walter de Manny's was the fourth ship engaged, and he was speedily followed by the other vessels. Showers of arrows, quarrels, and other missiles fell on all sides; and as soon as the ships came in contact, the crews fastened them to each other by hooks and grapplings, when the men at arms, seizing their swords, lances, and hatches, a fierce hand to hand fight took place, in which the combatants performed numerous feats of valor, many having fallen, many being taken, and many rescued. The French displayed their usual bravery, having, says their conqueror, made a "noble defence;" but unable to resist the impetuous courage of their assailants, several ships in their van were boarded and carried with such immense slaughter, that four hundred dead bodies were found in one ship alone, and the survivors leapt headlong into the sea. Among the ships thus gallantly won, were the celebrated "Christopher," and three large cogs, called the "Edward," "Katherine," and "Rose," together with some French ships. The French banner was instantly struck; that of England again floated from the masts of the recaptured ships, and the "Christopher," "that fine and beautiful ship," was immediately manned with English archers, and sent to attack the Genoese galleys.

On the defeat of their van, the French seem to have abandoned all hope of success. Instead of their second and third lines maintaining the contest, they endeavored to escape; but finding themselves surrounded by English ships, the crews threw down their arms, and rushed into the boats, which, becoming overladen, sunk before they reached the shore, and about two thousand men are said to have perished. The fourth line, consisting of sixty vessels, mostly Genoese, under Barbenoire, and including the French barges, escaped.

The battle must have lasted for at least ten if not twelve hours, as Edward says, the enemy defended themselves all that day and the night after. At the close of the action the fourth line put to sea, and though followed until the middle of the night by some English ships, twenty-four not only made their escape, but they seem to have beaten off their assailants, and captured or destroyed two vessels of the English; for Hemingford says, "in this last battle," the ship containing the king's wardrobe was taken, and all on board, except two men and a woman, slain, together with a galley belonging to Hull, the crew of which had all been crushed by stones. Part of the twenty-four vessels which had effected their escape were, however, captured a few days after the battle.

According to some authorities, no less than twenty-five, and, according to others, thirty thousand French and Genoese perished on this occasion, including those who were slain, those who leaped into the sea on their ships being boarded, and those who were drowned in the boats.

No English writer specifies the loss of the victors, but all agree that it was comparatively small. One Flemish writer rates it at four thousand persons, among whom were twelve ladies. King Edward is said by Froissart to have proved himself, with his own hand, a very noble knight. The battle was not distinguished by any display of nautical skill on either side; but was simply decided by personal valor and strength, in hand to hand conflict. This great victory securely established the maritime superiority and naval renown of England. A truce was soon after concluded with Philip, and Edward returned to London.

Edward was soon drawn into action again by the death of the Duke of Brittany. Two claimants appeared for his dominions—the Count of Blois and the Count of Montfort. Edward warmly espoused the cause of the Count of Montfort, and as the other claimant was the nephew of the king of France, he found ready support from his uncle. Considerable preparations were made for the conveyance of troops into Brittany. Sir Walter Manny was appointed commander of the expe-

RELIEF OF HENNEBON BY SIR WALTER MANNY.

dition, and he seems to have sailed on the 20th of March, with about one hundred and twenty men at arms and a thousand archers. Owing to contrary winds, his ships were sixty days on their passage; but they arrived off Hennebon at a most critical moment. The Countess of Montfort, "who possessed the courage of a man, and the heart of a lion," was then closely besieged in that town by the Count of Blois. Sir Walter speedily compelled the count to raise the siege, and his valor procured the sweetest of rewards—a kiss from the countess herself.

The Count of Blois had a powerful ally in Don Luis, of Spain, who brought a large squadron of Spanish and Genoese vessels to his assistance. This was at first very successful in its descent on the English coast and shipping, and obtained much booty. But it was attacked and entirely dispersed by Sir Walter Manny and Sir Amery de Clisson. Being informed of the support which the Countess of Montfort

28*

had received from the king of England, the Count of Blois sent Don Luis, Sir Charles Grimaldi, and Sir Otho Doria, off Guernsey to intercept her on her return to Brittany, with a squadron of thirty large ships, having on board three thousand Genoese, and a thousand men-at-arms. The English squadron, in which was Sir Robert of Artois, the Countess of Montfort, and a number of the English nobility, consisted of forty vessels of various sizes; but none of them was so large or so strong as nine of Don Luis's ships; besides which he had three galleys that overtopped all the others, and were severally commanded by the chiefs, Luis, Grimaldi, and Doria.

It was late in the afternoon when the two fleets came in sight of each other; and, as soon as the English sailors perceived the Spaniards, they exclaimed, "My lords, arm and prepare yourselves; for here are the Genoese and Spaniards approaching us." Then the English sounded their trumpets, displayed their pennons and standards with the arms of St. George, arrayed their archers, and advanced boldly towards the enemy in full sail. As they approached, the Genoese shot their crossbows and the English archers their arrows, inflicting many wounds; and when the ships came in contact, so that the lords, knights, and esquires could use their swords and lances, then was the battle hard and fierce. The countess, who was armed, was as good as a man, "for she had the heart of a lion," and bore a very strong and trenchant glaive, with which she fought with great courage. Don Luis in his galley, like a brave knight, anxiously sought his enemies, being desirous of revenging the injury he had sustained in this year at Quimperlé. The Genoese and Spaniards hurled large bars of iron and "archgays"* from their ships upon the English archers with great effect; but thick weather and the darkness of night soon rendered it impossible to distinguish one vessel from another, and the combatants separated without any advantage being gained on either side. Both fleets anchored, and dressed their wounded, preparing to renew the fight. A little before midnight, however, "so violent and so horrible a tempest arose, that the world seemed coming to an end," and the boldest wished themselves on shore, for the ships and barges clashed against each other with such violence, that it seemed they must be

* A sort of pike, or lance, borne by archers; but, according to Froissart, a machine which was thrown on an enemy.—*Roquefort*

EDWARD III. SAILING FOR FRANCE.

riven asunder. By the advice of their crews, the English lords determined to weigh and make for the land; and, reducing their sail to half a quarter of its usual size, the vessels bore away for Brittany.

Edward passed over to Brittany in October, 1342. Don Luis and the two Genoese admirals, were very successful in their attacks upon English ships carrying provisions for the army, and did great injury. It is an extraordinary fact, that within three years after the capture of the "Christopher" and the "Edward," and other large galleys at Sluys, England had not ships of war able to cope with the Spanish and Genoese squadron, which appears to have obtained an almost undisputed command of the narrow seas. A truce was concluded with France in January, 1343, which was to last for three years and eight months. Edward embarked for England towards the close of the same month, and a long and stormy passage, in which his life was frequently in imminent danger, landed at Weymouth, on the 2d of March.

The truce was soon broken by the faithless Philip; and Edward immediately prepared for another invasion of the French dominions. He embarked from the Isle of Wight on the 10th of July, 1346, and sailed on the 11th, with a fleet which has been estimated by some writers, at a thousand, and by others at sixteen hundred sail, eleven hundred having, it is said, been large ships, and five hundred small vessels. Edward was accompanied by the Prince of Wales, numerous earls, barons, baronets, and knights, four thousand men at arms, and ten thousand archers, besides Irish and Welsh foot soldiers; but, as has just been observed, the number of ships was probably exaggerated, or the amount of the troops much underrated. On the 12th of July, the armament arrived at Le Hogue, and the king landed as soon as the ships had anchored; but it was not until the 18th, that all the troops, horses, and stores were disembarked. A great part of the fleet was ordered to return to England; but two hundred ships, with one hundred men at arms, and four hundred archers, under the Earl of Huntingdon, were sent to ravage the coast. By the 30th of July, the English forces had destroyed more than a hundred sail of the enemy; some of these of a very large size.

In 1350, another wreath was added to the laurels won by Edward and his valiant son at Poictiers and Cressy. A Spanish fleet, under the command of Don Carlos de la Cerda, had captured and plundered several English ships during the truce, and then sailed to Sluys for merchandise. This, Edward resolved to attack, and punish so perfidious an enemy. Being informed of this, La Cerda armed his ships with every kind of artillery and missiles, among which were large bars of iron, and filled them with soldiers, cross bowmen, and archers. Edward embarked on the 28th of August with the Prince of Wales, the young Earl of Richmond, and a large number of the most distinguished of his nobles, in a fleet of fifty ships and pinnaces. The king made his arrangements as soon as he embarked; but he was compelled to remain at anchor three days, waiting for the Spaniards.

Having completed their rich cargoes, the Spaniards put to sea. They had forty large ships, all of the same class. Each mast was surmounted by the usual embattled "top," filled with stones and flint, and protected by soldiers. In number they were superior to the English, and felt confident of success. The battle took place on the 29th of August, 1350.

After a severe action, the Spanish fleet, which had, Froissart says, "given the king of England his people plenty to do," was entirely defeated. Twenty-four, if not twenty-six, large ships were captured, and the remainder took to flight. Edward then ordered his trumpets to sound a cessation of arms, and soon after nightfall his ships anchored at Rye and Winchelsea. The king and the Prince of Wales, with his young brother of Richmond, hastened to relieve the fears of the queen, who was lodged in an abbey about two leagues from the coast. Her attendants had seen the battle from the hills, and when they informed her that the Spaniards had forty large ships, she naturally felt the deepest anxiety about her husband and children. The night was spent by Edward and his knights in revelry with the ladies, conversing of love and arms; and the next day, when most of the barons and knights who had shared the honor of the engagement waited upon him, he thanked them greatly for their services, and, taking their leave, they returned to their homes.

In many of its features, the sea fight of "L'Espagnol sur Mer," stands unparalleled in English history. Equal valor and superior tactics have been displayed on many occasions; but never before was a sea fight marked by circumstances of so chivalrous and remarkable a nature. Not only the chief nobility of England were present, but they were led by their sovereign and the Prince of Wales, who both participated so largely in the dangers of the day, that they fought until their ships sunk under them. Even the king's second son, though but ten years old, was exposed to the perils of the day, and thus the renowned John of Gaunt made his first essay in arms on the element upon which British valor was so often triumphant. This was the first victory gained over a Spanish fleet by the English, and their king received the noble title of "King of the Sea."

The English squadron now commanded the neighboring seas, only interrupted occasionally by the small, but daring squadrons of Scotland. But their triumphs seem to have given too great a feeling of security; for, in 1360, so far was the navy neglected, that the French fleets ravaged the coasts of England with impunity. Military ardor was centred in the conquests of France after the memorable victory of Cressy, and the navy was sacrificed and the shores of England exposed for that object. At length, an attack upon Winchelsea and the barbarous acts there perpetrated by the French roused the people to action. A large fleet was equipped and placed under the command of Sir John Barclay, and the depredations of the French were fully retaliated.

It will be impossble for us to record every naval transaction of such an active maritime country as England, who was forced to employ fleets wherever it was necessary to transport troops to the continent or Ireland. Nor is it necessary to obtain a view of the progress and greatness of that navy. This will be made as evident from the most prominent achievements, and will save a great deal of uninteresting detail.

The triumphs of the early part of Edward's career form a humiliating contrast to the disasters which began towards its close, and continued during the whole reign of his successor. In April, 1372, a small squadron, under the Earl of Pembroke, was despatched from Southampton for the relief of Rochelle, which was besieged by the French. Being informed of this, the king of France sent the fleet of his ally, the king of Castile, consisting of forty large ships and thirteen barges to intercept the English squadron. The Spanish squadron was commanded by Ambrosio Bocanegru, and he was assisted by other naval commanders of great reputation.

Pembroke arrived off Rochelle on the 22d of June, and found the Spaniards lying at the mouth of the harbor. When the English and Poitevins saw that an engagement was inevitable, they encouraged each other, though they were not nearly equal, either in men or large ships, to the enemy, and prepared for battle, placing their archers in the bows. Besides great numbers of men at arms and brigands, who had cross-bows and cannon, the Spaniards had great bars of iron and leaden bolts. Having weighed and gained the wind, their large ships bore down on the English with loud shouts and great noise, which were responded to by similar cries; and Pembroke conferred the honor of knighthood upon some of his esquires "for honor." The fight was very severe, and the English were greatly pressed, or, as Froissart quaintly expresses it, had enough to do; for, as in the action off Winchelsea, the Spaniards derived great advantage from the height of their ships, as it enabled them to fling their missiles, with which they expected to sink their enemies, upon them with terrible effect. Pembroke, D'Angle, and the other knights, both English and Poitevin, gave many proofs of chivalry and prowess, and never did men act more valiantly. Inferior in numbers, and with much smaller ships, it was extraordinary that they could maintain so unequal a contest for so long a time. They fought, however, until night, with the loss of only two barges laden with provisions; and the two fleets then separated and came to an anchor.

As soon as the day dawned, and it was high water, the Spaniards disanchored, and sounding their trumpets, prepared for battle, and taking advantage of the wind to surround the English ships, bore down on them with all sail set. As soon as the ships came in contact the Spaniards fastened themselves to their adversaries with iron chains, and a fierce and cruel fight ensued. Pembroke's ship was attacked by four large Spaniards full of soldiers, under the command of Cabeza de Vaca and Don Fernando de Peon. The English, as on the preceding day, suffered heavily from the stones and iron bars which were thrown from the overtopping decks of the Spaniards, and Sir Aimery de Tarste, a gallant Gascon knight, and Sir John Lanton, a knight of the earl's body, were killed. After an obstinate resistance the Spaniards boarded and carried Pembroke's ship, and made him and his companions prisoners. Sir Simon Housagre, Sir John Mortaigne, and Sir John Touchet were slain; and Sir Robert Tinfort, Sir John de Gruières, and Sir John Tourson shared the captivity of their noble chief.

The battle, nevertheless, raged with great fury until nine o'clock,

SHIPS OF THE TIME OF RICHARD II.

and never did people at sea toil harder than did the Englisn and Poitevins on that occasion. Sir Guiscard d'Angle and Sir Otho Grandison, gallantly defended their ships against those of Bocanegra and De Rojas, but, at length, the English were completely beaten, and all the ships fell into the enemy's hands.

Not long after this complete victory the French obtained possession of Rochelle by capitulation. The Spanish fleet off Rochelle was soon increased in strength, and placed under the command of Evan of Wales and Don Rodrigo de Rosas. They then meditated an attack upon the English coast, and Edward made great exertions to equip a fleet capable of coping with them. At length, an armament was collected, and placed under the Earl of Salisbury. It sailed from Cornwall for the coast of Brittany, and entering St. Maloes, burned eight Spanish vessels and put their crews to the sword. Then proceeding to Brest, the French were compelled to raise the siege. But these successes were compensated by the burning of a large fleet of ships and barges in the Bay of Brittany, by the Spaniards. In June, 1337, Edward III. died, after a glorious reign of more than fifty years. The disasters in the latter part of his reign were caused by circumstances entirely beyond his control; as long as he possessed the means he was victorious.

When Richard the Second ascended the throne, the English navy was almost annihilated, the treasury exhausted, and the king of France preparing an expedition to invade the realm. But few preparations were made to resist, and the French landed at various points and committed great devastations. Occasionally a small squadron of English ships, under some daring commanders, obtained some slight advantage over the French. One gallant exploit is worthy of mention. Sir Thomas Percy, brother of the Earl of Northumberland, put to sea with one ship, two barges and several smaller vessels. Falling in with fifty ships, partly Flemish and partly Spanish, laden with merchandise belonging to the French; he desired the Flemish to separate themselves from their allies, as England was at peace with Flanders. This they refused to do, and Percy instantly attacked the whole convoy. Awed by his courage, and thinking he would be reinforced, they offered little resistance; and twenty-two ships having surrendered, he returned with his prizes to port. Sir Thomas Percy and Sir Hugh Calvely, a kindred spirit, were soon after this appointed admirals; and their courage and activity almost cleared the channel of the enemy's squadrons. But another disaster overtook the English. A violent storm destroyed a great part of their fleet, and deprived her of some of her bravest warriors.

In February, 1385, Charles the Sixth, king of France, who was then in the seventeenth year of his age and full of military ambition, assembled a fleet of six hundred ships for the invasion of England. The command of this formidable armament was given to Sir John de Vienne, admiral of France. The English sought to ward off the blow by negotiation, and obtained a truce of two months. In that time, ships were fitted out in all the English ports, and a fleet sailed under the two admirals, who were to guard the seas during the summer. They frequently saw the French armament; but dared not attack it. However, by the valor of the English garrison of Calais, a large number of the French vessels, which were separated from the squadron at various times, were captured, and their crews destroyed, or made prisoners.

In June, 1386, the English fleet, of more than two hundred sail, under the admiral, Sir Thomas Percy, put to sea, and the French fleet retired to Havre. France had never witnessed such extensive preparations as were made for the invasion of England in 1386. The spirit of William the Conqueror seemed to have revived in Charles VI. Every available vessel and soldier was pressed into the service. It is said that the fleet assembled at Sluys and Blankenburg numbered thirteen hundred and eighty-seven sail. The ruin of England was counted upon as certain. But after various attempts to get under way, the invasion was postponed until the next year—in spite of the murmurs of the soldiery. Soon after, the English fell upon the squadron, when it was almost deserted, and burned or captured the greater part of it. This broke up the expedition.

Something of the naval glory of England was revived at this time by the defeat and capture of a greater part of a Flemish fleet of one hundred sail, by the Earl of Arundel. This commander was very successful in his descents upon the coasts of the French provinces. He injured Normandy to the amount of two hundred thousand francs. Hostilities with France were at last terminated in June, 1389, by the treaty of Lenlingham.

The depredations of the English pirates upon the coast of Brittany roused the Bretons to take vengeance upon them, and in July, 1443, the English suffered a complete defeat. By the advice of Sir Oliver de Clisson, the constable of France, the Bretons collected twelve hundred men-at-arms and a great number of cross-bowmen and light troops, to intercept the English on their return home with their piratical spoil. They chose the Sire de Penhoet, Sir John, his son, admiral of Brittany, and Sir William du Chatel, all knights celebrated for their valor, for commanders, and embarked in thirty vessels at Chastel Pol, near Morlaix. The squadron weighed anchor on the 1st of July, and sending some small vessels to reconnoitre the position of the English, they discovered them at the extremity of the coast, in the Pace of St. Matthew, on the day after embarking. At dawn of day, the English steered towards home instead of seeking the Spanish at sea, and every exertion was made to bring them to action.

The Bretons formed their fleet in two divisions, one under Sir William du Chatel, and the other under his colleagues; and seeing this, the English divided their fleet in the same manner. The Bretons began the battle by boarding their adversaries with great impetuosity, uttering terrible cries; but they were received with equal courage, it not being easy to decide which displayed the most ardor, fought with the greatest rage, or sustained the battle with most bravery and constancy. After the action had lasted six hours, the English, finding that they could not keep their ground with their ships in two divisions, united them in one body. The French did the same, and the combat was renewed, both sides using all their engines and missiles, and then fighting hand to hand. The English maintained the combat until all their missiles were exhausted, when five hundred of their men being either slain or drowned, their courage gave way, and forty ships with sails and one carack surrendered. Some of the soldiers threw their weapons into the sea, with the hope of being put to a lighter ransom if they were taken unarmed, or more probably, to prevent them from falling into the hands of the conquerors; whereupon the Breton captains ordered these brave fellows to be thrown overboard after their weapons. One thousand prisoners, and all the English ships, were brought into port; and, after sending intelligence of the victory to their duke and to the French lords, the Bretons filled their ships with fresh soldiers to follow up their success, and carry the war to the shores of England.

Several unimportant actions took place between small squadrons of the French and English vessels, during the remainder of the reign of Henry IV.; and the coasts and commerce of both countries suffered continually. It seemed as if no truce or treaty of peace could prevent the vessels of France and England from entering into hostilities whenever an opportunity offered.

Few of England's monarchs took as much interest in her navy as Henry V. He ordered and superintended the building of larger vessels than the navy had ever possessed, with the determination to acquire the dominion of the sea. His efforts to restore and improve the navy were amply rewarded by success as glorious as that he achieved upon the land. Having asserted his right to the crown of France, and rejected all overtures for an amicable settlement, Henry collected a fleet of fourteen hundred vessels of various kinds, carrying about six thousand men at arms, and twenty-four thousand archers, and sailed from England on the 11th of August, 1415. The king and his forces disembarked near Harfleur, on the 14th, without meeting opposition. The town was immediately besieged and the fleet blockaded the harbor. After a gallant defence of thirty-six days, Harfleur surrendered on the 22d of September. The fleet was then sent back to England, while Henry boldly marched into the interior. After the great battle of Agincourt, the victorious king returned to England with a large number of prisoners.

In August, 1416, the Duke of Clarence sailed from Sandwich with three hundred vessels, full of English, men-at-arms and archers, and arriving off Harfleur, came in sight of the French fleet, under the constable of France. The English at once prepared for battle; and the French no less "eager for the fray," advanced boldly in their "sea-castles," to meet the enemy. The action began about nine o'clock on the morning of the 15th of August. The large ships then came violently into contact, and their crews fastened them to each other, by cables, chains, and hooks.

Three great caracks and many smaller vessels, with all their crews, were captured, and a hulk was sunk. The remainder of the French fleet escaped into Harfleur, whither the English were prevented from pursuing them, on account of the sands and other dangers on the coast. The largest of the caracks, which one writer says was called, from her ize, and, probably, also, from her color, the "Mountnegrie," and which is said by another writer to have been called the "Mother of

HENRY V. AT AGINCOURT.

all," in her efforts to escape, struck upon the sands and foundered. A carack which had been driven about some days before the battle, drifted from her anchors, and was likewise wrecked. Fifteen hundred of the French were killed, and about four hundred made prisoners; while the English did not lose more than one hundred men. For some days the corpses of the slain were seen floating on the sea, "as if they were seeking for other burial than that of the fishes."

Extensive preparations were made in February, 1417, for an expedition to Normandy, under Henry, in person; and an army of sixteen thousand four hundred soldiers, one thousand carpenters and other workmen, and fifteen hundred vessels assembled at Southampton. The French fleet, assisted by the Geonese, collected at Harfleur and scoured the channel occasionally. But their principal object was to intercept Henry's expedition. The king yielded to the remonstrances of his council, and concluded not to expose his person. He, therefore, sent a squadron to sea, under the Earl of Huntingdon, who defeated the French fleet on the 25th of July. Henry then embarked and sailed with his immense fleet for Normandy. He directed his course to the Seine, and disembarked at Tongue, about four miles from Harfleur. The fleet was then sent back and dispersed to the respective harbors which had contributed it. Henry returned to Dover, in February, 1421, and died in February, 1422, in the castle of Vincennes. During his reign the naval power of England commanded general respect, and the disasters of the preceding reign were forgotten in the glory of the great triumphs by sea and land.

The mode of fighting at sea underwent but little change under Henry V. Fleets still continued to come to close quarters, and the contest was decided by hand to hand conflict. Cannon were introduced into the navy, but their service was not rated high. In all hand to hand contests with the French, the English were victorious; and in view of this fact, it is strange that the French did not give more attention to the study and practice of tactics. The reason may lie in the chivalrous spirit of the day, which made courage to meet an equal foe on equal terms superior to the skill which triumphs by manœuvres.

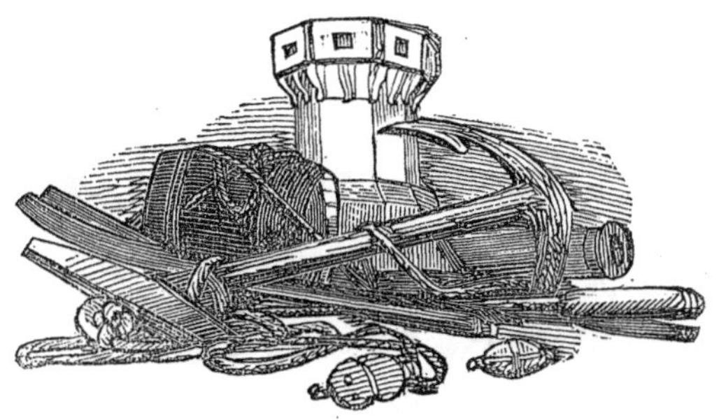

CHAPTER XXIV.

FROM THE DEATH OF HENRY THE FIFTH UNTIL THE REIGN OF CHARLES THE FIRST.

THE naval affairs of England during the early part of the reign of Henry VI. were unimportant; and the contest between the houses of York and Lancaster, distracting the attention of the nation, prevented the navy from receiving any consideration. No recollection of brilliant achievements could attract the care of the government to the navy. When the Earl of Warwick deserted the cause of Edward IV., he and a few followers seized some Flemish vessels, he found lying in the neighborhood of Calais, and sailed to the dominions of the Duke of Burgundy. There a reconciliation was effected between Warwick and Queen Margaret. A fleet was prepared to conduct them to England; and they sailed to Dartmouth. After landing, Warwick, (the kingmaker) had astonishing success, and in less than six days, he found himself at the head of sixty thousand men. Edward was forced to fly the kingdom. Having narrowly escaped his enemies, he embarked on board of a small fleet which lay off Lynn, in Norfolk. While at sea, he was chased by some ships belonging to the Hanse Towns, then at war with England. But he escaped all dangers

THE GREAT HARRY.

and landed in Holland. He returned to England nine months afterwards, and succeeded in crushing his enemies and securing himself upon the throne until his death.

After the Earl of Richmond had determined to dethrone the aspiring Richard III., he collected five thousand men, and set sail from St. Maloes. On arriving in England he received the news of the bad success of his adherents and returned to France. But he was soon joined by a large number of the Lancastarians, and assisted by the king of France; and after considerable preparation he set sail from Harfleur, and landed at Milford Haven, in Wales, on the 17th of August, 1485. Under the vigorous administration of Henry VII., all kinds of industry flourished, and the kingdom recovered somewhat of its foreign influence, which had been lost during internal convulsions. Henry was too avaricious to engage in any expensive naval expeditions. But under his direction some improvements were introduced in that important arm of warfare. The largest ship which had yet been built in England was constructed in this reign. It was called the "Great Harry," and cost fourteen thousand pounds.

Henry VIII. had not long been seated on the English throne before engaged in a war with France; ostensibly, for the purpose of recovering the provinces anciently annexed to the English realm. His arms were successful upon land; but not so upon the sea. A French fleet, under the command of Primauget, containing the "Cordelier," a vessel of extraordinary dimensions, and carrying six hundred men, sailed from the harbor of Brest. The English fleet of forty-five vessels, under the command of Sir Thomas Ruyvet, encountered the French squadron, and a hard fought battle ensued. "The Regent," was the largest ship in the English armament. Sir Charles Brandon, commanding an English vessel, attacked the Cordelier, but met with such a warm reception, that Sir Thomas Ruyvet, in the Regent, was obliged to hasten to his assistance. The combat then became obstinate. Primauget projected fire from his vessel to the Regent, and the flames soon communicated to the other; and the two ships were destroyed. The fleets then separated and returned to their respective ports, satisfied with each other's strength. The French were decidedly superior upon the sea during this short war, and were, therefore, able to balance the victories of the English land forces. Peace was concluded on the 7th of August, 1514.

The spirit of discovery which so excited the Spaniards and the Portuguese during the latter part of the fifteenth century, extended its influence to England. When the discovery of the new world was announced, a strong desire was manifested in England to participate in the glories of exploring it. In the reign of Henry VII., in 1497, John Cabot and his son, Sebastian, explored the coasts of America from Labrador to Virginia, and discovered Newfoundland. Two voyages for the discovery of a northwest passage to India were undertaken in the reign of Henry VIII., at the suggestion of a merchant named Robert Thorne; and the exploits and adventures of the subsequent English navigators, Sir Francis Drake, Cavendish, Frobisher, and others, are well worthy a place in the niche of Fame, by the side of those of Ferdinand Magellan. Their recital, however, would involve much repetition and, perhaps, be foreign to the purpose of this work.

The naval wars of Henry VIII. were of so desultory a character as to require no farther notice than this:—They were carried on against the French and Scotch; and such was the superiority of the English that their enemies were glad to avoid so unequal a contest. Henry

QUEEN ELIZABETH.

fully established the system of privateering which, in warfare has been pursued ever since. He invited skilful naval architects from foreign countries, and rewarded their labor munificently; so that ships of the best construction were launched in the English ports. An idéa of a first rate ship at this time, may be formed from the king's largest ship, called the "Henry, Grace á Dieu." It was of a thousand tons burthen. Its complement of men was three hundred and forty-nine soldiers, three hundred and one sailors, and fifty gunners; and it was armed with nineteen pieces of brass ordnance, and one hundred and three of iron. This amount of artillery may startle; but it must be remembered, that the cannon was much inferior in calibre to that which is now used. The largest ships had five masts, scantily supplied with sail; and the general appearance of one was very much like that of a Chinese junk of the present day.

As the reign of Henry VIII. presented few opportunities of testing the naval strength of England, there were fewer still under Edward VI. and Mary. The all-absorbing subject of religious reformation predominated at this period, and caused the state of the royal navy to be overlooked; at all events, we know that from the end of the reign of Henry VIII. to the accession of Elizabeth, it had greatly decreased. In consequence of this, the energetic queen found difficulty in sending a small fleet to the assistance of the Scotch reformers, in 1560, although it was a measure in which she took much interest. Even twenty years after her accession, the largest ship in her fleet was only one thousand tons burthen, while the smallest was scarcely sixty. But a sovereign like Elizabeth, and the increase of the resources of England, would have created a navy, if none existed.

We have already, in the history of Spain, given a description and history of the Invincible Armada, together with the attacks upon it by the English fleet. It is only necessary here to add, that the destruction of that formidable armament raised the reputation of the lord high admiral, Charles Howard, to a great height; and in 1596, a report being circulated that the king of Spain had again entered into preparations for an invasion of England, Lord Howard and the Earl of Essex sailed with a fleet of one hundred and seventy-four ships —twenty-four of which were Dutch—to destroy the Spanish fleet at Cadiz. The English arrived at Cadiz on the 12th of June; and on the following morning, they entered the harbor and commenced an attack upon the Spanish ships, which was carried on with great fury on both sides until noon, when the enemy's ships were much shattered, and rather than surrender them, they came to the desperate resolution of setting them on fire. This was done with such precipitation, that numbers of the men were obliged to plunge into the sea, and would have perished had not the English rescued them. In the time of this conflagration, the Spanish admiral's ship and several others were blown up, with all their crews on board. The few vessels which were not sunk or burned, were run on shore. Cadiz was then taken by eight hundred men, under the Earl of Essex, and a large

SAILING OF THE EXPEDITION TO CADIZ.

SIR FRANCIS DRAKE.

number of merchantmen were burned by the Spaniards to prevent them from falling into the hands of the English. On the return of this most successful expedition, the queen conferred the title of Earl of Nottingham on the valiant Howard; and, afterwards, when the Earl of Essex threatened the kingdom with invasion, he was made lord lieutenant general of all England, and conducted the sea and land forces with signal ability.

Among the many illustrious naval commanders of the reign of Elizabeth, none ranks higher than Sir Francis Drake. He has the honor of being the first commander who circumnavigated the globe, and his daring procured him the reverence of all as "the English hero." So great was his reputation after his famous voyage round the world, in which he had done so much injury to the Spaniards, that, in the attack upon the Spanish Armada, a galleon surrendered to him at the mere mention of his name. His various adventures and exploits would fill a volume of themselves.

JAMES I.

In pursuing his peace policy, James I. did not neglect the navy. On hearing of the encroachments of the Dutch and French, in 1604, he despatched a fleet, under Sir William Monson, to maintain the rights which had been transmitted by his predecessors. This admiral obliged the Dutch and French to pay the accustomed honors to his flag in the narrow seas for a period of twelve years. He also cleared the seas of pirates. On the establishment of the East India Company, in 1612, they fitted out a fleet of four large ships, for war as well as trade, and sent them to India. There they were assailed by an overwhelming force of Spaniards and Portuguese; but completely defeated them. In consequence of this success, the company increased their force by building a merchant vessel of twelve hundred tons, named the "Trades' Increase," and sent it to India.

James increased the navy more than one-fourth during his reign, and caused a ship called the "Royal Prince," to be built, which was then reckoned a masterpiece of naval architecture. It was one hundred and fourteen feet in length, of fourteen hundred tons burthen, pierced for sixty-four pieces of ordnance, and richly adorned within and without with painting, carving, and gilding. The only expedition undertaken by James I. was that against the Algerine pirates, in 1620. Six royal and fourteen merchant vessels were sent on this errand, under the command of the vice-admiral of England, Sir Robert Mansel. On the arrival of the fleet before Algiers, a negotiation was opened with the governor, which terminated without any advantage to the English. The fleet continued in the Mediterranean during the winter; and in the spring the admiral resolved to make an attack upon Algiers. The attempt was made in May; but from gross mismanagement, it failed, and the fleet returned to England. In the meantime, the Dutch were fast rising to naval power; and thinking themselves able to cope with the English, they frequently insulted their coasts by capturing enemies immediately under their batteries. Their punishment was reserved for another reign.

SEBASTIAN CABOT

CHARLES I.

CHAPTER XXV.

FROM THE DEATH OF JAMES I. TO THE ACCESSION OF GEORGE I.

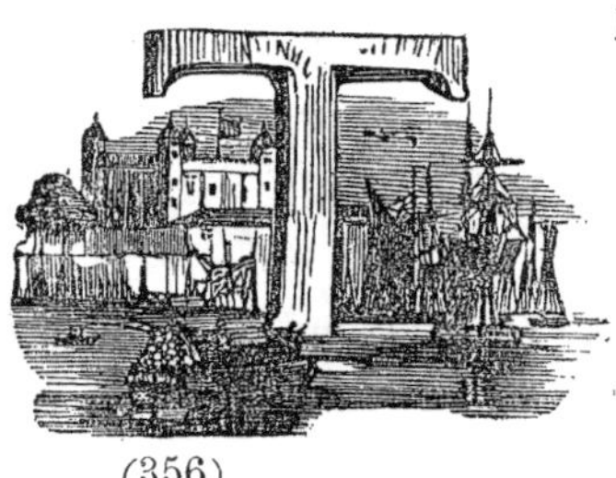

HE unfortunate reign of Charles I., was almost as barren of nautical events as his peaceful father's; so that only two expeditions worthy of notice were undertaken—those against Cadiz and Rochelle, both of which terminated in disgrace. In consequence of war being declared against Spain, an English fleet was fitted out, in 1625, to act in the Mediterranean, aided by the Dutch, the whole strength of which fleet amounted to more than eighty sail. It carried an army of ten thousand men, and was commanded by Lord Wimbleton. But such was the delay caused by the disputes between the naval and military commanders, that the Spaniards had time to fortify the city of Cadiz; and though it was finally taken, the enemy saved all their shipping. A disease soon after spread through the English fleet, and the armament was forced to return home—suffering all the consequences of a discomfiture. Another fleet of one hundred ships, under the Duke of Buckingham, was sent to the relief of the French Protestants at Rochelle. This was still more disgraceful to the English nation. It was undertaken to satisfy the pique of the Duke of Buckingham, against the French king. The French had no naval force which could meet this fleet at sea; and although the Spaniards reinforced them, they did not venture a battle. But the imbecility of Buckingham ruined all. He wasted time and resources in a hopeless siege of the port of St. Martin, in the island of Rhe; and finally was attacked by a French army and totally routed with the loss of two thousand men. The remainder of his forces returned to England.

But these unfortunate expeditions could not diminish the maritime supremacy of England. The French, Dutch, and Spaniards were successively forced to acknowledge it. When the rupture between Charles I. and the Parliament occurred, the latter obtained the command of the shipping; and were thus enabled to prevent the arrival of reinforcements for the king. But when the Earl of Warwick was displaced from the command, a large portion of the fleet deserted the cause of the Parliament, and placed itself under the command of Prince Rupert. Such was the order with which the contest was maintained at sea, that when the Parliament assumed the government, it could muster no more than fourteen ships of two decks. So great was the energy of the new administration, however, that three years after the execution of Charles, the Parliament had twenty-three ships of first, second, and third rates, thirty-two fourth rates, and fifty of inferior size. (1651.)

In 1652, a war with Holland broke out. The Dutch, by the practice and victories of half a century, had become the great maritime power of Europe. They possessed one hundred and fifty line-of-battle ships;

OLIVER CROMWELL.

and their resources were so extensive, that they could create fleets with a rapidity truly astonishing. They were thus far superior to the English at the commencement of the war. It is not our purpose to enter into the details of the contest any further than is necessary to show how the result was attained. The nature of the Dutch coasts forced them to construct their vessels with flat bottoms, to draw as little water as possible; while those of the English were larger, deeper, and swifter in sailing. The war was maintained for two years, and the English admiral, Blake, obtained several glorious triumphs. The Dutch suffered more in that time than during the whole of their eighty years' struggle with the Spaniards—expending six millions sterling, and losing eighty ships, twenty frigates, and seventeen hundred merchant vessels. They were also obliged to acknowledge the supremacy of the English upon the sea. Even with all the losses sustained during the war, England, at the end of it, possessed one hundred and fifty ships, more than a third of which had two tiers of guns.

The lofty views of Cromwell were directed to the establishment of the influence of England abroad. Two fleets were sent to sea under Blake and Penn; one was to proceed to the Barbary States and the other against the Spaniards at Hispaniola. The first fleet, under Blake, succeeded in capturing a richly laden Spanish flotila, sinking the vessels, and obtaining booty to the amount of six hundred thousand pounds sterling, with which the fleet returned to England. The second fleet, under Penn and Venables, failed in the immediate object of their expedition, but conquered the valuable island of Jamaica. So little, was this conquest valued, that, on their return, they were thrown into prison.

When Charles II. was restored to the throne, England possessed an almost irresistible navy, and the sovereign, himself, was skilled in ship building and naval affairs. A war with the Dutch, the only commercial rival, was immediately resolved upon. The commencement, however, was dishonorable to England. A fleet was sent to take possession of Cape de Verde, the island of Goree, and the settlement of New York, in 1664, without any declaration of war. This was accomplished. But the Dutch took active measures to recover their lost ground. The celebrated Admiral De Ruyter performed this service as speedily as they had been taken by the English. A powerful British fleet was soon at sea. It consisted of one hundred and fourteen ships of the line, and twenty-eight frigates and bomb-ketches, under the Duke of York. Soon after sailing it was encountered by a nearly equal Dutch force, under Admiral Oldam. Both nations fought with determined bravery, until Oldam's ship blew up, upon which the Dutch retreated, after losing nineteen ships; while the British lost but one fourth rate. The battle was fought off Lowestoff, on the 3d of June, 1665, and was the most signal victory the English had ever gained. The Dutch had six thousand men killed, and two thousand three hundred taken prisoners. The Dutch were, besides, unfortunate this year, in having the vice-admiral and rear-admiral of their East India fleet, and four ships of war, two fire ships and thirty merchantmen taken by the English.

The States were soon reinforced by France and Denmark, and in condition to contend with the victor. Their united fleet consisted of ninety-one ships of war, carrying five thousand seven hundred and

CHARLES II.

sixteen guns and twenty-two thousand four hundred and sixty-two men. The hostile fleets met on the 1st of June, 1666, in which the Dutch, under the famed De Ruyter, and the English, under Albemarle, maintained the conflict for four days, when the latter were partially defeated, and both were willing to retire and repair losses. After this great sea fight, the longest continued upon record, the Dutch had the credit of appearing at sea before their enemies and even braved them on their coast. But the English fleet of eighty sail and nineteen fire ships, under Prince Rupert and the Duke of Albemarle, was soon at sea, and encountered the Dutch on the 25th of June, off the North Foreland. A desperate battle was fought, and, although the Dutch were commanded by the great admirals De Ruyter and Van Tromp, they were completely defeated, with the loss of twenty ships, four admirals, many captains, and about four thousand men killed and three thousand wounded. The English loss is said to have been one ship burnt, and three captains and about three hundred men killed.

After this severe blow the Dutch were obliged to keep their ports during a whole year, while the English swept the seas, insulted the coasts of Holland, and even burned its ships within the protection of their harbors. Some efforts at negotiation were then tried by Charles, which the Dutch spun out in order to gain time to retaliate upon their enemies. The English in the full idea that peace was certain, had neglected their naval force, so that only two small squadrons were kept up to act against the Dutch. The latter then threw off the mask, rejected the proposals of Charles, while their fleet of seventy ships of war, besides fire ships, weighed anchor and arrived at the mouth of the Thames, June 7, 1667. Every obstacle was surmounted; Sheerness was taken, and the ships in the river were captured or destroyed. London itself trembled as the Dutch approached, and the worst fears of the inhabitants would have been realized, by an attack upon the capital, if the French king had sent his fleet, as agreed upon.

At last the country slowly recovered from this home thrust, and adopted measures to remove the hostile armament. A fleet, under Sir Jeremiah Smith, sailed northward to intercept a richly laden Dutch convoy, and De Ruyter was ordered by his government to follow and protect their commerce. The English were thus relieved from immediate apprehensions of danger. After this signal success on the part of Holland, terms of accommodation were proposed and ratified at Breda, August 24th, 1667.

Five years after the treaty at Breda, another war with Holland broke out This time, the French and English were united. In 1672, without a declaration of war, the pliant Sir Robert Holmes was sent to intercept a Dutch convoy of seventy sail, on its passage from Smyrna; and the fleets met at sea like those of two nations that were at peace with each other. The English admiral then commenced a furious onset, but was finally beaten off with much damage, and the

THE EARL OF SANDWICH REFUSING TO LEAVE HIS SHIP.

convoy proceeded in safety. After this shameful attack and defeat, war was proclaimed in regular style. The Dutch were prepared. They had ninety ships of the line, and fifty frigates and fire ships, with the brave and skilful De Ruyter to command them.

The first great naval encounter took place on the 19th of May, 1672, off Soleby. There the Dutch fought and defeated, after an obstinate battle, the English and French fleets, under the Duke of York and Mareschal d'Etreès. In this contest, the French are accused of having stood aloof while the English maintained the fight. The Dutch were prevented from gaining a more decisive victory by the bravery of the Earl of Sandwich, who, with the loss of both ship and life, covered the retreat of the English. This brave officer immortalized his name by refusing to leave his ship, when her destruction was certain. During the rest of this short war, several minor encounters took place, in which Holland, alone, was able to make head against her combined enemies. At length, the Dutch and English perceived that they were ruining each other's commerce, and advancing the ambitious projects of the French king. A peace was, therefore, concluded, independent of Louis XIV., in 1674. The only naval expedition of any importance during the remainder of the reign of Charles II., was the one sent against the corsairs of Tripoli, under Sir John Narborough. This was completely successful, destroying many of the fleets of the pirates and inflicting terrible chastisement upon the Barbary States in general.

Under such men as De Ruyter, Von Tromp, Blake, and Albemarle, the tactics of naval warfare were considerably improved. The most material alteration was that of making a battle depend, not upon a series of individual combats of ship against ship, but of squadron against squadron. More was made to depend upon manœuvering, and less upon the size and strength of ships. The principal missives used in the contest, were round shot, double-head, bar-spike, crow bar, case and chain shot; and, in addition to this, arrows, with fire works at the end, were sometimes shot from the windward against the sails. When the vessels neared each other, hand grenades and stink pots were hurled at each other to sweep the decks. After a mutual cannonade, if one squadron showed symptoms of yielding, fire ships were sent into the middle of it; and thus almost every battle was followed by a conflagration.

Under James II. the English navy was restored to a greater degree of efficiency than it had possessed under his predecessors, as from it, as Duke of York, he had derived his reputation. At the revolution, England had one hundred and seventy-three ships of various rates, requiring forty-two thousand seamen to man them. A force like this, under proper management, would have rendered invasion impossible. But the miserable administration of James lost him the confidence of the nation; and when William of Orange landed at Torbay there was no fleet to oppose him. The accession of William established a closer union between England and Holland, which, of course, operated against the views of the ambitious Louis of France. That monarch espoused the cause of James, and sent a fleet of eighty ships of the line, five frigates, and thirteen other vessels, with a powerful land force, to reinstate him on the throne. The fleet sailed to Ireland, and the army was landed in safety. The French fleet of twenty-four ships of the line, was attacked in Bantry Bay, by Admiral Herbert,

JAMES II.

with twenty-two ships of the line and five smaller vessels. The action was kept up for some hours with great spirit; but as Herbert was unable to bring all his ships up to the work, and found the contest very unequal, he did not risk a close fight. This prudent conduct was rewarded by King William by creating him a peer, with the title of Earl of Torrington.

This was but a slight experiment on the part of France; for in 1690, Louis, who had skilfully concentrated his naval forces while the other fleet was at sea, unexpectedly sent an armament of seventy-eight ships of war and twenty-two fire ships to sea, as an invading

WILLIAM III.

force. To oppose this large armament, Lord Torrington could only collect thirty-four ships, which were joined by a Dutch fleet of twenty-two sail. The English admiral was unwilling to risk the nation's honor, and therefore, held off until he received the order of Queen Mary, to fight at all events. In obedience, he bore down on the enemy, on the morning of the 3d of June; but from the inferiority of the combined fleets they sustained a severe defeat off Beachy Head, the English losing two, and the Dutch six of their largest ships. The Dutch were indignant, as having borne the weight of the contest; and to appease them, Lord Torrington was sent to the Tower of London.

The popular fear was this time the means of England's safety. Every naval preparation was made, and the French were reduced to shelter in port, while the English fleet, under Russel, kept possession of the sea.

Louis now prepared for a decisive naval effort. But he miscalculated the strength or activity of the English and Dutch. His fleet of sixty-three ships of the line, prepared for the invasion of England, was opposed by a fleet of one hundred English and Dutch ships, and in a battle near La Hogue, the French were so terribly defeated, that the few ships which escaped sought shelter in their harbors, while their enemies rode the sea in triumph. The English, in the confidence of victory, now began to remit their naval vigilance; while Louis made great efforts to repair the damage his navy had sustained. He was enabled to send into the Mediterranean, in the next year after the defeat of La Hogue, a fleet of seventy-one ships of war, besides bomb ketches, fire ships, and tenders, under command of Marshal Tourville. This great armament was then triumphant, and the British fleet, under Sir George Rooke, was encountered off Cape St. Vincent, and after a hard fought battle, completely defeated, with the loss of a convoy, the value of which was one million sterling. Sir George, however, brought off the greater part of his ships of war. A number of minor disasters befell the British flag, and the French destroyed a considerable quantity of shipping at Malaga, Cadiz, and Gibraltar.

Early in 1694, a powerful English and Dutch fleet, under Russel, was sent to sea, to cover a descent in Camaret bay; but the expedition was defeated, with severe loss from the batteries erected by the celebrated Vauban. These advantages led the French to style themselves *lords of both seas*—that is, the Atlantic and Mediterranean. In June, a more powerful English and Dutch fleet was sent to the Mediterranean, upon the approach of which, admiral Tourville retreated to Toulon. From this time till the close of the war, the French were unable to contend with their combined enemies, and in the series of minor engagements which followed the English, under Rooke, Benbow and Shovel were triumphant, and kept the coast of France in constant alarm. But the small squadrons of the French swift sailing vessels committed great depredations upon the commerce of the English. Their ships were considered as the best models. In the desultory system of warfare to which Louis was forced to resort, he was completely successful; and obtained a peace soon after on more favorable terms than he had expected—the only advantages gained by the English were the recognition of William III., as king of England, and the supremacy of the English navy.

The dearly purchased peace was not of long duration. Louis espoused the cause of the son of James II., and war was again declared. The English and Dutch fleets, under Sir George Rooke, and vice-admiral Benbow, kept the French coasts in awe and maintained the supremacy of England in the West Indies, in 1701. On the accession of Anne, in the next year, she appointed her consort, Prince George of Denmark, lord high admiral. Sir George Rooke, who had been appointed admiral of the fleet, and vice-admiral of England, took command of the great fleet of thirty English and twenty Dutch ships of the line, exclusive of small vessels, which made in all about one hundred and sixty sail, with fourteen thousand troops on board, under the Duke of Ormond. This armament put to sea on the 19th of June, 1702, and appeared before Cadiz, but the attempt miscarried. The English, however, were completely successful in their attack upon the French and Spanish squadrons in the harbor of Vigo. The French, unable to resist the attack, sunk and burned a number of ships; but ten ships of war and seven galleons were taken, together with a great amount of treasure, which inflicted a severe blow upon the enemy and added to the fame of the allies. Sir George Rooke returned in triumph to England, and the fortifications to the harbor of Vigo were demolished by Sir Cloudesly Shovel.

In the next year no important naval operations occurred. In 1704, Sir George Rooke, and Sir Cloudesly Shovel were again sent to the Mediterranean to look after the French fleet, when they resolved to make an attempt upon Gibraltar, which was attacked and carried with trifling loss on the 25th of June. The English fleet then proceeded up the Mediterranean, and on the 9th of August, the French fleet was seen and chased; on the 13th it was overtaken. A furious engagement followed which was maintained until night, when the French bore away to the leeward. The English admiral attempted to renew the contest on the following day, but the Count de Toulon declined, and at last disappeared. The English fleet in this action consisted of fifty-three ships of the line, exclusive of frigates; and the French fleet numbered fifty-two ships of the line and twenty-four galleys. The loss was equal; though not a ship was taken or destroyed by either. After the battle, the English fleet sailed to Gibraltar to refit; and leaving a squadron under Sir John Leake, Sir George Rooke returned to England, where he was received with all the demonstrations of respect due his long services.

The French made an attempt to recover Gibraltar in the succeeding October, in the absence of the English squadron; but on its return they were forced to withdraw with the loss of two frigates, and a number of smaller vessels. In January, 1705, they made another attempt for the same purpose; but were still more unfortunate; for Sir John Leake and Sir Thomas Delkes having arrived with a powerful fleet, they almost annihilated the French squadron. In the course of the summer, the English fleet assisted at the capture of Barcelona, and in every quarter the navy maintained its wonted superiority. The French navy was reduced to about thirty ships, and was unable to appear at sea. Peace was concluded at Utrecht, after eleven years of destructive warfare, in which the achievements of Marlborough upon land, and Rooke, Russel and others upon the sea, contributed to the glory of the English reputation. The navy of Britain, at this period, stood pre-eminent. The former great naval powers, Spain, Portugal, and the northern kingdoms, had now declined into a state of insignificance. The French were humbled, and the Dutch were in close alliance with the invincible power which truly ruled the sea.

ADMIRAL BLAKE.

QUEEN ANNE.

CHAPTER XXVI.

FROM THE PEACE OF UTRECHT TO THE PEACE OF PARIS IN 1783.

AFTER the peace of Utrecht, the different powers of Europe set about repairing and increasing their navies. Spain, especially, actively prepared for another contest. The overwhelming superiority of England was so manifest, that if they had done so, she would have swayed Europe at will. The death of Queen Anne and the accession of George I. in 1714, were the immediate causes of another war. The active and able Cardinal

Alberoni, who presided over the councils of Spain, directed his efforts to the creation of a navy, and such was the persevering character of his proceedings, that, only three years after the peace of Utrecht, Europe was astonished at the appearance of a Spanish fleet of thirty ships of war in the Mediterranean, destined for the reduction of Sardinia. The English government despatched a squadron of twenty-two ships into the Mediterranean, under Sir George Byng, to maintain the British authority. The ambitious Alberoni, expecting active hostilities, increased his exertions. Five hundred transports, which carried a formidable land force, were protected by a fleet of twenty-seven ships of various rates, two fire ships, four bomb-ketches, and seven galleys. But this fleet was met by Sir George Byng, off Cape Passaro, on the 11th of August, 1710, and so utterly discomfited, that all the ships were taken except three, which were saved by the conduct of their vice-admiral, a native of Ireland.

Alberoni now thought the most effectual method of annoying Britain was by espousing the cause of the Pretender; and as his naval resources were diminished, he hoped that an invasion of Scotland, on behalf of the Stuarts, might be accomplished successfully with a very moderate force. The Duke of Ormond was chosen to conduct the expedition; and he obtained from the Spanish court a fleet of ten ships of war, and transports having on board six thousand regular troops, with arms for twelve thousand more. This armament sailed from Cadiz in the latter part of 1718, but was dispersed and the greater part destroyed by a storm off Cape Finesterre. These schemes were so much beyond the resources of Spain, that a great outcry was raised, and Alberoni was dismissed. Peace was then concluded with England. (June, 1721.)

Having thus controlled the old monarchy of Spain, England was next called to employ her power against the youthful and rising empire of Russia. A fleet was sent into the Baltic, under Sir John Norris, to act against the Czar Peter, if he did not accede to the proposals of peace with Sweden. The czar was much enraged at the interference of England; but no sooner did the red cross flag appear in the Baltic than the Russian fleet withdrew, and peace was soon secured. The same interference had the same effect in 1726.

Although there was a cessation of hostilities between England and Spain, there was no cordial feeling of amity between them, and they seemed but waiting for an opportunity to injure each other. The English fleets commanding the seas committed many outrages upon the Spanish coast and their shipping; and the Spaniards had not the means of retaliating. The naval history of the reign of George I. was thus void of interest, merely because there was no opposing power to excite a display of strength. But this tide of undisputed success now threatened to become fatal to England, by creating an excess of confidence, which rejected the idea of improvement; and thus, while the French and Spaniards were busy in improving their marine architecture, the English doggedly adhered to the old principles of ship building. Their vessels were very heavy in their sailing, awkward in stowage, and confined in their decks. Yet with such ships the English mariners could and did annihilate the fleets of their opponents.

The many attacks upon the British trading vessels by the Spaniards whom no treaty could bind while they had wrongs to revenge, at last, in 1739, caused the English government to adopt active measures against them. Admiral Vernon, who was sent with a fleet to annoy the Spanish trade in the West Indies, had often boasted that he could take Porto Bello, with only six ships; and being permitted to try the experiment, he succeeded, by a combination of extraordinary temerity and good fortune. Commodore Anson was sent with a squadron to distress the enemy in the South Seas, and a more formidable armament was placed under the command of the hero of Porto Bello. But scarcely had the foolish delirium on account of this exploit subsided, when the English were equally depressed by the failure of the expedition against Carthagena, in which a noble fleet and land force were miserably sacrificed, between the blunders and dissentions of the two English commanders. Even the return of Lord Anson, with all the treasure he had captured in his voyage round the globe, was insufficient to heal the irritation of the people.

COMMODORE ANSON.

The French, who had looked smilingly on the disasters of their ancient rival, were now eager to share in the anticipated triumphs of Spain. They, therefore, resolved upon an invasion of England on behalf of the Pretender. An army of fifteen thousand soldiers, under the command of the celebrated Count Saxe was to be escorted to England by a strong convoy, under Admiral de Roquefeuille, and landed upon the coast of Kent. The armament set sail in January, 1743, but the measure, which depended so much upon secrecy for success, was discovered, and an English fleet, under Sir John Norris, sailing to meet them, the enemy were obliged to put back into port. France then declared war against England.

We can but mention the principal events and the general character of this war. The united fleets of France and Spain, after having been blocked up in the harbor of Toulon, was encountered by Admiral Matthews, on February 11th, 1744, with a very superior force. The battle consisted of a series of skirmishes through four successive days; but such was the confusion of purposes between the British commanders, that the result was wholly indecisive, although from the strength of the English fleet the destruction of their enemies seemed inevitable. A court martial was held in England upon this occasion, at which Matthews, who had gallantly rushed upon the enemy, was dismissed from the service, and the second in command, who had stood aloof, refusing to co-operate, was promoted immediately and entrusted with the command of a powerful armament of sixteen sail of the line, eight frigates, and two bomb-ketches, together with a land force of five thousand eight hundred efficient men. L'Orient was the object of attack; but from mismanagement, this expedition completely failed.

In June, 1755, Louisbourg, in the isle of Cape Breton, which the French had fortified at a vast expense, was taken by Commodore Warren. A few days after the surrender of Louisbourg, two French East India ships, and a Spanish ship, laden with treasure, sailed into the port, on the supposition that it still belonged to France, and were taken by the English. In addition to this territorial loss, the French, in October, 1747, suffered a severe naval defeat. Rear-admiral Hawke, with fourteen ships of the line, fell in with nine ships of the enemy, besides frigates, under the command of De Letendeur, in the latitude of Belle-isle. The English admiral immediately gave chase and the two fleets were soon in contact. The battle was well con-

CAPTURE OF THE TREASURE SHIPS OFF LOUISBOURG.

tested, and lasted from noon till night, when all their ships struck, except two, which escaped in the dark.

Amidst these important movements, a minor warfare, in which the strength of the French was chiefly exerted, had been kept up by privateers and cruisers. As the combined navies of France and Spain did not muster above fifty ships of the line, they wisely avoided general engagements, in which they could have no hope against the superior strength of the enemy. Instead of this, they harassed the British trade by flying squadrons, and compelled their enemies to keep watch in every sea, and waste their strength in destructive efforts to capture fortresses. Such were the exertions of the belligerents to annoy each other, and so far did they succeed, that both parties were glad to conclude a peace at Aix-la-chapelle, in 1748. The French obtained better terms than might have been expected from the relative strength of the parties at the commencement of the war.

The history of the relations of France and England may be characterized as a long war, with an occasional truce. In 1755, symptoms of the renewal of hostilities were plainly evident. At Brest and other French ports, there was a suspicious refitting and mustering of ships; and while it was avowed that this armament was intended to act in North America, the British were amused with professions of peace until it had actually set sail. Upon this, admiral Boscawen was sent out with eleven ships of the line, and one frigate, to watch the motions of the enemy. He was soon reinforced by six ships of the line and one frigate, and repaired to the banks of Newfoundland, at which the French also arrived; but there was so thick a fog at the time that neither party was aware of the neighborhood of the other. After having thus missed each other, Lord Howe fell in with a part of the French fleet at cape Race, and in the action that ensued, he succeeded in capturing two of their ships. The French then proclaimed war; and in consequence of the increase of their marine, they were confident of success. But

LORD HOWE.

the British navy, already a match for the united navies of Europe, was augmented so rapidly, as to make these hopes ridiculous. Before the end of the first year of the war, the British cruisers had captured above three hundred merchant ships and eight hundred French seamen.

Irritated by these losses, the French now attempted to alarm the English by the threats of an invasion, and began to assemble a powerful armament at Toulon. The plan succeeded so effectually, that England was filled with groundless apprehensions. But although France was conscious of her inability to execute such a threat, her ships were not assembled at Toulon in mere idle bravado; and in the beginning of 1756, the fleet sailed on the expedition against Minorca, then occupied by an English garrison. The English had long been informed of the extent of the French preparations, but, for reasons which have never transpired, did not send a fleet to the Mediterranean. On the same day that the French sailed from Toulon, Admiral Byng was sent, with a very inadequate force, to oppose their matured preparations. His only chance of success was an arrival before them. But as the French arrived some weeks sooner, and without resistance landed an efficient army, the delay was fatal. The French fleet was more powerful and efficient than that of the British; but still Byng bore down upon it, and after an undecisive action, obliged it to withdraw and escape during the night. Byng had but a handful of men who had been sent to reinforce the garrison at Minorca, and he knew these could only add to the number of prisoners if landed, and he, consequently, deemed it useless. The garrison of Port Philip was forced to surrender upon honorable terms; and Byng returned to Gibraltar to refit for a second contest.

The conduct of Byng in these operations against the French made him the subject of a great deal of violent and totally unjustifiable reproach. It was alleged that he should have destroyed a superior fleet, which he had forced to leave its object. Such was the popular clamor, and the violence of party spirit, that Byng was court martialed, and in spite of the recommendation of his judges, that he had acted bravely, and, therefore, should be shown mercy, he was condemned to be shot, which sentence was carried into effect on the 14th of March, 1756. It is now generally agreed, that the execution of Byng was a "judicial murder."

In the following year, the British ministry determined upon a de-

DEATH OF ADMIRAL BYNG.

scent upon the coast of France, to counteract the effect of Byng's failure; and a fleet, consisting of eighteen ships of the line, besides frigates, fire ships, bomb-ketches and transports, under Sir Edward Hawke, with a formidable land force, under Sir John Mordaunt, was assembled for this purpose. The secret instructions of the British commanders were to attempt a descent at or near Rochefort, and after capturing it, to burn and destroy all the docks, magazines, and shipping they found there. They sailed in September, and landed at Aix, a small island at the mouth of the Charente, leading up to Rochefort, and finding there a paltry, half finished fort, they attacked and demolished it. After this, instead of proceeding directly to the main object of their commission, they spent several days in deliberating what should next be done, while the French, in the meanwhile, fortified themselves so strongly, that when Hawke and Mordaunt had finished deliberation, they discovered that the opportunity for action had been lost. They then returned home, having accomplished nothing with their expensive armament. Both commanders were tried by court martial, but acquitted.

In the early part of 1758, two naval deeds were achieved that redounded to the honor of England. Admiral Osborne had been for some time blocking up a French fleet in the harbor of Carthagena, when he saw four ships of war, under the marquis du Quesne, coming to its relief. He immediately sent a detachment of his fleet to encounter them: but they fled in different directions. Each English ship then selected its chase and pursued; the enemy were overtaken and compelled to stand at bay; and after a hard fight, the French were so completely worsted that only the smallest vessel of the squadron escaped by superior sailing. The other three large ships were taken or destroyed. A few days after this, Sir Edward Hawke attacked a French fleet of five ships of the line, six frigates, and forty transports, lying off the island of Aix, and having three thousand soldiers on board, besides a large quantity of provisions and stores, for the supply of their settlements in North America. As soon as Hawke stood in to attack them, the French ships slipped their cables and fled in different directions; but the greater number of them grounded in shoal water. There they threw their cannon, stores and cargoes overboard, that they might be warped nearer shore, and thus secured their escape. The destruction of the material, however, effectually defeated the object of the expedition.

The course of German affairs, to which those of England were generally subservient, rendered it necessary to make a diversion in favor of the allies, by a descent on the coast of France; and preparations were made for the attempt. Two squadrons were fitted out: one, of eleven ships of the line, under the command of Lord Anson and Sir Edward Hawke, was sent to the Bay of Biscay, to watch the enemy and harrass their navigation; the other, consisting of four ships of the line and seven frigates, under Commodore Howe, escorted a hundred transports conveying a powerful land force, under the Duke of Marlborough, (grandson of the great duke,) on the chief object of the expedition. Landing near St. Maloes, an attempt was made to carry that strong place, but the land forces could not act without the ships of war, and when the ships of war were ready, the French had made the town impregnable. The only thing effected by Marlborough was the destruction of some shipping and military stores; after which, the French mustering in superior force, compelled him to embark his troops. Several attempts were made to land at other parts of the coast, but contrary and violent winds prevented, and a scarcity of provisions compelled the armament to return to England.

In the following August, the attempt was renewed by the fleet and the army, under General Bligh; and although the French made a stout resistance, the English troops effected a landing at Querqueville, and destroyed the French line of defences. Elated by this success, the British commanders hoped to take St. Maloes; but still found it too strong for their combined forces. Bligh, however, was resolved not to leave the coast without doing some injury; and, therefore, he made a bold dash some miles into the country, and defeated the enemy in several light skirmishes. He then retreated slowly and with drums beating towards the beach of St. Cas, where the fleet waited to receive him. The French assembled in large force, and when the English reached the beach, and began to embark, they made a furious assault upon them. The English were put to flight in five minutes, and the greater portion of them bayoneted or driven into the sea. One thousand men were slain or taken prisoners in this embarkation; and England was astounded at the return of the baffled and disgraced armament. The French were highly elated by their victory.

After this unfortunate expedition, the war, as usual, dwindled for a time into deeds of privateering, in which the English sailors were so successful, that not a French ship could venture out of harbor without being taken. In the following year, the French, still meditating an invasion of England, collected a great number of flat-bottomed boats in the harbor of Havre de Grace; and in consequence of these and other preparations, two English fleets were fitted out for service, the one being placed under Rodney, and the other under Boscawen. The first of these admirals repaired to Havre, where he commenced a thundering bombardment, by which he overturned certain boats, and frightened the townspeople; while the latter made an unsuccessful attempt upon Toulon. After the English retired from Toulon, a French fleet stole out from that harbor, and Boscawen, hearing of the circumstance, immediately gave chase, and overtook it off the coast of Barbary. In the engagement which followed, the French were defeated, with the loss of four large ships, two of which were sunk, and two became important additions to the English navy. The British then established a system of close blockade that extended over the whole French coast. Thus Dunkirk was watched by Commodore Buys; Havre de Grace, by Lord Rodney; Toulon, by Boscawen, and Brest, by Sir Edward Hawke; while lines of British

ADMIRAL RODNEY.

cruisers connected these so closely, that not a single ship could issue from the hostile ports without notice.

The French were on the alert to discover an opening in the blockade. The blockading squadron off Brest was driven off the coast by foul weather, and obliged to return to England; upon which, Admiral Conflans, with twenty-one sail of the line and four frigates, pushed out in the hope of surprising and overpowering the smaller fleet blockading in the absence of Hawke. But just as the French admiral had almost succeeded in his purpose, Hawke suddenly reappeared and gave chase to the enemy. Although of equal force, the French fled to their own coast, hoping that the English would be wrecked among the shoals and rocks; but Hawke continued the chase and overtook them in the neighborhood of Belle-isle. Here a furious battle was fought on November 20th, 1759. It continued till night, and the French fleet, after considerable loss, hauled off and escaped to Rochefort. This victory not only ruined the hopes of invasion entertained by the French, but decided the fate of the war, as the French, after this blow, were unable to accomplish any important naval enterprise. The English naval power was also creditably displayed in the East and West Indies, in Africa, and North America. These operations were too extensive and complicated to detail; but it was made evident that at this time, England brooked no rival upon the throne of Neptune.

The death of George II., which occurred on the 25th of October, 1760, brought no intermission in the war which raged with unabated violence. In the following year, negotiation was tried, but suddenly broken off; and during the course of the negotiation, Belle-isle, on the west coast of France was taken by Commodore Keppel, and Major-general Hodgson, to the great triumph of the English nation. Wishing to deprive the British of the use of the Portuguese ports, France and Spain declared war against that country in January, 1762. This measure seemed only to redouble the efforts and successes of the British navy. Martinique, St. Lucia, St. Vincent, and Grenada were taken from the French. From the Spaniards, the fortress of Havana, in the island of Cuba, was taken, in which capture, the enemy lost nine ships of the line and four frigates, while the British obtained booty to the amount of three millions sterling. Manilla also fell into the hands of the British; and thus were their enemies deprived of their valuable foreign possessions by a superior navy. Such losses made the French and Spaniards desirous of peace, which was at length concluded at Paris, on the 11th of February, 1763. Most of the islands and territory acquired by the heroic achievements of the navy were surrendered to the former owners, at which the English nation were indignant.

The French only desired breathing time. The rembrance of their losses and defeats could not but make a brave and active nation anxious to retrieve them. They employed the interval in strengthening the marine; and an opportunity for renewing offensive measures was soon found in the rupture between Great Britain and her American Colonies. In February, 1778, the French acknowledged the independence of the United States, and entered into a treaty by which they engaged to assist them in attaining their object. At the commencement of this war, it was found, as usual, that confidence of success had produced a neglect of the navy. Intelligence was received that the French had a squadron of twelve sail of the line and six

ADMIRAL KEPPEL.

frigates ready to sail from Toulon, under command of the well known Count d'Estaing, to co-operate with the Americans in their efforts to obtain independence. Admiral Byron was sent to oppose this fleet on the 9th of June; but the boisterous weather effectually dispersed the English fleet, and d'Estaing arrived at New York in safety.

The French had made extensive preparations to carry on the war. Another powerful fleet of thirty-two sail of the line, and a large number of frigates, was being equipped at Brest, under the Count d'Orvilliers. The English ministry were not aware of the strength of this armament. They despatched Admiral Keppel, with only twenty sail of the line and seven frigates and smaller vessels, to watch its motions and protect the English commerce in the Channel. Having captured a lookout frigate, the admiral learned the real strength of the enemy, and returned to Portsmouth for reinforcements. Ten sail of the line were added to his fleet, and he was then a match for his adversary. Unaware of this addition to the British fleet, d'Orvilliers sailed from

Brest to attack it; but when he found it had increased in strength, he endeavored to avoid an engagement. Keppel followed his adversary through the manœuvres of several days, and at length brought him to action on the 27th of July. The action was maintained with great vigor upon both sides; but in consequence of the conduct of Sir Hugh Palliser, the second in command, in failing to come up at the signals of his superior, the English admiral was prevented from achieving a victory otherwise certain. As it was, the fleets parted, a number of the English ships being much disabled, and the loss in men being about equal.

In addition to France, Spain now declared war against England, and the united navies, consisting of sixty-five ships of the line and a great number of frigates, swept the English Channel, and would have taken Plymouth, but for a mistake in their geography. A Spanish fleet blockaded Gibraltar, and reduced the garrison to great extremities. To preserve this valuable conquest, Sir George Rodney was sent with a fleet to its relief, which he performed effectually by the famous victory of St. Vincent, in which six large ships were captured, one blown up, and the remainder of the squadron dispersed. But this success was counterbalanced by the loss of the rich East and West India fleets, which fell into the hands of the enemy. An attempt at invasion was made by the French in January, 1781. They landed eight hundred men upon the island of Jersey, and compelled the governor to surrender. But the commander of the troops and volunteers, Major Pierson, suddenly rushed upon them and defeated them with great slaughter. The expedition then returned.

The Dutch were soon numbered among the enemies of Britain. They were the enemies the English had most reason to fear upon the sea. They displayed a prowess worthy of their former reputation. Admiral Zoutman, who was protecting a rich convoy, was met by Admiral Hyde Parker, with an equal force, off the Dogger bank, in August, 1781, upon which an engagement ensued, unparalleled for desperation among the events of war. For three hours and a half the two fleets continued to cannonade each other, until they sustained so much damage that they lay like logs upon the water, incapable of farther annoyance. At last, the Dutch admiral was able to bear away for the Texel, which he accomplished with difficulty, succeeding in saving his convoy. In the following year, the chief naval event was the victory gained by Admiral Rodney, between the islands of Guadaloupe and Dominique, in which De Grasse was defeated, with the loss of eight of his best ships. By this success, the junction of the French and Spanish fleets was prevented and the island of Jamaica saved. In the same year, Gibraltar was attacked by a fleet of the allied powers, but relieved by Lord Howe, with a much inferior force. The gains and the losses during the war had been so equal, that neither party could boast of obtaining any decisive advantage; and accordingly, each believing that a continuance of the war would result disasterously for itself, a peace was concluded in 1783, by which, after mutual restitution, the different powers found themselves in the same condition as at the commencement of the war, except that their resources were nearly exhausted.

EARL ST. VINCENT.

CHAPTER XXVII.

FROM THE PEACE OF PARIS IN 1783 TO THE PRESENT DAY.

HE peace was continued until the breaking out of the French revolution, by which another war was precipitated—England upon one side and France and Holland upon the other. The English fleets obtained the laurel of victory in the West Indies, where they captured several islands belonging to the French.

The enemy confined their efforts to privateering; and in this they were so successful, that in the month of May, alone, (1793,) they captured ninety-nine British ships, while only one of theirs was taken in return. Necessity at last compelled them to risk a general encounter at sea. As the return of a large fleet of merchantmen, laden with grain from the West Indies, was expected, Admiral Villaret was sent with the Brest fleet to protect the arrival of this valuable convoy. Lord Howe, who had been watching this armament for a long period, suspected its destination, and went in pursuit with twenty-six sail of the line. As soon as the French, who were of equal force, saw the approach of the enemy, they formed the line of battle and occupied the first day in preliminary skirmishing. On the next, May 29th, 1794, an engagement took place, without advantage on either side, after which, in consequence of a thick fog for two days, nothing could be attempted. But on the 1st of June, Howe, who had now gained the weather-gage of the enemy, renewed the encounter, broke their line, and after a terrible cannonade, completely defeated them; capturing seven ships and sinking another. The French, however, saved their convoy. The English fleet was so much crippled by the encounter, that instead of giving chase, Howe was obliged to return to port.

During the same year, two naval engagements upon a smaller scale took place. They were equally honorable to the British flag. While cruising with five frigates off Guernsey and Jersey, Sir John Borlase Warren descried, off the latter island, a squadron of four large French ships under M. Desgareux. The French commander offered battle; and the British commander, who had gained the weather-gage, and placed his squadron between the enemy and their own coasts, engaged them to great advantage. The conflict lasted three hours, at the end of which, two of the French ships struck their colors; the others attempted to escape; but one was overtaken and captured, and the others got clear off. The other affair was in the East Indies, where two British ships encountered and defeated four ships of the enemy, off Mauritius, in October. The French escaped in a crippled state.

In 1795, Parliament voted one hundred thousand seamen for prosecuting the war; and an expedition, under admiral Elphinstone, was sent against the Dutch possessions in Africa. The Cape of Good Hope was obliged to surrender, and this important acquisition was obtained with the loss of only seven men. An expedition was also sent to Quiberon bay to assist the French royalists, by a descent in that quarter. But the renowned Hoche attacked and defeated the troops as soon as landed. In March, 1796, an engagement took place in the Mediterranean, between a British fleet, under admiral Hotham, and one of France, under admiral Richery, which was indecisive. In June, admiral Cornwallis sustained a running fight, with five ships, against thirteen of the enemy; and this last fleet was defeated off L'Orient, by Lord Bridport. As in former times, the French were successful as long as they confined their efforts to privateering, in which the more scientific structure and superior sailing of their vessels gave them decided advantages; and they were victorious as long as they did not seek to meet the British in a general encounter. In consequence of the rapidity of her victories and conquests by land, France could now avail herself of the resources of other nations; and Spain was compelled to lend her ships for the purposes of her enemy.

A Spanish fleet of twenty-seven sail of the line endeavored to effect a junction with the French and Dutch armament at Brest, from whence the united fleets were to sail for the invasion of Britain. To prevent this union, Sir John Jervis set sail to meet the Spanish fleet, and met it near Cape St. Vincent, on the 14th of February. Though numbering but fifteen sail of the line, the English fleet, principally through the heroic disobedience and exertions of Nelson, obtained a splendid victory. Four ships were captured and about seven hundred of the enemy killed or wounded. The loss of the British was three hundred men killed or wounded. This victory created considerable elation in England, on account of the great disparity of the forces engaged in it and the consequent skill and daring displayed in the achievement. Sir John Jervis received his title of Earl of St. Vincent, a pension of three thousand pounds sterling a year and other marks of distinction, in consequence of this victory.

But while Britain had reason to be proud of her ocean bulwarks, an event occurred which she had greater cause to fear than the most perilous naval defeat. This was the mutiny in the fleets, which first broke out at Plymouth, on the 17th of April, 1797. There had been a spirit of discontent among the seamen for some time, caused by their being defrauded in the quantity and quality of their provisions, in the midst of their heroic exertions. The seamen refused to proceed to

BATTLE OF CAPE ST. VINCENT.

sea. They appointed delegates from every ship, and drew up petitions to the admiralty and the House of Commons, in which they stated their wrongs and demanded redress. Their reasonable demands were obtained by their firmness, upon which they returned to their duty. But while the mutinous spirit was thus quelled at Spithead and Sheerness, it was far otherwise at the Nore. At this station they went further in their demands, and whatever might be their justice, resolved to maintain them by force. They took possession of the ships, chose officers from their own number, and proceeded to shut up the mouth of the Thames, and interrupt the national commerce. The government stood firm, and, at length, the mutineers relented and returned to duty—their leader, Richard Parker, being tried and executed. Had not the appearance of a hostile armament recalled the seamen to their sense of duty, the co-operation or even the neutrality of the fleets during an invasion by the French, might have proved fatal to Britain.

THE DUTCH ADMIRAL DE WINTER SURRENDERING TO ADMIRAL DUNCAN.

Having failed in their proposed invasion of England, the French resolved to make a descent on Ireland, by the aid of the Dutch navy. A Dutch fleet, under Admiral De Winter, lay in readiness, in the Texel. Admiral Duncan, who had blockaded this force for a considerable time, was forced to retire for a short time, upon which De Winter seized the opportunity to push out to sea. He was soon overtaken by the active Duncan, with an equal force, upon which the Dutch fleet formed in order for action between Camperdown and Port Egmont, with the shore at nine miles distance. Duncan threw himself between the enemy and the shore, and ordered each of his ships to close with an antagonist, without waiting for forming an order of battle. This daring and novel plan was fully successful, and the victory of Camperdown became one of the brightest in English annals. Eleven of the largest

BATTLE OF THE NILE.

Dutch ships were taken, including that of De Winter. On board the British admiral's ship, Duncan was the only man on deck unwounded.

In the meantime, the French Directory made extensive preparations, with the ostensible object of invading England; but, really, for the conquest of Egypt. The English were completely deceived, and a large army, under Bonaparte, was embarked at Brest, escorted by a fleet under Admiral Bruyes. Bonaparte arrived off Egypt on the 13th of July, and landed his troops. The fleet lay moored off Aboukir. But its destruction was at hand. Lord Nelson had been sent in pursuit of the armament, whose destination was then unknown. After a long and fruitless chase, in which he visited Corsica, Naples, Malta, and even Egypt before the French arrived there, he returned to the latter coast on the 1st of August, where he descried the whole naval force of the enemy at anchor and drawn up in the order of battle. This was all Nelson sought. By the bold manœuvre practised at the Camperdown, he got between the enemy and the shore, broke their line, and gained, what he justly termed, not a victory, but a *conquest.* Of the whole French fleet only two ships of the line and two frigates escaped. Never, since the days of antiquity, was a naval victory attended with more important consequences. It broke the ascendancy of France in Europe, and ruined her hopes of conquest in Asia. The hitherto invincible Bonaparte was shut up in Egypt, where he could receive no reinforcements. This great victory, called generally, the "Battle of the Nile," raised Nelson to the reputation of being the greatest of naval commanders. Honors of all kinds were heaped upon him by the different courts of Europe.

As a counterpoise to such advantages, the power of Britain was less successful in other quarters. Minorca was captured by a British armament without the loss of a man; but at the end of the same year, the British were obliged to abandon all their strong positions upon the coast of St. Domingo. A fleet, under Admiral Mitchell, entered the Zuyder Zee, when an attempt was made to drive the French out of Holland, upon which, Storey, the Dutch admiral, surrendered his fleet of twelve ships without resistance; but the army under the Duke of York, was so injudiciously disembarked and subsequently so unskilfully commanded, that, after many disasters, it was glad to purchase the liberty of retiring. Indeed, by land, the genius of Bonaparte was irresistible. But every part of France was blockaded, and the British were triumphant upon the other element. Up to the year 1800, the navy had destroyed or taken eighty sail of the line, one hundred and eighty-one frigates, two hundred and twenty-four smaller ships of war, seven hundred and forty-three French privateers, fifteen Dutch, and seventy-six Spanish ships.

A formidable combination against the British maritime supremacy, had been matured by the efforts of the French. The Czar of Russia was drawn into it by Bonaparte, and the accession of Denmark and Sweden soon followed. This coalition was matured in 1800, when the northern powers began their hostile operations against the British commerce, and the czar laid an embargo upon all the British ships in his ports, to the number of three hundred, the crews of which he threw into prison. The naval resources of the three powers apparently justified such a step. Russia had eighty-two sail of the line, and nearly forty frigates; Denmark, twenty-three sail of the line and fourteen frigates; and Sweden, eighteen sail of the line and fourteen frigates, not including the smaller vessels of war of various denominations, which each of these powers possessed. Both sides of the Sound were fortified, and batteries were erected on the island of Amack, and on the Sproe, in the Belt, plentifully furnished with artillery men and red hot shot. Copenhagen appeared impregnable.

A British fleet of eighteen sail of the line, four frigates, and thirty smaller vessels of various kinds, commanded by Sir Hyde Parker, and under him, Nelson, the soul of the enterprise, set sail from Yarmouth, on the 12th of March, for the attack on Copenhagen. The fleet entered the Sound; and by keeping to the Swedish side, escaped the opposite batteries at Cronensburgh. On approaching Copenhagen, the road was found fortified with a strong line of ships and war vessels, mounting together six hundred and fifty guns, flanked by formidable batteries, and a strong chain was drawn across the harbor. After two days spent in reconnoitering, Nelson offered to lead the attack, and on the morning of the 2d of April, the battle of Copenhagen commenced. We cannot detail the numerous difficulties of navigation surmounted by Nelson, before his ships could be placed along side of the enemy, and the various changes of fortune which took place after the action commenced. The Danes fought with a spirit worthy of their ancestors. But on the side of their enemies, equal valor was directed by superior skill; so that after a terrible cannonade of five hours, the Danish fire slackened, at the end of which Nelson was in possession of most of their ships and batteries. Nelson then sent the Danes a note, entreating them for their own sakes, to desist from further resistance. The Prince Royal of Denmark yielded, and an armistice of fourteen weeks was agreed to.

Nelson, who was now invested with the chief command, resolved to follow up his successes by an attack upon Sweden; and on learning that a Swedish squadron of six sail of the line, was actually in readiness to join the Russian fleet, he shut up this small force behind the forts of Carlscrona, leaving a squadron sufficient to keep it in blockade. He then repaired to the Revel Roads, in which he anchored on the 14th of May, intending to give the Russian navy a "Nelson touch." But fortunately for that navy, the Czar Paul was assassinated, and his successor, disclaiming all hostility to the English, freed their shipping from embargo. All differences were soon after adjusted.

After these great exertions, the war dwindled into a series of petty encounters upon the sea, which generally resulted in favor of the British. An enterprise undertaken against the French coasts in August of this year, terminated unfortunately. As the object of the French still continued to be the invasion of England, they had collected a great number of gun boats and other vessels at Boulogne. In consequence of these preparations, Lord Nelson was sent to watch this station, with a considerable armament. He had already done the French flotilla some damage, and resolving to attempt its complete destruction, he sent a large force of gun boats and other vessels during the night, to make a sudden onset. But when the attack was made, it was found that a very strong netting was braced up to the lower yards of the French vessels, and that each was moored at the head and stern with iron chains, and defended by nearly two hundred soldiers, and land batteries and musketry from the shore. These difficulties baffled the valor and skill of the assailants, and after a loss of eleven hundred and seventy-two men, the British were obliged to retire. The success of the British fleet and army sent against the French in Egypt, under the command of Lord Keith, Sir Sindey Smith, and Sir Ralph Abercrombie, more than compensated for the defeat at Boulogne. The French were beaten, and compelled to evacuate the scene of their former conquests.

A treaty of peace between France and England was signed at Amiens on the 27th of March, 1802. The two nations seemed desirous of a more friendly relationship than had hitherto existed between them, and the conclusion of the horrors of war was hailed by the majority of the French and English with great satisfaction; but the flattering prospects of anticipations of long peace were destined to be disappointed. Bonaparte knew that when he ceased to dazzle and astonish, he could no longer be the idol of France; and, accordingly, he endeavored to bring about another struggle for supremacy. It was alleged that the English government had perfidiously broken the treaty, and the most active preparations for war were made in all the ports of France and England. War recommenced in May, 1802.

The fleets of Britain blockaded all the ports of their enemy, and captured a number of their foreign possessions. Bonaparte intimated his designs to invade the British isles, and collected and equipped an immense number of flat bottomed boats, at Boulogne. Before these could be used as transports, it was necessary to break through the blockade of the enemy. But having no navy adequate to the enterprise, the French were compelled to let their flotillas repose at their stations. Several attempts were made by the English to blow them up by means of a machine called a catameran; but they all failed. However, after creating a great deal of unnecessary alarm, the invasion was given up as hopeless by Bonaparte. Spain was soon induced to join the enemies of England, by the burning of four of her ships in the harbor of Cadiz, by an English captain.

The naval history of Great Britain, during the year 1805, was fraught with events of such magnitude as to command the attention of the civilized world. France, Spain, and Holland were leagued against her. There were British fleets stationed in the Texel, before Brest, Rochefort, Vigo, Ferrol, Cadiz, Carthagena, and Toulon; and the scene of operations extended from thence westward to Trinidad, the Antilles, and Jamaica. The French Toulon fleet, of eleven sail of the line and two frigates, under Admiral Villeneuve, ventured to sea on the last day of March, when the British fleet, under Nelson, had been obliged to anchor in the Gulf of Palmo. At the same time, the Rochefort squadron, six sail of the line, and two frigates, was equally fortunate in getting to sea. The Rochefort squadron sailed to the West Indies and committed some devastations; but as soon as it was known that admiral Cochrane had been sent against them, the French put back to Rochefort, which they reached in safety. The armament, under Villeneuve, had scarcely got to sea, before it was pursued by the active Nelson, who swept over the whole Mediterranean in quest of the enemy, but in vain. Villeneuve reached Cadiz in safety. There he was joined by a Spanish fleet, swelling his force to eighteen sail of the line, and with this armament the French sailed to the West Indies; but hearing that Nelson was in pursuit of him, he determined to return. There was destruction in the name of Nelson. The combined fleets of France and Spain, which now consisted of twenty sail of the line, three large ships armed *en flute*, five frigates and three brigs, pursued its homeward course without molestation till it was encountered off Cape Finisterre, on the 22d of July, by a British fleet of fifteen sail of the line, two frigates, a cutter and a lugger, under Sir Robert Calder. The French, notwithstanding their superiority, stood on the defensive.

The canonade continued four hours, and the British captured an

LORD NELSON.

eighty-four and a seventy-four; but they did not follow up their success. The remainder of the French fleet hauled off in safety. On his return to England with his prize, Sir Robert Calder was tried by a court martial, and reprimanded; which shows what the victories of Nelson had taught the nation to expect of an admiral.

Villeneuve reached Ferrol in safety; and receiving another reinforcement, he put to sea, and entered Cadiz, compelling Collingwood's small squadron to retire. In the meantime, Nelson had returned from a pursuit unexampled in history. During the short space of seventy-eight days, he had twice traversed the Atlantic ocean, without finding the enemy. He arrived at London on the 20th of August, and having learned there of the arrival of the French at Cadiz, he willingly accepted the task of encountering them. A powerful armament was fitted out, and on the 14th of September, he hoisted his flag on board the Victory, at Portsmouth, and proceeded on that expedition which was to be his brightest and his last. The chief difficulty was to get the French to sea; and to accomplish this object, Nelson was obliged to use a stratagem. He kept aloof from Cadiz, thereby offering them free passage; and to increase the inducement, he detached a squadron from his fleet, as a convoy to Malta, knowing that a reinforcement was on its way from England to join him. The plan completely succeeded. Villeneuve and the Spanish admiral Gravina, supposing Nelson had no more than twenty-one ships, boldly put to sea, on the 19th of October, with eighteen sail of the line and fifteen frigates. But Nelson had now received the expected reinforcement, and, on the 21st, he came up with the combined fleet, which was almost becalmed off Trafalgar.

Having telegraphed the glorious motto, "England expects every man to do his duty," Nelson bore down for battle at noon, at the head of the weather column, while Collingwood, at the same time, moved forward with the lee column. The lines advanced in the order of their sailing. The plan adopted by Villeneuve was admirable, and might have succeeded against another antagonist. Still conceiving that Nelson had only twenty-one sail, the French admiral had detached twelve of his ships to double upon the British after the action had closed, and thus place half of them at least between two fires. But when he discovered the real force of the enemy, he was obliged to alter this arrangement, and adopt that of a crescent convexing to the leeward.

The onset was commenced by Collingwood, breaking through the enemy's line, at the twelfth ship from the rear, and closing his vessels upon the French and Spanish ships, until the muzzles of their cannon were actually in contact. Nelson, with the weather column, had designed in the same manner, to break the van of the enemy, at the tenth or eleventh ship; but finding them lying too close together for such a purpose, he ordered each vessel to close with its antagonist. Thus the conflict became a hand to hand trial of courage and activity. The French and Spaniards fought desperately on the occasion; but the British, under their great commander, were determined to conquer, and nothing can withstand that determination when backed by superior

NELSON MORTALLY WOUNDED.

skill. Nearly every one of the crew of the Victory was either killed or wounded by the tremendous fire of the small arms of the French, and at half past one o'clock in the day, the heroic Nelson was mortally wounded, being shot through the backbone, while standing on the quarter-deck. After the battle had continued for about three hours with unabated fury, Gravina, the Spanish admiral, seeing many ships dismasted and a large number in possession of the English, collected all that could obey his signals and sailed away for Cadiz, as had been foreseen from the beginning of the day. The five headmost ships of the enemy's van, under command of Rear-admiral Dumanoir, were not able to avail themselves of this opportunity, their retreat being cut off; they therefore made sail on the larboard tack, keeping up a heavy fire upon every ship within their reach. Only one was arrested in the flight; and the battle of Trafalgar ended with the capture of nineteen sail of the line, of which nine were French, and ten were Spanish.

The battle of Trafalgar was the most destructive of all naval contests and was followed by a storm which continued for several days after, in which a greater loss of life occurred than in the desperate conflict. The victors made every exertion to rescue their subdued foes from the destructive elements. The British loss amounted to four hundred and forty-three killed, and twelve hundred and twenty-seven wounded. The loss of the enemy was very great. By the wreck and sinking during the battle, some thousands perished. In the captured ships, twenty thousand prisoners were taken, including the troops. Only four of the prizes could be brought into Gibraltar. The rest were wrecked, or destroyed by the victors. The relics of the French fleet, under Dumanoir, was met on the 2d of November, off Ferrol, and after a hard fight of three hours and a half, the whole force surrendered. This completed the annihilation of the French navy. The death of Nelson was felt as a public calamity; and even such a victory was thought dearly purchased by the loss of such a hero.

At the close of the year 1805, Bonaparte, anxious for the preservation of the French possessions in the West Indies, collected eleven ships of the line, and several frigates, and sent them to that quarter, under command of Villaumez and Jerome Bonaparte. A portion of this squadron was captured by Admiral Duckworth, and the rest were wrecked and every ship destroyed but that of Jerome Bonaparte, which succeeded in reaching L'Orient. In the meantime, a close blockade was kept up on the French coast. The British ships now boldly ventured to attack the French ships in the ports, under protection of batteries; and in this species of warfare, Lord Cochrane was particularly conspicuous.

The principal naval exploit of 1807, was the bombardment of Copenhagen and the capture of the whole Danish navy. The British government, apprehending, that, as the Danes were so much under the influence of Bonaparte, he would make use of their naval resources, determined to strip them of their shipping for a time. For this object, forty-two sail of the line, carrying twenty thousand men, set sail from England, while the British consul endeavored to convince the Danish government of the rationality of such a process. The Danes prepared for a stubborn resistance; but in spite of their gallant defence, Copenhagen was almost destroyed by a bombardment of several days, and the fine fleet of sixteen ships of the line, fifteen frigates, a multitude of brigs and gun boats, and an immense quantity of naval stores fell into the hands of the British. This cruel and destructive attack upon a nation at peace with the English cannot be justified by any of the laws of civilized nations. The Danish fleet was not restored until the conclusion of a general peace.

In 1809, Great Britain made extraordinary exertions to carry on the war, and sixty-four millions pounds were placed at the disposal of the government. In this year, the most powerful armament that Britain had ever fitted out, was despatched on the "unfortunate" Walachean expedition. Thirty-nine sail of the line, thirty-six frigates, and a multitude of smaller vessels, conveying an army of forty thousand men, would have promised success to any enterprise; but it was commanded by the inexperienced and incompetent Earl of Chatham. This mighty armament appeared off the coast of Zealand, on the 30th of July, and landed troops who met with no resistance till they came to the town of Flushing. Instead of leaving a small force to blockade that place, and pushing on to Antwerp, the British commander commenced a regular seige of it, and though he compelled it to surrender, the forces of the enemy had assembled so rapidly in the meanwhile, that the main object of the expedition was lost. Leaving fifteen thousand men to garrison Flushing, the armament which had cost twenty millions of pounds sterling, returned home. This was the worst conducted enterprise of the war.

The only interruptions in the career of naval triumph met with by the British were in the war with the United States. The notice of the victories achieved by the infant navy of the descendants of the English will be given in the history of that navy. Suffice it here to say, that the Americans were almost invariably successful. The English fleets found considerable employment in the operation against the Barbary States; where Lord Exmouth and a Dutch and English combined fleet almost destroyed Algiers, killed many thousands of the inhabitants, and compelled the dey to abolish Christian slavery forever. This wholesome chastisement was so effectual, that for seven years the Algerines refrained from their wonted piracies against the Christian powers; but this state of things was irksome to a people accustomed to plunder and violence, and in 1823, they resumed their old practices. An English fleet was sent against them, and fear this time reduced them to submission.

By a treaty signed at London, between Great Britain, France, and Russia, it was agreed to interfere in the struggle between the Greeks and the Turks. The British fleet, under Sir Edward Codrington, reached its station in February, 1827. An armistice was concluded between Sir Edward and Ibrahim, commander in chief of the Turkish and Egyptian forces, upon the faith of which, the Turkish and Egyptian fleet was permitted to anchor unmolested in the bay of Navarino. The French and Russian fleets soon joined the English, and some indications of a violation of the armistice being given by the Turks, the fleet of the allies weighed anchor and sailed in the form of a crescent towards the Turkish fleet. The opposing fleets were soon front to front, and the first gun being fired by the Turks, the battle of Navarino commenced. The close and heavy cannonade was continued for four hours. But the enemy, notwithstanding their numbers and ferocious courage, were no match for steady, European valor, backed by science and experience. Ship after ship, belonging to the Turks, was reduced to a wreck, or set on fire by its own crew; so that the whole bay was covered with wrecks, and enveloped in conflagration. The havoc and slaughter so peculiar to a sea fight seemed on this day to be exceeded in the bay of Navarino. One feature of the contest is particularly worthy of note. The French and British sailors, fought side by side and seemed to emulate the deeds of each other. Several times during the hottest of the fight, the French vessels saved their English allies from being overpowered by numbers, and the English fully reciprocated the conduct of those whom they had been taught to consider as their natural enemies. The Turkish and Egyptian fleets were almost annihilated, and the independence of Greece secured; but the gallant

BATTLE OF NAVARINO.

admiral, Sir Edward Codrington was not honored by his government for this splendid victory. Party spirit led to his recall from the command in the Mediterranean.

The battle of Navarino was the last great achievement in which the English navy has participated; and it was fully equal to the most glorious deeds of those who have been so long the rulers of the ocean. Latterly, the naval strength of the other great powers of Europe, and of the United States, has been so much increased, that they are in a condition to dispute the sovereignty so long held by England. At present, the navy of the United Kingdoms numbers upon the whole, nearly seven hundred vessels; one hundred and twenty-five of which are steamers, ninety-nine ships of the line, eighty frigates, and the rest smaller vessels. The great extent and distance from the mother country, of the foreign possessions, make such a navy an indispensable requisite for their preservation. The highest naval officer of Great Britain is entitled the "Admiral of the Fleet," who, when he embarks, is distinguished by the hoisting of the union flag at the main top-gallant mast head. The vice-admiral takes rank with the lieutenant-general of the army; the rear-admiral ranks with the major-general. Admirals, being commanders in chief of any squadron, carry their flags at the main top-gallant mast head, from which they are designated as admirals of the red, of the white, or of the blue. Ireland has four vice-admirals, Scotland one, and the governors of colonies, generally, hold a commission to preside over vice-admiralty courts, from which there is an appeal to the English court of admiralty. The principal naval stations and depots are Portsmouth, Deptford, Chatham, and Plymouth. At each of these there is a vast collection of the stores and equipments necessary for such a mighty navy.

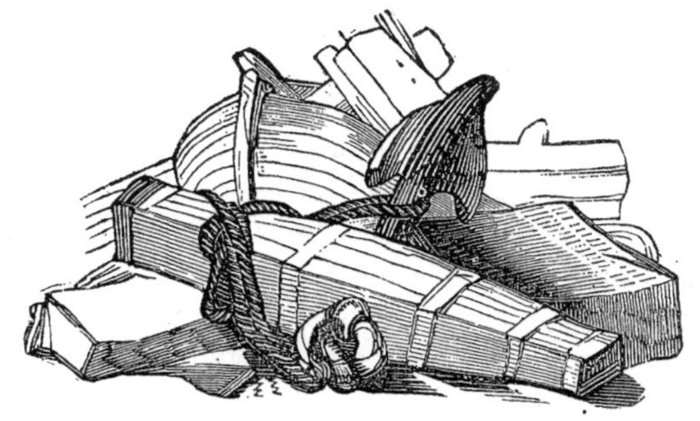

CHAPTER XXVIII.

FRANCE.

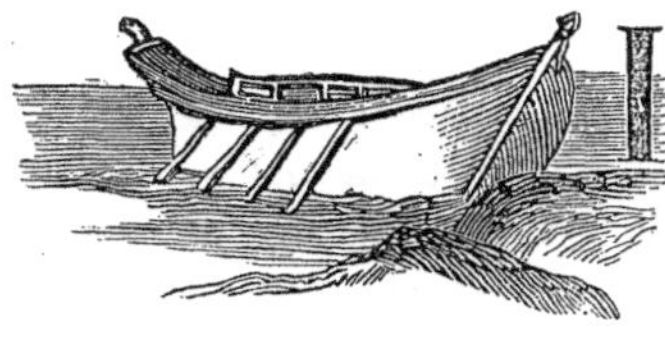

IN our history of the British navy we have unavoidably given a general idea of the rise, progress, and achievements of its often vanquished, but indefatigable rival of France. It but remains to notice that which had no connection with British history, and thus to fill up the picture. There will be found as noble an exhibition of skill and valor in French naval annals as in those of any other nation; and though for a long period held inferior in power to England upon the sea, the French vessels, were considered by the English themselves, as the best models, and the daring activity and skill displayed by a Renaud and a Thurot, forced admiration from their enemies, so capable of appreciating such qualities.

We are informed that Charlemagne was forced to create a navy to protect the coasts of France from the attacks of the daring pirates of the North, towards the close of the eighth century. The vessels composing this navy were, doubtless, of a construction similar to those of the Northmen and the Saxons, which have already been described.

But this navy does not appear to have been very efficient, or else was much neglected; for the attacks of the Normans were always successful, and they even sailed up the Seine as far as Paris, during the reign of Charles the Bald, the grandson of Charlemagne. Their retirement was purchased by heavy sums, which only made them more eager to return. Their fleets, at length, took possession of some islands in the Seine and Loire, which seemed as depots for booty and as points of departure for further conquest: and, finally, they obtained a permanent footing in France, under the celebrated Rollo.

The fleet used by William the Conqueror, in his invasion of England has already been described; but we may observe here, that the reported number and character of the vessels exhibit the naval power of the inhabitants of Normandy in a favorable light. The fleet is said by some to have consisted of three thousand vessels of all kinds and sizes, created principally by the contributions of barons of Normandy. The greater portion of the fleet was destroyed by William after landing his forces.

In the crusade in which Philip Augustus and Richard Cœur de Lion joined their forces, the French king was compelled to make use of the Genoese and Pisan galleys for the transportation of his followers, which seems good evidence that, at that time, (A. D. 1191,) France was without a navy. But after John had ascended the throne of England and had lost the greater portion of his continental territory, Philip prepared a formidable fleet for the invasion of Britain. This, however, was destroyed by the English mariners, as related in the naval history of Great Britain. In the crusade, undertaken by St. Louis, in the early part of the thirteenth century, a vast fleet was employed to convey the forces of the invaders. But the vessels were all obtained from Venice, Genoa, and Catalonia, each of which was considerably enriched by the necessity which compelled the crusade to make use of its maritime resources. This expedition to the Holy Land, though at first successful, afterwards met with a series of disasters, among which was the destruction of the greater portion of the fleet. Not more than one-third of those who embarked in it returned to France.

A second crusade was undertaken by St. Louis, in 1270. The French fleet was joined by thirteen English vessels, commanded by the Prince of Wales, afterwards Edward I. of England, and sailed from Aignes-Mortes on the 1st of July. From that moment every thing went wrong. The vessels had scarcely started before the water and provisions began to fail, and a mortality immediately broke out among the troops. The fleet first sailed to Tunis, where the Mahomedans were plundered and slaughtered without mercy. But a terrible retribution visited the barbarous ones who robbed and butchered under a banner of peace. A malady broke out, to which St. Louis and many of his distinguished followers, fell victims. At last, the remnant were relieved by Charles of Anjou, and the whole embarked to return home. But a terrible storm overtook them off Trapani, which wrecked eighteen of their largest ships, and a still greater number of transports, in which many knights and warriors, and an immense store of military equipments were swallowed up by the sea. The remainder arrived safely home.

For a long time after this expedition, the French monarchs purchased the use of the Genoese galleys whenever there was a necessity for naval operations. The inhabitants of the sea coast of Picardy and the other northern provinces were bold and skilful mariners, who were constantly engaged in piratical expeditions against the coast of England. With them, the French navy originated, and by their exertions was it for a long time an efficient arm of warfare. English fleets could make but little head at this time against the almost constantly allied fleets of France and Spain, and they sustained some notable defeats, more than compensating for the two naval victories of Edward III.

When war with England occurred in 1385, Charles VI. collected and equipped a tremendous fleet for the invasion of England. Every port, from Prussia to Spain, contributed to swell its numbers, till no fewer than thirteen hundred and eighty-seven vessels were assembled at Sluys, where the embarkation was to take place. But the dissentions of the French nobles and a disastrous shipwreck destroyed the hopes of the king; and all subsequent attempts during his reign ended in the same way. The admiral of the vast fleet was Sir John de Vienne, who was proven to have been one of the ablest and bravest naval commanders of his time.

The commerce of the Mediterranean was shared by Marseilles, Montepelier, and Beaucaire, during the latter part of the fourteenth century; and a great number of French vessels employed in it were occasionally formed into fleets for the service of the state. In the struggles which followed the appearance of Joan of Arc, this was especially the case. Fleets fitted out by the merchants of these French Mediterranean towns transported armies to various places upon the coasts of the British continental provinces, and contributed materially to the final expulsion of the invaders. After the death of Joan, one of these merchants, named Jacques Cœur, who had made the south redound with his commercial renown, contributed the greater portion of his enormous wealth and his trading vessels to the service of his king. This and his subsequent exertions in his country's cause, make him worthy of a place on the scroll of Fame, beside the warrior maid of Orleans.

During the war with the Venetian republic in the reign of Louis XII. the French fleet were equipped at Marseilles to act in concert with the land forces of the king. Contarene, the Venitian admiral, was encountered by a French cruiser, Prégent de Brideux, who came with his galleys into the port of Genoa, and pursued the Venitians almost to Civita Vecchia. This same naval commander was made admiral by Louis; and soon after defeated the English fleet in Brest harbor, and made several ravaging descents upon the coasts of the enemy. (A. D. 1513.) The battle in August of the same year between the largest ships in the French navy, under Primauget, and eighty of the English vessels has already been mentioned. The "Cordelier," the largest of the French galleys, which was burned in this action, is said to have carried twelve hundred men, beside her crew. No further trial of naval strength occurred during this war.

FRANCIS I.

The warlike ambition of Francis I., which brought him into contests with Charles V. and with Henry VIII. of England, made it necessary for him to maintain a considerable navy. The Genoese were generally in alliance with him, and their powerful fleets were often employed by him. When, in September, 1524, Marseilles was besieged by land and blockaded by sea, the Spanish fleet, under Admiral Moncarde, which had been

ANDREW DORIA.

compelled to give up the blockade, was attacked near Nice, by the French Vice-admiral, La Fayette, and the famed Genoese admiral, Andrew Doria; and after three of the galleys had been sunk, the remainder of the fleet was driven on shore, and burned by the Spaniards themselves, to save it from falling into the hands of the enemy. Andrew Doria was employed as an admiral for a long time by the French ministers; but being a frank, blunt sailor, he conducted himself too independently towards his employers. They caused the king to view him with suspicion, and treated his advice in naval affairs with disrespect. Finally, tempting offers induced him to enter into the service of Charles V., and became one of the most active and successful of the enemies of Francis.

In August, 1543, the French king received a valuable and timely addition to his naval strength by the alliance of the celebrated Barbarossa, who joined the fleet of the Count D'Enghien, with one hundred and fifty sail. The combined fleets forced an entrance into the port of Nice, took possession of that city and compelled the garrison to retreat to the fort. The crescent was displayed from the walls, side by side with the standard of France. The fort was bravely defended.

Barbarossa, offended at some demands of the French commander, and hearing of the approach of a hostile fleet under Doria, could not be induced to stay during a long siege, and accordingly sailed away to indulge his piratical propensities.

HENRY VIII.

Henry VIII. leagued with Charles V. against Francis, in 1544, and the allied monarchs invaded France at different points. Several towns were captured by Henry, with but little opposition. In the following year, Francis undertook the siege of Boulogne, the most important port of the English forces, and to prevent its being victualled by the English fleet, he equipped above two hundred sail, besides galleys, commanded by Admiral D'Annebaut, with which a descent on England was projected. D'Annebaut sailed to the Isle of Wight, where the English fleet was lying at anchor, at St. Helen's. It consisted of less than one hundred sail, and the admiral thought it wise to remain in that road, in order to decoy the French into the narrow channel and among the rocks. For two days, the fleets fired on each each other, but the damage done was inconsiderable. One of the largest English ships, the Mary Rose, went down, but whether from the enemy's fire, or from accident, was a matter of some doubt. The French fleet soon after returned, having effected nothing. A peace was concluded soon after this between the rival princes.

Henry II., the successor of the chivalrous Francis, did not neglect the navy. He entered into a league with the Turks against the emperor of Germany, and made extraordinary exertions to carry on the war vigorously. Thirty galleys equipped in the Mediterranean, were sent to join the fleet of Solyman; and twenty-five others were sent to cruise and blockade the ports of Spain or those of the Low Countries. The imbecility or neglect of the French admiral, Dragut, prevented the junction of the allied fleets, so that the Turks were left to combat the imperial fleet alone. This, however, they were quite e[illegible] to, and they succeeded in defeating the Admiral Doria. The French fleet was of litle service during the war. A truce was soon concluded, by which the French monarch obtained considerable territory.

Hostilities were renewed as soon as Philip II. had succeeded Charles V. as emperor. The same admiral continued in command of the French fleet, and although much more numerous, its operations were characterized by the same want of activity. In fact, the navy of France was always most shamefully neglected till necessity compelled the government to give it some share of its attention. The admirals were generally men of consideration and active politicians; but possessed little maritime knowledge or skill. The French were inferior in naval enterprise to the Spaniards and Portuguese, and the vast field for exertion opened by the discovery of the Cape of Good Hope and of America, did not excite their efforts. Internal dissensions occupied the thoughts of king and people.

When Louis XIV. ascended the throne, in 1650, he found the navy in a poor condition. While the English and Dutch covered the ocean with nearly three hundred ships of war, the whole maritime force of France consisted of fifteen or sixteen great barks, which the Duke de Beaufort had led against the pirates of Barbary, and when the states general summoned Louis to join his fleet with theirs in the war with England, there was in the port of Brest but one single fire ship, which the government was ashamed to order to sail, but which it was necessary to send in order to fulfil the engagements of the nation. The achievements of De Ruyter, however, enabled the allies to conclude a peace on favorable terms.

The vast schemes of Louis made the creation of a navy necessary. An alliance was formed with England by which that power agreed to send fifty-six ships to join a French fleet, and war was then declared against the Dutch; but their great admiral, De Ruyter, defeated the combined French and English fleets and maintained the command of the sea against them. The principal French naval commander at this time was the Count d'Estreés, who was an honor to the infant navy—being both brave and skilful. In 1674, the Chevalier de Vallette, with a few French frigates, broke the line of blockade, maintained before Messina by a Spanish fleet, and relieved the garrison. Shortly afterwards, a French fleet, composed of seven vessels, of sixty and eighty guns, together with many fire ships, appeared before the same place. The fleet was commanded by Duquesne, a mariner whom Colbert had selected. The Spanish fleet was beaten and driven from those latitudes, and Messina fell into the hands of the French.

Fortune seemed to favor the French on the sea. The court of Madrid courted the alliance of Holland; and De Ruyter was sent to the Mediterranean with twenty-three large ships. Duquesne had just put Toulon in a state of safety, while escorting a convoy to Messina. On the 8th of January, 1676, in sight of that city, between the islands of Stromboli and Salini, he met the combined Dutch and Spanish fleets, which endeavored to shut him up in the straits. A battle ensued, which was long and obstinate, but attended with no decisive results. Duquesne, leaving the enemy's fleet much damaged, proceeded to Sicily, entered the strait, and reached Messina. The allies, after vainly endeavoring to blockade the port, went to besiege Agousta. Duquesne followed, and came up with them near the Gulf of Catana. He had thirty-seven vessels under his command, and De Ruyter had thirty-nine. They fought for ten hours. The Dutch at last took advantage of the wind, and sailed to Syracuse. De Ruyter had received a mortal wound. Seven days after, the greatest of the naval commanders of Holland breathed his last. Deprived of their gallant chief, the combined squadrons could not long continue the contest with Duquesne; but they made a desperate effort. Twenty-seven vessels and nineteen galleys were assembled at Palermo. Duquesne and the Duke of Vivonne proceeded to attack them with twenty-eight men of war and twenty-five galleys. The allies experienced a complete overthrow. Their line of battle was forced at the first shock; half of their vessels were wrecked in the port; twenty-five ships were sunk, with five thousand men, and the remainder were either taken or dispersed; and the port of Palermo was devastated by the victors. This was the most complete naval triumph ever gained by the French. It opened to her magnificent views. The empire of the sea seemed to belong to her, where there did not exist a single Spanish vessel, and from which it was thought easy to exclude the English and Dutch forever. But Louis was more anxious for the success of his enemies than for that of his fleet.

In 1677, the Count d'Estreés captured from the Dutch the fortress on the island of Cayenne; and shortly afterwards he beat the Dutch Admiral

Bruck burnt his fleet, and captured the island of Tobago. These were the last naval achievments of this war, in which France combated the rest of Europe, and dictated the terms of peace. Louis XIV. reached the height of his fortune. When a general war recommenced in 1687, France had become a maritime power of the first rank. The military port of Brest was enlarged, that of Toulon created, at an immense expense, and rendered capable of containing a hundred vessels of war, with an arsenal and proportionate materiel. The like was done at Dunkirk, and on a still greater scale at Rochefort. Companies of coast guards were created, and sixty thousand new sailors were obtained from the mercantile shipping. In a short time, Louis XIV. had two hundred ships, and a hundred thousand men to man them. These mighty naval preparations were due to the activity of the Marquis de Seignelay, a son of the great Colbert.

To prove to Europe that this navy would be capable of maintaining its rank among its marine rivals, Louis sent his squadron, under the orders of Duquesne, to clear the Mediterranean of the pirates by whom it was infested. He avenged himself on Algiers by a new art discovered by a Frenchman. This art consisted in the employment of bomb ships, by means of which maritime cities could be speedily reduced to ashes. There was then living, a young man named Bernard Renaud, commonly known by the name of "the little Renaud;" and who, without having served in a ship, had become, from the force of his genius, an excellent mariner. Colbert loved to detect merit in obscurity, and had taken him into favor. It was chiefly by his exertions, the workmen succeeded in constructing galliots. He did not scruple to propose to the council, that Algiers should be bombarded by the fleet. The proposition was thought extravagant; and, of course, Renaud had to bear that contradiction and that unsparing ridicule which every inventor ought to expect; but the firmness and eloquence of this man induced the king to permit the experiment. In consequence of this decision, Renaud caused five vessels to be constructed, smaller than ordinary ships, but with stronger timbers, without a deck, with a false tiller in the hold, on which they formed masses of brick work, capable of receiving the mortars which were to be employed. With this preparation, Renaud sailed, under the orders of the old and successful admiral, Duquesne, who was entrusted with the command of the whole expedition. But the admiral and the

ALGIERS BOMBARDED BY DUQUESNE.

ADMIRAL DE TOURVILLE.

Algerines were not a little astonished in the sequel, to see the effect of the bombs. In a short period, a great portion of the city was consumed, or in ruins. This art soon found its way to other nations, and added to the instruments of destruction already in the hands of warriors. Thrice was Algiers bombarded by Duquesne and d'Estreés, and forced to give up all Christian prisoners and sue for peace.

Louis espoused the cause of James II. of England, when that monarch was forced to leave his dominions. He furnished the banished king with twenty sail of the line, with which he proceeded to Ireland. The Chevalier de Chateau Renaud, who had defeated the English fleet commanded by Admiral Herbert, had landed five thousand men in Ireland, and on his return, captured five Dutch ships. A fresh convoy afterwards left the ports of Brest, Rochefort, and Toulon. "The ports of Ireland and the English Channel were filled with French vessels." At length a fleet of seventy-two line of battle ships, and twenty fire ships, commanded by Tourville, vice-admiral of France, and having under his orders the Chevalier de Chateau Renaud, met, on the 10th of July, 1670, at Beachy Head, on the coast of Sussex, the Dutch and English fleet of sixty men-of-war and thirty frigates and fire ships, under Admiral Herbert. The engagement lasted ten hours; seventeen of the allied fleet were disabled, and either run aground or burnt; the remainder took refuge in the Thames and the Dutch harbors. Emboldened by this success, Seignelay, "who dared every thing," caused the galleys of the Mediterranean to be brought on the ocean—a novel spectacle for England. The fleet, revictualled at Havre, divided itself into many squadrons of cruisers; the galleys were made use of to effect a descent on Tynemouth, where they set fire to a number of men-of-war and merchant vessels. The French fleet was unable to prevent the passage of William III to Ireland.

After James had been defeated and returned to France, Louis caused a fleet of twelve ships of the line and ninety transports to sail from the harbor of Brest, in order to land a large army and a great quantity of stores in Ireland. The land forces, under General St. Ruth, were defeated at Aghrim, and then the French fleet, receiving the fugitives from that fatal field, returned to France. Seignelay left the navy in a flourishing state, and his successor, Ponchartrain, prided himself upon the excellent manner in which the marine was sustained. He had no difficulty in collecting three hundred transports between Cherbourg and La Hogue, in 1692. The defeat of the French fleet, under Tourville, has already been described in the naval history of England. Tourville was a brave and skilful admiral; and such was his conduct in the battle of La Hogue, that Louis XIV. gave him the baton of a marshal. The defeat was owing to the great superiority in numbers of the Dutch and English.

On the 29th of June, 1693, Tourville attacked, between Logos and Cadiz, a convoy of the Levant, escorted by twenty-seven ships of war, commanded by Admiral Sir George Rooke. But fifteen ships of the escort escaped. The rest were taken or sunk with the convoy, consisting of eighty sail. The victory cost the allies more than forty millions. But it was not so much the navies of France and Spain that damaged the commerce of England and Holland, as the corsairs, who were most active in their depredations. Squadrons, or single cruisers, commanded by Duguay Trouin, Jean Bart, Forbin, Nesmond, Pintis, Ducasse, enriched with the spoils of the merchants of London,

ADMIRAL DUGUAY TROUIN.

Cadiz, and Amsterdam, the privateers of Dieppe, Dunkirk, Havre, and St. Malo. In the course of nine years, the last mentioned city saw two hundred and sixty-two ships of war, and three thousand three hundred and eighty merchant vessels brought into its harbor. The Dutch had the mortification to see on their coast, a corsair from Dunkirk disperse their fleet, snatch from it a convoy of grain, which Louis had caused to be brought from the Baltic, and return to Dunkirk through the midst of an English squadron which blockaded that port.

In 1711, a fleet was fitted out by the French merchants, and placed under the command of the famous Duguay Trouin. This expedition was sent against Brazil. It forced an entrance into the port of Rio Janeiro, burned a Portuguese fleet, and compelled the city to pay a ransom of more than eight millions. No further naval operations took place until the peace of Utrecht, in April, 1713. After the death of Louis le Grand, the English held undisputed command of the watery realm. Feeble ministers, thinking only of their own pleasure and aggrandizement, left the navy to dwindle into insignificance. The celebrated Marshal de Saxe, maintained the glory of the French upon land, and effectually beat back her thick-coming foes.

In January, 1756, war with England commenced. A fleet was armed at Brest; and while the English were deceived by preparations, as if for an invasion, the Marquis de Montcalm set sail for Canada. A fleet from Toulon disembarked, unobserved, under the walls of Minorca, twelve thousand men, commanded by Richilieu. An English fleet, under Admiral Byng, attempted to relieve the garrison, but failed; and in the action with the French fleet, under La Gassompiere, was repulsed. The French fleet in the Indian Ocean was twice attacked by an English fleet, under Admiral Pocock, but the result was indecisive. The French fleet then returned home. Dubrais's successes and positive reverses had at this time almost destroyed the naval reputation of France.

But one brilliant effort threw a lustre over the French name Thurot, one of the first, if not the first, commanders in French naval annals, had for a long time, unfortunately for his country, held an inferior station. He was in command of a small squadron blocked up in Dunkirk by a superior force under Admiral Buys. But, watching his opportunity, he managed to issue from his confinement; and although his force consisted of only five small ships of war, and about fifteen hundred soldiers, such was his known skill and daring, that the news of his escape spread terror through the whole of England. So great, however, was the overwhelming force by which he was immediately pursued, that he was obliged to fly to the northern seas for refuge, where he endured incredible hardships. But indignant at the thought of returning home without performing some exploit worthy of his reputation, Thurot actually landed in Ireland, and took the town of Carrickfergus. This was the close of his brilliant career. On February 28th, 1760, he was attacked by Commodore Elliott, and slain in the engagement, upon which his ships surrendered; so much depends upon the life of a great leader.

The Seven Years' War gained for the English the reputation of being invincible upon the sea. But the ardor and prospects of the French were revived during the struggle of the American Colonies for independence. When Louis XVI. had concluded a treaty with the United States, he did not limit his manifestation of a favorable disposition to mere words; but hastened to send a fleet of twelve sail

RODNEY'S VICTORY OFF GUADALOUPE.

COUNT D'ESTAING.

of the line, under Count d'Estaing, to New York. The battle of Ouessant, fought July 28th, 1778, in which, during the whole day, Count d'Orvilliers sustained a contest, the force on each side being equal, tended to renew the naval ardor of the nation. The islands of St. Domingo, St. Vincent, and Grenada, were captured by d'Estaing; and Senegal was taken from the English. Sixty-six ships of the line, French and Spanish, cruised on the ocean. The West India fleet, under Count de Grasse, sustained a severe defeat on the 12th of April, 1782, off Guadaloupe. The English admiral, Rodney, triumphed chiefly by a bold manœuvre, before unknown to naval tactics —that of breaking through the enemy's line. The French fought bravely. Eight of their ships struck to the enemy and one blew up. Their loss was three thousand slain and double that number wounded. The loss of the British was much less. Little substantial advantage, however, was derived by the English from their victory. Admiral Graves, sailing home with the prizes, experienced a terrible shipwreck, and three thousand souls perished. Peace was concluded in 1783.

COUNT DE GRASSE.

The French revolution of 1789, involved that people in a war with most of the nations of Europe. At first the forces of the republic were every where defeated. The people of Toulon surrendered their town and fleet to the English. The revolutionary army approached, and, principally by the skill of Napoleon Bonaparte, then a lieutenant, compelled the English to evacuate the town. Before their departure, they burned most of the vessels which they could not bring off. The French met with an almost uninterrupted career of success upon land, while the English were equally victorious upon the sea. Almost all the French colonies in the West Indies were taken without difficulty.

In the course of the year 1796, the French made an attempt to invade Ireland, in order to assist the United Irishmen, who were discontented with the conduct of the British government. The fleet escaped from Brest, without being discovered by the English squadron. It consisted of a large number of transports, escorted by seventeen sail of the line and a number of frigates. But a train of circumstances occurred which rendered the expedition abortive. The time of sailing had been delayed beyond the proper period, and at the point of sailing, a dangerous mutiny broke out among the troops. After the ships left the harbor, two of them ran foul of each other; a large seventy-four was wrecked; and on the 23d of December, when the fleet reached the coast of Ireland, it was dispersed by a storm. Finding that the season for action had passed, the shattered squadron returned to its station at Brest. During the remainder of the war, the French were not able to get more than one fleet to sea, and that conveyed Napoleon to Egypt, and was annihilated in the battle of the Nile, already mentioned in the naval history of Great Britain. Napoleon compelled the Dutch and Spaniards to use their naval resources against the British, but they met with no success. The efforts of the French themselves were confined to collecting flotillas of gun boats, at Boulogne, in preparing to invade England. Like all the other attempts of the French for that purpose, this one ended in nothing.

The war was rekindled in May, 1802. Bonaparte made the greatest exertions to collect and equip a sufficient number of transports for an invasion of England. A vast number of flat bottomed boats were collected at Boulogne. But though the English people were considerably alarmed, the blockade of their squadrons prevented these extensive preparations from doing them any further damage. The escape of Admiral Villeneuve, with the Toulon squadron, through the blockading lines of the British, its reinforcements, chase and destruction by Nelson, have been detailed. In the great sea fight off Cape Trafalgar, Villeneuve and his Frenchmen did all that a brave and skilful commander could have been expected to accomplish. Had he continued with his first plan of battle, the result might have been different. The great loss of the French in ships and men must be attributed to the desperate valor with which they fought. It is true, nineteen of the French and Spanish vessels were taken; but not until they had inflicted a terrible loss upon the victors, and had a greater part of their crews killed or wounded. By the battle and the violent storm immediately following, the greater part of the naval force of France was destroyed.

After the battle of Trafalgar, Bonaparte was not able to effect much upon the sea. A fleet, under Admiral Villaumez and Jerome Bonaparte, which was sent against the English in the West Indies, was destroyed by Admiral Duckworth and a violent storm, and the vessel of Jerome Bonaparte alone escaped to France. The French then confined their enterprise to the land. The British held the sea against all except the infant republic of the United States.

After the fall of Bonaparte, and the restoration of tranquillity to

France, the navy was considerably enlarged and improved, and has been increasing in efficiency ever since. A fleet, under Admiral de Rigny, joined the English and the Russian fleets in the bay of Navarino, in 1827, and, in the great battle fought there, on the 20th of October, the French reputation, for bravery and skill, was nobly maintained. There they, who had long looked upon each other as natural enemies, fought with noble emulation, side by side; and the credit of that glorious victory belongs equally to both.

In 1845, the navy of France consisted of twenty-three ships of the line, thirty frigates, twenty-two sloops of war, one hundred and fifty-four other vessels, four steam frigates, and forty-one other steam vessels, all in active service; while twenty-three ships of the line, twenty frigates, three sloops of war, and two schooners were in the navy yards, and four steam frigates, and eighteen other steam vessels still on the stocks. The increase is very rapid. The principal naval stations are Brest, Toulon, Cherbourg and Rochefort.

CHAPTER XXIX.

THE NETHERLANDS.

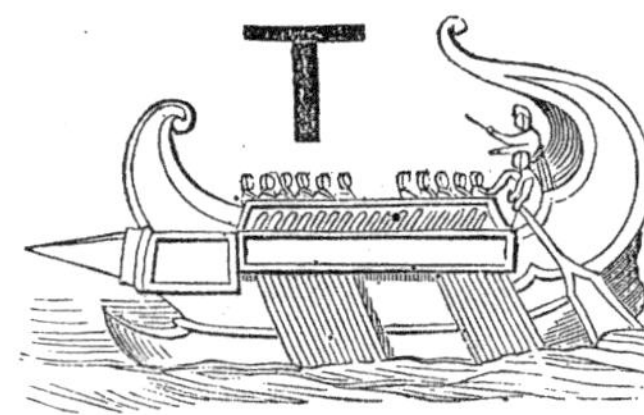

THE naval history of the country which produced such admirals as De Ruyter and Van Tromp, and which, for a time, rivalled the great power of Britain upon the ocean, cannot but be interesting. The Netherlands once comprised the Lowlands, or northwest declivity of the great basin formed by the forest of Ardennes, the Vosges, the Hunsdück, the Siegengebirge, the Spessart, Odenwald, and Hartz, in the valley of which the Rhine flows down through the Netherlands. The Northern portion of these countries, situated between the Meuse, the Ural, and the Rhine, was anciently called the islands of the Batavians. The part of the Netherlands, north of the Rhine, was inhabited by the Frisians, a brave nation who maintained a long struggle with the Romans, and subsequently, with the Franks, by whom they were subdued in the seventh century. The Frisians early engaged in commerce and piracy, and were involved in frequent contests with the Scandinavians.

The history of the Netherlands is essentially that of a patient and industrious population, struggling against every obstacle which nature could oppose to its well being. The extraordinary result, in which we see the capability of man, is due to the hardy stamp of character imprinted by suffering and danger on those who had the ocean for their foe. The Frisians, from the earliest period of their establishment in the country, maintained a commercial intercourse with England. They defeated the Romans upon the sea, but numbers and discipline finally subdued their spirit. When the country was brought under the sway of Charlemagne, the Frisians and the Flemings were united, and aided each other in the construction of dykes to keep back the ocean.

About the year 800, the Normans began their piratical descents upon the coasts of the Netherlands. The Flemings, under their great chief Baldwin, of the Iron-hand, successfully resisted the daring bands; but after the death of that brave chieftain, they succeeded in establishing themselves in the country. In 1066, the state of Flanders, then flourishing and powerful, furnished assistance, both in men and ships, to William the Bastard, of Normandy, for the conquest of England. Flanders maintained an extensive and profitable commerce with the northern nations, and the navy of the country was respected. The Counts who governed the Flemings were amongst the foremost in the expeditions to the Holy Land. It is said that the pope's nuncio found difficulty in preventing the women from embarking in these expeditions—so anxious were they to share the dangers and the glory of the men in combating the Saracens. Whole fleets of Dutch and Flemish merchant ships repaired regularly to the coasts of Spain and Languedoc, in the thirteenth century, such being the extent of their maritime prosperity and their influence upon the commerce of other nations The Flemings were the Genoese of the north.

A Flemish squadron decided the great sea fight near Sluys, between the French and English, in 1340. It remained a spectator during the contest of a whole day, and then hastening to join the English, completed the defeat of the French. In the latter part of the fourteenth century, after an obstinate contest, the Duke of Burgundy annexed Flanders to his dominions. But the spirit of the Flemings was that of republicans struggling against feudalism; and such was their strength, that the dukes of Burgundy were forced to allow them to continue their maritime connection with Great Britain, when they declared war against that kingdom.

The province of Holland, which enjoyed a degree of liberty almost equal to Flanders, declared war against the Hanseatic towns in 1450. Supported by Zealand, Holland equipped a fleet against the pirates who infested the coasts, and assailing their commerce, soon forced them to submission. Holland, Flanders, and Brabant continued to flourish and increase in maritime power during the wars between France, England, and the emperor of Germany; although their commerce was considerably annoyed by the French cruisers. Under the vigorous administration of Charles V., the spirit of the people of the maritime cities was encouraged, not oppressed; and all the evils inflicted by the naval depredations of the enemy were speedily remedied by industry and perseverance.

The Dutch and Zealanders distinguished themselves beyond all the other subjects of Charles V., in the two expeditions which the emperor undertook against Tunis and Algiers. The two northern provinces furnished a greater number of ships than the united quotas of all the rest of his states. From the death of Charles the increase of the commerce and maritime power of the Netherlands was astonishing. The opulence of the towns of Brabant and Flanders was without example in Europe. All the evils produced by luxury were fully demonstrated, and it was necessary to introduce sumptuary laws for their mitigation. The port of Antwerp was so crowded with vessels that each successive fleet was obliged to wait long before it could obtain admission for the discharge of its cargoes. The discovery of America opened a new field for the exertion of maritime enterprise, and the people of the Netherlands were ready to take advantage of it. They soon became worthy rivals of the Spaniards, Portuguese and English.

It was one of the objects of the crafty and cruel Philip II. to diminish the power of the people of the Netherlands. He visited the country; but his plans were discovered, and, for the time, defeated. A fleet, under the command of Count Horn, the admiral of the United Provinces, waited at Flessingue to form his escort to Spain. On the 20th of August, Philip set sail; turning his back forever on the country which offered a check to his despotism; and after a perilous voyage, he arrived in Spain. The perseverance and cunning of this lover of despotism at last succeeded in creating a revolution in 1566. He had aimed at this, in order to build his power upon the ruins of social happiness. Internal discord diverted the attention of the Netherlanders from their commerce—the source of their prosperity, and their maritime power rapidly declined. Pirates infested and ravaged the coast; and thus, from both sea and land, the whole extent of the Netherlands was devoted to carnage and ruin.

The naval force of the patriots began in 1570, to acquire that consistency and power which was so soon to render it the chief means of resistance. The privateers and corsairs which began to swarm from ports in Holland and Zealand, and which found refuge in those of England, sullied many gallant exploits by instances of the excess of desperation; so much so, that the patriotic leader, the Prince of Orange, was forced to withdraw the general command of the navy from the lord of Dolhain, and to replace him by Gislain de Fiennes, one of the exiled nobles of Antwerp. Many of these nobles and ruined merchants purchased or built, with the remnant of their fortunes, numerous vessels, in which they carried on a most productive warfare against Spanish commerce through the extent of the English channel, from the mouth of the Embo to the harbor of La Rochelle.

When John de la Cerda was appointed by Philip to succeed the tyrannical Duke of Alva in the government of the Netherlands, he appeared on the coast of Flanders, with a considerable fleet. On the 11th of May, 1572, the fleet was attacked by the patriots, and many of the vessels, with their rich cargoes, burned and captured before the governor's eyes. To avoid a rupture with Spain, the queen of England interdicted the Dutch and Flemish privateers from taking shelter in her ports. William de la Marck, Count of Lunoy, who now had the chief command of this daring force, was distinguished for his uncompromising hatred to the Spaniards. He bore the surname of "the wild boar of Ardennes." Driven out of the harbors of England he resolved on some desperate adventure; and on the 1st of May, he surprised and captured the town of Brille, in the island of Voorn. This was the first step towards the establishment of liberty and the republic. In a few days, in consequence of this exploit, every town in Holland and Zealand except Amsterdam and Middleburg, declared for

DEFEAT OF REQUESENS'S FLEET, JANUARY 29, 1574.

a republic. The single port of Flessingue contained one hundred and fifty patriot vessels, well armed and equipped: and from that period may be dated the growth of the first naval power of Europe, Great Britain alone excepted.

The Spaniards succeeded in taking the Hague; but they were repulsed before Alkmaer, and their fleet was almost entirely destroyed in a naval combat on the Zuyder Zee. The Count Bossu, the Spanish admiral, with about three hundred of his best sailors was taken in this fight. Alva was succeeded by Requesens in his office of governor, in 1576. At that time, Middleburg was besieged by the patriots, and reduced to great distress. Requesens resolved to relieve it. He assembled at Antwerp and Bergen-op-Zoom, a fleet of sixty vessels for that purpose. But Louis Boisot, admiral of Zealand, promptly prepared to attack this force; and after a severe contest, he totally defeated it, and killed De Glimes, one of its admirals. This battle took place on the 29th of January, 1574; and in the following February, Middleburg surrendered. All Zealand was now free; and the intrepid Admiral Boisot gained another victory on the 30th of May, destroying several of the Spanish vessels, and taking some others, with their admiral, Von Haemstede. Frequent naval enterprises were also undertaken against the frontiers of Flanders, harrassing the enemy at every vulnerable point.

In 1585, Antwerp was besieged by the celebrated Alexander, Duke of Parma, with a large army. He completely surrounded the city with his troops. But the success of the siege depended upon getting the command of the navigation of the Scheldt, a river of great rapidity and immense width. The only way to effect this was by throwing a bridge across it; and despite the great difficulties of the project, the duke and Barroccio, a celebrated Italian engineer, succeeded in accomplishing it. The bridge was completed, and defended by a large number of cannon. Resolving to save Antwerp, if possible, the states of Zealand sent forward an expedition, which, joined with some ships from Lillo, gave new courage to the besieged. Every thing was prepared for the destruction of the bridge—the only hope of the citizens. An Italian engineer, named Giambello, was at this time in Antwerp, and by his talents had long protracted the defence. He invented the terrible "fire ships," and with some of these formidable instruments and the Zealand fleet, the attack was at length made.

On the night of the 4th of April, the army of the besiegers was amazed by the spectacle of three huge masses of flame floating down the river, accompanied by numerous lesser appearances of a similar kind, and bearing directly against the prodigious barrier, which had cost them so much toil. Astonishment was followed by consternation, when one of the three machines burst with a tremendous noise. The second and larger fire ship burst through the bridge of boats and struck against one of the estocades. The effects baffle all attempts at description. The bridge, men, cannon, and the huge machinery employed in the various works were blown into the air and dispersed in all directions. By flood and flame, the Marquis de Roubais, other officers, and eight hundred soldiers perished. The river, forced from its bed at either side rushed into the forts erected by the besiegers, and drowned numbers of the garrison, while the ground far beyond shook as with an earthquake. Had the Zealand fleet come in time to the spot, the whole plan would have been crowned with success; but by some want of concert, it did not appear, and the town received no relief. Another attempt was made to destroy the bridge rebuilt by Alexander, by sending an enormous vessel, called the "End of War;" but this floating citadel ran aground; and, after a siege of fourteen months, Antwerp capitulated on the 16th of August. The Prince of Parma was elevated by the triumph of his valor and perseverance to the highest pinnacle of military renown.

The United Provinces were enabled to send constant aid to Henry IV. of France, in his war with the League; and nothwithstanding this drain, their armies and fleets augmented every day. Prince Maurice had succeeded William of Orange as captain-general, and his conquests were uninterrupted, now that the Duke of Parma, the great general of that age, was dead (1597.) After the establishment of peace, the United Provinces were without a rival upon the sea. In Europe alone, they had twelve hundred merchant vessels in activity, and upwards of seventy thousand sailors constantly employed. They built annually two thousand vessels. In the year 1598, eighty ships sailed from their ports for the Indies or America. In short, the people of the Netherlands found in all quarters of the globe, the reward of their skill, industry, and courage.

War was renewed in 1600; and being unsuccessful at first upon land, the states-general determined to undertake a naval expedition, greater than any hitherto attempted. A fleet of seventy-three vessels, carrying eight thousand men, was soon equipped, under the orders of Admiral Vandergoes; and after a series of attempts on the coast of Spain, Portugal, Africa, and the Canary Isles, this expedition, from which the most splendid results were anticipated, was shattered, dispersed, and reduced to nothing, by a succession of mishaps. During the siege of Ostend by the royalists, begun in 1601, the contest was maintained with vigor upon the sea. The siege was principally conducted by the brothers, Frederick and Ambrose Spinola. Frederick was killed in one of the naval combats. Ambrose adopted such vigorous measures, that after a siege of three years the town was reduced to ruins. The garrison fought as long as they had foothold. The town was taken in September, 1604.

In 1605, a Dutch squadron, commanded by Hautain, admiral of Zealand, attacked a superior force of Spanish vessels, close to Dover, and defeated them with considerable loss. But the victory was sullied by an act of barbarity. All the soldiers found on board of the captured ships were tied two and two, and flung into the sea. Some contrived to extricate themselves, and gained the shore by swimming; others were picked up by the English boats, whose crews witnessed the scene. The British seamen could not remain neuter at such a moment. The Dutch vessels, pursuing those of Spain, which fled into Dover harbor, were fired upon by the cannon of the castle and forced to give up the chase. In this year, also, the Dutch captured the chief of the Dunkirk privateers, which had so long annoyed their trade, and they cruelly ordered sixty of the prisoners to be put to death. But the humanity of the people prompted them to rescue them from the authorities.

The maritime enterprise of Holland, forced by the imprudent policy of Spain to seek a wider career than in the narrow seas of Europe, were day by day extended in the Indies. To ruin, if possible, their increasing trade, Philip II. sent out the Admiral Hurtado, with a fleet of six galleons and thirty-two galleys. The Dutch squadron of five vessels, commanded by Wolfert Hermanersóon, attacked them off the coast of Malabar, and his temerity was crowned with great success. He took two of their vessels, and drove the remainder from the Indian seas. He then succeeded in establishing the connection between the Dutch and the natives of some of the islands of the East Indies.

The Dutch naval operations during 1607, were more brilliant than those on land. Admiral Hautain, with twenty ships, was surprised off Cape St. Vincent, by the Spanish fleet. The formidable appearance of their galleons inspired a perfect panic among the Dutch sailors. They hoisted their sails and fled, with the exception of one ship, commanded by Vice-admiral Kleazoon, whose desperate conduct saved the national honor. Having held out until his vessel was quite unmanageable, and almost his whole crew killed or wounded, he prevailed on the few remaining to agree to his resolution, knelt down on the deck, and putting up a brief prayer for pardon for the act, thrust a light into the powder magazine and was instantly blown up. Only two men were snatched from the sea, and these, dreadfully mangled, died breathing curses on the enemy.

This disaster was soon forgotten in the rejoicing for a brilliant victory, gained the following year by Heemskirk, so celebrated for his voyage to Nova Zembla, and by his conduct in the east. He set sail from Holland in March, determined to signalize himself and honor the Dutch reputation by some great exploit. Receiving intelligence that the Spanish fleet lay at anchor in the bay of Gibraltar, he prepared to offer them battle. Before the combat began, he held a council of war, in which he urged upon his officers the imperative necessity for them either to conquer or die. He led on to battle in his own ship, and to the astonishment of both fleets, he bore down against the enormous galleon in which the flag of the Spanish admiral was hoisted. As Heemskirk approached, D'Avila cut his cables and attempted to escape under shelter of the town. The Dutchman pursued him through the whole Spanish fleet, and soon forced him to action. At the second broadside, Heemskirk had his left leg cut off by a cannon ball, and he almost instantly expired, exhorting his crew to win the fight or perish. Verhoef, the captain of the ship, concealed the admiral's death; and the whole fleet continued the action with a valorous spirit. The victory was soon decided. Four of the Spanish galleons were sunk or burned; the remainder fled. The death of Heemskirk paralysed the victors, as soon as made known. They sailed back to Holland with the body of their lamented chief, without thinking of any further exploits.

In 1617, the United Provinces seem to have successfully claimed the honorary empire of the sea. The Dutch sailors were even daring enough to violate the British territory, and set fire to the town of Crookhaven, in Ireland. The peace-loving James I., passed lightly over this outrage, intended to provoke a contest with England. After the accession of Frederick Henry to the power enjoyed by the celebrated Maurice, of Orange, the Dutch concluded treaties with England and France, and assisted both kingdoms with the loan of their ships. They maintained a strict neutrality in the war between France and England, which subsequently broke out; but prosecuted with activity and success the war against Spain. Their triumphs over the Spanish fleets were brilliant and decisive.

The West India Company confided the command of their fleet to Peter Hein, a most intrepid and intelligent sailor, who proved his abilities on many occasions—two of them of an extraordinary nature. In 1627, he defeated a fleet of twenty-six vessels, with a much inferior force. In the following year, he had still greater fortune, near the Havana, in the island of Cuba, in an engagement with the great Spanish armament, called "The Money Fleet," to indicate the great wealth it contained. The booty was carried to Amsterdam, and the whole of the treasure, in money, precious stones, indigo, &c., was valued at twelve million florins. This was, indeed, a victory worth gaining; and it relieved the republic from embarrassment. Hein perished in 1629, in combating the indefatigable pirates of Dunkirk. In every quarter, upon their favorite element, the Dutch were successful and extended their power.

The great victory of Van Tromp, known by the name of the battle of the Duoro, from being fought off the coast of England, on the 21st of October, 1639, raised the naval reputation as high as it could be carried. Fifty ships taken, burned, and sunk were the proofs of Van Tromp's triumph, and the Spanish navy never recovered the loss. The victory was celebrated throughout Europe, and Van Tromp was the hero of the day. He continued to be the chief admiral of the navy, both in fame and rank, during the remainder of the war, which ended in 1648. The Spanish government, after an eighty years' contest, acknowledged the independence of the states-general, and entered into commercial relations with them.

The time had now arrived when the wisdom, the courage, and the resources of the republic were to be put once more to the test, in a contest only paralleled by ancient history. The naval wars between

ADMIRAL VAN TROMP.

Holland and England had their real source in the inveterate jealousies and grasping ambition of both nations, reciprocally convinced that a joint supremacy at sea was incompatible with their interests and honor, and each resolved to perish rather than yield. The passage of the famed navigation act by the parliament of England precipitated the war. Ships were seized by the Dutch in reprisal, and every thing being prepared, they commenced hostilities in earnest.

In May, 1652, the Dutch admiral, Van Tromp, commanding forty-two ships of war, met the English fleet, under Blake, in the straits of Dover; the latter ordered the Dutch admiral to strike, which order was answered by a broadside. A bloody contest of five hours followed. The English fleet was inferior in number of vessels, but superior in their size. One Dutch vessel was sunk, another taken, and night parted the combatants. Soon after this battle, Blake put to sea with a numerous fleet; Van Tromp followed with a hundred ships; but a violent tempest parted these furious enemies, and retarded for a while the encounter they mutually longed for.

ADMIRAL DE RUYTER.

On 16th of August, a battle took place between Sir George Ayscue and the renowned De Ruyter, near Portsmouth, each having about forty ships; but with no decisive results. On the 28th of October, Blake, aided by Bourn and Penn, met a Dutch squadron of nearly equal force off the coast of Kent, under De Ruyter and De Witt. The fight which ensued was desperate and bloody; but although the Dutch had the worst of it, the battle was not decisive. In the Mediterranean, the Dutch admiral, Van Galen, defeated the English captain, Baddeley, but bought the victory with his life. And on the 29th of November, another bloody conflict took place between Van Tromp and Blake, near the Goodwin Sands. In this determined action, Blake was wounded and defeated; five English ships taken, burnt or sunk; and night only saved the fleet from destruction. After this victory, Van Tromp placed a broom at his mast head, to intimate that he would sweep the channel free from English ships.

To retrieve the national honor, the English sent eighty sail to sea, under the command of Blake, Dean, and Monk. Van Tromp and De Ruyter, with seventy-six vessels, were descried on the 18th of

February, escorting three hundred merchantmen up the Channel. Three days of desperate fighting ended in the defeat of the Dutch, who lost ten ships, of war and twenty-four merchant vessels. Several of the English ships were disabled; one sunk; and the carnage on both sides was nearly equal. Van Tromp acquired the highest honor by this battle; having succeeded, though defeated, in saving almost the whole of his immense convoy. On the 12th of June, and the day following, two other actions were fought; in the first, the English admiral, Dean, was killed; in the second, Monk, Penn, and Lawson revenged his death by forcing the Dutch to regain their harbors, with loss. On the 21st of July, the last of these desperate contests for superiority was fought. Van Tromp issued out once more, determined to conquer or to die. He met the enemy, commanded by Monk, off Scheveling. Both fleets rushed to the contest. The heroic Dutchman, animating his sailors, with his sword drawn, was shot through the heart with a musket ball. This event, and this alone, decided the battle, which was the only decisive contest of the war. The English captured or sunk, nearly thirty ships. The body of Van Tromp was carried with great solemnity to the church of Delft, where a magnificent mausoleum was erected over the remains of the hero of the sea.

This memorable defeat and the death of this great commander, added to the injury done to their trade, induced the states-general to seek for peace; but Cromwell insisted upon conditions which the Dutch could not recognise. At last, an inglorious peace was concluded. In 1656, it became evident that a new war could not be avoided. Denmark, the ancient ally of the republic, was threatened with destruction by Charles Gustavus, king of Sweden, who held Copenhagen in blockade. The interests of Holland were in imminent peril should the Swedes gain the passage of the Sound. De Witt persuaded the states-general to send a fleet to the Baltic, under command of Admiral Opdam. This intrepid successor of the immortal Tromp, soon came to blows with a rival worthy to meet him. Wrangel, the Swedish admiral, with a superior force, defended the passage of the Sound; and the two castles of Cronenberg and Elsenberg supported his fleet with their tremendous fire. But Opdam resolutely advanced: though suffering extremely from an attack of gout, he had himself carried on deck, where he gave his orders with admirable coolness and precision. The rival monarchs witnessed the battle. A brilliant victory crowned the efforts of the Dutch admiral, dearly bought by the death of the brave De Witt, and Peter Florizon, another admiral of note. Relief was poured into Copenhagen. Opdam was replaced in his command by the still more celebrated De Ruyter, who was already greatly esteemed for his valor and skill; and after a nine months' contest, the king of Sweden was compelled to consent to peace on favorable terms.

These transactions raised the United Provinces to the pinnacle of naval reputation. The Algerines were swept from the seas by a series of small but vigorous expeditions. Trade and finance were reorganized, and every thing seemed to promise peace and prosperity. Cromwell had died, and was succeeded by Charles II. That monarch, instead of entering into an alliance with the people who had sheltered him in adversity, was carried away by the commercial jealousy of the English; and after many acts intended to provoke hostility, war was declared on the 22d of February, 1665. A great battle was fought on the 31st of June. The Duke of York, afterwards James II. commanded the British fleet, and had, under him, the Earl of Sandwich and Prince Rupert. The Dutch were led on by Opdam; and the victory was decided in favor of the English, by the blowing up of that admiral's ship, with himself and his whole crew. The loss of the Dutch was nineteen ships. De Witt, the pensionary, then took command of the fleet in person. He soon gave proof of the adaptation of genius to a pursuit hitherto unknown, by the rapid knowledge and practical improvement he introduced into naval tactics.

The republic exerted its utmost energies. The harbors were crowded with merchant ships, and De Ruyter was ready to lead the fleet. The English also prepared boldly for the shock. The Dutch fleet, commanded by De Ruyter and Tromp, the gallant successor to his father's fame, was soon at sea. The English, under Prince Rupert and Monk, were equally active. A battle of four days' continuance, one of the most determined and terrible upon record, was the consequence. The Dutch claim, with the appearance of justice, to have had the advantage. But a more decisive conflict took place on the 25th of July, when the English triumphed, the Dutch having three admirals killed. In this desperate contest, De Ruyter, when certain of defeat, strove to meet his death; but exposed to a thousand bullets, none struck him.

De Witt now amused the English with negotiation, while a powerful fleet was equipped. It suddenly appeared in the Thames, under command of De Ruyter. This daring admiral took Sheerness, and burned many ships of war; almost insulting London itself in his predatory excursion. He then returned to Holland, and peace was concluded in July, 1667, the palm of superiority belonging undoubtedly to the Dutch. But they soon had to contend with a greater power. An alliance was formed between Charles II. and Louis XIV., the object of which was, the humiliation of the United Provinces. A base and piratical attack upon the Dutch Smyrna fleet, by a large force, under Sir Robert Holmes, on the 13th of March, 1672, was the first act of hostility by the English. Through the prudence and valor of the Dutch admirals, the attempt completely failed. A declaration of war immediately followed.

When the French army invaded the United Provinces, De Witt took active measures for defence. He equipped a fleet of nearly a hundred ships of the line, and half as many fire ships. De Ruyter, now, without exception, the greatest commander of the age, set sail with force in search of the combined English and French squadrons, commanded by the Duke of York and Marshal D'Estreés. He encountered them at Solebay, on the 6th of May, 1672. A bloody engagement followed. Sandwich, on the side of the English, and Van Ghent, a Dutch admiral, were slain. The Dutch had the advantage; but the victory was not decisive; Holland was now forced to submerge her fertile soil to save it from the ravages of the successful French land forces, and she sued for peace. The terms proposed by the two hostile monarchs were so dishonorable, that the Dutch, driven to desperation, resolved to perish rather than accede to them. Under the great Stadtholder, William III., Prince of Orange, they made every exertion for defence as well as for aggression.

Two desperate battles at sea on the 28th of May and the 4th of June, in which De Ruyter and Prince Rupert distinguished themselves, only proved the valor of the combatants, leaving victory doubtful. England became ashamed of the unjust war, and Charles was forced to make peace on the terms proposed by the Dutch, who were now free to pursue the war against France. The campaign of 1675, offered no remarkable event. But in the following year, the great De Ruyter was killed in an action with the French fleet in the Mediterranean. The constant maritime rivalry between England

and the United Provinces was diminished in 1675, by the marriage of the Prince of Orange and the daughter of the King of England. Peace was attained in August of the same year.

On the 21st of October, 1688, the Prince of Orange, with an army of fourteen thousand men, and a fleet of five hundred vessels, of all kinds, set sail from Helvetsluys; and after some delays from bad weather, he safely landed his army in Torbay, on the 5th of November. His object was the dethronement of James II. He had been invited over by a large majority of the English people, tired of the tyranny of bigotry, and anxious for a Protestant ruler. In a few weeks, William was triumphant in all quarters, and was crowned, with his wife Mary, in February, 1689. He still preserved his title of Stadtholder of Holland, and thus was the monarchy and the republic united in the same individual.

War against the power of Louis XIV. was the favorite project of William. He soon returned to the continent and put himself at the head of the forces destined to act against the French. During this war the naval transactions were unimportant. The French privateers were generally successful in their attacks upon the English and Dutch vessels, and obtained much booty and greater renown. Peace was concluded in September, 1697. But it was of short duration. The ambitious designs of Louis were still cherished, and precipitated another contest. William III. died in 1701, leaving the pensionary of Holland, Heinsius, to carry out his plans of resistance to the French.

The powerful genius of Marlborough made the war a series of brilliant triumphs for the Dutch and English, upon land. The naval operations of Holland offer nothing remarkable. The States had always a fleet ready to support the English in their enterprises; but no eminent admiral arose to rival Rooke ,Byng, and Benbow. The principal Dutch commanders were admirals Allemonde and Waponaer. During the thirty years following the peace of Utrecht, concluded in 1713, the republic attained the summit of its power. At peace internally and externally, there was leisure for giving more attention to trade and commerce, and to the improvement of the army and navy.

The attempt to despoil the Empress Maria Theresa of her splendid possessions, which was made by Frederick the Great, of Prussia, caused another European war, in which Holland and England sided with the empress, and France, with her enemies. No naval operations of importance were undertaken by Holland during the war; and from this period may be traced the decline of the maritime greatness of the once rival of England. Holland was compelled to submit to various indignities offered to her commerce by the jealousy of the English, which, in the time of Tromp and De Ruyter would have resulted in war.

The American revolution seemed to revive the spirit of the Dutch. The right of search was resisted, and war declared against England in 1781. The British Navy was triumphant in the East Indies, where the Dutch lost several valuable islands, the fruits of their enterprise and courage. An effort was made to deprive Holland of the Baltic trade. A squadron of seven vessels, commanded by Sir Hyde Parker, was encountered on the Dogher Bank, by a Dutch squadron, of equal force, under Admiral Zutman. An action of four hours followed, maintained with the courage of ancient Dutch heroes. A storm separated the combatants, and saved the honor of each; for both had suffered alike, and victory belonged to neither. The peace of 1784 terminated this short, but to Holland, fatal war. The commerce of the republic had suffered greatly during the struggle. But it was destined to suffer still more. Holland was overrun by the republican armies of France, in 1797, and forced to join in the war against England. Her marine was nearly annihilated, and some of her most valued possessions in India were taken by the invincible fleets of Britain.

On the 11th of October, 1797, the English admiral, Sir Adam Duncan, with a superior force, encountered the Dutch fleet, under De Winter, off Camperdown, and chiefly, by a bold and successful manœuvre, defeated him, and took the admiral and ten vessels. A series of severe and well contested engagements took place near Bergen, in which the whole of the Dutch fleet was captured and conveyed to England. Napoleon annexed Holland to France, in 1810. He introduced the conscription law, by which the naval forces were much increased, at the expense of the national industry. Evils of all kinds afflicted the country until the rise of the people and the proclaiming of William, Prince of Orange, as king of the Netherlands, in 1814. The regeneration of Holland was then rapid and complete.

In May, 1816, a Dutch fleet, under Admiral Van der Capellan, joined the English, under Lord Exmouth, in the bay of Algiers, and compelled the Dey of that piratical people to recognise the laws of nations. Nothing further of a naval character occurred until 1823, when the king established premiums for the encouragement of naval architecture; since which time, the navy has been constantly improving in size and efficiency. When the Dey of Algiers, in violation of the treaty of 1816, renewed, in 1824, his demands for presents, the commander of the Dutch fleet in the Mediterranean, Admiral Wolterbeck, replied, that his government had no intention of yielding to them; and at the same time threatened to begin hostilities if the Dey persisted. Whereupon the pirate sovereign renewed the treaty of 1816.

At present, Holland and Belgium are separate states. The navy of Holland consists of nine ships of the line, nineteen frigates, and thirty-seven sloops of war, brigs, &c., fourteen steamers, and eighty-seven gun boats. Besides these, the Dutch have twenty-one vessels of war in the East Indies. Flushing is the great naval station and depot of the kingdom. The regulations for the government of the navy are very much the same as those of Great Britain. Except a few gun boats, Belgium has no navy.

CONSTANTINOPLE.

CHAPTER XXX.

TURKEY.

HE account of the naval operations of the Turks becomes important after the capture of Constantinople, in 1453. They were then brought into contact with the Christian nations of Europe, who were anxious to prevent the extension of their conquests, and whose principal arm of warfare was the navy. The immense fleet which Mahomet II. employed in the attack and capture of Constantinople has been described in the conclusion of the history of the Roman empire. It was superior in number of vessels to any fleet which could have been fitted out by either of the Christian nations; but inferior in the construction of the galleys and in the skill of the seamen.

The harbor of Constantinople was made the naval station and rendezvous of the Turks. In 1455, the enterprising Mahomet sent a fleet against the islands of Rhodes and Chios; but the attempt on both failed. However, the island of Cos was reduced, and this was a little satisfaction to the ambitious sultan. Fleets were employed by the same monarch in his wars against the heroic Scanderbeg, and in the conquest of the Morea and Negropont; but no naval contest of importance took place. The successors of Mahomet II., Bajazet II., and Selim I., were warlike monarchs, and gave the army and navy constant employment. The Turks at this period possessed a maritime power, before which, even that of the Venitians was forced to yield. Fleets, irresistible from the number of vessels composing them, kept the sea, and conveyed the large armies upon their expeditions of conquest. Egypt several times felt the power of the sultan, and was forced to succumb.

Solyman II., surnamed the Magnificent, ascended the throne in 1519. He was as ambitious and war-loving as any of his ancestors. In 1522, he invested the city of Rhodes by sea and land. The fleet consisted of four hundred sail, and the army of one hundred and forty thousand men. The siege lasted more than six months, and an immense number of the Turks fell before the heroic knights by whom Rhodes was defended. But they were at length so reduced in number and strength, that a capitulation was agreed upon, and Solyman entered the city on Christmas day, 1522.

Barbarossa was the most celebrated of the Turkish admirals up to this period. He ravaged the coasts of Italy, and took the cities of Bisertia and Tunis, in Africa. But in 1536, he was forced to retire before Charles V. of Spain, who retook the city of Tunis. Solyman then turned his forces against Italy; which country was in danger of being overwhelmed, when, a Venitian captain having taken and burned some Turkish vessels, the sultan changed his design and resolved to chastise the Venitians. Several trifling encounters took place upon the sea, in which the superiority of the Venitians was quite evident; but peace was concluded in 1540.

A Turkish fleet, under Barbarossa, assisted the forces of Francis I.

of France, in his operations against Charles V. It appears, at this time, the power of Solyman was as much dreaded upon the sea as upon land. A large number of his subjects were constantly engaged in piratical expeditions; and, in time of need, therefore, he could collect a large and efficient naval force in addition to that maintained at the government expense.

In September, 1571, the greatest naval contest in which the Turks were ever engaged took place. The Sultan Selim, the successor of Solyman, had involved himself in a difficulty with the Christian powers, and they resolved to punish him, if possible. The Christian fleet, of Papal, Spanish, and Venitian vessels, collected in the port of Messina. It consisted of two hundred and fifty ships, manned by fifty thousand men, and was placed under command of Don John of Austria, natural son of Charles V., for whom the title of *generalissimo* was then invented. The pope, having proclaimed a general season of fasting and prayers throughout Christendom, sent a strong corps of ecclesiastics to officiate in the fleet, and a consecrated standard to be displayed from the admiral's ship. Absolution was promised to every sinner who should fight for the faith, and Heaven was opened to the slain. Don John was urged to give immediate battle and to feel sure of victory. Selim, on the other hand, was not backward in preparing to meet the danger, though part of his forces were employed in reducing the island of Cyprus. He equipped a fleet much larger than that of the enemy. It was entrusted to the Pacha Ali, who proved himself well worthy of the charge. The sultan animated his subjects with the promises of the Mahomedan paradise, if they fell, and tempting rewards if they won the battle. The two fleets met in the Gulf of Lepanto. What the Christians wanted in numbers they made up in superiority of equipment. The prows of their galleys were closer, and better defended, and their soldiers better provided with offensive and defensive weapons. They made general use of helmets, coats of mail, and fire arms, whilst many of the Turks defended their bodies with large leathern shields; and had no more destructive missiles than arrows. Moreover, fortune turned against them at the moment of onset; for the wind, which had hitherto been favorable to them, now blew in the sails of the Christians.

The battle, as of old, began with the admirals, Don John and Ali, after a short cannonade, closed, and grappled. Both crews rushed

BATTLE OF LEPANTO.

DON JOHN OF AUSTRIA.

to the contest, meeting in desperate struggle, upon the gunwales. Three times did the Spaniards gain the deck of their adversary, and as often were they driven back. Perhaps the Turks would have followed up their advantage to complete victory, had not Don John, in the critical moment, received a reinforcement of two hundred men. By their assistance, the Turk was again boarded, and with success. The slaughter was indiscriminate and terrible—the crescent being lowered and replaced by the cross. The head of Ali, planted on a pole, and hoisted at his own mast head, filled the breasts of his followers with momentary consternation. Scarce was this result manifest, ere the cry of "*Victoria! victoria!*" pealed from the Christians—and led on by a host of heroes,—a Colonna, a Veneiro, and a

Doria,—they rushed upon the enemy. Nor did the Turks tamely yield the victory. The ships grappled; the enemies fought hand to hand, and sword to scimitar. Turks and Christians had never fought so valiantly; even in that heroic age. At length, whilst the result was still in suspense, the Turkish galley slaves, taking courage at the efforts of their fellow Christians, suddenly rose, broke their chains, and attacked their masters with them, and repaid them, in a few moments, for years of cruelty. In an opposite manner, the criminals who performed the same office at the oar in the Spanish and Italian galleys, having asked leave of their officers, and been unchained and armed, boarded the enemy with a fury rendered irresistible by despair, and the hope of obtaining liberty or martyrdom. At length the few Turks that remained, began to think of flight. Thirty galleys only escaped to Constantinople, through the skill of the intrepid corsair, Ulucciali, who carried away the standard of Malta as a trophy, and one prisoner, the Spanish poet, Cervantes. A few reached the neighboring shore and abandoned their ships; one hundred and thirty were taken; the rest were either sunk, burnt, or battered to pieces; ten thousand Turks were taken; twenty-five thousand slain; fifteen thousand Christians were released from the servitude of the oar. Nor was the victory cheaply purchased; ten thousand Christians were among the victims. Europe resounded with the shouts for this glorious victory. When the news reached the pope, he is said to have exclaimed, in ecstacy, "There was a man sent from God, and his name was John." Don John was pronounced the greatest warrior of the age.

Notwithstanding the prodigious loss sustained by the Turks in the conflict of Lepanto, the confederates reaped but little advantage from the victory; and next year, Kalij Ali Pasha, who had succeeded to the post of high admiral, fitted out a fleet of two hundred and fifty galleys, with which he ravaged the coasts of Christendom, and maintained his ground so well wherever he came, that the confederates could gain no advantage over him. The Turkish power, however, declined from this period. The increase of the civilization and power of the western nations not only prevented the extension of the Turkish dominion, but made it a matter of extreme difficulty to retain the country first conquered. The navy continued on a respectable footing during the reign of the successors of Selim, without being involved in any notable contest. The Venitians alone opposed the Turks upon

SAILING OF THE VENETIAN FLEET UNDER ADMIRAL FOSCARI.

the sea; and generally with success. The numerous wars with the Germans and Russians, and the constant internal dissensions, made the necessity for a powerful army and navy apparent.

Amurath the III., the sixth emperor of the Turks, was constantly waging war against either the Persians, the Germans, or the Venitians. In 1594, he was at peace with the Venitians and the Persians; but at war with the emperor of Germany. A fleet was sent into the Adriatic to besiege Zegna, a city under the sway of the Germans. The better to effect this, Amurath sent an ambassador to the Venitians, to request them to permit the fleet to pass along the Adriatic and have the use of their ports, as need should require. This request the Venitians refused, fearing the treachery of the Turks. Thus baffled, the Turkish admiral landing his men in various parts of Italy,did much harm, but especially in Calabria, where he surprised the town of Rhegium and burned it. Not far from Messana, four ships were taken, and some few shots exchanged with galleys from the East. The Neapolitans, for the safety of their coast, put to sea thirty galleys, to which were joined the galleys of the pope, the Duke of Florence, the Genoese, and the knights of Malta. The provident Venitians, also, put to sea a fleet of about a hundred sail, some being ships, and some galleys, under the leading of Foscari, their admiral. These fleets were too powerful for the Turks to encounter, and delivered the inhabitants of the coast from fear. The sultan could command the services of an immense number of vessels and seamen, but not such as could contend with able Venitians; and a battle was never ventured except when the Turks had a greatly superior force.

In 1770, a year in which the Russian arms were crowned with success in the war with the Turks, a Russian fleet of sixteen or eighteen ships, entered the Mediterranean, and landed a body of troops on the Morea. Hearing that a Turkish fleet had passed the Dardanelles, the Russians sailed to meet it. This fleet consisted of fifteen ships of the line, of from ninety-six to sixty guns, three large frigates, and seven large armed vessels, besides galleys. A battle ensued, in which the Turks were defeated; and having imprudently retired into a neighboring harbor, they were, next day, entirely destroyed by the Russian fire ships; one ship of sixty-four guns, was taken. After this triumph, the Russian fleet blocked up the mouth of the Dardanelles, interrupted the Turkish trade, prevented provisions from reaching Constantinople by sea, and raised contributions from most of the islands on the Archichipelago. No Turkish fleet could be found to resist them.

In March, 1821, the fire of liberty was kindled in Greece. The people of that country had long suffered from the cruel, merciless oppression of the Turks. They formed the bravest of the soldiers of the empire, and their corsairs were the most active and skilful seamen. Upon the waves the Greeks were generally successful—achieving many brilliant exploits. The blue and red flag soon waved on one hundred aad eighty vessels, mostly of ten or twelve guns. The Hydriots cruised in the Turkish waters, and blockaded the ports. On the Achaian Sea, the Greek pirates frustrated the plans of the navarchs of Hydra, and the European powers were forced to protect their vessels by cruisers. The Turkish navy, at this time, was in a wretched state, and certainly, in no way fitted to contend with the bold seamen and swift vessels of the Greeks.

When the first Turkish squadron left the Dardanelles, May 19th, 1821, the Greeks constantly pursued it with their fire ships, avoiding a general engagement; and June 8, they attacked a vessel of the line, which had got ashore at Tenedos, burned it, and compelled the rest of the squadron to return to the Dardanelles. Another great fleet, under the pacha, Karu Ali, strengthened by Egyptian, Tunisian, and Algerine vessels, drove away the Greek flotillas, supplied the Turks in the Morea with provisions, arms and reinforcements, and burned and captured a number of Greek fishing vessels, but it effected nothing decisive. Hardly had it returned to the Dardanelles, when the Greek fleets renewed their blockade, and became, as formerly, masters of the Ægean Sea and the Gulf of Saloniki.

In 1822, a Turkish fleet, under Hali Bey, was sent to reinforce the garrisons in the Morea. But the attempt to reduce the country utterly failed. In revenge, the fleet sailed to Scio, and landed troops, who reduced the island from a paradise to a desert, massacreing the unresisting as well as those who attempted to defend themselves. Some of the people escaped in their vessels, but the greater portion were either butchered, or sold into slavery. Ipsara, Tine, and Samos were threatened with the same fate. But the, Ipsariots, having already made preparations to send their families to the Morea, hovered round the Turkish fleet with seventy small vessels, among which were several skilfully constructed fire ships. Forty-three Ipsariots and Hydriots, devoting themselves to death, rowed with their *scampavias*, a kind of gun boat, into the midst of the fleet of the enemy, as it lay in the road of Scio; and in the night of June, 1822, Captain George attached fire ships to the ship of the capudan pacha, and to another vessel of the line. The former blew up, with two thousand two hundred and eighty-six men; the latter was saved. The Turks were at first stupified; but their rage soon broke out, and the last traces of cultivation, the mastic villages, were destroyed.

After an obstinate contest, the Turks were forced to abandon the greater part of Greece by August, 1822. The Turkish fleet, which had laid at anchor four weeks in the Gulf of Lepanto, and had bombarded Missolonghi without success, set sail with the plague on board. An unsuccessful attempt was made to break through the line of fifty-seven Greek brigs, which blockaded Nauplia; and then the fleet came to anchor at the entrance of the Dardanelles, off Tenedos. On the 10th of November, seventeen daring sailors of the band of forty Ipsariots, dressed like Turks, conducted two fire ships under full sail, as if they were flying from the Greeks, whilst two Ipsariot vessels pursued them, firing blank cartridges, into the midst of the Turkish fleet, and fastened one of them to the admiral's ship, and the other to that of the capitana-bey. Both were soon in flames; the former narrowly escaped; the latter blew up with eighteen hundred men; the capudan, however, got on shore before the explosion took place. Three frigates were wrecked on the coast of Asia Minor, one thirty-six gun vessel was captured: storms destroyed a part of the Ottoman fleet, and of thirty-five vessels, only eighteen returned, much injured, to the Dardanelles. The seventeen Ipsariots were rewarded with naval crowns by the ephori. The Greeks were once more masters of the sea, and renewed the blockade.

Both parties prepared for a war of extermination in 1823. An immense army and an efficient fleet were raised by the exertions of the sultan. The Greek minister of the marine, Orlandi, organized the navy which consisted of four hundred and three sail, with cannon; the largest was the Hercules, of twenty-six guns. The rich Hydriot, Miaulis, was admiral, and there were three vice-admirals. The disputes of the government with the Hydriot monarchs had a bad effect on the naval operations. The Greek fleet, however, gained a victory on the 22d of March, 1823, over an Egyptian flotilla, destined for

Candia; but it was unable to prevent the landing of Turkish troops; and the daring expeditions of the Ipsariots and Samiots on the coast of Asia Minor, were without important results. When the fleet of the capudan-pacha finally appeared in June, the Greek ships retired and contented themselves with supplying their garrisons with fresh troops and provisions.

The Turkish fleet, again having the plague on board, sailed to the Archipelago, avoided the Greek islands, delivered Saloniki from blockade, and returned to the Dardanelles, after a few indecisive engagements with the Greeks. Mavrocordato conducted a division of the Hydriot fleet, to the Gulf of Lepanto, in November, and compelled the Barbary fleet, which was blockading Missolonghi, to withdraw. The campaign terminated in favor of the Greeks. The Porte, though much exhausted, had greater resources for the next year than the patriots, who were weakened by quarrels of the different chieftains. A great number of the transport ships of the Russians, Austrians, and others were hired by the capudan-pacha, in April, 1824, and they sailed out of the Dardanelles, to destroy Ipsara and Samos. Mehemet Ali, Pacha of Egypt, was induced to send twenty-thousand men, disciplined by French officers, under his son Ibrahim, and a large fleet, to reduce the Greeks to submission.

Ismael Gibraltar, admiral of the Egyptian fleet, subdued Candia, and the capudan-pacha succeeded in relieving the Turkish garrison of Negropont and took possession of Attica. The small, but strongly fortified, rocky island of Ipsara, had made itself formidable to the Porte, by the number of its vessels and fire ships, in which the most daring of the islanders carried terror and destruction into the Dardanelles. Khosru, the capudan, obtaining exact information of the state of the island, resolved to attempt its capture; but first, he offered pardon and protection to the Ipsariots. They rejected his proposals, and prepared for the combat. Khosru left the shores of Mitylene early in July, with two ships of the line, six frigates, ten corvettes, several brigs and galliots, a great number of newly built gun boats, and more than eighty European transport ships. The fleet surrounded the island. The men-of-war began to fire upon the town and forts, and a landing was effected on the opposite side. The Ipsariots had put the old men, women, and children on board of their vessels; these were taken or sunk by the Turks. The city was attacked on all sides.

The Greeks fought from street to street, and yielded but with their lives. After a desperate struggle, two forts, the last foothold of the Ipsariots, were blown up by themselves, and heroes and conquerors found an equal grave.

This terrible blow united the Greeks more firmly and stung them to more daring activity. Hydra and Spezzia manned their ships, and Ipsara was retaken by the brave Admiral Miaulis, and the ships there saved. In all directions, the Turks were beaten by forces far inferior. In the meantime, the second part of this bloody campaign began. The Egyptian fleet, comprising nine frigates, fourteen corvettes, forty brigs and galliots, and two hundred and forty transports, with eighteen thousand land troops, set sail from Alexandria, July 19. Ibrahim was instructed to bring reinforcements to Candia, and then invade the Morea.

The Egyptian and Turkish fleets united in the Gulf of Bondroun, in September, and some battles took place with the Greek fleet. The battle at Naxos, on the 10th of September, lasted the whole day. The intrepid Kanaris blew up, by his fire ships, an Egyptian frigate of forty-four guns and a brig. The Greeks lost ten small vessels. At length, the Ottoman fleet broke off the contest, and retired to Mitylene, with the loss of several transports. Khosru then turned back to Constantinople, with fifteen sail, and Ibrahim, with the rest of the fleet, to the Gulf of Bondroun. Miaulis soon after attacked the latter off Candia. Ibrahim lost a frigate, ten small vessels, and fifteen transports. Weakened by the plague, which visited the fleet, he drew back to the harbor of Rhodes, where the well known admiral, Ismael Gibraltar, died. The attack on the Morea was frustrated for this year.

After such activity on the part of the Greek fleet, the internal dissensions once more weakened the operations of the army and navy. The campaign of 1825 was opened by the landing of Ibrahim Pacha in the Morea. Missolonghi was besieged at the same time, and the capudan aided both with his fleet. When Ibrahim laid siege to Navarino, in May, Miaulis attacked his fleet on the night of the 12th, and burned an Egyptian frigate, two corvettes, three brigs, and many transports. But the inactivity of the Greek capitani caused the capitulation of Navarino. The capudan lost several ships in May, near the cape D'Oro, in an engagement with the Greek Admiral Sactouri, and could not arrive in time to support the siege of Missolonghi. During the terrible struggle at that place, Miaulis arrived with his fleet, burned several Turkish ships and forced the rest to retire.

The campaign begun under such favorable auspices by the Turks and Egyptians, had an unsuccessful termination. The capudan-pacha had received the command of the Egyptian fleet at Alexandria, about the end of August. There the brave Kanaris had, with three fire ships, in vain forced his way into the harbor, with the intention of burning the fleet. The affairs of Greece now appeared hastening to ruin. The fleet of seventy-three men of war and twenty-three fire ships, arrived too late to save Navarino; and the capitani squandered the money with which they were to provide troops. However, a new naval force was equipped at Hydra, and strengthened by this accession of vessels, Miaulis appeared in January, 1826, in the waters of Missolonghi, and defeated the fleet of the capudan-pacha. But all attempts to supply the garrison with provisions and reinforcements failed. Another engagement between the fleets took place in the Gulf of Patras, on the 27th and 28th of January, when the Greek fire ships, under Kanaris, destroyed a frigate and many small vessels; and then Missolonghi was relieved. Five times had this heroic garrison repulsed the immense numbers of the besiegers; but it fell, after a glorious struggle, April 22d, 1826.

Lord Cochrane arrived in Greece, and took chief command of the sea forces, in 1827. After many attempts at negotiations, the Greeks renewed hostilities with undaunted activity. On the 9th of September, 1828, the Turkish-Egyptian fleet entered the bay of Navarino. A British squadron, under Sir Edward Codrington, appeared on the 13th. To this, a French squadron, under Admiral Rigny, and a Russian, under Count Heyden, united themselves on the 22d. They demanded from Ibrahim Pacha a cessation of hostilities. He promised this, and went out with part of his fleet, but was forced to return, and he continued his devastations of the Morea. The three squadrons then entered the bay, where the Turkish-Egyptian fleet was drawn up in order of battle. A shot was fired and two Englishmen killed. This was the signal for a deadly contest, (October 20, 1827,) in which Codrington nearly destroyed the Turkish armada of one hundred and ten ships. One part was burned, another driven on shore, and the rest disabled; none struck their flag.

An involuntary suspension of hostilities now ensued, during which, the depredations of pirates became more serious. The admirals of the three squadrons remonstrated with the Greek government, and after a number of capital punishments, the safety of the sea was secured.

In March, 1828, the war between Turkey and Russia began. The Russian admiral, Ricord, with one ship of the line and three frigates, blockaded the Dardanelles, in order to prevent supplies from reaching Constantinople. The Greeks fitted out a great number of privateers. Operations were suspended during the progress of negotiations, and peace was signed at Adrianople on the 14th of September, 1829. The independence of Greece was achieved; and the power of Turkey humbled.

The Turkish navy now numbers ten ships of the line, ten frigates, and a number of other vessels. The chief officer bears the title of *capudan-pacha.* Constantinople is the principal station and rendezvous for all vessels employed in the service of the empire. The naval regulations and discipline have undergone considerable alteration by the exertions of the sultan to adopt the European customs; but they are still very inferior in efficiency, even to those of Egypt. The decline of the empire is rapid and steady.

CATHARINE II.

CHAPTER XXXI.

RUSSIA.

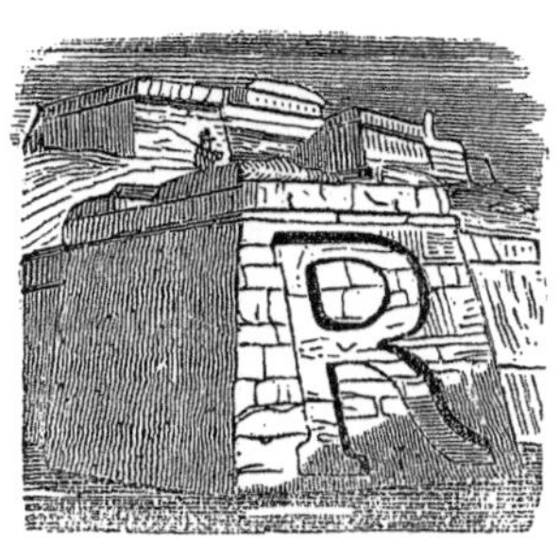

USSIA has but a trifling distinct naval history. In the numerous wars against the Turks which she has waged, her fleets have been found serviceable, and have been victorious; but as yet she has won no laurels like those which have crowned the English navy, nor produced any commander worthy of high rank as a conqueror. The navy of Russia began, as her power and her European influence began, with Peter the Great.

When Peter had resolved to make an effort to gain the throne, in opposition to his half sister, Sophia, he collected an army of twenty thousand men, and at the same time engaged himself in creating a naval force. He easily succeeded in seating himself upon the throne,

PETER THE GREAT GAINING A VICTORY AT TWERMUNDE.

and then resolved to carry out his plans for the formation of a large army and naval force. A Dutchman, named Karsten Brand, was appointed perpetual ship builder, and in 1693, the emperor sailed to Archangel in his own ship, the St. Peter. In 1694, he entered Archangel with several Russian vessels, and appointed Prince Romanadowiske, admiral of the fleet. The new ship yard at Woronesch, on the Don, furnished the emperor, as early as 1696, with a fleet of twenty-three galleys, two galleases, and four fire ships, with which he defeated the Turkish fleet, near Azoph. When Azoph fell into his hands, he ordered fifty-five ships of war to be built, and sent a number of young nobles to Holland and Italy, to learn the art of ship building. Thus he hoped to keep possession of the key to the Black Sea. In 1697, Peter went to Holland, and, under the name of Peter Michaeloff, worked at ship building for more than two months. Having completely mastered the art, he went to England, and visited the royal ship yard. He returned to Russia, in September, 1698.

During the war with Charles XII. of Sweden, Peter distinguished himself by capturing a large number of Swedish vessels of war, and attained the rank of rear-admiral. His next object was to distinguish himself in such a manner as to merit the title of vice-admiral. Having obtained a naval victory at Twermunde, and entered St. Petersburg in triumph, the Admiral Romanadowski saluted him with "Hail! vice-admiral!" and thus his ambition was gratified.

In 1716, the imperial admiral took command of the combined Russian, Danish, English, and Dutch fleets, numbering eighty vessels of war, and gained the command of the Baltic. Subsequently he succeeded in devastating the coasts of Sweden, despite the opposition of the English, Swedish, and Danish fleets. In July, 1724, he conducted his fleet against Sweden, and having succeeded in achieving his object, he returned to Cronstadt in triumph. The Russian navy now consisted of forty-one ships of war, with two thousand one hundred and six cannons, and fourteen thousand nine hundred and sixty sailors.

Catharine, the sucessor of Peter the Great, was principally occupied with the internal affairs of the empire, during her short reign. Nothing remarkable occurred in Russian naval history until 1762, when the able Catharine II. took possession of the throne. She increased the land and naval force of the empire, and invited distinguished foreign commanders to enter her service. The Turks were defeated in several encounters upon the sea. But the Swedes defeated the Russian fleets in a subsequent war. During Catharine's active reign, the Russian fleets acquired considerable influence in the Mediterranean, and complete control in the Black and Caspian seas. In August, 1828, the Russian fleet on the Black sea destroyed a Turkish flotilla, and the batteries on the coast near Constantinople. In February, 1829, another Turkish flotilla was destroyed near Nicopoli, and the fortress of Sizeboli, on the Gulf of Bourges, was taken by a Russian fleet, under Admiral Greig.

At present, the naval power of Russia is only inferior to that of Great Britain and France, and is constantly increasing. Her fleets command the eastern Mediterranean, and the Black and Caspian seas, in the south, and the Baltic sea in the north. Cronstadt is the principal naval station on the Baltic, and Sebastopol on the Black sea. The navy consisted, in 1840, of fifty-six ships of the line, carrying from seventy-four to one hundred and twenty guns, forty-eight frigates, carrying from forty-four to sixty guns, and a large number of sloops of war, brigs, and steamers.

THE EXCHANGE, ST. PETERSBURG.

A CHINESE JUNK.

CHAPTER XXXII.

CHINA.

THE history of the Chinese is of all others the most singular and interesting. Generations after generations have passed away, and still the customs and modes of life prevalent two thousand years ago hold undisputed sway. China changes but her generations, remaining in all else the same. Possessing an extensive sea coast, with many fine harbors, and being enterprising and industrious, the Chinese have ever been a commercial people. It is more than probable that the most important instruments of modern warfare and navigation were the inventions of the Chinese. It is generally conceded that the destructive gunpowder was long known in the East, before its introduction into Europe; and the use of the magnetic compass can also be traced to the same quarter.

The first certain information concerning maritime or commercial affairs which has been handed down, is the account of the construction of several extensive canals for the convenience of inland commerce, in the seventh century after Christ. The vessels used in this commerce, which was very extensive, were flat bottomed, because of the greater facility in drawing them over the embankments of the singular locks, without unloading them. They were built high and commodious.

In the early part of the thirteenth century, the celebrated Tartar chief, Zinghis Khan, subdued the greater part of China, and his greater son, Kublai, completed the work. As the Tartars approached the imperial city, the whole court fled in consternation, and went on board of some barks which were lying near the mouth of Canton river. Some Tartar vessels were sent in pursuit of the wretched fugitives, whose terror, at the sight of the hostile fleet, seems to have amounted to madness; for one of the grandees, seizing the infant emperor in his arms, jumped with him into the sea, and was instantly followed by the empress and chief minister—who thus all perished. Kublai Khan was then acknowledged as Emperor of all China, which at this time must have included the greater part of Asia, if the records of the conquest of Zinghis and Kublai are to be believed.

Kublai seems to have paid more attention to commerce than any of his predecessors; and to him the Chinese are indebted for the stupendous national work, the Grand Canal, connecting Pekin and Canton. There were none capable of resisting his power upon sea or land; and, therefore, we see no mention of a navy regularly organized existing under his reign. Once only, a fleet was sent against the Japanese to reduce them under the sway of Kublai; but a storm destroyed it, and the attempt was not renewed.

It was in the reign of the twelfth emperor of the Ming, or native dynasty, that the rapid progress of navigation which followed the discovery of America and the Cape of Good Hope, first brought the European ships to the shores of China. The Portuguese, who were the great navigators of the age, having made several voyages to India, ventured still farther eastward, in 1516, and reached the port of Canton. Some alarm was created in Canton at the appearance of strangely built vessels, and it was supposed an invasion was intended. Consequently, the fleet of eight vessels was surrounded by Chinese war junks, and it was with difficulty that the admiral, Pedro de Andrada, obtained permission to proceed with two ships, up the river to Canton.

Leave was obtained to establish a factory on the coast, and to send trading vessels to Canton once a year; and thus was a regular commercial treaty concluded between Portugal and China.

Not long after, the Spaniards, on the "errand of gain," sent out ships to China, and the Phillipine islands. The coasts of China had from time to time been infested with pirates, who were the terror of all the maritime towns, and who sheltered themselves in the islands of the adjacent seas. One chief, by the name of Limahon, made an attack on the town of Manilla, and treated the inhabitants with the greatest cruelty. A Chinese fleet, under Admiral Omnicon, was sent in search of the formidable corsair; but he had already been defeated and driven from the China seas by the Spaniards, in return for which, the admiral consented to introduce a number of the foreigners into a Chinese city.

The Dutch also sent ships to China, and established several factories; and thus was a regular maritime intercourse completed between China and the principal commercial nations of Europe. One of the most formidable opponents of the Tartars in their second conquest, about 1644, was a maritime chief, named Koshinga, a noted character in the history of those times, not only for his loyalty to the Chinese royal race, but also for his exploits against the Dutch. Ching-che-hong, the father of Koshinga, one of the richest merchants in China, fitted out a fleet at his own expense, to support the native prince; but after the accession of the Tartar, Shun-che, he accepted the offer of a high post at court, leaving the command of his fleet to his son, who remained faithful to his native sovereign. This chief was the terror of the Indian seas, where no foreign vessels dared to appear during the wars. At length, the Tartars having taken Nanking, laid siege to Cantòn, which, by the aid of Koshinga's fleet, was enabled to hold out for eight months; but was at the end of that time, obliged to surrender, by the superior skill and valor of the Tartars.

Koshinga openly continued his resistance to the new dynasty. He formed the bold project of conquering the island of Formosa, and landed on it with twenty thousand men. A desperate conflict took place with the Dutch, and in the end they were forced to abandon Formosa and take refuge with the Japanese. Koshinga then retained the sovereignty of the island until his death. His son was equally active and skilful upon the sea. He constantly ravaged the coasts; and the naval force of the empire not being strong enough to contend with the pirates, the emperor was forced to order the inhabitants of the sea shore to retire towards the interior, and leave a barren country to the invaders. A great number of sea coast villages were destroyed, and much distress produced. Formosa was surrendered to the emperor by a grandson of the chief Koshinga.

Hea-King, who ascended the throne in 1795, was an unpopular emperor, and his dominions were constantly in a state of insurrection. The pirates of the Ladrone islands renewed their depredations on the coast. Among these was a noted chief, named Ching-yih, who was no less famed and feared than Koshinga had been. He levied contributions on all vessels that appeared in the Chinese seas, plundered villages on the coast, and did not hesitate to give battle to the imperial fleet. He had a most powerful force at his command, and committed all sorts of devastations with impunity. Ching-yih was accidentally drowned; but his lawless practices were continued by his widow, who took command of the fleet, and fought with the bravest of the rovers. For some time, this pirate queen maintained her rule of the Chinese seas; insomuch that no merchant ships could navigate them, without a pass from her, and the payment of a certain amount of toll. At length, disputes arose among the pirate captains; and the chieftainess, finding her position a dangerous one, entered into a regular treaty with the governor of Canton, retired with distinguished honor and then the pirates submitted.

In 1839, the difficulties with the British merchants concerning the opium traffic commenced. Lin, the Chinese governor, blockaded the British factories and vessels on the Canton river, and demanded that twenty thousand chests of opium, then on board of the vessels, should be given up to be destroyed, according to the order of the emperor. To save the factories, the merchants agreed to surrender the drug, and it was accordingly landed, and destroyed by the governor. Soon after, the British merchants retired to Macao, a settlement belonging to the Portuguese. A quarrel occurring between some British and Chinese sailors, and one of the latter being killed, it was demanded that the murderer should be given up. This the English refused, and Captain Elliott removed the whole fleet of English vessels to the island of Hong Kong. The High Commissioner Lin, then decreed that all trade between the British and Chinese should cease.

The Chinese fleet, under Admiral Quan, a gallant veteran, much respected by friends and foes, then prepared to attack the British fleet, as it lay in the harbor of Hong Kong. But the Chinese were driven back with great loss, several of their vessels being destroyed in the

THE EMPEROR OF CHINA.

action. This defeat was a serious blow to the authorities of Canton, who had placed much dependence upon Admiral Quan. The emperor was for a time deceived into the belief that Quan had been victorious, and under this impression, he bestowed a high Tartar title upon him.

However, the admiral was continued in command of the fleet, even when the emperor was truly informed of the circumstances; but Lin was removed from his office of governor.

In the meantime, edicts were daily issued, threatening to close the ports forever against the English, if they continued to act in defiance of the imperial command. Lin and his successor exerted themselves to strengthen the fleet, by building a number of gun boats of larger size, and superior in construction to the generality of the war junks. Nothing of importance occurred until June, 1840, when an armament arrived from India, under Admiral Elliot, which joined the British fleet, already assembled at Hong Kong. A bold attempt was made by the Chinese to destroy the whole fleet by sending fire ships among the vessels; but most of them exploded before coming near enough to do mischief, and the experiment failed. This disappointed greatly the mandarins, who were so confident of success, that a proclamation had been issued, warning all other vessels to keep clear of the British fleet.

The fire ship scheme having failed, high rewards were offered to any who would kill or capture the English or take their ships. In consequence of this temptation, a large number of prisoners—soldiers, sailors, and one female—were captured; but were released in a few months, by a treaty between Admiral Elliot and Keshen, the high commissioner. The English took possession of the island of Chusan, in July, without opposition. The emperor, furious at these proceedings, commanded the viceroy to repair at once to Pekin and answer for his neglect. He also wrote to the governor of Ningpo, commanding him to cause to be constructed some vessels upon the English model. The governor forwarded the order to the head of the naval department at Ningpo, who, being utterly ignorant of the construction of English ships, and fearing the consequences of disobedience, killed himself in despair.

Towards the close of 1840, Admiral Elliot sailed up the Peiho river, to hold a conference with the high commissioner Keshen. This wily politician detained the English fleet at Canton, in amicable negotiation, and at the same time, strengthened his forces for an attack upon Chusan. At length, the English admiral, growing impatient, sent word to Keshen that if the treaty was not confirmed by eight o'clock on the morning of the 7th of January, 1841, hostilities would be renewed. No answer was returned, and, therefore, upon that morning, some of the Bogue forts were assaulted and taken, with a dreadful slaughter of the Chinese.

The appearance of a hostile fleet above these forts, caused great consternation at Canton. Seventeen war junks were burned, or blown up. Keshen then entered into a treaty with the English admiral, and the Bogue forts and all the captives were returned to the Chinese, together with the island of Chusan. Another article of the treaty provided that compensation should be made for the destruction of the opium. This, the Chinese would not fulfil; and Elliot was again compelled to proceed to attack the forts of the Bogue, a narrow pass in the Canton river. An immense number of the Chinese and Tartars were collected in them and their vicinity. The attack was successful, after a brave resistance from the band of Admiral Quan, who was killed in the struggle. The emperor was much grieved at the loss of his able and veteran admiral, and had him buried with great honors. Keshen now represented to the emperor that there was no hope of contending with the enemy unless other ships were built and cannon cast. For this and other *offences*, he was deprived of his office and disgraced.

Orders were now issued to the high admiral to sweep the barbarians (the English) from the seas; nothing less would satisfy the emperor. Early in May, the Chinese made several attacks upon the shipping in Canton river, and captured, plundered, and burned the British and Dutch factories. It was now resolved to make a direct attack upon Canton; and while a part of the fleet sailed up the river to invest it on that side, the rest, under General Sir Hugh Gough proceeded by another branch of the stream to a different point. The siege proceeded rapidly, and there is no doubt Canton would have been taken; but Elliot preferred making terms with the authorities for its ransom, and a treaty was accordingly concluded. The arrangements of the English admiral not being approved by his government, he was superseded by Sir Henry Pottinger, who arrived at Macao, in August, 1841.

The new commandant gave the Chinese authorities to understand, that they must either accede to all the demands of the English government, or expect that they would be forced into compliance. A fleet, consisting of thirty-four vessels, most of them steamers, appeared off the strongly fortified fort of Amoy on the 6th of August, and

BURNING OF THE BRITISH FACTORIES BY THE CHINESE.

summoned the city to surrender. This was done, and the British took possession of it. Chinghae, a large and populous city at the mouth of the Ningpo river, was also strongly fortified; but more desperately defended. The city was bombarded by the British fleet, and a great number of the inhabitants killed. Chinghae was taken on the 10th of October, and on the following day, the fleet proceeded up the river to Ningpo, which was taken without resistance.

HONG KONG.

In March, 1842, the Chinese attempted to recover Chinghae and Ningpo, by land attacks, and Chusan, by a fleet of junks; all three attacks were repulsed. The British fleet then proceeded up the Yang-tse-keung river, or "Child of the Ocean," and captured several large cities, after much fighting with the brave Tartars. About the middle of August, the fleet came within sight of Nankin, the ancient capital of the empire, where a treaty of peace was concluded, by which the British obtained all their demands, just or unjust. Five important ports were opened to the commerce of the invaders, and Hong Kong ceded to them forever.

For several centuries the Chinese have made no progress in ship building. Their vessels have neither mizzen, bowsprit, or topmast. They have only a main and foremast, to which is sometimes added a small top-gallant mast. The mainmast is placed almost in the same part of the deck as in European vessels; but the foremast stands much further forward. They use mats for sails, strengthening them with whole bamboes, equal in length to the breadth of the sail, and placed about a foot from each other. Two pieces of wood are fixed to the top and bottom of the sail; the upper serves as a sailyard, and the other keeps the sail stretched when it is necessary to hoist or lower it. No pumps are used. The anchors are made of the hard wood called *iron wood*, which, the Chinese say, is much superior to the metal, because the latter will bend; but the former never does. The Chinese are acquainted with the art of manœuvring a vessel, and make excellent coasting pilots, but very bad sailors in the open sea. There are two orders of mandarins, who superintend all maritime affairs—the Hai-tao, who inspect the sea coasts, and the Y-thuen-tao, who keep the harbors in repair, and have the care of the emperor's vessels. A large number of vessels can always be commanded for the service of the government, but their bad construction, and the miserable character of their seamanship, render them of little service against the men-of-war of the western nations. Doubtless, as the intercourse of the Chinese with other nations increases, the policy of adopting their vessels and warlike instruments will be made clearer, and national vanity will not interfere with the means of national safety.

CATHARINE II.

CHAPTER XXXI.

RUSSIA.

USSIA has but a trifling distinct naval history. In the numerous wars against the Turks which she has waged, her fleets have been found serviceable, and have been victorious; but as yet she has won no laurels like those which have crowned the English navy, nor produced any commander worthy of high rank as a conqueror. The navy of Russia began, as her power and her European influence began, with Peter the Great.

When Peter had resolved to make an effort to gain the throne, in opposition to his half sister, Sophia, he collected an army of twenty thousand men, and at the same time engaged himself in creating a naval force. He easily succeeded in seating himself upon the throne,

Towards the conclusion of 1775, it was determined by Congress to fit out a naval force to assist in the defence of American independence, and an anxious search was made for friends able and willing to act as officers on board of their vessels. The celebrated Paul Jones offered his services, and was immediately appointed first lieutenant of the Alfred, one of the only two ships belonging to Congress, and on board that vessel, at Philadelphia, he hoisted the *pine tree and rattlesnake* flag—the first banner of independence—with his own hands. In the course of an active and successful campaign, having found means to gain the confidence of the marine committee, he had not served many months, before he received a captain's commission.

In November, 1777, Captain Jones sailed for France, in the Ranger, a new sloop of war of eighteen guns, with despatches of the victory of Saratoga. It was intended as a reward for his services, that he should be appointed to the command of the Indian, a fine frigate, built for Congress, at Amsterdam; but the American commissioners thought it best to assign this vessel to the king of France, and Jones continued with the Ranger. Having convoyed some merchant ships to Quiberon bay, he there received the first salute that was given to the flag of Congress by a foreign power. Eager to retaliate upon Britain her depredations upon the American coast, Jones soon after entered the Irish Channel, and approached his native shores as an enemy. This cruize lasted twenty-eight days, and he returned to Brest, with two large vessels of war as prizes, besides having destroyed many valuable ships and thrown the whole coast into a state of alarm.

The French ministry, to testify their good will towards the United States, had promised to furnish Jones with a ship, in which he was to display the American flag. At length, after much delay, and having applied in person, at Paris, he obtained command of the Duc De Duras of forty guns. The name was changed to "*Le Bon Homme Richard,*" in compliment to the saying of Poor Richard, in Franklin's almanac, "If you would have your business done, come yourself; if not, send."

In this vessel, badly manned, and not much better furnished, Paul Jones sailed as commodore of a little squadron, consisting, besides his own ship, of the Alliance of thirty-six guns, the Pallas of thirty-two, the Serf of eighteen, the Vengeance of twelve, and two privateers, which requested leave to share the commodore's fortunes. After

LE BON HOMME RICHARD, AND THE CAPTURE OF THE SERAPIS.

taking several prizes, the Serf, the privateers, and at length the Alliance, deserted the squadron. The commodore's good fortune, however, did not desert him. On the 15th September, he was, with his own ship, the Pallas, the Vengeance, and several prizes, at the entrance into the Firth of Forth, where they made every necessary disposition to seize the guard ship, and two cutters, that rode at anchor in the roads, and to lay Leith, and perhaps Edinburgh, under contribution. The wind, which was fair in the night, opposed them in the morning. However, on the 16th, the little squadron continued all day to work up the Firth. At this time, a member of the British parliament observing them from the coast of Fife, and mistaking them for the king's ships, sent off a boat to inform the commodore that he was greatly afraid of Paul Jones, and to beg some powder and shot. Our hero, much amused with the message, sent him a barrel of gunpowder, with a civil answer to quiet his fears, and an apology for not including shot in the present.

Next morning at daybreak, every thing was in perfect readiness to commence the engagement, and two tacks more would have brought the strangers alongside their enemies, when, at a critical moment, a sudden gale of wind swept down the Firth, raging with such violence, as completely to overpower them, to sink one of the prizes, and drive all the rest of the squadron fairly out to sea. By this failure, the captains of the Pallas and Vengeance were so much disheartened, that they could not be prevailed on to renew the attempt.

Continuing their cruise, after various adventures, the squadron suddenly discovered the homeward-bound British Baltic fleet, off Scarborough castle, escorted by the frigate Serapis, and the Countess of Scarborough. After a long engagement, in which Paul Jones displayed the most astonishing skill, intrepidity, and presence of mind, the Countess of Scarborough struck to the Pallas, and the Serapis to the Bon Homme Richard, which latter ship was reduced to so shattered a state, that next morning, after all hands had left her, she went to the bottom. The Serapis was not in much better condition, the commodore having, with his own hands, lashed the two ships together, to prevent the enemy from availing himself of his superiority in weight of metal.

This was the most obstinate naval contest on record. The Serapis was commanded by Captain Pearson, a brave and skilful officer. Jones

COMMODORE JOHN PAUL JONES.

had not only to contend with a superior vessel; but, in the heat of the battle, his vessel received several shots from the Alliance, as is supposed, in mistake. Nothing but the most determined courage and superior ability could have triumphed under the circumstances. Jones now took command of the Serapis, erected jury masts, and with some difficulty, conveyed his prizes to the Texel. There he took command of the Alliance; and the Dutch being summoned to deliver him up as a pirate and a rebel, he was forced to put to sea. He contrived to make his escape, passing the Isle of Wight and Dover, in the very face of the English fleets.

Towards the close of 1780, Captain Jones sailed for America, and having encountered in his passage, the Triumph, an English vessel of twenty guns, he forced her to strike. By permission of Congress, the king of France conferred upon the daring captain, the cross of the order of military merit; and Congress passed a vote of thanks for his services. Surely this was a brilliant commencement of a naval career. A large number of privateers were fitted out at Philadelphia and other ports, which constantly annoyed the commerce of Great Britain. Captains Alexander Murray, John Barry, Nicholas Biddle, Joshua Barney, and others, distinguished themselves by their activity and daring, either in eluding the large fleets of the British or in capturing their single vessels. Many vessels were destroyed even in the British seas, by a light squadron, under Captain Wickes, and the English merchants thrown into a state of constant alarm. But few large vessels of war were within the command of the marine committee; and the majority of the individual exploits were accomplished by vessels with letters of marque, or by those fitted out by the different colonial governments.

So destructive to the navigation of England did the privateering system become, that the government resolved to refuse to exchange any more of the seamen that fell into their power. By acting on this policy, they collected a large body of prisoners, in 1780, sending them to England in their return ships, and sensibly affected the nautical enterprise of the Americans, who had but a limited number of seamen. By the fall of Charleston, the regular American marine was much reduced; but the alliance with France brought the large and powerful French fleets to the coasts, and Congress thought it unnecessary to make any effort to increase the number of its vessels. Several well contested actions were fought during 1780, between single ships, in all of which the superiority of the Americans was clearly manifest. The Trumbull, twenty-eight, under Captain James Nicholson, senior officer of the navy, encountered the Watt, 34 or 36 guns, on the 2d of June, and for two hours and a half the vessels lay within a cable's length, cannonading with effect. An accident—the mainmast falling—prevented Nicholson from securing a complete victory. However, the ships separated, the Watt having lost ninety-nine men in killed and wounded, and the Trumbull but thirty-nine. The Watt was in all respects, except sailing, the superior vessel.

In March, 1782, the Delaware was much infested by the barges and small cruisers of the enemy. With a view to keep the navigation open against the marauders, the State of Pennsylvania determined to fit out a few vessels at its own expense. With this object, a small ship, named the Hyder Ally, unfit for any thing but commercial purposes,

CAPTURE OF THE GENERAL MONK.

was purchased and an armament of sixteen six-pounders put aboard of her. Lieutenant Joshua Barney was selected as her commander. Convoying a large fleet of merchantmen, the Hyder Ally got into the Delaware on the 8th of April, and soon after was attacked by the General Monk, of twenty guns, commanded by Captain Rodgers, while a British brig witnessed the action. The battle lasted but half an hour, when the General Monk struck, the two vessels remaining foul of each other. This was one of the most brilliant achievements of the American navy, and Captain Barney received great praise for the skill and daring he had displayed, in attacking such a superior force. The fleet of merchantmen was saved.

The country was too much exhausted by the war of the revolution to incur the expense of a marine during a time of peace. But the rapid growth of the commerce, and its unprotected state, excited the cupidity of the Dey of Algiers, who captured the schooner Maria, of Boston, in July, 1785. This outrage was succeeded by others, until the government of the United States found the necessity of arming. This decided measure was taken after the organization of the government under the new constitution, and during the presidency of Washington. Six frigates were ordered to be constructed, and the keels of the following vessels were laid :— the Constitution, forty-four, United States, forty-four, President, forty-four, Chesapeake, thirty-eight, Constellation, thirty-eight, and Congress, thirty-eight. This was the commencement of the permanent marine of the United States. These frigates were not launched until some years afterwards, in consequence of the arrangement of the difficulties with Algiers; but the officers appointed to command them were continued in the service.

COMMODORE BARNEY.

The President in his annual speech to Congress, in December, 1796, strongly recommended laws for the gradual increase of the navy. The general war in Europe proved very injurious to the commerce of this country, and French cruisers even captured British and American vessels in our own waters. All attempts to obtain redress failed; and in April, 1798, the President submitted to Congress, a plan of armament and defence intended to check these aggressions. Twenty small vessels were ordered to be built, and in the event of an open rupture, it was recommended to Congress to authorize the building of six ships of the line. The United States, forty-four, was the first vessel got afloat, under the present organization of the navy. Congress authorized the building of twelve vessels, none of which was to exceed twenty-two guns; and on the 30th of April, 1798, a regular navy department was formally created. The whole naval force authorized by law, on the 16th of July, 1798, consisted of twelve frigates; twelve ships of a force not exceeding twenty-four guns; and six smaller sloops, besides galleys and revenue cutters, making a total of thirty active cruisers.

The Ganges twenty-four, under command of Captain Richard Dale, was authorized to cruise along the coast and capture all French vessels there to be found with hostile intentions; and the Constellation, thirty-eight, Captain Truxtun, and the Delaware, twenty, Captain Decatur, went to sea in June, 1798, to cruise along the coast, south of Cape Henry. Decatur, when a few days out, captured a French privateer schooner, Le Croyable, fourteen guns, and sent her into the Delaware. This vessel was altered and called the Retaliation. The activity of the American government now astonished those who had thought that it would submit to almost any insult. By the close of the year, three frigates, eleven sloops, and brigs, and nine smaller vessels were at sea, under the orders of the government. Most of these were employed in the West Indies, or in convoying between the islands and the United States. The Retaliation was recovered by the French frigate Volontaire, in November of this year; but other privateers were captured by the United States and Delaware.

A number of efficient vessels were got afloat at the commencement of 1799, several being built by the different principal cities and presented to the general government. On the 9th of February, the Constellation, thirty-eight, Commodore Truxtun, while cruising on her prescribed ground, encountered the French frigate L'Insurgente, forty, one of the fastest sailing ships in the world, commanded by the brave and skilful Captain Berrault. A close contest of more than an hour ensued, at the end of which, the Constellation being in a raking position, L'Insurgente struck her colors. In this brilliant engagement between well matched forces, the French ship was much cut up, and sustained a loss of seventy men in killed and wounded. The Constellation suffered in her upper works, but was not much damaged in the hull, and had but three men wounded. With much difficulty, L'Insurgente with all her crew as prisoners on board, was conducted into St. Kitts, after being three days separated from the Constellation.

This victory rendered the navy still more popular with the people of the United States, and the new ships were constructed as fast as possible. The Congress, thirty-eight, and the Essex, thirty-two, sailed at the close of 1799 to convoy vessels as far as Batavia. The Congress was much damaged by a gale and forced to return; but the Essex, Captain Preble, proceeded on her cruise, carrying her pennant, for the first time, to the eastward of the Cape of Good Hope.

CAPTURE OF L'INSURGENTE.

The largest American squadron was forced to cruise in the vicinity of the island of Guadaloupe, in consequence of the number of French privateers proceeding from that place.

On the 1st of February, 1800, the Constellation, thirty-eight, Commodore Truxtun, was again off Guadaloupe, when a French frigate, La Vengeance, fifty-two, Captain Pitot, came in sight. Although the French vessel was so much superior, Truxtun bravely prepared for battle. It commenced at eight o'clock in the evening, and was continued with obstinacy for five hours, within pistol shot. Both vessels were so shattered, that they separated about one o'clock without coming to a decisive result. Truxtun succeeded in reaching Jamaica in safety, and Pitot got into Curaçoa in a sinking condition. In this hard fought battle, the Constellation had fourteen men killed and twenty-five wounded—eleven of the latter afterwards dying of their injuries. Her antagonist had fifty killed and one hundred and ten wounded. It is said, that La Vengeance struck her colors three times during the action, but seeing that no notice was taken of it, they were hoisted again. Considering the disparity of force, the action must be con-

COMMODORE TRUXTUN.

sidered as in every way honorable to the Americans. Truxtun gained a great name by this, his second brilliant affair. Congress voted him a gold medal, and he was given the command of the President, forty-four. The Insurgente soon after went to sea, under Captain Fletcher, and nothing more was ever heard of her.

The year 1800 was actively employed on both sides in the West Indies. The French captured a considerable number of merchant vessels, and the Americans a large number of their privateers—upwards of fifty sail. Peace was concluded between France and the United States, in February, 1801; and thus ended a struggle, in which the marine of the United States was permanently established, and most of the officers afterwards celebrated, commenced their career. At the peace with France, the cruising vessels in the service were thirty-four in number, and of these, when the law reduced the navy to a peace establishment, fourteen of the largest were retained.

COMMODORE DALE.

CHAPTER XXXIV.

FROM 1801 TILL 1812.

ON the 14th of May, 1801, war was proclaimed against the United States by the Bashaw of Tripoli, in consequence of the refusal to pay tribute. Algiers and Tunis followed the example. Before it was known that Tripoli had actually declared war, a squadron was ordered to be fitted out and sent to the Mediterranean to overawe the Barbary powers. This squadron consisted of the President, forty-four, Philadelphia, thirty-eight, Essex, 32, and Enterprise, 12, at the head of which was Commodore Dale, an officer already greatly distinguished. On the 1st of July, 1801, the squadron anchored at Gibraltar, and thus prevented the Tripolitan admiral from getting into the Atlantic.

The appearance of this squadron quieted the resentment of the rulers of Algiers and Tunis. The Enterprise soon after captured a polacre-rigged ship of fourteen guns, called the Tripoli, after a desperate fight, in which the Turk thrice hauled down his flag and as often renewed the contest. The President appeared off Tripoli on the 24th of August, and after some small captures the prisoners were exchanged with the enemy, with whom Commodore Dale was desirous of concluding a truce. The President then left her station and proceeded to Gibraltar. She was succeeded by the Essex. The return of Dale's squadron was ordered by the 1st of December; but discretionary power being given, he left the Essex and the Philadelphia in the Mediteranean; the first to guard the Straits, and the other to watch the Tripolitans, making Syracuse her port of resort. Thus ended the first year of the Tripolitan war. Although little was done towards bringing the enemy to terms, much was effected in raising the discipline of the navy.

Early in 1802, Congress provided by law, for shipping crews for two years. Preparations were made for sending out a relief squadron, consisting of the Chesapeake, thirty-eight, Constellation, thirty-eight, New York, thirty-six, John Adams, twenty-eight, Adams, twenty-eight, and Enterprise, twelve. Commodore Truxtun was selected to command this squadron. The vessels composing it did not sail together, but proceeded singly and at long intervals to the Mediterranean. The Constellation, under Captain Murray, blockaded the port of Tripoli, and had an engagement with a number of gun boats belonging to the enemy. The gun boats were a good deal cut up, but succeeded in escaping. After waiting for a reinforcement, Captain Murray was compelled to quit his station, and Tripoli was again left without blockade.

On the 3d of May, the John Adams was sent to blockade Tripoli, and was soon joined by Commodore Morris, with the New York, Enterprise, and Adams. An attack was then made upon a fleet of vessels laden with wheat, and guarded by some gun boats. These vessels

CAPTAIN MURRAY.

succeeded in reaching the shore, where they were protected by batteries. They were attacked in that position, however, and although the Americans failed to destroy them, they suffered considerably. Commodore Morris then made an effort to negotiate a treaty, but did not succeed. He left the three vessels before the fort, in command of Captain Rodgers, of the John Adams, and sailed to Malta.

On the 22d of June, the Enterprise, under Lieutenant Hull, gave information of the approach of a Tripolitan corsair of twenty-two guns, with a large number of men, and succeeded in keeping her off from the shore until the John Adams came up. A number of gun boats full of men went to the assistance of the Tripolitan vessel, and their cavalry lined the shore. The John Adams opened her fire upon the ship, and the Enterprise then occupied the attention of the gun boats. A smart cannonade was maintained for forty-five minutes, when the men of the corsair abandoned their guns, and great numbers leaped overboard and swam ashore. The vessel then blew up, and the gun boats escaped to the shore. The squadron, soon after this affair, visited several Mediterranean ports. Commodore Morris was recalled, and being thought guilty of neglect of duty, was dismissed from the service. This measure was considered by many as high-handed and unjust. Captain Rodgers was temporarily left in command in the Mediterranean.

The government soon became convinced of the necessity of some light cruisers, to render a blockade effective; and accordingly, four finely modeled vessels, carrying from twelve to sixteen guns, were constructed. A new squadron was selected and despatched to the Mediterranean. It consisted of the Constitution 44, Philadelphia 38, Argus 16, Siren 16, Nautilus 12, Vixen 12, and Enterprise 12. Commodore Preble was selected to command this force, and he arrived in the Mediterranean in September, 1803. This excellent officer soon made preparations for bringing Tripoli to terms. But before the squadron could assemble for this purpose an accident happened which must be mentioned here. The Philadelphia, Captain Bainbridge, in chasing some small Tripolitan vessels, ran aground near Tripoli. Every exertion was made to get her off; but she was soon surrounded by the gun boats of the enemy, and after a sharp contest, Bainbridge surrendered, having previously made the vessel useless, by boring holes in her bottom. The prisoners were plundered of every thing valuable, and conducted to the bashaw.

The Tripolitan ruler now had power to propose higher terms of peace. He expected a high ransom for the officers and crew of the Philadelphia. That vessel was secured, her leaks stopped, her guns remounted and she was then anchored within a mile of the bashaw's castle. Commodore Preble soon received information of the capture of the Philadelphia, and letters from Bainbridge suggesting plans of destroying her. Preble mentioned the project to Lieutenant Stephen Decatur, commander of the Enterprise. The exploit had strong attractions for the ardent and daring temperament of Decatur, and he had just before taken a ketch which offered the means of success. The attack was planned by the judgment of Preble, and Decatur appointed to

BURNING OF THE PHILADELPHIA.

execute it. Sixty-two men were picked, as being most active, and a number of midshipmen volunteering, the whole force which embarked in the ketch, Intrepid, was seventy-four men.

The Siren and Intrepid came in sight of Tripoli on the afternoon of the 9th of February, 1804. During the night, a reconnoisance was made; but a violent gale prevented the execution of the project and drove the ketch out to sea. On the 16th of February, the attempt to enter the harbor was renewed, and the attack arranged judiciously by Decatur. Fire arms were only to be used in the last extremity, and the watchword was to be, "Philadelphia." The greater part of the men lay upon deck, secured from the sight of the Tripolitans, and as the vessel entered the harbor in the evening, but ten or twelve were visible, the Philadelphia then lay a mile from the town, and near several corsairs and gun boats. The ketch was hailed, and the interpreter amused the Turks until she was swung alongside of the Philadelphia. In an instant the men sprang up, and led by Decatur, Morris, and others, were soon upon the deck of the frigate. The surprise was as perfect as the assault was rapid and earnest. The Turks leaped into the sea, when driven from the stern of the vessel, and the resistance was trifling. The combustibles were then passed up from the ketch, and the firing was so rapid that some of the Americans who went below were almost smothered before they had time to ascend. All escaped, however, and the Intrepid pushed off from the frigate, as the flames burst out from every part of her. Three hearty cheers were then given by the daring crew, and they took to their sweeps. This aroused the Turks and all their batteries were at once opened. The Intrepid sustained no injury and was soon beyond the reach of the enemy's guns. The success of this undertaking laid the foundation of Decatur's reputation, and he was immediately made a captain. It also raised the confidence of the American seamen.

It was July 21st, 1804, when Commodore Preble was able to sail from Malta with his whole force, to join the vessels cruising off Tripoli. The blockade had been kept up for some months with vigor, and the commodore felt the time had arrived for more active operations. He had with him, the Constitution, Enterprise, Nautilus, two bomb-ketches, and six gun boats. To these were joined before Tripoli, the Siren, Argus, Scourge, and Vixen. Opposed to this force, the Tripolitans had one hundred and fifteen guns in battery, and two large

BOMBARDMENT OF TRIPOLI.

galleys. two schooners and a brig, all well manned, were moored in the harbor. The only advantages possessed by the assailants in the attack, were those of spirit, discipline and system. The attack began on the 3d of August, 1804, by two bombards, and then the fire on both sides began to roar. The gallant Decatur headed a desperate attack upon the gun boats of the enemy, and besides being severely wounded, came near losing his life in a hand to hand contest with a Tripolitan. He was only saved by one of his men devotedly interposing his arm, which received the blow intended for the daring captain. His brother, Lieutenant James Decatur, nobly emulating his brother's example, was shot through the head. The commander of another boat, named Trippe, also engaged in a hand to hand fight with the Turkish leader of a gun boat crew, and killed him, after a desperate battle, in which the gallant American received eleven sabre wounds. Several of the enemy's gun boats were captured, and the rest forced to seek safety in flight. The bombardment and cannonade were continued with effect by the squadron, and then, satisfied for the time, Preble hauled off with his prizes.

The attack was renewed on the 7th of August, and several gun boats destroyed, and batteries silenced. The bombs were of little use, on account of the crippled state of the vessels. On the 16th, Preble, who had been waiting for a promised reinforcement, resolved to begin another and more vigorous attack. The positions of the enemy were carefully reconnoitered by Decatur and Chauncey, and every prudent preparation made to render the assault effective. On the 28th, a favorable position was taken before the town of Tripoli, and the gun boats, under seven of the most intrepid commanders, proceeded in the night to their stations. At dawn on the 29th, the enemy opened their fire, and thirteen of their boats engaged those of the Americans in the former desperate manner. One of them was sunk, two were run ashore, and the rest retreated. The fire of the Constitution frigate was tremendous, and did terrible execution in the town. One shot passed within six feet of Captain Bainbridge, the captive commander of the Philadelphia. After withstanding and returning the heavy fire of the Tripolitan batteries for a considerable time, the Constitution hauled off, and the gun boats followed.

On the night of the 4th of September, the Intrepid, which had been converted into an "infernal machine," sailed into the harbor, under the conduct of Captain Somers and a daring crew, who had volunteered for the service, which was, the destruction of the enemy's vessels. She was perceived; a fire opened upon her, and in a few minutes an awful explosion took place, and not one of her devoted crew escaped to tell her fate. The campaign terminated with this destructive effort. Commodore Preble had exhausted his ammunition, and the season was so far advanced, that it was dangerous to remain on that exposed coast. The commodore had displayed all the qualities of a great naval commander, and was deserving of the thanks voted him by Congress. A powerful fleet was maintained in the Mediterranean, and Preble was succeeded by Commodore Barron.

The blockade of Tripoli was continued during the bad season of 1804–5, but no attack was attempted. A large reinforcement of bomb-ketches and gun boats was received early in 1805. A treaty of peace was concluded in June, by which the prisoners in the hands of the bashaw were ransomed for sixty thousand dollars; but no tribute was to be paid in future. The influence of the Tripolitan war upon the American navy was incalculable. It raised its character among for-

AFFAIR OF THE CHESAPEAKE.

eign nations, to a degree that secured our commerce respect, and afforded many noble examples of heroic daring almost unparalleled. After the settlement of the relations between the United States, Tripoli, and Tunis, the Mediterranean squadron was gradually withdrawn—no fear of any further demonstration on the part of those powers being entertained.

The frequent insults offered to American vessels, and the Chesapeake and Leopard, and the President and Little Belt affairs especially, created a growing hatred between England and the United States, and led to the second war between the unnatural mother and her offspring. The Chesapeake, under Commodore Barron, sailed from Hampton Roads for the Mediterranean on the 22d of June, 1807. She had a new, undisciplined crew, and was totally unprepared for a sea fight. A British squadron was stationed at the mouth of Chesapeake bay, watching some French vessels. One of the vessels of this squadron, the Leopard frigate, 56, proceeded to meet the

Chesapeake, and sent a boat to her, with a request to search the vessel for deserters. Commodore Barron returned answer, that there were no deserters on board of his vessel, and his orders would not allow him to let his people be mustered by any officers but their own. The Leopard, then, being in all respects as ready for action as the Chesapeake was unfit, fired a broadside into the American vessel, wounding Commodore Barron and his aid. Every exertion was made to get the guns ready; but the means of discharging them were absolutely wanting. For twelve or fifteen minutes the Leopard poured in her fire upon an unresisting ship. But one gun was fired from the Chesapeake, and then she hauled down her colors. Three men were then taken by the Leopard as deserters, and the Chesapeake allowed to go into Hampton Roads. This affair aroused a feeling of indignation in the breasts of the American people. Commodore Barron was tried by court martial, acquitted of cowardice, but found guilty of neglect in not clearing his ship for action.

After Congress met, the President interdicted all British vessels of war from entering the American waters. On the 18th of December, a law was passed authorizing the construction of one hundred and eighty-eight gun boats, a force only useful for defensive purposes. The number of seamen was increased to nearly seven thousand. It was also thought necessary to begin to construct a naval force for operations on the lakes; the English having already a force on lakes Erie and Ontario, and, accordingly, gun boats were placed on Lake Champlain, and a brig of sixteen guns on Lake Ontario.

The British cruisers continued their impressment of American seamen, under pretence of searching for deserters, and all American vessels were subject to a constant annoyance. In the spring of 1811, the President 44, Commodore Rodgers, when within six leagues of the land, southward of New York, came in sight of a British ship of war—the Little Belt 18, Captain Bingham. Chase was immediately made, to get within hail; but the Little Belt stood away southward. On getting within gun shot, Rodgers hailed the British vessel. No answer was returned; but a single gun was fired by the Little Belt, and then her whole broadside. The President, of course, returned the fire, with interest, completely disabling the British vessel. Thirty of her people were killed or wounded. The encounter caused great excitement both in England and the United States. Captain Rodgers and Captain Bingham told different stories of the affair, and particularly, in regard to firing the first gun. But as the statement of Captain Rodgers was made upon oath before a court martial, and that of Captain Bingham was not, the former was entitled to the most credit. The consequence of this affair was, an increased alienation of the people of the two countries, which made it evident that an open rupture was at hand. A large majority of the people of the United States cherished an intense hatred of the English government, and eagerly sought every occasion to add to the flame of discord.

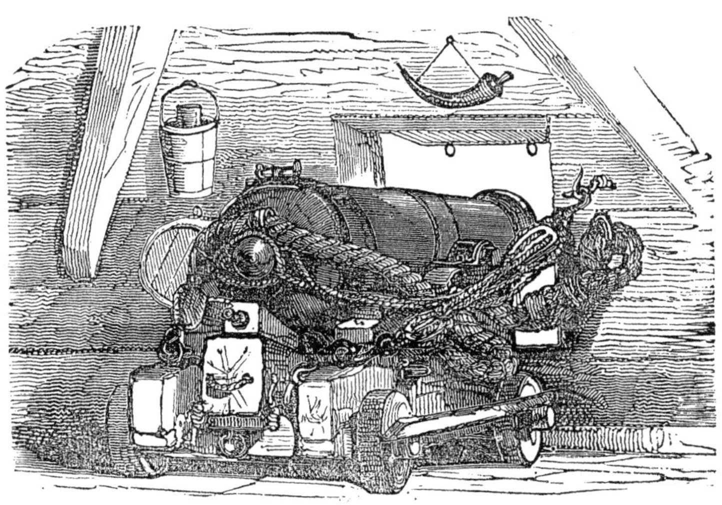

CHAPTER XXXV.

THE NAVAL OPERATIONS ON THE OCEAN OF THE WAR, FROM 1812 TO 1815.

AT the commencement of the struggle with Great Britain, on the 18th of June, 1812, the contrast of the two navies was remarkable. Great Britain had between seven hundred and eight hundred efficient cruising vessels, the greater number of which could be directed against the United States. To oppose this powerful force, the United States had three frigates of forty-four guns each, three of thirty-eight guns, one of thirty-six, one of thirty-two, three vessels of twenty-eight, two of eighteen, three of sixteen, three of fourteen, and one of twelve guns. The English bore the reputation of being invincible upon the sea, and the general feeling in America was that of distrust of their own ability.

Commodore Rodgers was soon at sea, with the President, United States, Hornet, Congress, and Argus. It was determined to make a dash at a large fleet of Jamaica-men, then expected northward. In moving towards the gulf stream, the President, being ahead of the rest of the squadron, fell in with the British frigate Belvidera, of 36 guns, Captain Byron. The President fired the first shot of the war, and then both vessels poured their destructive thunders into each other. The Belvidera was enabled to haul off much injured and with seven killed and wounded. The President suffered less in injury to the vessel, but had twenty-one killed and wounded. The Jamaica fleet succeeded in eluding the American squadron, which then put into Boston. During the whole cruise of seventy days, seven merchantmen and one letter of marque were captured.

The British collected a fleet as soon as they received the intelligence of the declaration of war, and a force, consisting of the Africa 64, the Shannon 38, Guerriere 38, Belvidera 36, and Æolus 32; all under orders of Captain Broke, sailed with the hope of meeting this squadron of Commodore Rodgers. The British squadron captured the Nautilus 14 guns, after a long chase, early in July; and thus was an active cruiser lost to the American service.

On her return from a run to Europe, the Constitution 44, Captain Hull, had gone into the Chesapeake. Here she shipped a new crew, and on the 12th of July, sailed southward. On the 17th, being out of sight of land, a British frigate, in company with other vessels, was descried. Sail was immediately made, and at dawn on the 18th, the squadron of Commodore Broke was made out. They soon closed, and the Constitution had two frigates on her lee quarter, and a ship of the line, two frigates, a brig, and a schooner astern. Every preparation was made for a contest, and several shots exchanged with the nearest vessels. It seemed as if the British squadron would overwhelm the Constitution as she tacked, and gliding away, was followed by the whole force. The chase was continued, the Constitution gaining on the enemy, for three days and nights, and then the English squadron hauled off to the northward. Throughout this long and trying chase, the Constitution and her noble crew, extorted admiration from the enemy. A few days after, the English squadron separated, in the hope of meeting the American frigate in single combat.

The Essex 32, Captain Porter, captured the Minerva frigate 36

ESCAPE OF THE CONSTITUTION FROM THE BRITISH SQUADRON.

guns, with one hundred and fifty soldiers on board, during a cruise to the southward from New York; and soon after, the Alert 20 guns; another British ship was taken by the stratagem of disguising the Essex as a merchant vessel. The Essex continued to cruise to the southward of the Grand Bank, running considerable risk from the number of the enemy's frigates, and then put into the Delaware for supplies.

The Constitution was not idle. Hull sailed from Boston on the 2d of August, and stood to the eastward, hoping to meet some of the enemy's cruisers. Several small vessels were captured, and burned, and a privateer and a prize American brig were taken and sent into port. The Constitution then stood southward, and on the 19th, came in sight of a frigate which proved to be the Guerriere 38, Captain Dacres. Chase was made, and the Englishman shortened sail, and

COMMODORE HULL.

prepared for battle. The Constitution withstood the fire of the Guerriere, without returning it, as she could have done, until close enough to do it with effect. The vessels were soon side by side, pouring a heavy fire into each other, and as they touched, both parties prepared to board; but the fire was too heavy, and neither had the opportunity. The Constitution shot ahead and secured a raking position. Just then, the foremast and mainmast of the Guerriere fell, leaving her a helpless wreck. She then, of course, surrendered. It being found impossible to keep the British frigate afloat, her crew was removed, and the vessel blown up. Hull then returned to Boston, encumbered with his wounded and prisoners. In this, the first single combat of the war, the Constitution suffered in her rigging and sails, but little in her hull. Her loss in men, was seven killed and seven wounded.

CAPTURE OF THE GUERRIEEE.

COMMODORE DECATUR.

On the other hand, the Guerriere was completely dismasted, had seventy-nine killed and wounded, and received thirty shot as low as five sheets of copper beneath the bends. The battle lasted two hours, but the greater part of the execution was done in one-fourth of the time. The moral effect of the victory was remarkable. Although the Constitution was the superior vessel: the fact of her having conquered a British frigate of nearly equal force in a regular engagement, destroyed the charmed circle of invincibility so long existing around the British reputation.

The Constitution was soon ready, for sea again, and sailed, under Captain Bainbridge, in September. Congress did nothing of importance towards increasing the navy during the year 1812, and it was left to the officers to demonstrate their ability to maintain the honor of their country before it would confide to them sufficient means. The United States 44, under Captain Decatur, encountered the British frigate Macedonian 38, Captain Carden, on Sunday, October 25th, in lat. 29° N., long. 29° 30′ W. The firing commenced when the vessels were within a mile of each other, and was continued for more than an hour—the Macedonian suffering greatly, and the United States but trifling injury. On taking possession of the British vessel, Decatur found that she was fearfully cut to pieces, having received one hundred round shot in her hull alone. Of three hundred men on board, thirty-six were killed and sixty-eight wounded. The United States had five men killed and seven wounded. Although heavier in armament than her opponent the results of the contest were vastly disproportioned in favor of the United States. The frigate and her prize sailed for New York. The previous brilliant reputation of Decatur was confirmed and heightened by the bravery and skill which he exhibited in the action.

COMMODORE JONES.

A more equal conflict took place in October. On the 13th of that month, the Wasp, a ship of war of 18 guns, Captain Jones, sailed from the Delaware to clear the coast, and get in the track of vessels steering north. On the night of the 17th, a convoy of six English ships, under the charge of a heavy brig of war, was descried. The commander of the brig seemed desirous of a combat, and shortening sail let the convoy proceed. The vessels were soon near enough to pour in their broadsides. The fire of the English vessel was rapid, but that of the Wasp was deliberate and deadly. The vessels closed, and the impetuous crew of the Wasp sprang upon the deck of the enemy; but there was little opposition. There was scarcely twenty of her people left unhurt. Lieutenant Biddle lowered the flag, and the officers threw down their swords in submission. The battle lasted forty-three minutes. The prize proved to be the Frolic, a sloop of war of 18 guns, Captain Whinyates. The Wasp was much cut up aloft, and had five

UNITED STATES AND MACEDONIAN.

WASP AND FROLIC.

men killed and five wounded. The Frolic had been hulled at almost every discharge, and her masts fell, as the vessels separated. Her loss in men is not precisely known; but Captain Whinyates' statement leaves us to infer, that the number of killed and wounded reached between ninety and one hundred. The result occasioned much exultation in America.

These brilliant achievements followed each other in rapid succession. Scarcely had exultation for one victory gladdened the hearts of the Americans when another was reported equaling or excelling it. Victory seemed chained to the American flag; bound to follow wherever it floated. South of St. Salvador, on the 29th of December, the Constitution, "Old Ironsides," under Captain Bainbridge, fell in with the British frigate, Java, 38 guns, Captain Lambert. The battle commenced at 2, P. M., with a furious cannonade from both sides. Considerable manœuvring to gain a raking position followed; but neither vessel succeeded, and they were finally brought alongside—yard arm and yard arm. The fire was destructive for a while, and then the

43*

COMMODORE BAINBRIDGE.

vessels got clear of each other, and the fire ceased—the American captain thinking the enemy had struck. He busily employed his men in repairing the damage in his rigging, and in about an hour, observing an ensign still flying aboard the Java, the fire was renewed, and the enemy struck. This battle lasted about two hours, and was well contested. Although there was more manœuvring than common, the Java was literally picked to pieces by shot, spar following spar, until she had not one left. Her hull was also greatly injured; and her loss in men was sixty killed and one hundred and one wounded. The Constitution did not lose a spar. Of her crew, nine were killed and twenty-five wounded. The Java was blown up, and the Constitution made way to St. Salvador, where her prisoners were landed on parole.

On the 24th of February, the Hornet, 20 guns, Captain Lawrence,

CONSTITUTION AND JAVA.

CAPTAIN LAWRENCE.

fell in with the brig Peacock, 20 guns, Captain Peake, near Demarara river. Having got the weather gage, the Hornet poured such a tremendous fire into the enemy, that she struck and hoisted a signal of distress, in thirty minutes. The Peacock was found to be rapidly sinking, and every exertion was made by the Hornet's crew to remove the prisoners. In spite of this, however, nine of the Peacock's and three of the Hornet's crew went down with the wreck. In this short battle, the British had their captain and four men killed, and thirty-three wounded. The Hornet had one man killed and two wounded, in addition to two men badly hurt by the explosion of a cartridge. The Hornet was superior in the weight of her metal; but there was the same disproportion in the amount of execution done as in the affair of the Constitution and Java.

These successes procured Captain Bainbridge and Captain Lawrence medals, swords, and votes of thanks from the different legislatures, and served to increase the popularity of the navy. On the 2d of January, 1813, Congress passed an act, authorizing the building of four ships, to rate not less than 74 guns each, and six ships, to rate at 44 guns each; and soon after, another act authorized the building of six sloops of war on the sea board, and as many vessels on the lakes as would be required.

The Essex frigate, Captain Porter, left the Delaware in the latter part of October; but did not meet an enemy for several weeks. Having crossed the equator in long. 30° W., however, she fell in with and captured a British brig, 10 guns. This brig was put in possession of a prize crew, with directions to proceed to Boston. On its passage it was overtaken and captured by a British frigate; and thus the Essex lost her first prize. Captain Porter then cruised for some time in the neighborhood of St. Salvador, and not finding the Constitution and Hornet, he resolved to sail for a cruise in the Pacific. This was in January, 1813. On the 5th of March, he anchored off the island of Mocha, not having met an enemy for two months. Hearing that Chili had thrown off the Spanish authority, and being in great want of supplies, Captain Porter put into Valparaiso, where he remained a week. Upon resuming his cruise, he captured a Peruvian cruiser, in search of American vessels, and two merchant ships. Two privateers of 18 guns each, were captured, one of them, the Georgiana, was equipped as an American cruiser.

It was soon found the Essex and Georgiana could not keep company, in consequence of the bad sailing of the latter. A number of other captures were made, and Porter increased his force to nine sail. With these, he swept the seas of the enemies of America, and established his reputation as a great naval commander. In January, the Essex, and the Essex Junior, a prize converted into a cruiser, arrived at Valparaiso. The rest of the prizes were sent home. Near Valparaiso, the British frigate Phœbe 36, Captain Hillyar, and the Cherub 20, Captain Tucker, were met, and Porter was anxious to bring the Phœbe to action, though a superior vessel. But the attendance of the Cherub prevented the prudent commander from attaining his object. Having

CRUISE OF THE ESSEX.

heard that several other British cruisers were expected at Valparaiso, Porter determined to go to sea. In this attempt, a squall carried away the main topmast, and drowned several men; and under these circumstances, nothing remained but to regain the port, or fight both the enemy's ships, in a crippled state. The British vessels soon saw their advantage, and approached the Essex to engage her. The fire was opened at four, P. M., and was destructive to the American vessel. However, both of the enemy's vessels were compelled to haul off to repair damages, so well were the guns of the Americans served. The attack was renewed under more favorable circumstances. The Essex ran down on her enemies, and though her decks were strewn with killed and wounded, returned their fire with tremendous effect. But the Phœbe possessed an immense advantage in her long guns, and she was enabled to haul off, and play upon the Essex at pleasure. The slaughter on the American vessel was horrible. Porter fought till the greater part of his crew were shot down, his vessel a wreck and on fire, and no officers living but himself to command her. He then felt it his duty to strike his colors.

In this desperate battle, the Essex had fifty-eight men killed and sixty-six wounded—nearly one-half of those on board at the commencement

COMMODORE PORTER.

of the action. Thirty-one were missing, most of whom were drowned, in attempting to swim ashore, while the ship was on fire. The English ships were cut up more than could be expected under the circumstances, the Phœbe receiving eighteen twelve pound shot below the water line. Their loss was five killed and ten wounded. The Essex Junior was converted into a cartel, and with the prisoners on board, sailed for New York, where Captain Porter succeeded in escaping to Long Island. Thus terminated this great cruise. Its end was as disastrous, as its commencement was fortunate; yet, at all times, it was a display of almost unequaled spirit, perseverance, and resources.

The victorious career of the American vessels was destined to receive a severe check.

THE CHESAPEAKE SAILING OUT OF BOSTON HARBOR.

The Chesapeake 38, Captain James Lawrence was lying in Boston harbor in the latter part of May, 1813. The British had stationed two frigates, the Shannon 38, and Tenedos 38, off Boston, to watch for American vessels. When it was understood that the Chesapeake was ready to sail, Captain Broke, of the Shannon, sent Lawrence a challenge to meet his vessel in equal combat. The high spirited Lawrence, although his crew were mercenary and mutinous, resolved to accept the challenge. He sailed out in the bay, and at five o'clock, P. M., on the 1st of June, the battle began, the vessels soon being yard-arm and yard-arm. For six or eight minutes, the cannonade was fierce and destructive on both sides. The Shannon was enabled to sweep the upper decks of the Chesapeake, and soon the American frigate was left without an officer. Lawrence, and Ludlow, his first lieutenant, were mortally wounded. The British boarded, and took complete possession of the ship, with but little resistance. Lawrence was carried below, and earnestly besought his crew not to yield. But the men had not the means of resistance. Few naval battles have been more bloody than this. It lasted but fifteen minutes, yet both vessels were charnel houses. The Chesapeake had forty-eight men killed and ninety-eight wounded. The Shannon had twenty-three killed and fifty-six wounded, principally by the broadside of the Chesapeake. Captain Broke was badly wounded. As soon as the ships were clear of each other, they both made sail for Halifax. Captain Lawrence died of his wounds on the 6th of June, and with Lieutenant Ludlow, was buried by the enemy with military honors.

The capture of the Chesapeake produced a degree of exultation on the part of the British, and of depression on the part of the Americans, which shows to what a state each had been accustomed during the war. The British were overjoyed, because the victory was unusual; the Americans were depressed, because they looked upon victory as certain. Captain Lawrence rather gained than lost in his reputation by his bravery. It was evident, he did all a commander could do under the circumstances.

The Enterprise 14, Lieutenant Burrows commanding, left Portsmouth, N. H., on the 1st of September, 1813, and steering to the eastward, in quest of privateers, reported to be near Manhagan. On opening the bay, near Penguin Point, a British brig of war came in sight, and both vessels at once prepared for a struggle. The combat lasted from twenty minutes past three, P. M., until four. It was hot and vigorous, and was distinguished by a novel manœuvre on the part of the Enterprise. Having a stern chaser in position, Burrows kept his vessel playing upon the bows of the enemy, while she was ready at any moment to meet a change of position on their part. The colors of the British vessel were nailed to the mast, and she could only be surrendered by hailing to the Enterprise to stop her destructive fire. The brig proved to be the Boxer 14, Captain Blythe, an officer of merit, who was nearly cut in two by an eighteen pound shot. Her loss in killed, was supposed to be heavy, but was not ascertained; there were fourteen men wounded. The Enterprise had one man killed and thirteen wounded, of whom three, including her gallant captain,

ENTERPRISE AND BOXER.

subsequently died. The Boxer was much cut up in hull and rigging; the Enterprise suffered but little. The vessels were carried into Portland on the 7th, and Lieutenant Burrows and Blythe were both burried with the honors of war. This victory is considered as the fair triumph of skill and bravery—as the opposing forces were equal.

In June of this year, the brig Argus 20 guns, Captain Allen, which had caused the British merchants much alarm by cruising in their own seas after the manner of Paul Jones, and Captain Wyckes was captured by the brig Pelican, Captain Maples, a vessel one-fourth larger than the Argus. The crew of the Argus were exhausted from their constant exertions to escape the British frigates, and also intoxicated at the time of the capture, from having partaken too excessively of the freight of a vessel from Oporto, laden with wines. Yet in spite of this state of things, the Argus was not surrendered until Captain Allen was mortally wounded, and his first lieutenant, Watson, severely hurt. The second lieutenant, W. H. Allen, continued the struggle manfully, until no longer possible, and then struck. The Argus had two midshipmen and four men killed, and seventeen wounded, in an action of three quarters of an hour. The Pelican had seven men killed or wounded. The loss of this active cruiser was severely felt

CAPTAIN ALLEN.

by the Americans. But when all the circumstances of the action are considered, it could not be thought a humiliation.

Shortly after the commencement of the war, the British had a hundred vessels in the American seas. About twenty of these were in the Chesapeake. When either of the vessels approached the land in a favorable position for attack, there were always flotillas of gun boats ready to annoy her; and one of the frigates came near being captured on one occasion. She was saved by the interposition of another vessel of the fleet. The attack was made by fifteen gun boats, under Captain Tarbell, the fire from which was very effective.

In the summer of 1814, several new ships were put into the water; among them were the Independence 74, the Guerriere and Java, 44 each, and the Wasp, Frolic and Peacock, ships of war. The Frolic

CAPTAIN BLAKELY.

was soon captured by the British frigate Orpheus 36, Captain Pigot. There was no action—the disparity of force being too great.

On the 28th of June, 1814, the Wasp 18, Captain Blakely, in the neighborhood of the British Channel, fell in with the Reindeer 18, Captain Manners. After a destructive cannonade, the vessels closed, and the English made several trials to board the Wasp, led by their commander in person; but they were repulsed with steadiness. Two or three desperate efforts having failed, Blakely gave the order in turn to board the Englishman, and in an instant, their flag was lowered. The contest lasted twenty-eight minutes. The loss of the Reindeer was twenty-five killed and forty-two wounded; among the slain was Captain Manners. The Wasp had five men killed and twenty-two wounded. The Reindeer was reduced to a wreck. The Wasp was hulled six times, and was filled with grape. Blakely put a portion of his wounded on board a neutral, and proceeded himself to l'Orient; the prize was burned.

After being detained in port until the 27th of August, the Wasp sailed on another cruise. She made three or four captures of merchant vessels, and on the night of the 1st of September, encountered a British brig of 18 guns, and after an action of thirty-six minutes, compelled her to strike. Before the Wasp could lower a boat to take possession, another brig of the same size came in sight, and she was forced to abandon her prize, and prepare to meet the new-comer. The brig came up and threw in her broadside, but the vessel which had struck firing signals of distress, she went to her assistance. The Wasp left so suddenly that she did not learn the name of her prize. She had two men killed and one wounded; the latter by a wad, which proves the closeness of the combat. Her hull was much injured, and her rigging cut up. It is now known that the vessel captured was the Avon 18, Captain Arbuthnot. She sunk, and her people were saved with difficulty. Her loss in the action was supposed to be between thirty and fifty. The Wasp captured three other vessels, one of which, the Atalanta, 8 guns, was sent to America, under command of Midshipman Geisinger. The Atalanta arrived at Savannah, November 4th, and this was the last that ever was heard of the gallant Wasp and her noble crew. Doubtless, however, the insatiable ocean took them for its own.

The Peacock 18, Captain Warrington, went to sea from New York in March, 1814, and proceeding southward, cruised in the vicinity of the coast of Florida. On the 29th of April, she met the sloop of war Epervier 18, Captain Wales, and a close and well fought action ensued. There was no opportunity for manœuvring, and the battle was decided in forty-two minutes, by gunnery alone. The Epervier was reduced to a mere wreck, and had forty-five shot in her hull. Twenty-two of her men were killed or wounded. The Peacock received slight injury, and had but two men wounded. She was the heavier vessel, but, as usual, the disparity in loss was far greater than that of the forces engaged. Specie to the amount of one hundred and eighty thousand dollars was captured in the Epervier. As soon as the vessels could be got ready, they were, with difficulty, conducted to Savannah—the sea swarming with British cruisers.

THE PEACOCK AND THE EPERVIER.

CAPTAIN WARRINGTON.

The President, Congress, and the other five frigates, were at sea many months; but could not succeed in bringing a single vessel to contend with them. Their prizes consisted entirely of merchantmen. The predatory excursions of the British in the Chesapeake, gave rise to many skirmishes with the detached militia of the country, in some of which boats were taken from the enemy, and many of their number killed or wounded. But the superiority of the English in their large vessels, gave them power to choose their time and mode of attack, and their success was in proportion. The government had equipped a large flotilla to protect these waters, the command of which was given to Captain Joshua Barney, an officer distinguished for his capture of the General Monk, in the revolutionary war. His operations were boldly planned and executed; but he could not prevent the advance

RAVAGES OF THE BRITISH ON THE SHORES OF THE CHESAPEAKE BAY.

of the British ships up the bay. The seamen and marines did all that could be expected of brave men both on land and sea; the numbers and discipline of the enemy were overwhelming. When Washington was taken, the inhabitants destroyed two vessels, then on the stocks, together with a considerable quantity of naval stores, to prevent their falling into the hands of the enemy.

In all the operations in the defence of New Orleans, the navy bore a full and highly creditable share. The flotilla of gun boats was placed under the command of Lieutenant Thomas ap Catesby Jones. On the 15th of December, this force was attacked by the English, in forty or fifty barges, and after an obstinate conflict, in which the assailants lost more than a hundred men, they succeeded in capturing the whole flotilla. The result, however, was considered as a triumph on the part of the Americans. Several large men-of-war aided the efforts of the defenders upon land, by their effective fire, and contributed in no slight degree to the glorious result of the short campaign.

CHAPTER XXXVI.

NAVAL OPERATIONS ON THE LAKES.

THE English government had long maintained a small naval force on the great lakes; though much the larger portion of Champlain being within the jurisdiction of the United States, it had kept no cruiser on that water. On Lake Ontario, however, the force was efficient. The naval station on the American side of that

COMMODORE CHAUNCEY.

lake, was at Sackett's Harbor, not far from the commencement of the St. Lawrence. The United States had built one vessel of sixteen guns, called the Oneida; but the superiority of the enemy, prevented it from taking any active measures. When hostilities were fairly begun between the United States and England, Congress selected Captain Isaac Chauncey, to take command of the American forces on Lake Ontario, and to superintend the construction of a number of vessels sufficient to cope with the enemy.

A number of schooners were armed and equipped for service, until the regular war vessels could be completed. With the Oneida, the entire flotilla that could be made available, mounted forty guns, and was manned by four hundred and thirty men, marines included. The British, at that time, had a force in guns more than double that

THE CITADEL OF KINGSTON, FROM THE ST. LAWRENCE.

under Chauncey's orders; and as cruising vessels, their squadron possessed many advantages over those of the Americans. Commodore Chauncey first appeared on the lake on the 8th of November, with his broad pennant flying on board of the Oneida 16, having in company, the Conquest, Hamilton, Governor Tompkins, Pert, Julia, and Growler, each carrying four guns. The object of going out was to intercept the return of the enemy's vessels, which were known to be conveying supplies to Kingston. The flotilla had scarcely taken its station at the islands, known as the False Ducks, when the Royal George 22, much the largest ship that had yet appeared on the lakes, was discovered near the shore. Chauncey immediately gave chase, and actually followed this ship, of such superior force, until it took refuge under the batteries of Kingston.

It was then determined to attack the batteries and the Royal George at the same time. The American vessels gallantly sailed into the harbor, and delivered their fire with effect, receiving in return the fire of five batteries and the guns of the Royal George. The action was

CAPTURE OF THE CALEDONIA AND DETROIT.

maintained for half an hour, when the weather looking threatening, and the pilots refusing to be responsible for the vessels, Chauncey ordered the flotilla to haul off, intending to renew the attack next morning. In this spirited affair, the Americans suffered less than might have been expected, considering the disparity of forces employed. The Oneida had one man killed and three wounded; the rest of the flotilla came off still better, having but a few wounded. The vessels shortly after returned to port, bringing with them two or three small prizes. From this time until December, the American commander had undisputed possession of the lake; although so much superior, the British squadron could not be brought to action.

The United States had no war vessels on Lake Erie until the 9th of October, when they obtained one through the gallant exertions of Lieutenant Elliot, of the navy. This officer, being at Black Rock, and seeing two British vessels lying under the guns of Fort Erie, determined to cut them out. With this object, he embarked at midnight, accompanied by fifty volunteers, and, in a very few minutes, carried both of the vessels by boarding. The current, however, was so

SACKETT'S HARBOR.

strong, that they were run aground; and one of them, an armed vessel, called the Detroit, was afterwards burnt. The other, a merchant brig, called the Caledonia, with a valuable cargo of furs, was secured under the batteries of Black Rock. The whole affair was honorable to Lieutenant Elliot and his brave associates, and clearly indicated what the enemy might expect, when the Americans should have greater means at their command on the lakes.

Both parties employed the winter of 1812--13, in building. In the course of the autumn, the Americans had increased their force to eleven sail, ten of which were small schooners bought from the merchants on the lake. Neither of the ten was fit to cruise; but in attacking batteries and covering batteries, they were found to be exceedingly serviceable. On the 26th of November, a new ship, pierced for 24 guns, and called the Madison, was launched at Sackett's Harbor, and the keel of another large one laid. About the same time, the enemy made choice of Captain Sir James Lucas Yeo, to command their lake forces.

On the 22d of April, 1813, the squadron being ready, General

CAPTURE OF FORT GEORGE.

Dearborn embarked seventeen hundred men. The troops were very much crowded; the Madison, alone, had six hundred men in her. On the 25th, the squadron got out, and sailed for York, where it arrived next day without accident. The squadron was anchored about a mile from the shore, and during the attack upon York, covered the movements of the troops by a rapid fire. York was taken and remained in possession of the Americans until the 1st of May, when they evacuated it to proceed upon other duty. The Duke of Gloucester, a vessel which had been undergoing repairs, was captured, and a vessel of 20 guns burnt upon the stocks; a considerable quantity of naval and military stores was destroyed or taken to Sackett's Harbor.

About the middle of May, Chauncey began to make preparation for a descent upon Fort George. He reconnoitred the coast near that port, himself, and having every thing skilfully planned, the squadron weighed anchor on the 27th of May. Captain Perry was the sea officer second in rank, and Chauncey confided to him the duty of

QUEENSTOWN.

attending to the landing of the troops. The marines of the squadron were embodied in the regiment of Colonel Macomb. When all was ready, the advance vessels swept into the stations ordered them, and opened their fire with effect. The boats, with the troops under Colonel Scott and Captain Perry, dashed in, and the forces were landed without difficulty. Three hours after the landing was effected, the town and fort were in quiet possession of the Americans—the British retiring to Queenstown. In this brilliant affair, the navy had but one man killed and two wounded. The trifling loss of the assailants must be attributed to the covering fire of the squadron.

In revenge for the blow at York, Sir James L. Yeo and Sir George Prevost determined to strike a home thrust at Sackett's Harbor. On the 28th of May, the Wolfe, Royal George, Morra, Prince Regent, Simcoe and Seneca, with two gun boats and a strong brigade of barges and flat bottomed boats, appeared off that station. A conflict with some gun boats followed, and twelve were driven ashore and taken after being abandoned by the Americans. The British troops, under Sir George Prevost, then landed, and at first carried all before them. But some regulars coming up, the enemy were driven to their boats, with loss. The American squadron was of little assistance in this affair. Had it acted as at Fort George, the result would have been a more disastrous defeat for the enemy. But as it was, they were allowed to carry away twelve boats used for transporting troops.

The General Pike, pierced for 26 guns, was launched on the 12th of June. This raised the entire strength of Commodore Chauncey's fleet to 108 guns. This force, however, was not all available. On the 7th of August, the British squadron, consisting of two ships, two brigs, and two large schooners, was seen to the northwest of the mouth of the Niagara. Chauncey immediately put his fleet of thirteen sail in motion, and it was expected a regular battle would ensue. As both commanders knew how much depended upon the struggle, they were anxious to get as much advantage as possible. After many manœuvres, a few shots were exchanged, and a gale springing up, two of the light American schooners were capsized and, all of their crews but sixteen men were drowned. After this accident, another long series of manœuvres followed, no advantage being gained by either party. Twice was the line of battle formed and altered, and by the last disposition, two schooners, the commanders of which let their zeal run away with their judgment, were captured by the large ships of the British squadron. Chauncey then thought it wisest to return to his station, at Sackett's Harbor, in consequence of his inferior force, and a violent gale.

The squadron arrived at Sackett's Harbor on the 13th, and the wind failing, it took in supplies, and immediately started upon another cruise. No important operations took place, however, and violent storms again forced the vessels to return to the Harbor. On the 18th of August, a new schooner, named the Sylph, was launched and equipped with extraordinary expedition. She mounted 10 guns, and was considered weatherly. On the 28th, Chauncey sailed again. The enemy was not seen until the 7th of November, when he was discovered off the mouth of Niagara. Pursuit followed, and for six days the American squadron endeavored to bring the British to action, but without success. On the 11th, the enemy was becalmed off the Genesee; when the American vessels got within gun shot before the

BUILDING OF THE FLEET ON LAKE ERIE.

English took the wind. A running fight of three hours ensued; but the enemy escaped to Amherst Bay by superior sailing. As the Pike succeeded in getting several broadsides at the enemy, he did not escape without injury. According to his own report, an officer and ten men were killed and wounded. The Pike sustained but trifling injury.

All attempts to bring the enemy to a decisive action failed until the 28th of September, when Chauncey succeeded in getting him into such a position near York Bay, as would force him to fight, or acknowledge his inferiority. Sir James Yeo resolved to fight. A sharp contest of about half an hour followed, sustained upon the part of the Americans by the Pike and Madison. So well were the guns served that the English squadron was forced to retreat, and a chase of two hours ensued; but the superior sailing of the enemy's vessels enabled them to escape. Chauncey, satisfied with having beaten his opponent, then hauled off to the Niagara. The Americans lost five men, killed and wounded by the fire of the enemy, and had twenty-two killed or wounded by the bursting of a gun. The loss of the enemy was very heavy, but is not accurately known. It is understood that two small vessels struck their colors, but the Pike, eager for nobler prey, declined taking possession of them. After this action, several of the small vessels of the British were captured together with about two hundred and fifty men. The Americans had undisturbed possession of the Lake until winter closed all naval operations.

In the course of the winter of 1812–13, Captain O. H. Perry, volunteered for the lake service. Commodore Chauncey gladly availing himself of the presence of an officer of his rank, and known ability, and sent him to command upon the upper lakes. From this time until the navigation opened, Captain Perry was actively employed in creating and organizing a force which might be sufficient to contend with the enemy for the mastery of the waters of Lake Erie. By the 20th of June, 1813, Perry appeared on the lake, with a squadron, consisting of the Caledonia brig, and the schooners Somers, Tigress, and Trippe. At this time, Captain Finnis, the British commodore, had as a cruising force, the Queen Charlotte, a large ship of seventeen guns; the Lady Prevost, a schooner mounting thirteen guns; the brig Hunter, mounting ten guns, and three or four lighter cruisers. A ship of five hundred tons, to be called the Detroit, was building at Malden.

The American force was soon increased by two brigs of twenty guns each, and some schooners; but was blockaded in Erie harbor by the British, under Captain Barclay, who succeeded Finnis. Perry, however, managed to get his vessels out during the temporary absence of his enemy, and when he returned, he found the Americans so well prepared to receive him, that he hauled off. The American squadron then moved upon the offensive. On the morning of the 10th of September, the squadron was lying in Put-in Bay, when the enemy was discovered to the northwest. All the vessels were soon under weigh, and an attempt was made to get the weather-gage of the enemy; but it failed. The line of battle was formed when the fleets were three leagues asunder. Captain Barclay formed his line, with the Chippeway, armed with a gun on a pivot, in the van; the Detroit, his own vessel, next; and the Hunter, Queen Charlotte, Lady Prevost, and Little Belt astern, in the order named. To oppose this line, the Ariel, of four long twelves, was stationed in the van, and the Scorpion, of one long and one short gun on circles, next her. The Lawrence, Captain Perry, came next; the two schooners, having no

BATTLE OF LAKE ERIE.

COMMODORE PERRY.

quarters, keeping on her weather bow. The Caledonia, the Niagara, Tigress, Somers, Porcupine, and Trippe were next astern in the order named.

The wind was very light. The English line of battle was perfectly formed, and the vessels made an imposing appearance. The American vessels could not be kept within the required distance of each other, on account of the vast difference of their sailing qualities. About twelve o'clock, the Detroit threw a twenty-four pound shot at the Lawrence. The American vessels closed up, and the firing soon became animated. The Lawrence appeared to be the principal aim of the enemy, and suffered dreadfully. At the end of a cannonade of two hours and a half, the enemy having filled, and the wind increasing, the two squadrons drew slowly ahead, and the Lawrence fell partially out of the combat, her place being filled by the Niagara. Perry now left the Lawrence, and proceeded in an open boat through the enemy's fire, to the Niagara, and the devoted vessel soon after hauled down her colors, being a mere wreck, with but fourteen sound men on board. The enemy then thought the day was gained, and gave three hearty cheers. A short cessation of firing followed, as if each party was preparing for a desperate final effort. When the Americans again opened their fire and proceeded to close action, they gave three cheers also; and that was the knell of hope to the enemy. The firing became tremendous, and the conflict as close and deadly as possible between squadrons followed. This was necessarily short. In fifteen or twenty minutes after the renewal of the fire, the enemy struck their colors. The action had lasted three hours, and terminated in the capture of the whole British squadron.

In this obstinate conflict, so far as the people were concerned, both squadrons suffered in an equal degree; the Lawrence being cut up almost beyond example. The total loss of Perry's force was twenty-seven killed and ninety-six wounded—of which, twenty-two were killed and sixty-one wounded on board the Lawrence, and twelve were quarter-deck officers. The injury sustained by the English, though more divided, were necessarily great. They had forty-one killed and ninety-four wounded, including twelve officers. The forces of the hostile squadrons were thought to be about equal under the circumstances of situation and wind. Each commander displayed considerable skill in forming the line of battle and bringing the vessels to action; but the triumph of the Americans was the result of superior manœuvering towards the end of the battle, and a firm resolve not to yield the day as long as there was hope. For his gallant conduct, Captain Perry received a gold medal from Congress, Captain Elliot, of the Niagara, received a gold medal, and rewards were bestowed upon the officers and men generally. It was a decisive triumph, of which the nation had reason to be proud. Captain Perry soon after resigned the command on the upper lakes, and Captain Elliot succeeded him.

Powerful fleets were constructed by both parties upon Lake Ontario. The Superior, the American vessel, under Commodore Chauncey's orders, mounted sixty-two guns, and the whole squadron carried two

BURLINGTON BAY.

hundred and twenty-eight. The English had a force slightly inferior. Thus had these inland seas become the scenes of the evolutions of mighty armaments, where, but a few years before, nothing larger than the Indian's canoe ruffled their waters. No operations of importance, however, took place, the English being too wary to be drawn into an engagement.

As in the autumn of 1814, the British determined upon an invasion of the northern states by the route pursued by Burgoyne, in 1777, the command of Lake Champlain became an object important to be attained. Until this season, neither nation had a force of any consequence upon that water. But the Americans soon saw the necessity of a squadron, and commenced several large vessels and some gun boats. The English also began to collect and construct a number of vessels. Captain McDonough commanded the American force.

When the British army advanced against Plattsburg, in the early part of September, McDonough's force consisted of the Eagle, a brig of twenty guns, the Saratoga, a ship of twenty-five guns, the Ticonderoga, a schooner of seventeen guns, the Preble, a cutter of seven

BATTLE OF LAKE CHAMPLAIN.

guns, and ten galleys, or gun boats, six of which mounted a long twenty-four apiece, and four, a long twelve apiece. On the 6th of September, hearing of the approach of the enemy, McDonough formed his squadron in two lines, distant forty yards, in Burlington Bay, a little to the south of the outlet of the Saranac. The force of the enemy was materially greater than that of the Americans. It consisted of the Confiance, a frigate of thirty-seven guns, the Linnet, a brig of sixteen long twelves, the Cherub, a sloop of ten guns, the Finch, a sloop of eleven guns. Besides these, there was a force of thirteen galleys, mounting twenty-one guns. Captain Downie commanded the whole force.

On the 11th of September, the enemy approached, McDonough being resolved to fight at anchor. He came on abreast, and for a while there was a deep silence aboard the American vessels. Suddenly, the Eagle discharged rapidly four guns. In clearing the decks of the Saratoga, some hen coops were thrown overboard, and the poultry permitted to run at large. Upon hearing the report of the guns, a cock flew upon a gun slide, and crowed. This slight occur-

COMMODORE MCDONOUGH.

rence strangely animated the men, and they gave three cheers. The enemy came on, confident of superiority, and the battle opened. The Confiance suffered from the American fire, which was directed to disable her especially, being so far superior to any of the American vessels. McDonough's ship, the Saratoga, also suffered from the broadside blaze of the Confiance. The battle now became a steady, animated, and gradually increasing cannonade. The men in the different galleys, made several desperate attempts to board the smaller vessels of the squadrons, but could not succeed. The Saratoga was, at length, left in the middle of the battle, without a single available gun; and it was only after the greatest exertions that McDonough succeeded in changing her position, so as to return the fire of the Confiance. After an obstinate conflict of two hours and a quarter, the Confiance struck her colors, and the rest of the British squadron followed the example.

In this bloody contest, the American squadron had fifty-two killed and fifty-eight wounded. The Saratoga was hulled fifty-five times, and the Eagle, thirty-nine times. Several valuable officers were among the killed and wounded, and the gallant McDonough sustained the reputation he had acquired at Tripoli, for intrepidity. He was struck down two or three times; but not dangerously wounded. The loss of the British could not be ascertained. There can be no doubt, however, that the loss on board of the Confiance alone was equal to that of the whole American squadron, and it is thought that the entire loss of the enemy in killed and wounded, was at least two hundred men. The Confiance received one hundred and five shot in her hull, and was reduced to a wreck. This must be considered a more brilliant triumph than that gained by Perry upon Lake Erie. The force of the English was so decidedly superior, that the victory could only have been gained by superior skill and persevering bravery. Besides the usual medal from Congress, Captain McDonough received compliments and gifts from the various states, and was promoted. The consequence of the victory was, the immediate retreat of the British troops from Plattsburg, and the safety of the northern frontier, during the remainder of the war. After this battle, the transactions upon the lakes cease to be important. The Americans had the vantage ground, and the remembrance of their triumphs stimulated them to keep it. Commodore Chauncey had to the last, retained the confidence of his government, as a judicious and active commander, and although he had not the opportunity to connect his name with the lustre attaching to a brilliant victory of squadron over squadron, it was only because the vigilant and judicious Sir James Yeo feared to meet him.

SURRENDER OF THE BRITISH FLEET ON LAKE CHAMPLAIN.

CHAPTER XXXVII.

FROM THE COMMENCEMENT OF 1815 TO THE PRESENT DAY.

TWO triumphs of the American navy upon the ocean during the war with Great Britain remain to be mentioned. They were fit to terminate such a series. On the 17th of December, 1814, the Constitution, under Captain Charles Stewart, left Boston, and cruised eastward, even to the Bay of Biscay, making a narrow escape from a British seventy-four. On the 20th of February, two large vessels were seen in company, and proving to be enemies, the Constitution gave chase, hoping to engage them separately. This being impossible, Stewart still resolved to fight both; and succeeded in getting in such a position, that the three vessels formed an equilateral triangle. In this masterly situation, the battle commenced; the three vessels keeping up an incessant fire for about three-quarters of an hour, when that of the enemy sensibly slackened. Some manœuvering followed, by which, the Constitution secured such a position, and delivered her fire so effectually, that one of the vessels struck, and on taking possession, was found to be the British ship,

Cyane 24, Captain Falcon. The other vessel had hauled off, in consequence of the crippled condition of her rigging; but at the end of an hour, ignorant of the fate of the Cyane, she came up and met the Constitution coming in search of her. Broadsides were exchanged immediately, and the English ship, finding her opponent too heavy, endeavored to escape. In trying this, however, she received a fearful raking, and at last, hauled down her ensign. Lieutenant Shubrick was sent aboard to take possession, and found that the prize was the Levant 18, Captain Douglas. During this cruise, the Constitution mounted fifty-two guns, and carried four hundred and seventy men. The Cyane was a frigate built ship, carrying thirty-four guns. The Levant was a new ship, carrying twenty-one guns. The united force of men in the two British vessels, was about three hundred and fifty. Their loss was ten killed and twenty-eight wounded. The Constitution had three killed and twelve wounded. Captain Stewart gained great praise from nautical men, for the manner in which he handled his ship on this occasion; it being an unusual thing for a single ship to engage two enemies and escape being raked. The whole series of manœuvres is amongst the most extraordinary in naval annals. It is due to the British commanders to say, that they conducted their vessels gallantly and well. Stewart proceeded with his prizes to Port Praya, where he arrived on the 10th of March. On the return home, the three vessels were chased by a British squadron, under Sir George Collier, but succeeded in eluding it, by skilful manœuvring. This was the last exploit of the Constitution. She had been in three obstinate battles within three years, and had captured five vessels of war. The reason of her success was, that she was always well manned and commanded.

In the middle of January, 1815, the President, under Commodore Decatur, left New York for a cruise. During a violent gale the vessel struck near Sandy Hook, and suffered considerable damage. A large British blockading force was in the offing, and as soon as the President appeared, she was chased by the whole squadron. A running fight followed in which the Endymion, the nearest British vessel was much cut up and would have been taken but for the presence of the rest of the squadron. At length, after a long and close cannonade, Decatur was compelled to surrender. The President had twenty-four men killed and fifty-six wounded. She was a good deal injured in

HORNET AND PENGUIN.

her hull, and most of her spars were badly damaged. The Endymion had eleven killed and fourteen wounded. Decatur was shortly after paroled, and he and all his surviving officers and men were subsequently acquitted with honor for the loss of the ship.

The Hornet, Captain Biddle, followed the President to sea, and sailed to the island of Triston d'Acaunha, which Decatur had appointed as a rendezvous. Off the island, on the 23d, the Hornet fell in with a British brig of eighteen gun rate, called the Penguin. After a fifteen minutes' cannonade, which proved very destructive to the enemy, he closed with the intention of boarding; but the attempt to board failed. When it was thought that the enemy had surrendered, Captain Biddle sprang upon the taffrail to inquire if such was the case. Two marines on board the Penguin discharged their muskets at him, one ball from which wounded him in the neck. This exasperated the crew of the Hornet, and as the vessels separated, they poured a terrible fire into their enemy. Even when twenty of the British seamen came to the side of the vessel and raised their hands for quarter, the crew of the Hornet could scarcely be restrained from giving them another broadside. In this conflict, the vessels were fairly matched; being of the same size, and carrying the same number of guns and nearly the same number of men. Yet with the advantage of the wind, the Penguin was taken in twenty-two minutes. Her loss in men was fourteen killed and twenty-eight wounded; among the slain was Captain Dickenson. The Hornet had one man killed and ten wounded, including the captain and first lieutenant. Though the Penguin was hulled many times and was much cut up in sails and rigging, the Hornet was not hulled once, and suffered little in her upper works. This was the crowning triumph of the war. It clinched the nail before driven, and the superiority of the American navy, in every respect but numbers, was incontestably established. The Hornet had a narrow escape from a British 74, on her return home. She was only saved by the perseverance of Captain Biddle, under circumstances which would have induced most other commanders to surrender their vessel.

Thus terminated the war as far as it was connected with the American marine. The result had produced a degree of confidence in the American people, only equalled by the astonishment and humiliation of those so long accustomed to rule the sea. In all the different encounters of the war, there had been displayed by the infant navy, a brilliancy

ESCAPE OF THE HORNET.

and rapidity of manœuvring, and an accuracy of gunnery which commanded the admiration of all capable of judging of such things. But to these qualities must be added, the determined and indomitable spirit peculiar to a free people. This conquers where skill fails.

No sooner had the war with Great Britain ended, than it became necessary to employ the naval arm against Algiers. Taking advantage of the American cruisers being excluded from the Mediterranean by the British fleets, the Dey of Algiers began his depredations upon the little of our commerce that remained in and near that sea. No sooner was peace concluded, than Congress passed an act authorizing hostilities against Algiers, and an efficient squadron sailed for the Mediterranean, on the 1st of May, under the command of Commodore Decatur. On the 17th of June, the squadron captured the Algerine frigate, Mishouri 46, Admiral Rais Hamida, after a running fight of twenty-five minutes. The Algerines had their admiral and thirty men killed and a great number wounded. None of the American vessels sustained any damage, except the Guerriere, which had four men wounded, in addition to between thirty and forty-five men killed and wounded by the bursting of a gun. So energetic were Decatur's operations, that the Dey was compelled to sign a treaty of peace forty days after the squadron left New York. The Americans obtained their own terms. Tunis and Tripoli were also visited and made prompt restitution for injuries done to American commerce.

After the conclusion of peace with the Barbary powers, the United States government seemed to feel the necessity of increasing the strength of its marine. Several ships of the line were soon begun and measures adopted for a regular increase. From that time until the breaking out of the war with Mexico, in 1846, a period of thirty-one years, the navy became gradually most powerful and efficient. Squadrons were soon maintained in the Mediterranean, on the coast of Brazil, in the West Indies, in the Pacific, and in the East Indies. Though not of great force, these were quite equal to the task of protecting the commerce which was constantly increasing in value. A home squadron was not thought necessary until of late years. In 1837, the Pennsylvanian 120, the largest ship of the line afloat, was launched at Philadelphia. Besides this great floating battery, there were then in the water four ships of 80 guns, and three of 74.

During the war with Mexico, which commenced in May, 1846, the United States squadrons were only of use in the transportation of troops and in assisting the attacks upon the Mexican coast towns. Their enemies had no navy worthy of the name. On the determination of the government to resent what was called an invasion of the territory of Texas, orders were sent to Commodore Sloat, commanding the Pacific squadron, to take possession of the principal ports of California. He had under his orders, the frigate Savannah 52, the sloops of war Portsmouth, Cyane, and Levant, each of 22 guns, with the Warren of 24. To this force was afterwards joined, the Congress 52, the sloops Saratoga, Dale, and Preble, and the razee Independence. On the 7th of July, 1846, Commodore Sloat appeared before Monterey, in the flag ship Savannah, and took possessi of the town and defences, without difficulty. At the same time, the Portsmouth took possession of San Francisco. Commodore Sloat was relieved by Commodore Stockton on the 29th of July. The latter officer immediately commenced active operations upon land, and within a month had complete possession of Upper California, while his vessels were stationed at every port. His subsequent operations during the insurrection of

CAPTURE OF MONTEREY.

the Californians do not belong to naval history, though the seamen and marines formed the greater part of the army which defeated the enemy in two battles, thus proving that their zeal and valor wanted but opportunity to display themselves upon the sea.

In February, 1847, great preparations were made for a descent upon Vera Cruz and the Castle of San Juan de Ulloa. The Gulf squadron, under Commodore Conner, then consisted of three steamers, three gun boats, and two schooners. This force had attacked the town of Alvarado in October; but the grounding of a steamer produced such a derangement of plans, that the attempt was abandoned. A large number of merchant vessels were subsequently destroyed at Tobasco, by Commodore Perry. Early in March, the United States army, under General Scott, embarked on board the Gulf squadron, to proceed upon the attack upon the city of Vera Cruz. On the 7th, the fleet arrived at Anton Lizardo, when Commodore Conner and General Scott made a reconnoisance of the coast, and selected a portion of the beach, west of the

VERA CRUZ.

Isle of Sacrificios, as a suitable spot for landing. This was effected in beautiful style, and without opposition, on the 9th. Commodore Conner permitted the marines to join the army as a part of the third regiment of artillery. On the 22d of March, General Scott opened fire upon the City of Vera Cruz; and at the same time, the small vessels of the squadron approached near enough to throw a smart fire into the castle of San Juan de Ulloa; but it was thought expedient to withdraw them the next morning from their daring situation. Commodore Perry succeeded Commodore Conner in command of the fleet before Vera Cruz, and actively co-operated with the land forces, and contributed to the triumphant result of the siege. Towards the close of the war, detachments of the Pacific squadron captured Guaymas and Mazatlan, towns upon the Mexican coast. Indeed, the greater portion of the Mexican coast on the Pacific was kept under a strict blockade by the United States vessels of war, successively under the orders of Commodores Stockton, Shubrick, and Biddle. Since the conclusion of peace between the two republics, no important naval operations have been undertaken.

With regard to the present condition of the United States marine, we may observe, that it is about one hundred fold more efficient than it was at the commencement of the war of 1812. Steam vessels of war are fast taking the place of the ships of the line; being found to possess such great superiority in rapidity of movement, and combining strength with lightness of construction. The active naval force consists of ten ships of the line, thirteen first class frigates, two second class frigates, twenty-three sloops of war, eight brigs, eight schooners, nine steamers, and four store ships; and additions are constantly being made. There is no higher rank than that of post captain. Among officers of the same rank, seniority determines precedence. The principal naval depots and stations are at Norfolk, Philadelphia, Brooklyn, and Pensacola. In all parts of the globe, as extensive as our commerce, is the range of its protecting arm—the navy; and of nothing has our country more reason to be proud. Hallowed by the recollection of its achievements—even in its infancy reminding us of the infant Hercules—we cannot give it too much of our attention and admiration.

THE CORACLE.

CHAPTER XXXVIII.

NAVAL CONSTRUCTION.

ALTHOUGH, in the course of the work, we have alluded to the gradual improvement in the art of naval construction, it has been in so slight and scattered a manner, that it will fail in giving that clear understanding of the subject which is so desirable. It is not so essential to this, that we should trace naval construction in the history of all maritime countries. The progress of the British navy affords the most complete idea of the art—from the skin boat of the early Britons to the war steamer of the latest day; and of that history we make use, to give the required information.

The vessels dignified by the ancient Britons with the name of ships, were a sort of coracle constructed of twigs, covered with ox hides, capable of holding three or four persons, and in summer, of passing over to Ireland or Gaul. A small sail on a single mast, a paddle, like the ancient clavus, over each quarter, for a rudder, and a few

ANCIENT BRITISH VESSEL.

oars, seem to have completed the furniture of these frail barks. The canoe, consisting of the trunk of a tree, hollowed out and hewn into a shape fitted for cleaving the waves, or a boat of birch bark, is the more primitive vessel of the Indians of America.

The next improvement of naval architecture was the galley of one, and then two, banks of oars. This was introduced by the Romans; and was essentially the same kind of vessels used by ancient Grecians. The following engraving will explain the distinction between these galleys and the *ships* of the ancient Britons. The prow of the galley was made strong and sharp, in order to sink the vessels of the enemy, by striking them with all the impetus of oars and a sail. There was a single mast in the middle of the vessel, and a square sail, raised and supported by a transverse pole, or yard, was extended across the mast, not far from the top, to which ropes were attached; and it was made

ROMAN GALLEY.

to slide up and down freely, by a wooden hoop being placed in its centre. The rudder, of which galleys sometimes had two, was affixed to the side of the vessel, the handle being passed through a staple. It was like an oar with a very broad blade. Over the poop of the vessel, was a fan-shaped ornament, made of plants, called the *Aplustre.* Behind this, the standard, or pennon, was placed, as seen in the cut. This was the galley so long in use in the southern seas of Europe. By the inventive genius of the Grecians and Romans, they were much enlarged and improved. The line of battle ship was the quinquereme, or galley of five banks of oars. The general features, however, were the same.

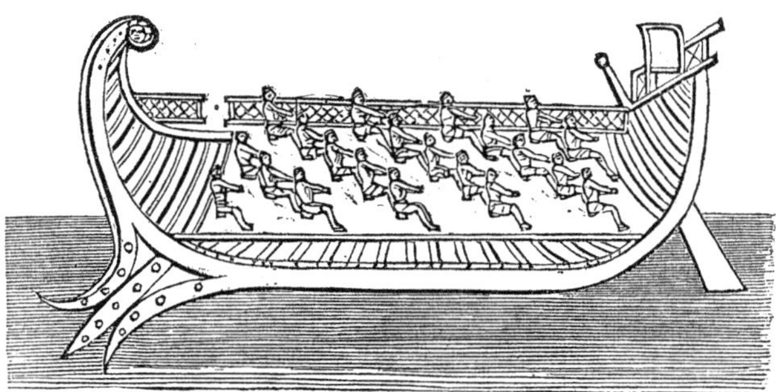

SECTION OF A QUINQUEREME.

The vessels used by the Saxons, in their piratical excursions, were very light, and so built as to weather out a storm, in which a larger and stronger ship would be in danger of perishing. They were, generally, swift sailers, in order that the pirates could assail any foe, and escape if met by overpowering force. They would even dare the seas in little skiffs, like those of the Britons. But for important expeditions, the Saxons had large and strong ships. They were built of very stout planks, laid over each other in the manner practised at the present time. Their prows and sterns were very erect, rising high out of the water, and the prow was ornamented by the uncouth head of some animal. To the single mast was attached a large sail, which, from its nature, could only be useful when the vessel went before the wind. The vessel was steered by a large oar, and is supposed to have carried about fifty or sixty men, though those used by Alfred the Great were much larger.

The vessels used by William, of Normandy, to transport his army to England, resembled greatly those of the Saxons. We have described them in one of our chapters on the British navy. During the Norman period, it does not appear that much alteration occurred in the mode of naval construction. The vessels began to be made larger. *Le Blanche Nef,* in which the children of Henry I. were wrecked, is said to have held one hundred and sixty persons. The vessels used by Richard Cœur de Lion, in his famous expedition to the Holy Land, possessed no features distinct from those of William the Conqueror. The sails were sometimes painted, and emblazoned with heraldic devices, to make as

imposing an appearance as possible; but the principles of construction were not changed. Afterwards, the custom of adorning the head of the vessel with the likeness of the head of an animal was dropped, and both stem and stern made alike, as in the preceding engraving

A manuscript in Bennet College, Cambridge, supposed to have been executed by Matthew Paris, in the thirteenth century, gives a spirited representation of an attack upon a fortress by sea. The ship is particularly interesting, as it shows the height of the stem and stern, and the curious wooden stage erected for archers and slingers, at the stern. Another kind of vessel used about the same time, was

ATTACK UPON A FORTRESS BY SEA.

the *vissier*, which was large and flat, being principally used for transporting horses, yet was furnished with a prow armed in such a manner, as would make it formidable in attacking an enemy. This vessel was used by the French and Venetians, in their attack upon Constantinople, in 1204. In that case, they were filled with archers and slingers.

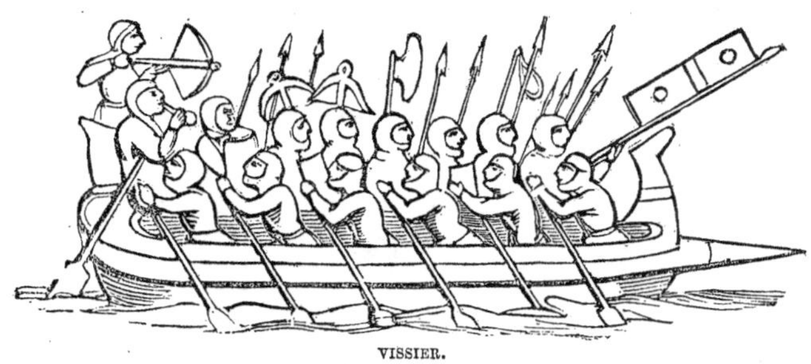

VISSIER.

Top castles were used in the vessels of King Richard. They were placed upon the top of each mast, and held one or more warriors, armed with slings, stones, or javelins. This was an exposed and dangerous position for soldiers. The archers of that period were sure marksmen, and the mischief done by these top-men, drew the attention

TOP-CASTLES.

of their enemies to them especially. The largest vessels at this time in use, had two masts, (fore and mainmast,) with two square sails; but they had no bowsprit, and the foremast raked considerably over the bows. The bows and stern of the vessel were alike. A short fighting deck, termed the *bellatorium*, or fore and stern castle, surmounted the extremities of the ship. The standard was erected in the forecastle, and the trumpeters were stationed in the stern-castle. Beneath the stern-castle, sat the steersman, who still guided the vessel with his side paddles. The cabins were reached by descending beneath the castles, and the principal cabin was termed the *Paradise* —a prostitution of the term.

VESSEL WITH FORE AND STERN-CASTLES.

Great doubt has long existed in regard to the time of the invention of the modern rudder. No antiquarian has succeeded in tracing the use of the rudder any further back than the time of Edward III. of England, in the early part of the fourteeth century. All agree, however, that the paddles were not abandoned until long after the rudder was known and used. On the curious seal of the city of Damme, attached to a charter in the year 1328, is a ship, with fore and stern-castles, in which the crew are holding banners. It has only one mast; but there is a short bowsprit, with a rope from the outer end leading in over the bows. At the stern is the present rudder, with pintle and gudgeons; and the tiller is shipped over the rudder head, instead of being placed in a cavity in it. The vessels used by Edward III., at the battle of the Sluys, in 1340, had rudders of the same description attached, as will be seen in the following engraving, taken from the seal of John Holland, Count of Huntingdon. It will also be observed, that in this ship, the castles are not raised from the deck, upon platforms.

In the opposite engraving we have a representation of vessels of war used in the time of Edward III. of England, going upon one of the many naval expeditions, in which that monarch engaged. The larger one, it will be seen, is highly decorated, the musicians being stationed in the stern, and the bow occupied by a castle, filled with men. The smaller vessel has an armed prow, and is propelled by oars alone. Her stern is decorated with elaborate carving.

ONE MASTED VESSEL USED BY EDWARD III.

The Genoese and other southern maritime powers had vessels of a much larger capacity than those of the English at the same period; they were called caracks, and some of them were vessels of even five hundred tons. After cannon began to be used in naval warfare,

GENOESE FOUR MASTED VESSEL.

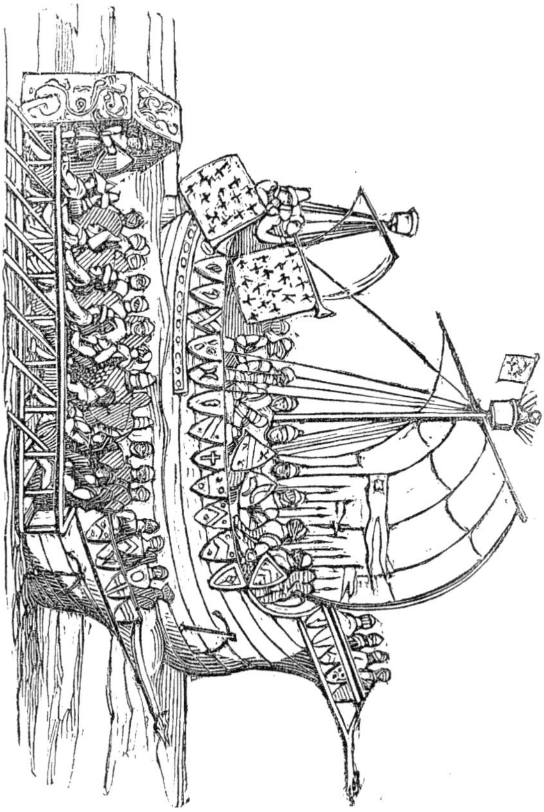

VESSELS IN THE TIME OF EDWARD III.

about 1338, the Genoese built powerful men of war, some of which had four masts, as the one in the annexed engraving. This vessel is remarkable for many peculiarities of construction. It is from a manuscript preserved in the British Museum, in which it is said that such vessels as this were hired for the service of the English Earl of Warwick, Richard Beauchamp, surnamed the "Kingmaker." The fighting deck has here given place to a covered poop, from whence the rudder is guided, as in a modern vessel. The general improvement in the construction of ships is evident from the engraving.

In the sixteenth century, ship building had greatly improved, and the large size of the vessels which were now constructed, completely threw the old single masted ships into disuse, as men of war or trading vessels; although exceptions to this rule may be met with, they occur only in the early part of the sixteenth century. But before dismissing the old single masted vessel, we will present the reader with one more example of a war ship of the fifteenth century, because it is a very good specimen of the craft; and it will also aid by its contrast with the modern improvements, in showing how much has been gained

WAR SHIP USED IN THE FIFTEENTH CENTURY.

in appearance and utility. The engraving is taken from an illuminated copy of Froissart's Chronicles, preserved in the British Museum. It is peculiarly valuable as giving a bird's-eye view of the deck of the ship. The turreted forecastle with its windows, and trumpeters, will be noticed in front; the single mast in the centre, with its top-castle and its one sail furled in the yard. Behind is seen the raised poop with the door leading to the cabins. The ship is one in which the Dauphin of France is about to embark with his soldiers.

Henry VIII. captured a large ship of war from the Scotch, in 1511. It was called the Lion, by its builders; but the king of England changed its name for that of "The Regent." Another ship still larger was built by the Scottish king the same year. This vessel was two hundred and forty feet in length, by fifty-six in breadth; dimensions, however, which were much diminished by the thickness of the planking, which was not less than ten feet. It carried thirty-five guns, all upon the upper deck, besides three hundred smaller pieces of artillery, and a complement of three hundred seamen, one hundred and twenty gunners, and one thousand soldiers. The principal vessel in possession of the king of England at that time—the Regent being blown up a few months after she put to sea—was the Great Harry—an engraving of which we have given in one of the chapters on the naval history of Great Britain.

During the wars of Henry VIII. a light pinnace was used for the

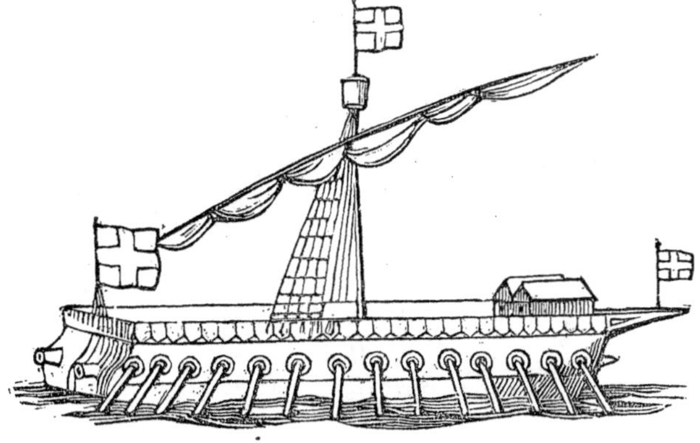

LIGHT PINNACE.

disembarkation of troops, of which we give an engraving. It is a vessel square at the stern, carrying some few guns there and in the head, and propelled by rowers. It has a single sail, like the Genoese boats, and is decorated at the sides with painted shields, in imitation of the time when the soldiers' shields were ranged round the vessels.

These pinnaces sometimes served the same purpose as the modern gun boats.

The continental vessels still continued small, if not used for long journeys, or expressly built for ships of war, in the more modern style. The cut here given, copied from a German print, dated 1540, is a capital specimen of a war galley, a mere coasting vessel for the transport of troops. It has but one sail, above which is the old top-castle, well armed with darts. The sail, it will be perceived, is still guided by the man at the helm. In front of the vessel is placed a large cannon, upon a portable carriage. There are galleries at the sides for rowers, and the centre is closed, packed with troops. Mounted high upon the stern, the fifer and drummer, in place of

COASTING VESSEL.

trumpeters, strike the inspiriting strain, and thus gaily and boldly does the vessel speed upon her errand of battle. On reaching an enemy, the position of things is altered. Anxious for the man to man strife, the vessels near each other as in the opposite engraving. Boats are grappled and a combat still like that upon land, in its essential features, ensues; but upon the sea, "grim-visaged war," is more terrible.

The vessels used for commercial and pleasure purposes, were of a different construction. They were in no way fitted for a contest with an enemy. The deck was covered, and the rowers worked upon the top of the cover. The helmsman still sat in a covered recess, as his predecessors had done from the earliest times, managing the sail. Improvement in this department was very slow, in consequence of the proverbial prejudice of sailors against any thing new in the way of navigation.

MERCHANT VESSEL.

The discovery of America exercised a vast influence upon the art of naval construction. Necessity, and the hope of gain, were the

NAVAL COMBAT.'

parents of invention. The spirit of enterprise reached England in the time of Elizabeth, and a galaxy of great navigators sprang up to add new glory to a reign distinguished as one of the greatest periods of English history. The war ships of Elizabeth were, like those of her father, of high build, with raised deck, two stories in height, much the same as the Chinese war junks of the present day. They were furnished with double rows of guns; and although clumsy looking, were very picturesque. This may be seen from the cut of the great seal of Charles Lord Howard, of Effingham, the lord high admiral of England. The seal exhibits a first rate man-of-war. The sail of the mainmast is painted. The top-castles are large, particularly the centre one, where the old fashion of surrounding it with shields of arms is still continued. The vessel, upon the whole, has a stately look.

GREAT SEAL OF HOWARD.

Drawings have been preserved, representing some of the vessels composing the "Invincible Armada." One, in particular, represents a vessel with high decks, four masts, and external galleries, at the stern. Such ships were very unwieldly, and smaller ones had frequently the advantage over them. Stormy weather, too, made them difficult and dangerous to manage.

VESSEL OF THE SPANISH ARMADA.

We have now traced the progress of the "camels of the sea" from the coracle of the early Britons, to the large and stately structures of the time of Elizabeth. There is but little difference between the ships of the latter time and those of the early part of the seventeenth century, a specimen of which, we give in the annexed engraving, copied from one of the maps of Abraham Ortelius, the famous geographer. The high decks, and general aspect of the "Great Harry," are here visible, with all that quaint and clumsy construction which was then followed by the naval architects. There is a striking similarity in all European vessels of this period. The increase of commercial intercourse may be mentioned as the cause. The general build was the same, but it was varied to suit the requirement of peculiar localities. Strength appears to have been the aim of the ship builders; beauty of appearance, or swiftness, and ease of. movement, were things left out of view. In the following engraving of a vessel which

SHIP OF THE EARLY PART OF THE SEVENTEENTH CENTURY.

conveyed the Duke of Anjou to Antwerp, in 1582, we see how much of the old style was retained. The raised forecastle, the pendent hang-

DUKE OF ANJOU'S SHIP.

ing from the fore and top yard, and the covered place for the helmsman, are still found in vogue.

In 1609, the East India Company of Englishmen, built the largest merchant vessel ever constructed—its burthen being variously estimated at from a thousand to eleven hundred tons. This ship was named the "Trade's Increase," by the king, who, with all his court, attended the launch. Soon after, a man-of-war, called "The Prince," of fourteen hundred tons burthen, and carrying sixty-four guns, was constructed for the protection of the interests of the same company.

The form of the Dutch ships of war, used by the celebrated Admiral Van Tromp, in the battle with the English, under Blake, in 1653, is preserved in accurate drawings by Hollar. The heavy build, which

DUTCH WAR SHIP OF 1653.

characterizes these vessels, has been, to this day, the general feature of the vessels of that nation. Great strength, but great clumsiness, is apparent, and these heavy monsters could be easily surrounded and captured by lighter, but more rapidly moving vessels. The English had, thus, an important advantage over them.

At this time, it was the common practice, to bestow much labor and

DUKE OF YORK'S PLEASURE BOAT.

cost on the decoration of ships. The ingenuity of the wood carver carried out tbe taste of the ship builder, and enriched the vessel

DUKE OF YORK'S SHIP.

wherever it was possible. The bow and stern were covered with a profusion of carved work, including the royal arms, emblematic figures, nymphs, and sea horses. The following representation of the ship of the Duke of York, used in the ceremonies of bringing Catharine of Braganza to England, about a year after the restoration of Charles II., is a good example of a ship of that period. The duke, was lord high admiral of England, and, therefore, his vessel was a first rate man-of-war. The smaller vessels have the same general appearance as the first rates. The same heavy build, is discerned among them. The "Duke of York's pleasure boat," copied from a series of prints by a Dutch artist, named Stoop, will give an idea of the similarity between such craft and the more important vessels. It is the "yacht" of the seventeenth century.

From a print of 1680, we obtain a very excellent specimen of the first rate man-of-war of that time. The critical reader, will observe many variations in the build of these vessels, and those of our own day. The entire front of the vessel, as well as the carved sterns, and

MAN-OF-WAR OF 1680.

side galleries, do not belong to our ships; but, independently of these things, modern improvements in ship building do not make this vessel differ much from those in which Nelson and others "spread their glory o'er the waves."

We have thus traced the art of constructing vessels from the first rude invention to the commencement of the seventeenth century. From that time to the present, improvements have been rapidly brought into use, and the modern ship of the line combines strength, swiftness, and beauty in an extraordinary degree of perfection. There is no necessity for giving specimens; they are abundant, and easily obtained by all. Nothing can be more beautiful and impressive than the sight of one of these mighty ships under full sail. Like a great, white-winged bird, she seems to move along the deep and skim the "heaving way." Freighted with the heavy instruments of death and defence—a floating battery—a ship of war is a thing to awe and compel.

The application of steam as a motive power to purposes of navigation, has, of late years, created a vast revolution in ship building. The superiority of steam vessels for naval warfare, is as apparent as their advantages for commercial purposes; while from the invention of Paixhan guns, and other terrible instruments of destruction, it is probable that the ships of the line, so formidable at present, may be thrown into disuse. A small steamer, of little weight of metal, is more than equal to a ship of thrice its force. Its rapidity of movement, and its ability to act, as well with or without the once high-rated advantage of the weather-gage, must give it an invaluable superiority. This revolution in ship building for warfare, will be much accelerated by the introduction of bomb-cannon, an invention which must soon be perfected. Light, quick vessels, will then be the best required; since large ships present many times the surface of the others, without a commensurate advantage in the number of cannon and rapidity of manœuvering. Ten bombs, projected from the side of a vessel, would be as surely the destruction of an enemy, if rightly directed, as a hundred. As forming part of a system for coast defence, bomb-cannon, mounted upon steamers, would be terribly formidable. Peaceful nations will be the gainers by the change, and the establishment of peace generally, will be much facilitated, by diminishing the power of numbers. May such be the result. No consummation could be more devoutly wished, when the attendant evils of all kinds of warfare are considered. But, patriotism will glory in naval achievement, until that end is attained.

Within the last twenty years, there have been introduced upon the Atlantic ocean, lines of steam vessels, opening a rapid and constant communication between Europe and America. The initiative in the enterprise was taken by a British company—the Messrs. Cunard & Co.; and their means and profits increased so rapidly, that the merchants of New York became desirous of entering into competition with them. Accordingly, an American company—the Messrs. Collins & Co.—was formed, and several splendid steam ships placed upon the route between New York and Liverpool. Another line connects New York and Bremen. The vessels of the Cunard line are large, commodious, and elegant, and in every way creditable to the enterprise, liberality, and judgment of the proprietors, and all concerned in their construction. The same remark applies to the vessels of the opposition line. The advantages resulting from the improvements of the means of intercourse between the two countries, are too obvious to need mention here. The ultimate tendency of all such improvements, is to draw closer the bonds of peace and friendship, and by creating new ties and new interests, to lessen the cause of hostilities.

CHAPTER XXXIX.

NAVAL ANECTDOTES.

N this, the concluding chapter of the present work, a few anecdotes, illustrating the more remarkable traits of naval character, and exhibiting some striking naval events are given. These could not have been introduced into the body of the work, without interrupting too much the course of the narrative. We commence with the affair of the Gaspee.

AFFAIR OF THE GASPEE.

IN 1772, the brave sailors of Rhode Island gave the British a small specimen of the naval spirit of the colonists.

The commander of the Gaspee, an armed British schooner stationed at Providence, had exerted much activity in supporting the trade laws and punishing the increasing contraband traffic of the Americans; and had provoked additional resentment by firing at the Providence packets, in order to compel them to salute his flag by lowering theirs as they passed his vessel, and by chasing them even into the docks in case of refusal. The master of a packet conveying passengers to Providence, June 9, which was fired at and chased by the Gaspee for neglecting to pay the requisite tribute of respect, took advantage of the state of the tide (it being almost high water,) to stand in so closely to the shore, that the Gaspee in the pursuit might be exposed to run aground. The artifice succeeded; the Gaspee presently stuck fast, and the packet proceeded in triumph to Providence, where a strong sensation was excited by the tidings of the occurrence, and a project was hastily formed to improve the blow and destroy the obnoxious vessel. Brown, an eminent merchant, and Whipple, a ship master, took the lead in this bold adventure, and easily collected a sufficient band of armed and resolute men with whom they embarked in whale boats to attack the British ship of war. At two o'clock the next morning, June 10, they boarded the Gaspee so suddenly and in such numbers, that her crew were instantly overpowered, without hurt to any one except her commanding officer, who was wounded. The captors, having despatched a part of their number to convey him together with his private effects and his crew ashore, set fire to the Gaspee and destroyed her with all her stores. The issue of this daring act of war against the naval force of the king, was as remarkable as the enterprise itself. The British government offered a reward of five hundred pounds, together with a pardon if claimed by an accomplice, for the discovery and apprehension of any person concerned in the treasonable attack on the Gaspee; and a commission under the great seal of England appointed Wanton, the governor of Rhode Island, Peter Oliver, the new chief justice of Massa-

DESTRUCTION OF THE GASPEE.

chusetts, Auchmuty, the judge-admiral of America, and certain other persons, to preside upon the trial of the offenders. But no trial took place. No body came forward to claim the proffered reward; some persons, who were apprehended in the hope that they might be induced by threats and terror to become witnesses, were enabled, by popular assistance, to escape before any information could be extracted from them; and in the commencement of the following year, the commissioners reported to the British ministry their inability, notwithstanding the most diligent inquisition, to procure evidence or information against a single individual.

THE BURNING OF FALMOUTH.

N 1795, a British naval force burnt Falmouth. Congress having intimated to General Washington that an attack upon Boston was much desired, a council of war was called, October 18, but unanimously agreed that it was not expedient, at least for the present. On the same day, Captain Mowat destroyed a hundred and thirty-nine houses, and two hundred and seventy-eight stores and other buildings, the far greatest and best part of the town of Falmouth, (now Portland, Maine,) in the northern part of Massachusetts. The inhabitants, in compliance with a resolve of the provincial congress, to prevent tories carrying out their effects, gave some violent obstruction to the loading of a mast ship, which drew upon them the indignation of the admiral.

Captain Mowat was despatched in the Canceaux, of sixteen guns, with an armed large ship, schooner, and sloop. After anchoring toward the evening of the 17th, within gun shot, he sent a letter on shore, giving them two hours for the removal of their families, as he had orders to fire the town, they having been guilty of the most unpardonable rebellion. A committee of three gentlemen went on board, to learn the particular reasons for such orders. He answered, that his orders were, to set on fire all the seaports between Boston and Halifax; but agreed to spare the town till nine o'clock the next morning, would they consent to send him off eight small arms, which was immediately done. The next morning the committee applied afresh; he concluded to spare the town till he could hear from the admiral, in case they would send him off four carriage guns, deliver up all their arms, ammunition, &c., and four gentlemen of the town as hostages. That not being complied with, about half past nine, he began to fire from the four armed vessels, and continued it till after dark. With shells and carcasses, and about thirty marines whom he landed, he set the town on fire in several places. About a hundred of the worst houses escaped destruction, but suffered damage. The inhabitants got out a very considerable part of their furniture, and had not a person killed or wounded, though the vessels fired into the town about three thousand shot, besides bombs and carcasses.

General Lee reprobates their cowardice, in admitting such a paltry party to land with impunity, and set their town in flames, when they had at least two hundred fighting men, and powder enough for a battle. In the private letter wherein he expressed these sentiments, he made no mention of the sailors being repulsed with the loss of a few men; though this might happen in the close of the day, and give occasion for its being related by others. The burning of Falmouth spread an alarm upon the sea coast, but produced no disposition to submit to the power and mercy of the armed British agents. The people in common chose rather to abandon the seaports that could not be defended, than quit their country's cause; and, therefore, removed back, with their effects, to a safe distance.

LANDING ON ST. MARY'S ISLE.

GENEROSITY OF PAUL JONES.

IN the life of Paul Jones, we find numerous instances of daring intrepidity as well as the most chivalrous generosity of spirit. The following anecdote is in point.

In cruising off the coast of Galloway, it occurred to him, that, if he could get into his power a man of high rank and influence in the state, he should be able, by retaining him as a hostage, to insure to the American prisoners of war more lenient treatment than was threatened by the British government. Knowing that the Earl of Selkirk possessed a seat in St. Mary's Isle, a beautiful peninsula at the mouth of the Dee, and being ill informed with regard to the political connections of that nobleman, he destined him for the subject of his experiment. With that view, he landed on the Isle, about noon, with two officers and a few men; but, before they had proceeded far, he learned that his lordship was from home, and that

PAUL JONES RETURNS LORD SELKIRK'S PLATE.

there were none but ladies at the house. Finding his object frustrated, he now wished to return; but his crew were not so easily satisfied. Their object was plunder; and as they consisted of men in a very imperfect state of discipline, and with whom it would have been dangerous to contend, he allowed them to proceed. He exacted from them, however, a promise that they should be guilty of no violence; that the men should not enter the house, and that the officers, after having made their demands, should accept of what might be put into their hands without scrutiny. These conditions were punctually obeyed. The greater part of the Selkirk plate was carried off in triumph by the crew, and Paul Jones was, for a time, stigmatized as a freebooter: but he nobly vindicated his character, by taking the earliest opportunity of purchasing the whole of it, out of his own private funds, and remitting it safe to its original owner, without accepting the smallest remuneration. National prejudice has misrepresented this transaction; and in order to heighten the popular indignation against our hero, it has been common to state, that this attempt on the person, and as it was supposed the property, of Lord Selkirk, was aggravated by ingratitude, his father having eaten of that nobleman's bread. Nothing can be more false. Neither Mr. Paul, nor any of his kindred, ever was in the earl's employ, or had ever the most distant connection with his lordship or his family; and in a correspondence which took place between our hero and the Lady Selkirk, relative to the restitution of the plate, a most honorable testimony was gratefully paid by the latter to the captain's character.

NELSON SAVED BY HIS COXSWAIN.

LORD NELSON.

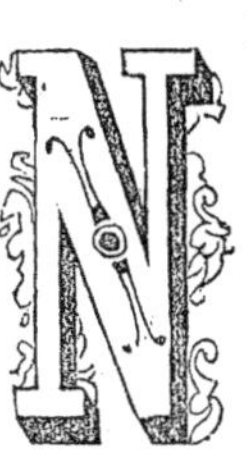

NELSON lost the sight of one eye at the seige of Calvi, by a shot driving the sand and gravel into it, and he lost his arm by a shot in an expedition against Teneriffe; but the most dangerous of his daring exploits were, boarding the battery of San Bartolomeo, boarding the San Joseph, the boat action in the bay of Cadiz, and the famous battles of the Nile and Trafalgar. Of these, perhaps, the boat action during the blockade of Cadiz was the most severe. While making an attempt against the Spanish gun boats, he was attacked by D. Miguel Tregayen in an armed launch, carrying twenty-six men; fearful odds against his ten bargemen, captain, and coxswain. Eighteen Spaniards were killed, the rest wounded, and the launch captured.

The Spaniards were more than two to one, and yet, he beat them. But it was a hard and desperate struggle, hand to hand, and blade to blade. Twice did John Sykes, the coxswain, save Nelson's life, by parrying off blows that would have destroyed him, and once did he interpose his head to receive the blow of a Spanish sabre; but he would willingly have died for his admiral.

Poor Sykes was wounded badly, but not killed.

When Nelson's health was established, after the loss of his arm, he sent to the minister of St. George's, Hanover Square, the following desire to offer up his thanksgiving:—"An officer desires to return thanks to Almighty God for his perfect recovery from a severe wound, and also for the many mercies bestowed on him." He was humble enough to be thankful to God; and continued so in the midst of all his successes.

The following is an instance of his coolness in the hour of danger. The late lieutenant-general the Hon. Sir William Stewart, as lieutenant-colonel of the rifle brigade, embarked to do duty in the fleet which was led by Sir Hyde Parker and Nelson, to the attack of Copenhagen in 1801. "I was," says he, "with Lord Nelson when he wrote the note to the Crown Prince of Denmark, proposing terms of arrangement. A cannon ball struck off the head of the boy who was crossing the cabin with the light to seal it. 'Bring another candle,' said his lordship. I observed, that I thought it might very well be sent as it was, for it would not be expected that the usual forms could be observed at such a moment. 'That is the very thing that I should wish to avoid, Colonel,' he replied, 'for if the least appearance of precipitation were perceptible in the manner of sending this note, it might spoil all.' Another candle being now brought, his lordship sealed the letter, carefully enclosed in an envelope, with a seal bearing his coat-of-arms and coronet, and delivered it to the officer in waiting to receive it. It is said that the moment was a critical one, and that Lord Nelson's note decided the event."

ANCIENT NAVAL FIGHT ON LAKE ERIE;

OR, A PIECE OF WYANDOTT HISTORY.

[Communicated by Stanley Griswold, Esq., for the National Intelligencer.]

DURING my residence at Detroit, I had the following story from the chiefs of the Wyandott nation, (called by the French, Hurons,) and principally from Walk-in-the-Water, a man of superior penetration and eloquence.

Near two hundred years ago, as well as I could recollect, their nation resided on the north shore of Lake Ontario, and the St. Lawrence river. Opposite to them, on the south side of those waters, resided the Senecas. A woman, as happened among other nations, was the cause of a terrible war between them, which terminated in the expulsion of the former from the country. She was the wife of one of the Seneca chiefs, to whom the Wyandott prince took a strong liking, and by stratagem carried her off.

The war immediately ensued, and was prosecuted with great cruelty and slaughter for a long time. At last, a final battle came on, (upon the northern territory,) in which the Wyandotts were worsted, and were obliged to fly with great rapidity. The greater part took a course to the west, and their antagonists followed them vigorously till they came to the straits of lakes Huron and St. Clair. The fugitives calculated to pass on the ice, but found it just broken up, and then floating down the strait. Their only alternative was, to throw themselves upon it, and leaping from cake to cake, they all safely reached the opposite shore. Their pursuers, not choosing to encounter the risk, returned home.

The nations among whom the Wyandotts now found themselves, namely, the Potawattamies, Ottawas, and Chippewas, received them with friendship, and gave or lent them land to settle on. At the solicitation of the strangers, they even went so far as to fit out a fleet of large and excellent birch canoes, with a view to meet the Senecas, whom they expected on with a fleet from the east. These canoes were chiefly built on the straits and higher lakes, and came to a rendezvous about where Malden now is. It is said they made a grand show. The Senecas not having as good materials, were obliged to make use of log canoes, hollowed out of the trunks of trees. These were far more clumsy and unmanageable than those made of the birch bark; the latter being superior to our best skiffs, and may safely brave the surges of the lakes.

The Wyandotts and their allies set out from their rendezvous, coasting the north side of Lake Erie till they came to Long Point, within twenty or thirty miles of the eastern end of the lake. Here they made a halt, not deeming it prudent to double the point till they had looked around it. For this purpose, they despatched a few men across the point, who happened to meet midway, with about the same number of the enemy, dispatched for a similar object. Each party retreated to their fleet, except one or two Wyandotts, who ascended trees to ascertain the situation and number of their enemy and the nature of their craft, which they found to be logs.

Now a grand manœuvre was set on foot—the birch canoe party proceeded to the end of the point, and in full view of their enemy, put out directly into the lake. The Senecas immediately pursued, and when they had reached about midway of the lake, the birch canoes turned upon them and gave them such battle as could not be withstood. All the Senecas were slain but one man, who pretended to be dead, but was afterwards found alive, and was permitted to go home to tell the catastrophe to his nation.

Thus closed the war, and the Wyandotts remained in peace in their new station. This is supposed to have been the first naval action on the lakes.

Several circumstances conspire to gain credit to this relation.

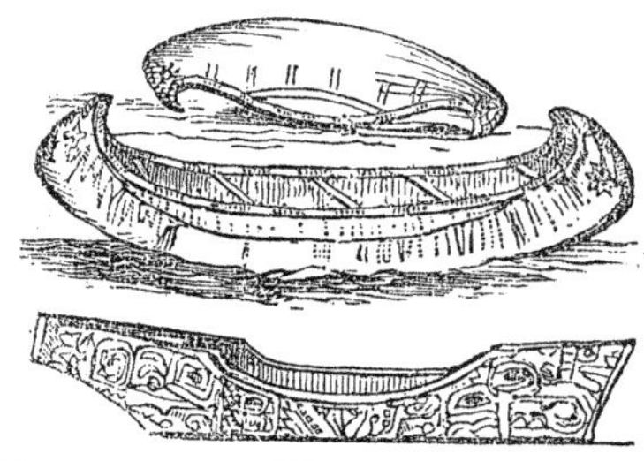

GALLANT ACTION OF THE PRIVATEER GENERAL ARMSTRONG.

IN the last war between the United States and Great Britain, many gallant actions were performed by the American sailors in the privateer service, which have almost entirely escaped the notice of history. The following will serve as a specimen.

The private armed schooner General Armstrong, Captain Champlin, of eighteen guns, being within five leagues of the mouth of Surinam river, on the 11th of March, 1814, discovered a large sail to be at anchor under the land. The crew of the General Armstrong supposed her to be an English letter of marque, and, consequently, Captain Champlin bore down with the intention of giving her a starboard and a larboard broadside, and then to board her. The stranger, in the meantime, had got sail on her, and was standing out for the American. Both vessels thus approaching each other, had come within gun shot, (the Englishman firing the guns on his main deck,) when the General Armstrong discharged both the contemplated broadsides, and discovered too late, that her antagonist was a heavy frigate. She nevertheless, kept up her fire, though attempting to get away, but in ten minutes she was silenced by the enemy. The last shot of the General Armstrong brought down the enemy's colors, by cutting away her mizzen gaff, halyards, and her mizzen and mainstay; and Captain Champlin, presuming that she had struck, made preparations to possess her; but the frigate opened another heavy fire upon the schooner, killed six, and wounded the captain and sixteen of her men; shot away the fore and mainshrouds, pierced the mainmast and bowsprit, and struck her several times between wind and water. In this condition she laid upwards of forty-five minutes, within pistol shot of the frigate; but, by the extraordinary exertions of the crew and the aid of sweeps, she got out of the enemy's reach, and arrived at Charleston on the 4th of April.

The following account of the capture of the General Armstrong, is from Mr. Perkins's History of the Late War.

"On the 26th of September, 1814, the American privateer brig General Armstrong, Captain Reid, came to anchor in the port of Fayal, one of the Azores, a Portuguese island in the Atlantic. On the same day, the Plantagenet seventy-four, and the Rota and Carnation, British ships of war, suddenly appeared in the roads. At dark, Captain Reid warped his ship in under the guns of the fort for protection; at eight o'clock, he observed four boats from the ships filled with armed men approaching him; after warning them to keep off, he fired into the boats, killed seven men, and compelled them to return. At midnight, twelve large boats armed with swivels, carronades, and muskets, attacked the brig, and after a severe action of forty minutes, the contest ended in a total defeat of the party, a partial destruction of the boats, and a severe loss of men. Among the killed were the first lieutenant of the Plantagenet, the commandant of the party, and two lieutenants and one midshipman of the Rota. It was estimated by the spectators on shore, that the boats contained four hundred men, and that more than half of them were killed or wounded. Several boats were destroyed, two remained along side of the Armstrong, loaded with their dead and dying, only seventeen from these two boats reached the shore. The British acknowledged a loss of one hundred and twenty killed. The sloops Thais and Calipso, were loaded with the wounded and sent to England.

"Immediately after the first attack, Mr. Dobney, the American consul, applied to the governor of Fayal, to enforce the privileges of a neutral port in favor of the American ship. The governor expressed his indignation at what had passed, but was unable with his means to resist such a force. His remonstrances to the British commander were answered by an insulting refusal.

"On the morning of the 27th, one of the ships took a station near the shore, and commenced a heavy cannonade on the brig. Captain Reid, finding further resistance unavailing, partially destroyed the brig, and went on shore with his crew; the British then set her on fire. In this attack, not only the privileges of neutrality, but the safety of the town was wholly disregarded. Several of the inhabitants were dangerously wounded, and a number of houses destroyed."

ADMIRAL KEPPEL AND THE DEY OF ALGIERS.

WHEN Admiral Keppel was sent to the Dey of Algeirs, to demand restitution of two ships which the pirates had taken, he sailed with his squadron into the bay of Algiers, and cast anchor in front of the Dey's palace. He then landed, and attended only by his captain and barge's crew, demanded an immediate audience of the Dey. This being granted, he claimed full satisfaction for the injuries done to the subjects of his Britannic Majesty. Surprised and enraged at the boldness of the admiral's remonstrance, the Dey exclaimed, "that he wondered at the English king's insolence in sending him a foolish, beardless boy." A well-timed reply from the admiral, made the Dey forget the laws of all nations in respect to ambassadors, and he ordered his mutes to attend with the bow string, at the same time telling the admiral, he should pay for his audacity with his life. Unmoved by this menace, the admiral took the Dey to a window facing the bay, and showed him the English fleet riding at anchor, and told him, that if he dared to put him to death, there were Englishmen enough in that fleet to make him a glorious funeral pile. The Dey was wise enough to take the hint. The admiral obtained ample restitution, and came off in safety.

COURAGE OF AN IRISH SAILOR.

HEN the British ship Tonnant was in close action with the French rear-admiral's ship Algesiras, the latter had her bowsprit over the chess-tree of the former, so as to admit of a raking fire from the Tonnant, which did great mischief to the enemy. The foretop of the Algesiras was full of French riflemen, who, commanded, by an incessant fire, the upper decks of the Tonnant, which the marines on the poop, and officers and men on the quarter deck, were suffering from considerably. In the midst of this carnage, an ordinary seamen, named Fitzgerald, made his way from the main rigging of the Tonnant, by the sprit-sail yard of the enemy, to the bowsprit of the Algesiras, and with his knife cut down the French jack, amidst the loud cheers of his shipmates and the shouts and groans of the Frenchmen. Notwithstanding the heavy fire of musketry, and many hand-grenades thrown out of the foretop of the enemy, he had regained the main rigging of the Tonnant, where his gallant exploit terminated from a grenade, which struck him in the back: he sunk between the two ships, with the tri-colored winding-sheet under his arm, accompanied by the admiration and regret of every officer and man in the ship. This fine fellow was an Irishman, of the humblest origin; but the greatest man of the great house of Fitzgerald, never displayed more intrepidity or coolness in the hour of danger than this poor Fitzgerald did.

ADMIRALS HAWKE AND RODNEY.

ADMIRAL HAWKE has the reputation of being not only brave, but also circumspect; to the most consummate courage and active spirit, he added a temper cool and deliberate; accident ruffled him not; sudden misfortune seemed not to take him by surprise. The following is one instance of his coolness and steady self-possession. When his flag was on board the Royal George, the ship once took fire, owing to a collection of soot in the funnel of the stove of the great cabin. A man of less presence of mind would have given an alarm instantly to the whole ship; but, instead of this, Sir Edward, who was at the time dressing himself, went on deck without manifesting any emotion, and taking aside the first-lieutenant, said to him in a low tone, "Sir, the ship is on fire in my cabin; give the necessary directions for putting it out."

Capital! capital! Why, we should have cried out fire! as loud as we could scream.

And by that means have gathered round you those who would have only been in each other's way. I have given you an instance of coolness in Admiral Hawke. The following is an example of fidelity and integrity in Admiral Rodney.

After many instances of bravery and skill, he unfortunately engaged in election contests, and became so poor that he was obliged to retire to France to escape from the pursuit of his creditors. When in this forlorn situation, the Duke de Biron invited him to his house, treated him very hospitably, and then hinted, that if he would enter the French navy it would be greatly to his advantage. But the blue jacket that would fight against his country, even to be lord high-admiral of an enemy's navy, would deserve to be tarred and feathered. Rodney began to think that the duke was a little deranged in his intellects, but what was his surprise when the duke told him, that he was commissioned by his royal master, the king, to offer him the command of a French squadron, with unbounded advantages, should he accept the appointment.

This was his reply to the duke. "My distresses, sir, it is true, have driven me from the bosom of my country, but no temptation whatever can estrange me from her service. Had this offer been a voluntary one of your own, I should have deemed it an insult, but I am glad that it proceeds from a source that *can do no wrong*."

There is that in an upright and noble action which commands respect. The brave respect the brave, and the faithful respect the faithful all the world over. The duke was so struck with admiration of the British tar's patriotism, that he instantly became his friend.

NELSON'S PRAYER AT TRAFALGAR.

AT the battle of Trafalgar, Collingwood, in the Royal Sovereign, led the lee-line of fourteen ships, Nelson, in the Victory, was at the head of the weather line, consisting of fourteen ships. Besides these, there were four frigates. The ships of France and Spain opposed to the British were in number thirty-three, with seven large frigates. The odds were great against the English, but the superior tactics, and well known bravery of Nelson, clothed him with power, and more than made up the difference. When every thing was prepared for the engagement, Nelson retired into his cabin alone and wrote down the following prayer.

"May the Great God, whom I worship, grant to my country, and for the benefit of Europe in general, a great and glorious victory, and may no misconduct in any one tarnish it, and may humanity after victory, be the predominant feature in the British fleet! For myself, individually, I commit my life to Him that made me; and may His blessing alight on my endeavors for serving my country faithfully! To Him I resign myself, and the just cause which is entrusted to me to defend. Amen! Amen! Amen!"

THE SINKING OF THE ROYAL GEORGE.

THE SINKING OF THE ROYAL GEORGE.

HE Royal George was an old ship; she had seen much service. Her build was rather short and high, but she sailed well, and carried the tallest masts and squarest canvass of any of England's gun ships. She had just returned from Spithead, where there were twenty or thirty ships of war, a large fleet, lying under command of Lord Howe. It was on the 29th of August, 1782. She was lying off Portsmouth; her decks had been washed the day before, and the carpenter discovered that the pipe which admitted water to cleanse the ship was worn out, and must be replaced. This pipe being three feet under the water, it was needful to heel, or lay the ship a little on one side. To do this, the heavy guns on the larboard side were run out of the port holes as far as they would go, and the guns on the starboard side were drawn up and secured in the middle of the deck; this brought the sills of the port holes on the lowest side nearly even with the water. Just as the crew had finished breakfast, a vessel called the Lark came on the low side of the ship to unship a cargo of rum; the casks were put on board on that side, and this additional weight, together with that of the men employed in unloading, caused the ship to heel still more on one side; every wave of the sea now washed in at her port holes, and thus she had soon so great a weight of water in her hold, that slowly and almost imperceptibly she sank still further down on her side. Twice, the carpenter, seeing the danger, went on board to ask the officer on duty to order the ship to be righted; and if he had not been a proud and angry man, who would not acknowledge himself to be in the wrong, all might yet have been well. The plumbers had almost finished their work, when a sudden breeze blew on the raised side of the ship, forced her still further down, and the water began to pour into her lower port holes. Instantly the danger became apparent; the men were ordered to right the ship: they ran to move the guns for this purpose, but it was too late. In a minute or two more, she fell quite over on her side, with her masts nearly flat on the water, and the Royal George sank to the bottom, before one signal of distress could be given! By this dreadful accident about nine hundred persons lost their lives; about two hundred and thirty were saved, some by running up the rigging, and being with others picked up by the boats which put off immediately from other vessels to their assistance. There were many visitors, women, and little children on board at the time of the accident.

THE BLOWING UP OF THE ROYAL GEORGE.

HEN the dreadful event which has just been related occurred, the Lark sloop, which had brought the cargo of rum, was lying along side of the Royal George: in going down, the main yard of the Royal George caught the boom of the Lark, and they sank together, but this made the position of the Royal George much more upright in the water than it would otherwise have been. There she lay at the bottom of the sea, just as you have seen small vessels when left by the tide on a bank. Cowper, when he heard the sad tale, thus wrote:

"Her timbers yet are sound,
And she may float again,
Full charged with England's thunder,
And plough the distant main.

"But Kempenfelt is gone,
His victories are o'er,
And he, and his eight hundred
Shall plough the wave no more."

Admiral Kempenfelt was writing in his cabin when the ship sank; his first captain tried to inform him of their situation, but the heeling of the ship so jammed the cabin doors, that he could not open them: thus the admiral perished with the rest. It seems Cowper thought that the Royal George might be recovered; other people were of the

THE BLOWING UP OF THE ROYAL GEORGE.

same opinion. In September of the year in which the ship sank, a gentleman named Tracey, living in the neighborhood, by means of diving machines, ascertained the position and state of the ship, and made proposals to government to adopt means of raising her and getting her again afloat. After a great many vexatious delays and interruptions on the part of those who were to have supplied him with assistance, he succeeded in getting up the Lark sloop. His efforts to raise the Royal George were so far successful, that at every time of high tide she was lifted from her bed; and on the 9th of October, she was hove at least thirty or forty feet to westward; but the days were getting short, the boisterous winds of winter were setting in, the lighters to which Tracey's apparatus was attached were too old and rotten to bear the strain, and he was forced to abandon the attempt. The sunken ship remained, a constant impediment to other vessels wishing to cast anchor near the spot, for nearly fifty years, when Colonel Pasley, by means of gunpowder, completely demolished the wreck: the loose pieces of timber floated to the surface; heavier pieces—the ship's guns, cables, anchors, the fire hearth, cooking utensils, and many smaller articles were recovered by the divers. These men went down in India rubber dresses, which were air and water tight; they were furnished with helmets, in each side of which were glass windows, to admit light, and supplied with air by means of pipes, communicating with an air pump above. By these means they could remain under water more than an hour at a time. Large hollow vessels, called cylinders, were filled with gunpowder, and attached by the divers to the wreck, these were connected by conducting wires with a battery on board a lighter above, at a sufficient distance to be out of reach of danger when the explosion took place. Colonel Pasley then gave the word to fire the end of the rod: instantly, a report was heard, and those who witnessed the explosions, say that the effect was very beautiful. On one occasion, the water rose in a splendid column above fifty feet high, the spray sparkling like diamonds in the sun; then the large fragments of the wreck came floating to the surface; soon after the mud from the bottom, blackening the circle of water, and spreading to a great distance around; and with it rose to the surface great numbers of fish, who, poor things, had found a hiding place in the wreck, but were dislodged and killed by the terrible gunpowder.

THE EARL ST. VINCENT, LORD DUNCAN, AND LORD HOWE.

VINCENT, Duncan, and Howe, are great names as naval commanders. One of the most brilliant victories mentioned in English history was achieved by Vincent. He went to sea at ten years of age. When posted, he was appointed to the Gosport. Afterwards, he captured the Pallas, a French frigate, and was present in Admiral Keppel's action with the French. Under Admiral Barrington he chased and fought the Pégase, a French seventy-four, capturing her without the loss of a single man. With his flag on board the Victory, of one hundred guns, he came face to face with his enemy on the 14th of February, 1797, fighting one of the most famous battles, and achieving one of the most splendid victories ever recorded in the roll of fame.

Duncan's victory over the Dutch fleet off Camperdown was a gallant affair, and it has handed down his name in the list of Britain's warriors. Assembling his crew in the presence of the captured Dutch admiral, he kneeled down at their head to offer up his thanksgiving to the God of battles.

Admiral Lord Howe, when a captain, was once hastily awakened in the middle of the night by the lieutenant, who informed him, with great agitation, that the ship was on fire near the magazine. "If that be the case," said he, rising leisurely to put on his clothes, "we shall soon hear a further report of the matter." The lieutenant flew back to the scene of danger, and almost instantly returning, exclaimed, "You need not, sir, be afraid, the fire is extinguished." "Afraid," exclaimed Howe; "what do you mean by that, sir? I never was afraid in my life;" and looking the lieutenant full in the face, he added, "Pray, how does a man feel, sir, when he is afraid? I need not ask how he looks."

www.ingramcontent.com/pod-product-compliance
Lightning Source LLC
LaVergne TN
LVHW021106110826
845150LV00001B/185

* 9 7 8 1 4 2 5 5 6 5 1 2 1 *